✜ SLAVES AND OTHER OBJECTS

SLAVES

AND OTHER OBJECTS

PAGE DUBOIS

THE UNIVERSITY OF CHICAGO PRESS

CHICAGO AND LONDON

PAGE DUBOIS is professor of classics and comparative literature at the University of California, San Diego. Her articles and essays have appeared in journals such as *Theatre Journal, differences, Classical Philology,* and *Arethusa,* among others, as well as in edited collections. She is also the author of six books, most recently *Trojan Horses: Saving the Classics from Conservatives; Sappho Is Burning; Torture and Truth;* and *Sowing the Body.*

The University of Chicago Press, Chicago 60637
The University of Chicago Press, Ltd., London
© 2003 by The University of Chicago
All rights reserved. Published 2003
Printed in the United States of America

12 11 10 09 08 07 06 05 04 03   1 2 3 4 5
ISBN: 0-226-16787-9 (cloth)

Library of Congress Cataloging-in-Publication Data

duBois, Page.
   Slaves and other objects / Page duBois.
      p.   cm.
Includes bibliographical references and index.
   ISBN 0-226-16787-9 (alk. paper)
   1. Slaves—Greece—History.   2. Greece—Civilization—
To 146 B.C.   3. Slavery in literature.   4. Slavery in art.
I. Title.

HT1234.D83   2003
305.5'67—dc21

2002152496

⊗ The paper used in this publication meets the minimum requirements of the American National Standard for Information Sciences—Permanence of Paper for Printed Library Materials, ANSI Z39.48-1992.

❖ *For John*

❖ CONTENTS

ILLUSTRATIONS

❖ PREFACE

HAVING written about slaves, and torture and truth, and wanting to think more about slavery in ancient Greece, I began this book in 1991. Soon afterward I encountered a book of photographs called *Material World: A Global Family Portrait*.[1] Published by the Sierra Club, this volume was meant to commemorate the United Nations International Year of the Family in 1994 and echoed *The Family of Man*, a collection of photographs produced by Edward Steichen in 1955. The more recent text assembles photographs of "average" families from each of thirty different countries, pictured outside their homes and surrounded by all their belongings. These photos have some comic aspects, not least because everyone and everything stand outdoors, inventory to be registered by the camera. The images include a family in Mali (where the average annual per-capita income is $251): a man, his two wives, their seven children, and their baskets and pots. Also featured is a family of four in Texas (the U.S. average annual per-capita income is $22,356) whose possessions include a dune buggy and two other motor vehicles, two televisions, a microwave oven, a washer, a dryer, a stove, and all the other necessities of life in the metropolis. Though not unexpected, disparities between the photographs still have the power to shock: all the possessions of the Malians could fit into the Range Rover of the Texas family, and cost a fraction of the monthly payment on the auto loan.

Interested in questions of everyday life and slavery in classical Greece, and the presentation of these features of that society, I was struck by the fact that *Material World* contains no photograph of a household in Mauritania, where it is now known that some people possess slaves.[2] How would one represent such a "family"? There would be people and their things, and then there would be the people who are themselves in some sense things, possessions, commodities, or property. The slaves often resemble the people who own the house, the household implements, the cars, and the animals—yet they are not owners or possessors but things possessed.

In historical cultures not so distant from our own, the "material world" included not just people and their inanimate objects but also many human beings who were somehow objects themselves, things to be traded or bought and sold. In this awkward case, human beings constituted both members of the family and some of its possessions. It also occurred to me that as a sort of snapshot of the world, *Material World* could register only the world of 1994. What would it be like to provide a portrait of historical cultures? And especially that of such a society as ancient Greece, where, as in contemporary Mauritania, among the material possessions of a household were other human beings, slaves, persons who would be included in the image not as members of a family but as belongings, belonging in another sense, objects of possession?

One of my concerns in *Slaves and Other Objects* is to point to the ways in which the slaves of ancient Greece have been both ubiquitous and invisible—ubiquitous because there is no scene of life in that society that is not informed by slaves, yet invisible to some who commemorate ancient Athens as one of the founding sites of Western civilization. Slaves are invisible also to those who visit museums exhibiting the great works of art of classical Greece. They are invisible sometimes even to those who make the study of Greek antiquity their professional concern. In writing the chapters that follow, I have thought that slaves seemed often like furnishings of Greek life: useful objects for the conduct of everyday life, yet often difficult to manage and incessantly reminding the free of the possibility of their own enslavement—a fact of life sometimes impossible for their masters and for latter-day scholars to recognize, precisely because of the anxieties it raises concerning the practice of slavery.

I have referred often in this book to the experience of American culture and its recent history of slavery, not because of historical likeness or even analogy between the highly various and historically distinct racial slavery of the United States and the slavery of Greek classical culture but rather because I believe the memory and defining consequences of that institution in this country have affected classical scholarship's relationship to the practice in the ancient world. I am convinced that we cannot have an unmediated direct experience of classical Greece; all we know of the ancient past comes to us in our present situation, affected by all that has happened in between, all that defines our lives in postmodernity. Disregarding our own historical, social, and geographical situation would mean imagining immediate perfect access, a purely antiquarian visit to the past, a fantasy of fusion with Perikles and Sokrates on the Akropolis of ancient Athens. I argue here for another perspective: one that locates scholarship in a present distant from the ancient past, critical and conscious of investments personal, political, and cultural in a certain idea of ancient Greece.

To that end, I have organized the book in two parts: Objects and

Texts. Part 1 considers the exhibition of the artworks of the Greeks, and the presentation of the material evidence of their everyday life. It looks at how the civilization of ancient Greece is portrayed in museums, and points to the difficulty of representing slaves and slavery in such contexts. Indeed, it argues for a troubling absence of slaves here, in the presentation of the visual remains of classical Greek antiquity, and in the history of art, and a disturbing ubiquity of the slave body as an object, a presence at every scene of ancient life. Included is a discussion of an instrument of erotic pleasure often depicted on Greek vases, and a consideration of how these objects figure within a history of sexuality that takes the ubiquity of slaves in ancient households into account. A discussion of the slave body as object concludes the section.

Part 2 focuses on textual materials, building on the issues formulated earlier in the book. Here the chapters take soundings of various genres and moments of classical Greek culture, and point to the difficulties slaves and slavery present for readings of ancient drama, philosophy, epic, history, and other texts received from antiquity.

❖ ACKNOWLEDGMENTS

I WOULD like to thank Michael Roth, Salvatore Settis, and the Getty Research Institute for the History of Art and the Humanities for inviting me to spend 1998 as scholar in residence, part of the group dedicated to "Representing the Passions." There, among pink flamingos and birds-of-paradise on Sunset Boulevard, I was blessed with a research assistant of great diligence and expertise, Chris Hudson, and with wonderful colleagues, especially Richard Meyer, Lesley Stern, and Debbie Silverman. It was a pleasure there to deliver a lecture in the Languages of Interpretation series for Beyond Beauty: Antiquities as Evidence, the exhibition inaugurating the new Getty Museum, on April 1, 1998. One of the chapters in *Slaves and Other Objects* found its beginnings in an essay written for *Representing the Passions: Histories, Bodies, Visions*, edited by Richard Meyer (Los Angeles: Getty Research Institute, 2003).

Thanks also to David Lloyd, for the invitation to lecture at Scripps College on the slave body for a series on the new ancient world; to Phiroze Vasunia, who organized "Sex and the City," a joint UCLA-USC conference at the University of Southern California, where I delivered the lecture "Slaves, Dildoes"; and to Susanna Braund, for her invitation to deliver "Irate Greek Masters and Their Slaves" at the Altertumswissenschaftforum in Heidelberg at the conference "Aspects of Anger in Antiquity." Thanks to the UCLA Center for Modern and Contemporary Studies, where I presented "The Will to Possess: Aristotle and Early Modern Slavery" at the conference "The Politics of Passions." Thanks to Donald Mastronarde, chairman of the Classics Department at UC Berkeley, where I read "Greek Slaves and the History of Sexuality" and met with spirited debate.

I am grateful for the opportunity to perform in the Life of the Mind series in 1994 at the University of Southern California, where I read a paper called "Slaves and Other Objects," an early version of the ideas that grew into this book. I benefited from the chance to comment on a panel discussing the body at the Archaeological Institute of America's annual convention.

Thanks to Cary Perloff, who asked me to contribute to a panel for the American Conservatory Theater in San Francisco that discussed the performance she directed of Euripides' *Hecuba*. Shadi Bartsch and Rob Nelson of the University of Chicago welcomed me to the workshop on the ancient Mediterranean, and to a conference, "The History of Culture." I was a keynote speaker for the "Silence and Expression" conference at Texas A&M University, and presented a paper at the College Art Association's annual meeting as a member of a panel on sexualities organized by Richard Meyer and David Joselit—occasions that helped me refine my ideas about slave bodies.

Raphael Newman brought me to lecture at the University of Washington in the series Incorporating Discourses: Body, Identity and Culture in Europe. Thanks also to Carlos Blanco and Jose Monleon for inviting me to participate in a symposium in Madrid, "Postmodernism's Challenge to the Social Sciences and the Humanities," jointly sponsored by the University of California and the Universidad Complutense de Madrid, in April 1997. I also appreciated the invitation to present the lecture "The Slave Plato" to the Comparative Literature Department at New York University.

I am grateful for the pleasure of being a plenary speaker at "After the Body," a conference at the Centre for Religion, Culture and Gender, Department of Religions and Theology, University of Manchester, and owe special thanks to Kate Cooper. Chris Connery and Daniel Selden offered hospitality and intellectual challenge at UC Santa Cruz.

Thanks to Giulia Sissa and Ellen D. Reeder for the invitation to participate in a conference inaugurating the Pandora's Box exhibition at the Walters Art Gallery in Baltimore. Thanks also to curators at the Dallas Art Museum for the opportunity to travel with the exhibition and deliver the paper "Plow, Stilus."

Mary Louise Hart and Karol Wight of the Getty Museum took me into the bowels of the Getty Villa; unwrapped precious glass, ceramic vases, and other treasures; patiently explained mysteries; and let me touch extraordinary relics of the Greek past. The intimate encounter with these objects had a transforming effect on my ideas about our relationship to antiquity. I want also to acknowledge the collegiality of archaeologists John Papadopoulos, formerly of the Getty Museum, and Sarah Morris, of UCLA.

Thank you to Mike Howard and Christa Acampora of the Philosophy Department at the University of Maine at Orono and to Steve Evans and Jennifer Moxley.

I owe many thanks to my colleagues Lisa Lowe and Susan Kirkpatrick, who supported this project in myriad ways, and whose work has long inspired mine. Thanks also to Helen Deutsch, whose enthusiasm and creativity are irrepressibly encouraging. Patrick Sinclair arranged for a weeklong seminar on this work in progress in the Critical Theory Program at UC Irvine, a stimulating experience. I continue to appreciate the moral and material support of Frantisek Deak, dean of humanities at UC San Diego.

I thank Froma Zeitlin, always.

Thanks to Leslie Kurke for reading my work on Aesop in an early draft, and for her example as a scholar. I extend my gratitude also to Michael Meranze, for trying to set me straight about American history, and for the pleasures of conversation. This is the place to acknowledge François Lissarrague and his brilliant work on the iconography of Greek vases, and Jean-Pierre Vernant, who made me a classicist.

I want to thank Charles Platter and Nancy Felson for their warm hospitality at the University of Georgia. It was there, in Athens, that I began to understand the complex entanglement of the American South, the classics, and that other Athens.

Thanks to my dear friend Fanny Howe. To Kaja Silverman. And to Kate Harper and Harper Page Marshall for love and shelter. I owe gratitude to Melvyn Freilicher and Joe Keenan for kindness and irony in times of calm and stress. I miss my colleague and friend, the late Sherley Anne Williams, author of the slave narrative novel *Dessa Rose*.

Thanks to Antonia Meltzoff, whose wise, generous, patient work has changed my life.

Most of all, I thank John Daley, poet, my hero and husband, who struggles every day against the consequences of slavery and racism, and whose love sustains me.

❖ SLAVES AND OTHER OBJECTS

INTRODUCTION

> Domestic slavery in the Southern states has produced the same re-
> sults in elevating the character of the master that it did in Greece and
> Rome. He is lofty and independent in his sentiments, generous, affec-
> tionate, brave and eloquent. . . . History proves this. . . . Scipio and
> Aristides, Calhoun and Washington, are the noble results of domestic
> slavery. Like Egyptian obelisks 'mid the waste of time—simple, se-
> vere, sublime,—they point ever heavenward, and lift the soul by their
> examples.
>
> —George Fitzhugh, *Sociology for the South* (1854)

The Tattooed Slave

THE ANCIENT Greek historian Herodotus tells the following story about events preceding the Persian Wars at the beginning
of the fifth century BCE:

> [V]arious causes of alarm were already making Aristagoras contemplate
> rebellion, when something else occurred to confirm his purpose; this was
> the arrival from Susa of a slave, the man with the tattooed scalp, sent by
> Histiaeus, urging him to do precisely what he was thinking of, namely, to
> revolt. Histiaeus had been wanting to make Aristagoras take this step, but
> was in difficulty about how to get a message safely through to him, as the
> roads from Susa were watched; so he shaved the head of his most trust-
> worthy slave, pricked the message on his scalp, and waited for hair to grow
> again. Then, as soon as it had grown, he sent the man to Miletus with in-
> structions to do nothing when he arrived except to tell Aristagoras to
> shave his hair off and look at his head. The message found there was, as I
> have said, an order to revolt.[1]

I have written about this intriguing anecdote before, in another context,
when discussing the metaphor of the writing tablet in reference to
women's bodies, which were inscribed by their masters', husbands' pe-
nises in intercourse.[2] Here the anecdote can be turned, mapped in another set of discourses, those referring to slaves and their bodies. Here

3

the skin of the slave, at the master's disposition, becomes a surface, a device for communication like the wax-covered wooden tablet that the Greeks used for writing. The skull of this nameless slave is like the wooden tablet, the skin of his scalp its wax.[3]

The master in Herodotus's story inscribes his message, "pricking," tattooing, or marking the slave's head. In the natural process of time the slave's hair grows, covering the inscription. The body of the slave, that of a human being, is usefully subject to such change over time, unlike a writing tablet. The slave passes over the watched roads, unsuspected by the Persians. He conceals a seditious message on his person, but it is carried secretly, marked on the body itself rather than borne as a discrete and separate object. When he, the message embodied, reaches the destination, the recipient of the message, he transmits verbally the clue that allows the recipient, the "destinataire," to read his body. This story communicates to the listener or reader not only that the original recipient should revolt but also that its bearer is a slave, that his body is taken for granted, that it passes through boundaries without interrogation, that it is in some way a surface, a thing without interiority. One of my concerns in this book is to point to the ways in which the other slaves of ancient Greece, like the tattooed slave of Histiaeus, have been invisible—corporeally, socially, and epistemologically invisible—and yet served as potential messengers for rebellion.[4]

The Tattooed Orator

In a mid fourth-century-BCE speech concerning an embassy to the Macedonian ruler Philip, the Attic orator Aeschines alludes to the bodies of slaves in defending himself against charges of treason. He uses the degrading image of the tattoo to stigmatize his rival and accuser Demosthenes, whom he has accused of descent from a Scythian, therefore "barbarian," grandmother:[5]

> But you find fault with my service as ambassador to Arcadia and my speech before the Ten Thousand there, and you say that I have changed sides—yourself more slave [*andrapododes*] than freeman, all but branded as a runaway [*kai monon ouk estigmenos automolos*]![6]

Aeschines, who had tried to convince the Arcadians to resist Philip but eventually advised them to make peace, represents Demosthenes himself as the traitor, like a slave abandoning his true master, the Athenians, to revert to his slavish, barbarian blood.[7] A *scholion* (commentary) on this passage in Aeschines adds helpfully that runaway slaves were tattooed on the brow, inscribed with the message *katekhe me, pheugo*, "stop me, I am a runaway."[8] If the scholiast's description is accurate, the slave's body was made to speak in his own first person, and his face was marked, inscribed like a tablet by the master who had written on him, tattooed him. This slave too, like Histiaeus's, is nameless, and bears a message that he himself can neither see nor read.

Most ancient readers read haltingly and aloud, spelling out the letters of words.[9] Like the inscriptions on ancient tombs, or statues accompanied by inscriptions speaking in the voice of the dead, the tattooed message would be read aloud by the viewer and given voice by the viewer's body.[10] The imperative written on the slave's forehead is addressed to the viewer, who reads the face of the person facing him and ventriloquizes the voice of the other's body. The speech of the inscribed body, articulated by the other, speaks against the interests of the fleeing body, exposing it to capture and return, as the surface of the body is forced to contradict and betray the intentions of the person who inhabits it.[11] With every encounter, facing another person, this tattooed slave's body carries signs of his revolt and flight, taken for granted in all situations of everyday life. The onlooker becomes the slave of the text written on the slave's body in that he must voice its message. The viewer speaks the repressive imperative, and then repeats aloud the essentializing characterization: "I am running away," "I am a runaway." The tattooed forehead of this slave embodies the contradiction of the ancient social relation between slave and free. The reader, as he speaks the damning inscription that marks the slave as object, as thing, as commodity, and as always already criminal, must take on that identity himself, speak its truth, saying, with his body, "I am a runaway," "I am running away." The free person, caught in this mirror relationship with the inscribed body of the other, must recognize his own danger, his own vulnerability to enslavement. He is always himself running away, running away from the possibility of slavery.

Much of the ideological effort, the cultural labor of this society, directly or indirectly strives to produce an inevitable, uncrossable, and natural line between one kind of body and another, a line which the reading of this message violates.[12] This tattooed slave carries with him all the contradiction of this culture: the necessity to maintain difference, the impossibility of such a task, and the anguished enactment of recognition that must be both repeated and suppressed, enacted and denied, in the face-to-face encounter between slave and free. Along with the invisibility of the slave to ancient free persons and postmodern readers alike, we must consider this problem of recognition of the slave by free persons—and of the ongoing cultural labor of affirming or suppressing recognition—in which every ancient act, every gesture, takes a position on the reification of this difference. If the freeman carries his body differently (Aristotle says in the *Politics* that "the intention of nature is to make the bodies of freemen and of slaves different," with the free body erect and serviceable for a life of citizenship [1254b]), the slave body must not be seen, and yet paradoxically must be seen, as serviceable: often as stooped, ugly, and defective.[13]

One result of the crucial place of slaves in the ancient Greek economy is the possibility that there were and are some humans at the beginnings of Western civilization understood to be more human than others; that being human is not an absolute condition but rather a gradual one, on a sliding scale on which some humans approach the status of things, of objects. This understanding of human being is somehow imperceptibly inscribed into enduring ways of thinking—about politics, about others, about our own bodies, about material existence.[14]

Classical Studies and the Slave

The classical historian Moses I. Finley stresses: "I should say that there was no action or belief or institution in Graeco-Roman antiquity that was not one way or other affected by the possibility that someone involved *might* be a slave."[15] This is a book about invisibility and ubiquity, about the troubling presence of slavery and slaves in ancient Greece, about how slavery informed every aspect of life in ancient Greek society, and how idealization of the Greeks has led modern scholars often to overlook both slavery and slaves.[16] My argument is that these phenomena determine one another, that invisibility and ubiquity are mutually constitutive, both for ancient thinkers and for modern scholars. "They," the free ancient Greeks, often were not actively conscious of slaves both because slavery and slaves were so much taken for granted as props, part of everyday life, the furnishings of their world, and because their ubiquity was often threatening and unnerving.[17] "We," in modernity, have difficulty recognizing slaves and slavery, perhaps because we have at times assumed the Greeks' overt perspective of disregard.

Readers and students of classical antiquity may share the ancient Greeks' uneasiness or indifference to these persons, or have taken for granted slaves as part of the landscape, as furnishings of everyday life, and failed to recognize this aspect of ancient culture, so different from our own. Readers fear being reductive about ancient economic relationships, not wanting to understand all culture in terms of class or economic relations, or striving not to be anachronistic in projecting modernity's and postmodernity's economistic categories onto ancient societies. Scholars at times uncritically construct the ancient Greeks as our ancestors, as the heroic inventors of philosophy and democracy, almost unconsciously finding a utopian past in antiquity, a site of democracy and philosophical conversation, one in which menial tasks and agricultural labor were invisibly performed by the unfree, those owned by the free with whom many readers identify. In the setting up of a society in the past to be praised for its philosophical and democratic equanimity, the unproblematic idealization of antiquity cannot be sustained if one recognizes the ways in which slavery permeates every aspect of ancient life. The misrecognition of slavery has contributed to a myth of origin for Western civilization; an inevitable and necessary occulting of the presence of slaves has occurred. Such an invisibility implicates both antiquity and modernity. Antiquity has been preserved as a domain of origin, of philosophical or democratic purity, in many of the discourses tracing a trajectory from an ancient source. And modernity, contaminated as it is both by actual slavery and by racisms, by the results of recent slavery, can refuse to acknowledge this contamination, misrecognizing it in the ancient past as well as in the present.[18]

The discipline of classics has often taken for granted a transparent, unmediated access and relationship to antiquity. Many classicists operate within a positivist, scientific model of truth seeking, in which knowledge is to be gathered and understood to be added to a sum of knowledge about ancient societies, in which the project of the scholar must be a further accumulation of facts and data in the unending search for a true and accurate representation of the past. Such a model presents difficulties in part because it fails to recognize the ways in which the concerns of the present affect a presumably innocent or inevitable approach to the object of inquiry. Feminism, for instance, has had its impact on the field of classical studies as the concerns of feminist classical scholars emerged from political struggles in the twentieth century. Women in antiquity had always been there, or not, to be studied and interpreted; it was the scholarly world, and its engagement with its present, that changed and produced new objects of scholarly inquiry in twentieth-century classical scholarship. Classical antiquity is in fact an unstable object, one that comes into being with each encounter; and our relationship to it changes as we come to terms again and again with the artifacts, objects, ruins, and fragmentary texts of the ancient Greek past.

Freud on the Akropolis

Sigmund Freud traveled to Greece in 1904; Freud's letter to Romain Rolland, written in 1936 on the occasion of Rolland's seventieth birthday, was a birthday gift, an offering, from an old man to a younger one, written when the world was on the threshold of war. It concerns the journey Freud and his brother took in southern Europe; offered at Trieste the possibility of traveling on to Athens, they both became inexplicably depressed and yet, like automata, they went on. Having arrived in Athens, Freud had what he calls a "disturbance of memory" on the Akropolis. In his recollection he writes:

> When, finally, on the afternoon after our arrival, I stood on the Acropolis and cast my eyes around upon the landscape, a surprising thought suddenly entered my mind: "So all this really *does* exist, just as we learned at school!"[19]

He was of two minds: one had doubted the very existence of the Akropolis, while the other was astonished, incredulous about this very doubt. Upon reflection, Freud concludes:

> [T]he whole psychical situation, which seems so confused and is so difficult to describe, can be satisfactorily cleared up by assuming that at the time I had . . . a momentary feeling: "What I see here is not real." Such a feeling is known as a "feeling of derealization." I made an attempt to ward that feeling off, and I succeeded, at the cost of making a false pronouncement about the past. (244)

What he called "derealization" is a defense, aimed at keeping something away from the ego, at disavowing it—just as, Freud reminds us, King Boabdil, the last Moorish king of Granada, disavowed the news of the fall of his last fortress by killing the messenger.

Freud decides that he could not bear the physical reality of Athens, of the Akropolis, of the Parthenon, and that his disturbance of memory stemmed from a "disavowal":

> It must be that a sense of guilt was attached to the satisfaction in having gone such a long way: there was something about it that was wrong, that from earliest times had been forbidden. It was something to do with a child's criticism of his father, with the undervaluation which took the place of the over-valuation of earlier childhood. It seems as though the essence of success was to have got further than one's father, and as though to excel one's father was still something forbidden.
>
> In addition . . . in our particular case, [t]he very theme of Athens and the Acropolis in itself contained evidence of the son's superiority. Our father had been in business, he had had no secondary education, and Athens could not have meant much to him. Thus what interfered with our enjoyment of the journey to Athens was a feeling of *filial piety*. (247–48)

A knowledge of classical antiquity signifies the gentleman, luxury, and an elite education, and marked the distance between these sons and their father.

Freud's letter stresses the impact of the material, physical, stony presence of the Parthenon on someone who knew so well the textual tradition of Greek literature, bringing up the matter of material culture: the fact that we may now self-consciously construct our narratives, our histories, but that nonetheless there are *things*—ruins, vases, bones—that stubbornly remain from people who lived before us. How do we integrate them into our narratives about the past?[20] One issue in the discipline of classical studies has been a division of labor between those scholars who deal with the material world, and those who treat the supposedly immaterial world of texts—tragedy, poetry, philosophy. The material world contains dirt, bones, ruins, fragments (those fragments, in fact, sometimes bearing texts), all the detritus of the ancient world. The world of literary studies, and cultural studies in general, seems to seek to protect itself from acknowledgment of the decay, ruin, and fragmentation of the material world encountered by archaeologists. Philologists, unless they are engaged with the difficult work of examining papyri and manuscripts, find the works of the great masters of the ancient world in sanitized, purified form, printed in books or even further dematerialized on the Internet. Freud's visit to the Akropolis recalls that material dimension of the study of antiquity, the ruined stones of the Parthenon, the sacred site desecrated by centuries of unbelievers, by shelling, by tourists with their debris. I want in this book to insist on the precious and unsettling material remains of the ancient world, and on all their intervening history.

Freud's letter brings up other matters of interest here, among them the knowledge of classical antiquity as a marker of class, separating men of culture and leisure from those in commerce and trade, from women, and from workers. Part of the European tradition of class and gender distinction rests on a privileging of Greek antiquity as an object of elite education. The cultivated knowledge of Latin and Greek passed from generation to generation as a hermetic initiation among men of the upper classes, eventually producing intellectuals and imperial bureaucrats.[21] In *Separate Tables*, an English post–World War II film, David Niven passes himself off as a retired major in a small seaside boardinghouse, makes an error in citing Horace, and reveals his belief that the Roman poet Horace wrote in Greek. His ignorance gives him away as an impostor. The film is ironic about the snobbery and condescension of the man who recognizes his error, but nonetheless records the power of such markers of class even as they wane.

Registering a difference of class between one generation and the next, then, in terms of an appreciation of classical antiquity, Freud addressed the crucial matter of the son's going beyond his father, his having surpassed his father in education and in professional status; and his anxiety has its bearing on some of the matters discussed in this book. Classical scholarship has had its obligations, gratitude, debts to be paid to its ancestors, its intellectual filiations that may replicate forms of blindness just as much as they transmit erudition and skills. Generations of scholars follow in the footsteps of their scholarly predecessors, perpetuating blindnesses, with oblivion, shame, or resistance governing their treatment of the issue of slavery, for example. The tradition of Hellenic studies has only with some difficulty acknowledged the traumatic presence of slaves in the ancient world, even as other scholars have celebrated Greek antiquity precisely for the freedoms invented and sustained for citizens in a world also occupied by slaves.[22]

In discussing his disturbance of memory, Freud presents the issue of disavowal, which is central to the concerns in this book. *Disavowal* is defined by Laplanche and Pontalis in their dictionary of psychoanalysis as "a mode of defence which consists in the subject's refusing to recognise the reality of a traumatic perception—most especially the perception of the absence of the woman's penis."[23] Disavowal is connected to Freud's version of fetishism, caused by the simultaneous disavowal of "castration" and the recognition of an absence; such a complex reaction to the female body, supposedly castrated, produces a psychic "splitting" and, in some, the erotic attachment to such substitutes for the phallus as feet or silks. The analogous fetishizing of antiquity as a site of origin for Western culture may require the simultaneous recognition and disavowal of such a problematic feature of ancient societies as slavery. For some early classicists of the antebellum South, for example, a fetishization of ancient Greece permitted an overt or covert celebration of slave-holding in the guise of appreciation for heroic, exemplary ancestors. These themes, of class, filial piety, material culture, and disavowal, called up by Freud's retrospective interpretation of his own reaction to the remains of ancient Athens, persist through my discussion of the place, or absence, of slavery in classical studies.

The name of Freud and of his important follower, Jacques Lacan, stand for the recognition of a troubled, split, fragmentary access to knowledge. Disavowal, like the themes of the unconscious, projection, transference, and countertransference, adduced by these thinkers to account for the operations of the human mind, acknowledges the difficulties, even the impossibility, of a pure, immediate access to our objects of inquiry. Psychoanalysis tries to recognize and name, but never fully to master, all that inevitably interferes with a perfect, true, and objective knowledge of one's self, of others, of texts, of all that one encounters in life. Psychoanalysis, with its rich vocabulary for describing the troubling, noisy, interfering investments we bring to any object, opens up new kinds of reading. To the confidence of the positivist working toward a clear, unblemished account of the ancient past, I prefer the self-conscious, self-critical, self-reflexive mode of knowing recorded in Freud's memory of the Athenian Akropolis. As Freud and Nietzsche insist, every perspective is particular, internally troubled, marked by conscious or unconscious investments. One can never know or understand all the determinants of one's inquiry, never fully represent the object. There is no single, true, whole picture of the past.

Studying Antiquity

Classicists have traditionally adopted a commonsensical attitude toward antiquity, one unselfconsciously consistent with a positivist or scientific view of the project of history—that of course the ancient Greeks survive; that we can pursue them, as did generations of scholars before; that we can know more and more about the Greeks through such means as printed texts or through the study of ruins; that of course we can write about them without concern about our own writing, our own rhetoric; that our aim is eventually to reconstruct their reality; and that such a goal is sensible and realistic, with any other attitude being obfuscating and irrelevant to the discipline of classics. There are important exceptions to this norm—in queer studies, in the history of sexuality and pederasty, in the work of David Halperin and Jack Winkler, for example, and also in the literary studies of Daniel Selden and Jim Porter, scholars touched by the example of the renegade classicist Friedrich Nietzsche.[24] Yet the positivist assumptions noted above are taken for granted by many classicists who see themselves as modest historians of a particular moment of the past. There is much thoughtful, often brilliant work, sometimes hermetically contained within the field of classical studies precisely because it hasn't taken seriously, or perhaps been contaminated by, questions of textuality, rhetoric, critiques of developmental narratives, and the erosion of stable historical paradigms elsewhere in the humanities.

Rey Chow has written some suggestive pages on the melancholy of the sinologist that are relevant here.

> For Freud, we remember, the melancholic is a person who cannot get over the loss of a precious, loved object and who ultimately introjects this loss into his ego. . . . In the case of the sinologist's relationship with his beloved object, "China," melancholia is complicated by the presence of a third party—the living members of the Chinese culture, who provide the sinologist with a means of externalizing his loss and directing his blame.[25]

The classicist, on the other hand, has no living survivors of the culture she mourns, although she has at times consoled herself for her loss, assuaged her melancholy, by replacing the dead Greeks with living "natives," using contemporary anthropological work, ethnographies based on contemporary "primitive," "native," or "untouched" Mediterranean societies, to guide interpretations of the ancient Greeks. Classicists' mining of anthropological texts, and their comparative methods, can seem like a refusal to accept the loss of the Greeks. The Greeks are dead, but some modes of comparison find displaced forms of them, still-living exemplars, who can be interviewed. In the manner found wanting by Walter Benjamin and Paul DeMan, we can imagine some naïve symbolic fusion by extension with the ancient Greeks themselves, rather than the mournful recognition of ruin and the necessity of allegory. This solution to the problem of representing antiquity in the present seems as problematic as that of the neoconservatives who seek to preserve a fetishized, frozen ancient Greece without slaves or women or pederasts, for the moral edification of children.[26]

Within the humanities, the discipline of classics is anomalous with virtues and strengths inherent in its position. Because of its inherently historical perspective, the discipline often mounts a determined resistance to a version of cultural studies based entirely on contemporary culture.[27] It is committed to the preservation of philological integrity and knowledge of the ancient languages of Greek and Latin, and thus in this period of globalization goes against the grain of an English-only, presentist emphasis in the academy. Yet if it fails to respond to the critiques of transparent access to the past, of an unexamined relationship to history, classics could go the way of Egyptology, confined to a few universities' graduate programs and no longer part of the undergraduate curriculum.

Cultural studies, a more recently developed discipline for the study of culture than the traditional classics department, can itself be accused of a positivist orientation; it may have new objects of analysis, but often, like classics, fails to recognize rhetorical and textual issues, assuming an immediate access to its objects. And it rarely incorporates the self-conscious doubt about full, perfect knowledge that a psychoanalytic perspective brings. But a perspective informed by a historically self-conscious version of cultural studies, on the other hand, acknowledging a political engagement, attempting to address societies as problematic, heterogeneous, contradictory cultural fields, perhaps can come to terms more fruitfully with antiquity, with the complexity of the study of culture in other fields in the humanities, and with such matters as the everyday life of the ancient Greeks.

A Southerner in the Peloponnesian War

I see this book as a meditation on these issues, taking up the crucial matter of slavery, slavery in antiquity, and slavery in America. The field of classical studies in North America was from its inception informed, inhabited, and troubled by the question of slavery in the nation of the United States of America, and by the analogies made between the American institution and the slave societies of Greek and Roman antiquity. Some Northerners who fought in the Civil War against the Confederacy and were committed abolitionists, often informed by Christian ideas, had worked in the fields of rhetoric and had taught the ancient languages of Greek and Latin. Joshua Chamberlain, for example, professor of rhetoric and later president of Bowdoin College and governor of Maine, fought in the Union Army.[28] Before the Civil War, he taught Latin and Greek at Bowdoin, where he encountered Harriet Beecher Stowe, the wife of fellow professor Calvin Stowe, reading installments of *Uncle Tom's Cabin* to an assembled company at the couple's "Saturday Evenings," which Chamberlain attended. At the war's end, Chamberlain presided over the formal surrender of the Confederacy at Appomattox. The phrases he assembled concerning the struggle over slavery rarely refer to antiquity, except through the rare citation of Vergil; he says of the Confederacy: "it set slavery across the nation's way, and God,—in his wrath, in his justice, in his mercy, in his love, in his far purpose for man and earth,—swept slavery from the path, as the mighty pageant of the free people passed on to its glory."[29] Such figural language befits the nineteenth-century professor of rhetoric; the study of antiquity as a historical culture yields little in the way of intellectual or political support for abolitionism.

By contrast, the career of Basil Lanneau Gildersleeve can serve here to illuminate the profound and troubled connections between the foundation of classical studies as a professional discipline in the United States and the history of slave-holding in the southern states. Gildersleeve may stand as a case study; his biography provides another example of the complex relationship of modern American intellectuals to classical antiquity. The scholarly work and life of Gildersleeve have recently attracted notice; an *American Journal of Philology* Monograph in Classical Philology, published in 1986, was devoted to his life and works, a sign of the growing interest in the history of the discipline of classics.[30] While the connection between the field of classics and American slavery has often itself been rendered invisible, Gildersleeve's long and important career as an American classicist—present at the beginnings of the professionalization of the discipline; founder of its national society and its journal, which survive to the present; and his scholarly works, monuments in the field—bears with it the traces of his nostalgia for a lost southern culture, with its slaves, and for another lost world, that of the ancient Greeks, Spartan and Athenian, and their slaves.[31] Gildersleeve's career illustrates an early identification of professional classicists with the slave-holding societies of antiquity: one source of the fetishization of ancient Greece, and an aspect of ancient culture that has subsequently often been disavowed or elided in the field.

Although Greek and Latin had long been taught at American colleges, including Bowdoin, Harvard, and Yale, it was with the introduction of the model of the German university that classics achieved the status of professionalization as a discipline.[32] Gildersleeve founded and edited one of the discipline's most important journals, the *American Journal of Philology*, in 1880 at The Johns Hopkins University. In 1877–78 and again in 1909 he served as president of the American Philological Association, the principal scholarly organization of the field of classics, founded in 1869. Gildersleeve had graduated from Princeton in 1849, studied in Berlin and in Bonn, and received his Ph.D. from Göttingen in 1853. After this training in German methods and style of scholarship, he returned to the United States and taught at the University of Virginia, then was appointed to the chair of Greek at Hopkins in 1876, the first professor named at the new university. In the meanwhile, Professor Gildersleeve also served in the Confederate cavalry during the Civil War.

Gildersleeve's position on the American Civil War was deeply felt, carefully reasoned, and set down fully during the combat and in the years afterwards. In a letter written during the war, from a "camp Near Hamilton's Crossing" on September 10, 1863, Gildersleeve explains his views:

> As (crossed out) For myself (crossed out)/my part/ I will not allow myself to regret the outbreak of the war. I have no scruples with regard to the justice of our cause. We are in the right—and that solves all questions for me as to my personal duty.[33]

Later in his life, responding to an invitation to "make intelligible to the educated man of the North those springs of conduct that sent the young Southerner into the field with untroubled conscience and high sense of duty,"[34] Gildersleeve wrote two essays, "The Creed of the Old South," and "A Southerner in the Peloponnesian War."[35] In the letter explaining his response, he writes:

> The cause was one for which I wrote, prayed, fought, suffered but in the long agony I never was haunted by a doubt as to the righteousness of the

course which we followed and even if there had been a doubt as to the justice of our cause, the command of the State would have sufficed.[36]

The two essays, first printed in the *Atlantic*, were published in 1915 by Johns Hopkins University Press in a single volume as *The Creed of the Old South;* they reveal Gildersleeve's commitment to the Southern cause of states' rights, his complex relationship to the question of slavery, and his identification with both the Spartans and the Athenians in an extended analogy drawn between the American Civil War and the Peloponnesian War of the fifth century BCE.[37]

In the original essay, "Creed of the Old South," Gildersleeve recalls months of suffering on the battlefield. His language, like that of the classical authors he so much admired, is saturated with references to slavery, and, like the ancients, he understood many political questions through analogy with slavery. His defense of the Confederacy's position in the Civil War relies on such a parallel: "Submission to any encroachment, the least as well as the greatest, on the rights of a State means slavery. To us submission meant slavery, as it did to Pericles and the Athenians."[38] Here Gildersleeve alludes to the works of the ancient historians, and their frequent representation of an opposition between slavery and freedom, the basis of much political theory and debate in antiquity. The free Athenians' state found its definition in contrast with that of the Persians', characterized by what the Greeks saw as imperial despotism and a populace enslaved; submission to the Persians in the Persian War would have meant slavery, and the later Athenian struggle with the Spartans and their allies was cast in a similar light. Defeat by one's enemies meant not only literal but also metaphorical slavery.

Gildersleeve encodes the principle of "States' rights" (32) in analogous terms; surrender to the North meant slavery for all the South: "there was no lurking suspicion of any moral weakness in our cause. Nothing could be holier than the cause, nothing more imperative than the duty of upholding it" (38). Gildersleeve translates the literal slavery of African Americans into a matter of "States' rights," and interprets the greater struggle of the Civil War as a matter of local freedom for the Southern states: "Slavery was simply a test case, and except as a test case it is too complicated a question to be dealt with at the close of a paper which is already too long" (45). Evasive here, Gildersleeve, at least upon reflection in the years after the Confederate defeat, does not appear to have been a passionate advocate of slavery. He describes the variety of positions Southerners took on the question, and exhibits some sympathy for those who believed that African American freed slaves should return to Africa. Nonetheless, he found reasons for criticism of the slaves and former slaves: "the negro race does not deserve undivided praise for its conduct during the war. Let some small part of the credit be given to the masters, not all to the finer qualities of their 'brothers in black.' The school in which the training was given is closed, and who wishes to open it?" (48) Gildersleeve insists that the war was fought not for slavery but against the metaphorical "enslavement" of the Southern states to the North: "That the cause we fought for and our brothers died for was the cause of civil liberty, and not the cause of human slavery, is a thesis we feel ourselves bound to maintain" (51). But for this classical scholar, throughout his later life in the postbellum world, "the poetry of life will still find its home in the old order" (52). And this "old order," one of slaves and free, finds its analogues in utopian memories of classical Greece.

The nostalgia for the "Old South," for the world of slavery, recurs in the second essay published in the *Atlantic*, which appeared in 1897. In "A Southerner in the Peloponnesian War," Gildersleeve explores more fully a comparison between ancient and modern societies. The yearning for a lost past colored not just his relationship to the South of the antebellum years but also his relationship to ancient Greece. Throughout the essay, he compares two wars. The Peloponnesian War was not fought over the question of literal, corporeal slavery of part of the population of one of the combatants. Rather, Gildersleeve understood it as like the American Civil War in being about the enslavement, the domination, of one free state by another. Both wars, he argues, were fought between leagues, a northern union and a southern confederacy. They both involved a southern land power. The Athenian league was naval and "progressive," while the Spartan league was "conservative." The Athenians were in favor of centralization, he writes; the Spartans, of autonomy: "it would be possible to write the story of our Peloponnesian war in phrases of Thucydides" (73).

Gildersleeve experienced the American Civil War through the frame of his readings on the ancient struggle between the Spartans and the Athenians. The Spartans, analogous in his mind to the South in the American Civil War, were victorious in the ancient combat; and perhaps their victory, allowing for retrospective fantasies of the victory of the Confederacy, both during and after the Civil War, gave life to the analogy.

> I went from my books to the front, and went back from the front to my books, from the Confederate war to the Peloponnesian war, from Lee and Early to Thucydides and Aristophanes. (79)

Gildersleeve's postwar life as father and founder of the professional discipline of classics in the United States was shaped in some measure by his service in the Confederate cavalry:

[T]he war was part of my life, and it is not altogether surprising that the memories of the Confederacy come back to me whenever I contemplate the history of the Peloponnesian war, which bulks so largely in all Greek studies. (83)

He draws many parallels between his stint in the Confederacy soldiery and the accounts of the Peloponnesian War in ancient texts:

The war was a good time for the study of the conflict between Athens and Sparta. It was a great time for reading and re-reading classical literature generally, for the South was blockaded against new books as effectively, almost, as Megara was blockaded against garlic and salt. (84)

And the readings a classicist makes of ancient Athenian texts, since almost none survive from Sparta, reminded him of the defeated and their sufferings during war. He recalls the hungers of war, and Aristophanes' comedy *The Acharnians*, with its fantasy of a separate peace: "all our cry for sugar was but an echo of the cry for honey in the Peloponnesian war" (100). The later study of classical Athens became for him often a study and a recollection of war:

[A]ll these little details of daily hardship come back even now to the old student when he reopens his Aristophanes. No wonder that the ever present Peloponnesian war will not suffer him to forget those four years in which the sea of trouble rose higher and higher. (103)

Studying the ancients recalled his own war to Gildersleeve, but he performed a strange chiastic move in reading his war and the ancient war together. Although he identified with the Spartans, with their conservatism, their localism, their landed power, his allegiance to the defeated Southerner forced him to switch sides in the Peloponnesian War—to read the Athenians' suffering and defeat as his own.

Deborah Reeves Hopkins emphasizes that throughout his career as a classicist, Gildersleeve was reminded of his own career as a warrior:

Just as Gildersleeve spoke an eloquent and rational defense of the South in the Civil War in his essays, "The Creed of the Old South" and "A Southerner in the Peloponnesian War," so in his scholarly publications he revealed the scars of the lost cause. In his introduction to Pindar, he argued that "it was no discredit to Pindar that he went honestly with his state in the struggle . . . .the Greece that came out of the Persian War was a very different thing from the cantons that ranged themselves on this side and that of a quarrel which, we may be sure, bore another aspect to those who stood aloof from it than it wears in the eyes of moderns, who have learned to be Hellenic patriots." This was the Gildersleeve who stirred resentment among his professional colleagues, who would not surrender an opening for another word on behalf of his cause. Any opportunity for reminiscence of the Southern experience in the war was for Gildersleeve a partisan act his life long.[39]

Seth Schein comments on Gildersleeve's aversion to classical tragedy in his scholarly work, citing "an aristocratic bias in favor of traditional institutions and values, traditional forms of heroic excellence" perhaps incompatible with tragedy as a genre of the Athenian democracy.[40] Schein attributes to Gildersleeve's influence what he sees as a relative neglect of the study of Greek tragedy even up to the 1980s.

The complex identifications of Gildersleeve with the ancient Greeks colored both his interpretation of his own history and of classical Greece. His sympathy for the defeated, his understanding of the victorious, and his emphasis on war affected his autobiography, his classical scholarship, and the subsequent development of the discipline of classics in the United States. And, although he denied the relevance of the institution of slavery to the lost cause of the South, it does figure in his account of that lost society. Hopkins reminds us that "[a]s Gildersleeve expressed it, most Southerners believed that they were fighting for the cause of civil liberty and not the cause of human slavery. The biographer of William Gilmore Simms, W. P. Trent, had written in 1891 that such a view neglected the fact that it was human slavery which largely determined the nature of a Southerner's idea of civil liberty."[41]

Ancient Slavery, American Slavery

The entanglement of American history with ancient slavery precedes and exceeds the life and works of the classicist Basil Lanneau Gildersleeve.[42] As Louis Menand reminds us, "Cornelius Conway Felton, a professor of Greek at Harvard . . . who later became president of Harvard College, was proslavery and an opponent of antislavery agitation."[43] Felton subsequently, after the near fatal beating of Charles Sumner by a South Carolinian on the Senate floor, changed his views and turned against slavery (ibid.). Participants in the debates concerning slavery mined the histories of ancient Greece and Rome and set them up as examples of political excellence, sometimes defending freedom as a concept possible only in the context of slave-holding societies. In *The Making of New World Slavery*, Robin Blackburn writes:

[I]n the realm of philosophy, the Renaissance did little to weaken ideas supportive of the legitimacy of slavery. . . . The rediscovery of classical authorities did nothing to undermine belief in the lawfulness of slavery. Indeed, by diffusing a greater awareness of the cultural achievement of Antiquity and contributing to a sense that Christendom was its legitimate heir, the Renaissance could lead to a sense of shared cultural superiority which dovetailed with the classical Aristotelian doctrine that barbarians were natural slaves.[44]

David Brion Davis recalls that "in 1488 Pope Innocent VIII accepted a gift of one hundred Moors from Ferdinand of Spain, and distributed them among the cardinals and nobility."[45] Thomas More's *Utopia* contains slaves, in servitude for various causes. Davis further notes that "the Reformation brought no immediate change in the traditional ideas of servitude" (106), although of course the movement that eventually contributed to its abolition gained strength in this period. Yet, "the revival of classical learning, which may have helped to liberate the mind of Europe from bondage to ignorance and superstition, only reinforced the traditional justifications for human slavery" (107). Slavery was understood to be natural for "barbarians," that is, in some interpretations, for non-Christians, a corrective and a punishment for their lack of belief; and the idea is traced back to, and authorized by, the philosophical reasoning of the ancient Greek philosopher Aristotle.

The nineteenth-century American writer George Fitzhugh, for example, classically erudite in his advocacy of slavery, like many proslavery thinkers catalogued the wonders of ancient Greece and Rome to authorize claims about the benefits slavery bestows on human societies. Fitzhugh argued passionately for the enslavement of those unable to care for themselves:

> We conclude that about nineteen out of every twenty individuals have "a natural and inalienable right" to be taken care of and protected, to have guardians, trustees, husbands, or masters; in other words, they have a natural and inalienable right to be slaves.[46]

The benefits of slavery were evident to Fitzhugh; a good Aristotelian, he urged the dependency of the weak on the strong. Calling himself a "socialist," he represented slavery as a utopian protectorate for those who had become helpless victims in capitalist economies.

Of course, even in the more recent past, slavery advocates looked not only to classical, "pagan" antiquity but also to the Judaic and Christian traditions for authority. The May 8, 1996, edition of the *Los Angeles Times* reported on the recent activities of an Alabama politician:

> A white Republican state senator running for Congress wrote a speech in which he argued that slavery is justified by the Bible and was good for blacks. Charles Davidson, 61, had prepared the speech for a Senate debate

over his proposal to fly the Confederate battle flag over the Capitol. Davidson cited the Book of Leviticus—"You may acquire male and female slaves from the pagan nations that are around you"—and quoted 1 Timothy as saying slaves should "regard their own masters as worthy of all honor." "The truth is that nowhere on the face of the earth, in all of time, were servants better treated or better loved than they were in the Old South by white, black, Hispanic and Indian slave owners," Davidson wrote.[47]

Advocates, defenders, and apologists for slavery, past and present, find solace in ancient Israel as well as in Greece and Rome for their views.

The nineteenth-century Virginian Fitzhugh took an extreme position on the question of white slavery, but his turning to antiquity for support for his proslavery arguments was not unique. The proslavery thinkers of the American tradition referred often to the classics; they saw in ancient Greece and Rome philosophical greatness, the invention of freedom for the free, and linked the achievements of the ancient world with the institution of slavery. Anti-Jeffersonian conservatives advocated what Larry Tise calls "a full-scale salvaging of the classical tradition": "If a young man were steeped in the philosophy of ancient Greece, the political thought of Greece and Rome, and the classical languages, he would be insulated against all of the booby-traps of modern infidel thought."[48] In these thinkers' eyes, Jeffersonianism was democracy, and democracy was inspired by the French Revolution, and led inevitably to anarchy.

> The only true republics were those with rigidly structured societies, with clear-cut class differentiation, and with firmly established patterns of authority. Rome and Greece were obviously the foremost examples of republican societies. (226)

William Harper, an important proslavery ideologue of the 1830s who wrote a *Memoir on Slavery*, refers his readers to the models of Greece and Rome: "I may observe that the history of these great republics, from which the rest of the world learns wisdom, may be studied with double advantage and instruction by us" (340).[49] An anonymous Southern clergyman reinforces Harper's argument:

> How came the distinguished heathen Republics of Greece and Rome to flourish for many centuries, having the Institution of slavery as the foundation, as the palladium of their Constitutions? The Institution of slavery ever has been and ever will be the only sure foundation of all republican governments.[50]

As Eugene Genovese remarks: "The proslavery theorists never tired of proclaiming that the greatness of ancient Egypt, Israel, Greece and

Rome had been based on slavery, and the reading of ancient history and literature seemed to confirm the proclamation."[51]

Classicists and Slaves

Classicists may be unfamiliar with these aspects of the history of their discipline—the implication of such founding scholars as Basil Gildersleeve in the militant defense of the slave-holding Confederacy in the Civil War, and with the political deployment of antiquity in defense of slavery—but such a genealogy affects not only the polemical use of the example of classical societies in contemporary political debates but also classicists' own readings of antiquity, embedded as they are in an intellectual and scholarly tradition. The red herring of "political correctness" is used now to discredit any attempts to recognize class differences or forms of oppression in contemporary or historical cultures, and this too serves to reproduce the invisibility of ancient slaves to the modern gaze. The discipline of classics, since the time of its professionalization in the early nineteenth century, may have obfuscated the question of ancient slavery in part to protect itself from this nation's history with slaves and their descendants. Slavery is too recent and painful a memory for American culture, one which brings up difficult questions about hierarchy and racism in the present.

It may support my argument about American classical scholarship to observe that other national traditions in the field of classics have been differently attentive to issues of slavery and slaves. In the American tradition, where slavery and slave trading played a crucial role in eighteenth- and nineteenth-century economic development and politics, slavery has been a more vexed question. Important scholarship on the history of slavery emerged from the former Soviet Union and Germany, and also from Britain, which gave up slave trading before slavery ended in the United States; in France and Italy, the place of slaves in the economic development and intellectual history of antiquity has been granted a great deal of attention.[52] Neglect of the question of slavery may also be related to the anti-Marxist and conservative strains of American politics and academic institutions. Moses I. Finley, an important scholar of slavery, left the United States in the McCarthyist 1950s. In his introduction to Finley's book *The Ancient Economy*, reissued in 1999, Ian Morris writes: "By 1954 Finley was under considerable pressure at Rutgers for his and his wife's political connections with radicals. As a serious student of Weberian sociology, Finley would have made a strange communist, but he and his wife, Mary, decided to emigrate to Britain."[53] Finley spent the rest of his scholarly career in a more tolerant England.

The Historiography of Ancient Slavery

The Roman historian Keith Bradley, in his essay "'The Regular Daily Traffic in Slaves': Roman History and Contemporary History," responds to other historians' charge that "presentism," a recognition of the historian's situation in the present, of the setting of a historical agenda in the present, "distorts" our view of the past.⁵⁴ He accepts that distortion with resignation: "Distorted vision may be imperfect vision, but it is preferable to no vision at all" (134). Bradley makes a point of condemning ancient slavery: "The reality is that slavery at Rome was an evil, violent and brutalizing institution that the Romans themselves, across a vast interval of time, consciously chose to maintain, for which they themselves were responsible, and whose justification they never questioned" (136). He characterizes his own project as a gesture of solidarity with the silenced slaves of antiquity: "We will never know exactly, to be sure, what they thought, or felt; but to try to find out is, I believe, something that matters" (138). Paul Cartledge, who studies ancient Greek slavery, has argued that it is easier for Britons than Americans to adopt a "morally neutral or 'value-free' stance towards the very fact of slavery in classical Greece," but that such a stance ignores Britain's guilty role in transporting millions of Africans to slavery in the New World.⁵⁵ He poses a question in a 1993 essay: Was classical Greek slavery, though regrettable, the foundation of the ideal of freedom, and therefore not entirely "a Bad thing"? Or should we rather liken Greek slavery to Shakespeare's 'worm i' the bud'—"a cancre that ate the heart out of the efflorescent bloom of classical Greek civilization?"(168) Upon reflection, he concludes that Greek slavery *was* "like Shakespeare's worm" (177), that it "warped and poisoned the outlook of free Greek citizen men" (ibid.).

Both these scholars have contributed immensely to our understanding of ancient slavery, and their arguments are important programmatic declarations about their scholarship. Our relationship to modern slavery troubles our view of the ancient practices; the detailing of atrocities, assigning blame, accepting guilt, are matters of contemporary politics; apologizing for slavery in the New World is implicated in racial relations now. In addition to expressing solidarity with ancient slaves and indignation about ancient slavery, we need to consider the ways in which ancient slavery was inseparable from such practices as democracy and philosophy that begin in ancient Greece. I don't think we will ever have access to "what slaves thought or felt," especially in the case of Greece—no matter how much we mine our evidence, or try by analogy with antebellum slaves in the United States or slaves in the present, to invent a voice for the slaves of antiquity. Nor do I believe that slavery somehow "spoiled" a noble citizenry of Athens; slavery is constitutive rather than supplementary to or parasitic upon classical Athenian culture. The study of slavery should neither be dismissed as irrelevant to the great questions, nor confined to the work of what I call "slave-ologists," those scholars who use social-scientific methods to estimate how many slaves there were in antiquity in order to construct economic models of the ancient city, who see only slaves and slavery in a slave mode of production when they look at ancient culture.[56] I am interested rather in the inseparability, the *embeddedness* of slavery in all the phenomena of ancient Greek life.

Classics, Slavery, and Cultural Studies

Scholars have in the past often overlooked the presence, literal and metaphorical, of slaves and slavery in their evidence from Greek antiquity, merely noting them. Or they have studied only slavery, only slaves. In this book I want to attempt to register this split, to read some ancient texts in such a way that these presences are acknowledged differently, not smoothly integrated into readings but rather marked as difficulties.[57] I do not want to suggest that classicists have been oblivious to slavery, but rather that it has proved difficult in modern slave and postslavery cultures like Britain and the United States to measure its presence adequately in representations of the ancient world.[58] Many historical texts either cite slavery as a feature of ancient life when it impinges directly on their narratives, in the form of an "event" like the desertions of slaves during the Peloponnesian War, without considering its embeddedness in everyday life. Or they focus exclusively on slavery as their object. The great historian G. E. M. de Sainte-Croix wrote an immense, exemplary, encyclopedic volume on slavery in antiquity, *The Class Struggle in the Ancient Greek World*; other historians rarely integrate his findings into their narratives about ancient Greece.[59] For example, the British Museum's guide to everyday life in antiquity says dismissively, "The idea of slavery is repulsive to those who have been reared on the belief that all men are born free. We must judge the ancients in their own terms, however, and not by the moral standards of our own day."[60] The only survey history of Greek antiquity I know which does take seriously the central, informing presence of slavery for Greek society is Paul Cartledge's *The Greeks*, which devotes an entire chapter to the topic "Of Inhuman Bondage: Free v. Slave."[61] Such attention to slavery is the exception rather than the rule; cultural imperatives, pressures to preserve the study of antiquity as part of the curriculum of Western civilization, have led often to misrecognitions or occlusion of the troubling presence of slaves in almost every scene of Greek antiquity.

23

A cultural study of classical Greece might aim to recognize the so-called distortions, or rather what we might call in a psychoanalytic analogy the inevitable projections, disavowals, transference, and counter-transference of our own situation in recently slave-holding societies. Such a cultural studies approach, interdisciplinary, critical, self-critical, and attentive to the relations of power in the past and in the present, might describe antiquity by taking into account those inevitable "distortions"—our perspective from the present—neither stopping at the point of judgment and confession and guilt, nor isolating the study of slaves and slavery in economic or social history, but rather embedding it in our understanding of all domains of ancient life.[62]

Part of the difficulty of seeing, acknowledging, and weighing the presence of slaves in every scene of ancient Greek life is the structure of the discipline of classical studies itself.[63] Unlike other fields in the humanities, classics has been constituted as a historical entity; rather than studying "literature," or "history," classicists study ancient literature or ancient history. Although such a disciplinary shape might seem ideal for interdisciplinary work, and for a cultural studies that would take account of ancient Greek culture as a fragmentary, heterogeneous set of discourses, in fact the field often resembles a battlefield of disciplines. Epigraphers, papyrologists, archaeologists, and others, including many historians, have rarely been tempted by the almost revolutionary changes —the turn to textuality, for example—characteristic of other fields in the humanities. Methodological and theoretical questions have been neglected in the name of a scientific approach to hard data. The division of labor between scientific and cultural studies has been drawn with great vigor, and a certain contempt and condescension still govern the relationship between the empiricists and those more sympathetic to issues of interpretation, perspective, or hermeneutics, who are dismissed as dangerously vague and speculative. Issues of epistemology and interpretation, so important for literary and intellectual historians, are regarded by more empirical scholars as hopelessly amorphous and pointless, tossed out in the name of rigor. This chasm within the discipline of classics is one of the matters that concerns me here: how can we attempt to see ancient culture without replicating a disciplinary division of labor that cuts off history from culture?

So-called slave historians write immensely detailed factual studies on the numbers of slaves in ancient society, yet these are often disregarded by many scholars who work on literary cultural texts, focus on high cultural texts such as Greek tragedy, and attend to purely literary and aesthetic issues without considering the context of the drama's production within a slave-holding citizenry.[64] The intradisciplinary boundaries are defended with passion, most often from the bunker of the empiricists, to the detriment of understanding the ancient world; on the other side, many literary critics simply ignore the valuable empirical evidence produced by historians and archaeologists. I would like to call attention to this rift, and at the same time, following scholars like Sandra Joshel, Sheila Murnaghan, William Thalmann, and Danielle Allen, take account of the historical presence of slaves in the cultural landscape of antiquity.

My desire is not smoothly to integrate a recognition of slaves and slavery into accounts of the ancient object world, and of the textual history of antiquity. Rather, I see the value of the historical methods of Walter Benjamin, for example, in the confrontation of two worlds, that of ancient Greece and that of the United States in modernity and post-modernity. As Fredric Jameson has written, in a call for a more disjunctive, radical form of history than that commonly found in classical studies:

> We must try to accustom ourselves to a perspective in which every act of reading, every local interpretive practice, is grasped as the privileged vehicle through which two distinct modes of production confront and interrogate each other. Our individual reading thus becomes an allegorical figure for this essentially collective confrontation of two social forms.[65]

Greek Slaves

Part of the problem addressed here is that slavery appears in classical historiographical work, set off from cultural studies, as a closed, static system. Of course slavery itself has a history, as Moses Finley has pointed out.[66] It is a developing, dynamic element in ancient economies of various sorts, quite different in the Homeric world from its manifestations in the classical Greek *polis*, for example. And, as a feature of an ongoing social, cultural network, we must read it in its multiple, various being.

In this book, I have most often focused on Athenian slavery of the classical period, from which most of our textual evidence comes. But of course slavery itself is not monolithic, has its own histories, and covers a variety of situations. Moses Finley argued that the categories of unfreedom evolved from a wide spectrum of statuses, from free to unfree in the earlier historical periods, to a sharp opposition between slave and free citizen in the classical age.[67] The Greeks also made a distinction between helotry, the collective enslavement of conquered peoples who remained in their communities, typical of Sparta and some other cities, and chattel slavery, the individual status of slaves born into households, captured in war, kidnapped, or sold. There was a hierarchy of difference among slaves. Those born in Greek households, speaking Greek, serving as trusted members of households, differed from newly captive slaves, victims of kidnapping or prisoners of war, whose languages made them barbaric in the eyes of the Greek citizens, in comparison to the native slave population. The brutalized slaves who worked in the Athenian silver mines at Laurion, whose life expectancy was very short, no doubt resembled very little the educated and even elegant slaves of the wealthiest Athenian masters.

The second-century CE writer Athenaeus recounted the origins of chattel slavery, said to have begun on the island of Chios in the distant past: "The first Greeks, so far as we know, who made use of purchased slaves were the Chians. . . . the slaves whom the Chians own are derived from non-Greek peoples [*barbarous*], and they pay a price for them."[68] Athenaeus cited the account of the historian Theopompus, who went on to tell of these slaves' flight from slavery, and of their leader Drimakos, who negotiated with the Chians and managed the troupe of runaways. The Chian state put a price on his head; when he had grown old, Drimakos summoned his beloved (*eromenon*), and commanded the boy to behead him so he could collect the reward. After protests, the beloved did so, and then returned to his own country. The fugitive slaves remembered Drimakos as a hero, and offered the first fruits of their thefts on his shrine (265c–266e).[69]

There is substantial evidence for the ubiquity and value of slaves in ancient Greece and in Athens in particular. Artists and artisans represented slaves on artworks and everyday objects. Slave traders were important businessmen in the ancient economy, although they ran risks. Herodotus tells the story of one Panionios, who used to buy and castrate beautiful boys; one of these boys later forced Panionios to castrate his own four sons, who were then made to turn and castrate him (Herodotus 8.105–6). Thucydides recounts the enslavement of the women and children of the island of Melos, captured by the Athenians in the Peloponnesian War.[70] Slaves' testimony, obtained by torture, actual or threatened, figures in legal texts.[71] Advice on the proper administration of slaves abounds; a text attributed to Aristotle advises: "The principal and most essential form of property is that which is best and most central to managing a household: the human being. So the first thing to do is acquire good slaves";[72] this treatise also advises allowing slaves to have children, to serve as "hostages" (6). Some public slaves, Scythian archers, "originally lived in tents in the middle of the agora," and served as a police for Athens.[73] Other public slaves picked up the bodies of the dead found on the roads.[74] Although Solon had in the sixth century forbidden the sale of Athenian citizens and their families for debt (2; 6), other Greeks and barbarians lived among the Athenians as slaves. Speakers in court took the value of slaves into account when listing their assets: "my father, men of the jury, left behind two workshops, each with highly skilled craftsmen; one had thirty-two or thirty-three cutlers, each one worth five or six minae, and even the least skilled of them were worth not less than three minae. . . . Then there were twenty furniture-makers who had been given to him as security for an outstanding debt."[75] Their owners leased some slaves to work in Athens's silver mines at Laurion.[76] Skilled slaves, listed as "X belonging to Y," worked alongside Athenians and metics, non-Athenians resident in Athens, on such public buildings as the Erechtheion.[77] Wills included the disposition of the deceased's slaves; the putative will of Aristotle contained this provision: "Thales is to be given one thousand drachmae and a slave girl, in addition to the little girl I bought whom she has now" (Diogenes Laertius 5.14). Xenophon describes a husband's training of his wife, whose responsibilities in turn included training slaves, making them more valuable when sold (*Oikonomikos* 7.41). Law codes made provisions for establishing the status, slave or free, of persons; slaves could flee their masters and seek sanctuary in such shrines as the Theseion in Athens, and the law protected them from some forms of assault. "The Old Oligarch," an irritable conservative of fifth-century Athens, complained, "Slaves and metics are allowed the greatest license at Athens, and you are not allowed to strike any of them there, nor will a slave stand aside for you" (1.10).[78] All these details and many more of slave presence in Greek antiquity are registered on objects and in texts, yet somehow often fail to inform our sense of everyday reality, and of the context for literary and other cultural artifacts in Greek antiquity.

Despite the forgotten advocacy of slavery of the eighteenth and nineteenth centuries, or the disavowals, or their invisibility to scholars, slavery and slaves are everywhere in Greek antiquity: in the archaeological record, in the literary, historical, forensic, and philosophical texts that constitute our knowledge of the ancient world. Slavery enters into the very definitions of life, death, and human beings' relationship to the gods. Take, for example, a scene from Aristophanes' *Frogs. The Frogs* begins with a long exchange between Dionysos the god and his slave Xanthias, in which they mock other comic writers for their tired old jokes about how burdened the slave is. Of course he is burdened, his neck hurts, but he can't complain. This Xanthias regrets not fighting at sea, at the Battle of Arginousai, at which Athenian slaves fought so valiantly that they were subsequently freed. The two set off to the underworld, but the ferryman Charon refuses to carry a slave, so Xanthias has to go on foot around the lake that separates the world of the living from the underworld (190–91). They arrive at the door to the underworld, and Dionysos claims to be Herakles, but this earns him only threats from Aiakos the doorkeeper. Dionysos shits in fear, and then asks Xanthias to trade places with him. The slave is dressed as Herakles, while Dionysos, the god, will bear the luggage. When treats for Herakles are promised, they trade back again, and then again, when new threats are made. Xanthias offers his slave, Dionysos, for torture (616), by means of the piling on of bricks, stuffing his nose with acid, flaying, racking, hoisting him, and flogging him with a cat-o'-nine-tails. Dionysos, terrified, insists that he's the god and Xanthias the slave. Xanthias says that if he were a god, he wouldn't mind being beaten. And he argues that whichever of them takes the beating without flinching or crying out is the god, subtly obscuring the fact that the slave, an experienced victim of many beatings, would tolerate this beating more easily than a god. Aiakos proceeds to beat both onstage, and they steadily pretend indifference, masking their exclamations of pain as tears produced by onions, and as flights of song. Finally Aiakos concludes, "No, by Demeter, I can't find out which of you is the god" (668–69). He thinks his master and mistress, gods of the underworld, gods themselves, will be able to tell.

The scene presents this spectacle of beating, and a weird exchange of places between slave and god, with Dionysos as the more cowardly and ridiculous. The statuses of god and slave bracket that of the free mortal men in the audience, laughing at this mimesis of flogging, which serves strangely to reify and naturalize the place of slaves in this culture. If the nature of the gods is immutable and essential in its immortality, so the nature of a slave is fixed and naturalized as well. Even though the two can be comically changed one for the other onstage, in the end the god remains a god, and the slave a slave. Both are others, men who do not fit, somehow, in the world of the free. Gods, like slaves, are both invisible and ubiquitous. As Aristotle says, "a man who is incapable of entering into partnership, or who is so self-sufficing that he has no need to do so, is no part of a state, so that he must be either a lower animal or a god" (*Politics* 1253a).

Sokrates in Plato's *Phaedo* uses the analogy of slavery to account for his opposition to suicide:

> "The allegory which the mystics tell us—that we men are put in a sort of guard post, from which one must not release oneself or run away—seems to me to be a high doctrine with difficult implications. All the same, Cebes, I believe that this much is true, that the gods are our keepers [*epimeloumenous*], and we men are one of their possessions [*ktematon*]. Don't you think so?"
> "Yes, I do," said Cebes.

"Then take your own case. If one of your possessions were to destroy itself
without intimation from you that you wanted it to die, wouldn't you be
angry with it and punish it, if you had any means of doing so?" (62bc)

In this text, for the Sokrates of this dialogue, on the point of death, the
human condition is like slavery, enslavement to the gods, and the word
Sokrates uses here, "possessions," *ktematon*, suggests that all human beings are slaves, things owned; "we" mortal human beings are the gods'
slaves. For Plato, the analogy with slavery defines the human condition.

Overview of the Book

In this book, I consider various sites where slaves disturb the scene of
Greek antiquity in a heterogeneous set of soundings of various places
where the troubling representations, misrepresentations, or occlusions
of slavery occur. *Slaves and Other Objects* does not offer a continuous argument, and I cover a huge terrain here, reading across what have been
considered discrete cultural domains to try to come to something new.
Because it touches on so many objects and texts, the analyses in this
book cannot be as local, detailed, and specific as a positivist philologist
(or even I) might like them to be, and as the analyses of books devoted
to single texts or authors would be. As Bernard Williams writes in *Shame
and Necessity:* "The truth is that we all have to do more things than we
can rightly do, if we are to do anything at all."[79]

The mood, tone, and style of the chapters differ according to the subjects addressed. The first section of the book treats the occultation of
slavery in the presentation of objects in various institutions of classical
studies. I begin with the question of everyday life and with the exhibition of Greek antiquity in museums. This analysis is followed by a chapter on a particular kind of object represented on vases and in texts, the
dildo, which I connect with a chapter on bound, beaten, tortured, tattooed, and sexually available slave bodies. The second section of the
book deals with exemplary texts. The first chapter therein juxtaposes
discussion of a comedy of Aristophanes with consideration of the political rhetoric of freedom and unfreedom in ancient Athens. An essay on
women enslaved in Greek tragedy precedes a chapter on the ancient anecdote of the enslavement of Plato and on the *Meno*, the only Platonic
dialogue in which a slave speaks. There follow a chapter on the freed
slave and fabulist Aesop and the relationship between slavery and the
genre of the fable in antiquity, and another on Aristotle's work on the
question of slavery. The last chapter concerns slaves and the discourses
of anger in classical Greece, and returns to slavery in America.

Rather than writing an exhaustive historical or sociological account of slavery in Greek antiquity, I have sought to register the trouble slavery has caused for classicists, archaeologists, curators, and art historians who write about or represent the ancient world. Slavery and slaves, ubiquitous, informing, structurally necessary to ancient life, exist in a blind spot, obscured by modern investments in a narrative of origin, a certain denial about the present. I argue here for what might be called a "rhetorical" orientation to the ancient evidence of slavery, which considers representations as dynamic acts, performances in social situations. That is, slavery has a history, and every utterance, every statement, even every work of art that represents slavery is an intervention, an act to be understood in terms of this developing history. The acts we perceive in our evidence from antiquity, and that evidence itself, can be understood in terms of the dynamic maintenance of slavery as a fundamental asymmetry in antiquity's social relations. As in every society, power flows constantly among the human inhabitants of these ancient worlds. The asymmetry of the master-slave relationship must be actively sustained, maintained, reiterated, naturalized, and essentialized constantly. If there are sometimes challenges to this asymmetry, questions raised about the natural difference between master and slave, as in works of art, in certain moments of Aristophanic comedy or Euripidean drama, these questions are affirmed, answered, silenced, or drowned out by other sorts of acts, where the mutual recognition between master and slave is registered only to be truncated, cauterized, or aborted by a naturalizing of difference.

Scholarship on slavery, with its own rhetoric, implicated in the politics of its own day, can obscure this never-ending process, inevitable in any society marked by dramatic differences in the status of human beings. Scholarship can ignore slavery entirely. Or it can describe it as a static object in the past, relying on ancient texts, inscriptions, acts, and utterances as evidence of reality without considering the ways in which every utterance or representation is an act, a taking of a position in an ongoing struggle to maintain authority and mastery on the part of ancient slaveholders.[80] The slave is a sort of uncanny object, standing at a blind spot of modernity where the place of the subject and that of the object intersect. The slave is *a-topic*, eccentric, out of place, unnervingly both ubiquitous and invisible. And as such, the slave can and should destabilize, undo, unnerve the certainties of our knowledges about the ancient world. The slave pops up to defy the idealization of antiquity which has defined modernity's relationship to ancient Greece. If Gildersleeve idealized the ancient world, with its slaves, as a site of freedom and inspiration for the free, for a South founded on slave labor, post–Civil War America, as well as the European tradition, idealize another Greece, one from which the presence of the slaves has been erased, except for those few archaeologists and historians who concentrate on their existence. This double vision, overlapping idealizations, has served to obscure the presence of slaves for modernity. And in fact the ancient slave can stand as a figure for all the difficulties we face in trying to come to terms with ancient Greece. This past is fragmented, obscured by our investments in master narratives, in the masters' narratives, inaccessible except through the transmission and intervention of countless scholars. The slave can be glimpsed only through the veil of centuries, through the mask of racialized slavery in the more recent past, through anxieties about slavery and the persistent idealization of a democratic, philosophical Athens.

The distorted, beaten, whipped, tortured, tattooed, often comic body of the slave insists on its presence, and disturbs the tranquility of positivist historicism, of a serene and confident scholarly posture toward antiquity. The slave cannot be seen; the slave must be seen. This duplicity can undo the comfortable, comforting presentation of Greek antiquity by curators and classicists.

My claim is not to have given the truth about the Greeks, to have set the record straight, but rather to have tried to read the obstacles, to acknowledge the blind spots, to call into question an easy access to ancient reality, including slavery in my account of these ancient objects, but also pointing to how difficult it has been to see. It is as if, in order to avoid the celebration of ancient slavery produced by such thinkers as George Fitzhugh, modern scholars of antiquity have been forced either to isolate and denounce slavery, producing a history of slavery apart from its embeddedness in ancient societies, or to disregard it, naming it without taking into account the myriad ways in which it informs every relation, every space, all of everyday life and discourse in antiquity.[81] American history, the foundation of the discipline of classics, the period of slave trading and slave-holding in the United States, even the separation and the division of labor between sociologists and historians of slavery and other classicists, have contributed to producing an image of antiquity that the slave body, an unruly object, calls into question.

I   OBJECTS

1   COMMUNICATING WITH THE DEAD

Slaves and Everyday Life

WHAT WOULD it mean for the idealized celebration of the Western tradition to come into contact with artifacts of slaves and slavery in antiquity, the remains of everyday life of that age, the things of ancient societies? Walter Benjamin, the brilliant German Jewish critic who killed himself while fleeing the Nazis in 1940, once wrote:

> [*Dining Hall.*]—In a dream I saw myself in Goethe's study. It bore no resemblance to the one in Weimar. Above all, it was very small and had only one window. The side of the writing desk abutted on the wall opposite the window. Sitting and writing at it was the poet, in extreme old age. I was standing to one side when he broke off to give me a small vase, an urn from antiquity, as a present. I turned it between my hands. An immense heat filled the room. Goethe rose to his feet and accompanied me to an adjoining chamber, where a table was set for my relatives. It seemed prepared, however, for many more than their number. Doubtless there were places for my ancestors, too. At the end, on the right, I sat down beside Goethe. When the meal was over, he rose with difficulty and by gesturing I sought leave to support him. Touching his elbow, I began to weep with emotion.[1]

Benjamin's ominous premonitory dream, recorded in the twenties, evokes a passionate attachment to the traditions of German high culture, and to the material remains of classical antiquity: "An immense heat fills the room," signifying the pressure of this encounter with the past. He breaks down and weeps after touching the great dead man, like the urn from antiquity fragile, filled with meanings for him; the dream condenses for me the precious legacy of European poetry, of ancient objects, and the horror of slave camps and death camps awaiting Benjamin's fellow German Jews.

❖ ❖ ❖

I BECAME a classicist one day long ago. I was raised in a small town in California that had a little park in its center with a totem pole set in green grass. An old municipal museum stood at its heart, across the street from the house of my great-aunt, Auntie Bee. I was fascinated by her; she lived in a big house with a porch, a house with satin cushions embroidered with words. Her house had a special smell I associated with her great age. Her skin was very wrinkled, and she powdered it, and the powder sat in its wrinkles. I remember as a small child asking about that skin, those wrinkles, that powder, and being silenced.

The museum across the way, which I entered with a sense of wonder, displayed objects collected and donated by the citizens of the town. There was a huge, stuffed, and fraying Komodo dragon, a relic of someone's trip to what was once called the Orient. There were miniature rooms outfitted with the furnishings of moments in American history, usually Anglo-Saxon moments—George Washington's house, the parlor of John Adams, a pioneer cabin. There were some Native American relics, artifacts from the voyages of French beaver trappers of the eighteenth or nineteenth centuries, and remnants from the landholdings of the Spanish in old California.

But what I remember most vividly, what sealed my fate, was a cabinet displaying Roman glass. These vessels, small amphorae, perfume vases, and an alabastron, along with fragments and shards, had the characteristically complex surface of old glass; they were scaly, iridescent, pearly, and looked as if their skin itself had depths. They were pink and turquoise and pearly gray, mother-of-pearl, and gold. What really struck me, though, as a third-grader at Woodrow Wilson Elementary School, was that people long ago, now long dead, had blown that glass; touched it; filled it with liquids, oil, tears, perfume, or wine; had kept it whole; and that while they had died, the object, the beautiful pearly shape of it, fragile, frangible, breakable, thin-skinned as it was and remained, had survived from Roman times. I didn't understand how to measure the distance between myself and those ancient times; I had seen movies of people in togas riding in chariots, people who seemed very much like people I knew, with American accents and American body language. But I knew this glass was different, was old, and that the old dead Romans had made it and kept it and passed it on, and that it had lasted all the way down through time to sit here in this little museum, the oldest thing in the place, the oldest thing in the town besides the rocks, the oldest human-made thing I had ever seen. The glass survived to become artifacts, objects made with human labor, by some human hand. It looked so fragile, but it was tougher in its inanimacy, more durable than the soft, powdered, wrinkled skin of my Auntie Bee.

Deliberately or not, the dead passed that glass down to us, for me and others to see. It is the sensation of contact, a passion for such contact, like Benjamin's dream of the urn of antiquity and the dead Goethe, that makes me want to study the ancient things, the ancient world, in our world, which increasingly looks only at the present and toward the future, which throws old things away, or which fetishizes the masterpiece and separates it from those who made it, lived with it, used it long ago, locating it ahistorically within a set of masterpieces, framing it as utterly remote and inaccessible, a work of genius, like something passed to us from ancient gods. In fact, it may be everyday objects, like the Roman glass of the provincial museum's cabinet, like Benjamin's urn, which convey most vividly a sense of the dead, of their manufacture, the making by hand, their use, their users' treasuring of the things of ordinary life, these things that excite my passion, just as much if not more than the works of high art, which are now everywhere used as mechanically produced signs for high culture and the great European tradition. Everyday objects are "atopic," in the Greek sense, strange, eccentric, out of place, disturbingly inassimilable in narratives of high culture, aesthetic exemplarity, and the idealization of Greek democracy and philosophy.

A passion for the dead means thinking about those human beings, including slaves, who made, used, and lived with now ancient things when they were new. Objects from antiquity have the latent capacity to remind us that human beings were involved in their fabrication, their use, their preservation, and their descent to us, and can implicitly call into question the notion reigning in institutions of high culture, such as art museums, that only the great masterpieces, the finest, most aesthetically distinguished and perfect works of high art can excite passion in the viewer, communicate a sense of the past.

Art museums have focused on high art, on the cultural legacy of masterpieces that stand alone, often dissociated from any historical context. One of the acknowledged functions of the nation-state was the provision of aesthetic education for its citizens, and the museum was one of the sites of such education.[2] The great bronze statue of the ancient Greek god Poseidon (fig. 1), for example, holds price of place in the National Archaeological Museum of Athens. Its heroic masculine monumentality connects the national project of modern Greece with the glories of Greece's past; the bronze was preserved from the depredations of treasure seekers who took many of the great artworks from Greece in the eighteenth and nineteenth centuries, overlooked because it lay underwater, lost for centuries in a shipwreck. The middle class and the poor of early modern nations could not afford to own such masterpieces of antiquity themselves. The lower classes were encouraged eventually to come to museums, often formed around the private collections of the very wealthy, to cultivate their taste, to educate themselves about the

FIGURE 1. The Poseidon of Artemision. Statue, bronze, 460–450 BCE. Inv. #15161, National Archaeological Museum of Athens.

finest products of European civilization, and to know themselves as subjects of the nation-state.

Even though archaeologists have long been concerned with everyday life, and have excavated houses, middens, ordinary sites of human habitation, the space of most great museums has been occupied by works judged exceptional for their aesthetic value. The exhibition of antiquities, in this country and in Europe, has often meant the detachment of objects of cult that played a role, for example, in the public space of ancient Athens, the former site of their integration into the political and religious fabric of the city. Much of them physically severed from the temple itself, the fragments of the Parthenon frieze now in the British Museum and elsewhere once adorned the walls of Athens's great temple of Athena. They were literally cut off from its fabric and transported to be exhibited in isolation from the temple itself, a site of civic goddess worship. The gods of the ancient democracy were thus reframed, sometimes as part of the collections of wealthy aristocrats, redefined as exemplifying aristocratic, refined taste, and then used to form the aesthetic criteria of the new classes of the industrial world. In the process, the makers of these objects, and of other objects from the ancient world, were effaced; the works of art are named for the possessors, the modern collectors such as the British Lords Lansdowne or Elgin with whom they are still identified. The masons, sculptors, potters, painters, the artisans and laborers, slave and free, who made these objects are unknown, except in the rare cases, usually speculative, in which a maker's name is attributed to a work of art, in which an analogy with our modern notion of the artist can be established.

The display of everyday life in these contexts has had a meager history. The British Museum, for example, set up an exhibit devoted to Greek and Roman everyday life in the early part of the twentieth century. According to Ian Jenkins, who wrote the museum's companion guide to its "everyday life in antiquity" exhibit, those in charge of representing antiquity to the public in the eighteenth and nineteenth centuries had idealized Greek civilization. Toward the end of the nineteenth century, however,

> scholars came to realise that even the enlightened Greeks, those lovers of democracy, builders of the Parthenon and founders of modern philosophy, had their darker side. The study of ancient religion, in particular, revealed irrational and superstitious elements in the Greek mind which, it was soon recognised, were an integral part of the Greek way of life.
>
> The establishment of the first exhibition of Greek and Roman life at the British Museum in 1908, with its particular focus then, as now, on domestic life, may be seen historically as part of this development in Classical scholarship.[3]

The exhibit therefore contains objects of human rather than artistic interest, the things of domestic life, of women's work. At the time of my last visit in 2001, it grouped objects under such categories as "sacrifice," "gods," "reading and writing," "women," and "trade and transport." Not really the "darker side." No category of "slaves," or "foreigners," or "torture," for instance. And little recognition of the passionate interest some adult visitors to this room might bring to its exhibits, which are rigorously separated from the masterpieces of Greek art displayed on the floors below. In part, such a separation may derive impetus from a sense of the possible contamination of the masterpiece by the everyday, by the dirt and debris and fragmentation of archaeological remains. The blinding purity of Parian marble differs dramatically from the knucklebones and other vestiges of quotidian existence, marked by use and decay.

In the British Museum, as in many other museums and cultural institutions, curators and scholars present everyday life with a particular rhetorical tone, often with the voice of adults instructing the young. In Britain and America everyday life in Greece and Rome has most frequently been designated the province of children. For example, in a recent book on everyday life in ancient Greece, Anne Pearson presents an illustration of terra-cotta perfume bottles as a puzzle for her young readers (fig. 2).[4] Figure 3 is another representation of these containers. A photograph from the British Museum everyday life exhibit (fig. 4) displays ancient children's toys: a whip top, a dancing doll holding castanets,

MYSTERY
OBJECT

What do you think these are? They were found in the women's room, near makeup containers. Clue: they would have smelled pleasant. You will find the answer on page 32.

FIGURE 2. Mystery objects. Drawing, date unknown. From Anne Pearson, *Everyday Life in Ancient Greece* (New York: Franklin Watts, 1994), 14. Copyright 1994 by Scholastic Publishing Inc.

FIGURE 3. Scent bottles in the form of sandaled feet. Terra cotta, eastern Greece, sixth century BCE. Photograph copyright the Trustees of the British Museum.

FIGURE 4. A group of children's toys: whip top, terra cotta, eighth century BCE; dancing doll with castanets, terra cotta, Corinth, ca. 350 BCE; baby feeder, pottery, southern Italy, fourth century BCE; miniature wine jug, Athens, 425–400 BCE; rattle in the form of a pig, terra cotta, Cyprus, third–second centuries BCE. Photograph copyright the Trustees of the British Museum.

FIGURE 5. Two figurines: a woman grinding grain and another baking bread. Terra cotta, Greece, fifth century BCE. Photograph copyright the Trustees of the British Museum.

a baby feeder with the inscription "drink, don't drop," a miniature wine jug, and a rattle in the form of a pig.

The display of everyday life often depends on a strong gender division, one that was both produced and reproduced in the texts of books about everyday life written and published in the twentieth century. They are organized around women's work, and men's warships and weapons, a practice that encourages a conventional division of labor between the sexes. Terra-cotta figurines in one illustration show women grinding grain and placing food in an oven (fig. 5), while others concentrate on armor and appeal to boys as readers. One of these books on daily life, written in the thirties, begins:

> No boy or girl can understand what has happened in this England, or this Europe, or, as a matter of fact, America, unless they are prepared to tramp along the road that leads to Rome. Arrived there they will find they must continue their journey to the Athens of Pericles; but they need only travel in imagination, because the tale is well told on a few square miles of English land.[5]

Children see in their own lands the toys of ancient children; girls see
how ancient women spun and wove cloth and made garments for their
households, boys how men waged war. This image of ancient Greek
coiffures, from the same book (fig. 6), is one of the most common illus-
trations in books about everyday life in antiquity published during the

FIGURE 6. Greek hairstyles. From M. and C. H. B. Quennell, *Everyday Things in Ancient Greece* (New York: Putnam, 1954), 176, fig. 123.

43

1920s and 1930s, and it is repeated in contemporary books about the everyday life of Greek and Roman civilizations (fig. 7). Little girls, we are led to conclude, like to think about hair. Some of the cultural labor done by such books imitates, produces, and reinforces normal gender divisions for modernity.

Interest in everyday life as pursued by disciplines other than classical

FIGURE 7. Greek hairstyles. From Ian Jenkins, *Greek and Roman Life* (London: British Museum Publications for the Trustees of the British Museum, 1986), 26.

studies has not been confined to the domain of pedagogical literature. A concern for what is called everyday life, or daily life, or the quotidian, has not always been part of the discipline of history, but in the humanities in general, attention has turned in recent decades to a social history taking into account the lives of the long-silenced populations of the world: women, slaves, people of color, and laborers. Henri Lefebvre contends that everyday life only became visible or perceptible with the advent of capitalism and with the beginnings of the culture of modernity, arguing that before capitalism, life was lived as an undifferentiated whole. The things of the world had symbolic values, linking them to the meanings of existence; people lived with the rhythms of the day, the changes of the seasons. With the advent of modern, capitalist culture, what he calls "differentiation" began, as the world broke apart into functions, into apparently autonomous subsystems; art was separated from science, the public sphere from the private.

> [T]he concept of the everyday illuminates the past. Everyday life has always existed, even if in ways vastly different from our own. The character of the everyday has always been repetitive and veiled by obsession and fear. In the study of the everyday we discover the great problem of repetition, one of the most difficult problems facing us. The everyday is situated at the intersection of two modes of repetition: the cyclical, which dominates in nature, and the linear, which dominates in processes known as "rational." The everyday implies on the one hand cycles, nights and days, seasons and harvests, activity and rest, hunger and satisfaction, desire and its fulfillment, life and death, and implies on the other hand the repetitive gestures of work and consumption.[6]

Everyday life, according to Lefebvre, was recognized but despised in the nineteenth century; it was not until the period of the surrealists in the twentieth century that it became a domain of interest to artists. And to Sigmund Freud, who, in the *Psychopathology of Everyday Life*, for example, values everyday speech, forgetting, lapses and slips of the pen and the tongue because they provide access to the otherwise inaccessible realm of the unconscious. In his work, we find meaning residing in the everyday, in the stream of consciousness or in analytic speech, which points to other realms of signification.[7]

Social history has sought to restore to public view the invisible of the past, those social actors in the quotidian realm who have not had a voice—women, the poor, slaves. We find in the work of Fernand Braudel, in contrast with Lefebvre's, an attempt to point to the *longue durée*, a temporality characterized by the survival of historical features almost invisible precisely because they endure for so long, persist so far beyond individual human existences that they are taken for granted, become part of a naturalized landscape of human history, and must be excavated, revealed as not natural but rather part of a long process of change and transformation, of a geological slowness.[8] For Michel Decerteau, the everyday imposes itself as a site of resistance, a domain of social practices that ordinary people can turn back against their masters, thereby subverting the structures of the world of domination so that people forge their own paths in cities, use company time for their own pleasures and enrichment; he sees the everyday as an immense field of uncharted, unaccounted-for practices of ingenuity and defiance.[9]

Classics, because of its history as an academic discipline and its long-standing desire to preserve the remains of classical civilization, was long exempt from the general trend of attention to the quotidian, the everyday. Classicists have often been asked to provide the rationale for the foundational institutions of Western civilization, for democracy, philosophy, the law, and political theories of the republic.[10] The great institutions of the Athenian democracy and of the Roman republic and Empire have served as models, often polemically deployed to defend ideas in contemporary culture about the proper governance of the polity. The everyday life of human beings unknown heretofore, people without great names like Pericles and Julius Caesar, has occupied the minds of scholars less. In classical literary studies, scholars have concentrated on masterpieces, the great epic poems of Homer, for example, rather than on graffiti and such popular forms as the mime. Some philologically inclined classicists restrict their study of antiquity to the highest forms of ancient literary culture, such genres as Greek tragedy. In Aeschylus's *Oresteia*, for example, the Eumenides, the Blessed Ones who were once avenging Furies, bless the city of Athens in the elevated language of archaic lyric:

> Let there blow no wind that wrecks the trees.
> I pronounce words of grace.
> Nor blaze of heat blind the blossoms of grown plants, nor
> cross the circles of its right
> place. Let no barren deadly sickness creep and kill.
> Flocks fatten. Earth be kind.
>
> (*Eumenides* 937–42)

Greek tragedy contains many such moments of high diction, divine presence among mortals, and the imagination of a world without drought or hunger. Aeschylus's *Oresteia* is a masterpiece, a work of high culture, a synthesis of the archaic and of the highest aspirations of the new democratic culture of the city of Athens, confirmed in the archaeological record of great temples such as the Parthenon, which honors the goddess Athena. The classical ages of Greece and Rome, their monuments, and their highest genres, epic, tragedy, and philosophy, claimed the attention of the West for centuries.

Like literary classical studies, the beginnings of the study of ancient art focused on masterpieces. The Renaissance excavators who brought to light Roman sculpture to be admired and imitated by Mantegna and Michelangelo looked for masterpieces rather than for the details of everyday life. Even in the excavation of Pompeii and Herculaneum, where the trauma of the volcanic eruption cast a certain moment of everyday life into stone, the pathos of the petrified often overcame interest in Roman life in the first century. The disaster narrative overshadowed the details of quotidian existence made accessible by the ash and lava. In Greece, the early amateur excavator Heinrich Schliemann dug up the golden mask he assigned to the hero Agamemnon, and in so doing ignored much that might have shed light on the lives of ordinary people in the Mycenaean age.

Yet the field of classical archaeology, which grew out of such predatory excavations as Schliemann's, has served as a reminder of the importance of everyday life in the study of ancient civilization, demonstrating that it should not be just the province of children, relegated to displays in the British Museum's attic for field trips of the young. The passion for antiquity, specifically for the lost civilization of the ancient Greeks, can be formed and nurtured by an attention to the material civilization of Greece, its ordinary objects and simple domestic spaces. Classical archaeology and archaeologists, to some degree following the example of anthropologists and archaeologists working in other locations, on other cultures, have reminded literary and cultural scholars of how important attention to the ordinary, the everyday, the material, the object world of antiquity is, how we can know ancient culture not just through the highest of genres, the greatest of masterpieces, but also through what we can reconstruct or assemble of the ruins of everyday life in the past. Moreover, such attention may be just as valuable an enterprise as restoration, admiration, and awe before the works of the greatest artists of our tradition.[11]

Let me illustrate what I mean with some examples from the material remains of antiquity, and then consider how the attention of literary scholars and philologists to similar matters, including slavery, enriches our sense of the Greek past. Figure 8 shows an amphora made in Athens about 520 BCE. It depicts an olive harvest; two bearded men strike the tree with long poles while a boy below collects its fruit. Such a scene, while representing everyday labor and displayed in the museum along

FIGURE 8. Amphora depicting an olive harvest. Athens, ca. 520, attributed to the Antimenes Painter. British Museum, London. Photograph copyright the Trustees of the British Museum.

with toys and terra-cotta figurines of that era, nonetheless has its connections to high literary and political culture, the founding gestures of
some of the West's political and aesthetic traditions. Marcel Detienne has
written about the significance of the olive tree as a figure for the Athenian ephebe, the young man newly registered as a citizen.[12] The first
olive tree was the gift of the goddess Athena to the city of Athens, which
because of this gift chose her as its principal deity. The chorus of the
Greek tragedian Sophocles' *Oedipus at Colonus* sings its praise of Attica:

> Here . . .
> where the nightingale in constant trilling song
> cries from beneath the green leaves,
> where she lives in the wine dark ivy
> and the dark foliage of ten thousand berries,
> safe from the sun, safe from the wind
> of every storm, god's place, inviolable
>
> . . . .
>
> There is a thing too, of which no other like
> I have heard in Asian land,
> nor as ever grown in the great Dorian
> island of Pelops,
> a plant unconquered and self-renewing,
> a terror that strikes the spear-armed enemy,
> a plant that flourishes greatest here,
> leaf of gray olive,
> nourishing our children.
> It shall not be rendered impotent
> by the young nor by him that lives with old age,
> destroying it with violence,
> for the ever-living eye of Morian Zeus
> looks upon it—and gray-eyed Athene also.
>
> (768–802)[13]

Olive trees were said to survive for centuries; it was a capital crime to cut
down one of the sacred olives of the land of Attica.[14] From a ruined and
burned stump on the Akropolis, destroyed by the Persian invaders of the
early fifth century, miraculously, overnight, a new tree grew. A newborn
male child received an olive bough that was placed over the door of his
parents' house. Victorious athletes won oil from the sacred trees, and
crowns made from their leaves. A young man was imagined to grow in
the cultivated soil of his city like a sacred tree. The visual representations
carry this complex significance: the tree is sacred to the goddess, bearer
of nourishing fruit and oil, sign of the city and its soldiers. However, the
amphora serves to remind us also of the laborers, often agricultural
slaves, and of the labor required to fill vessels like this one with the oil

from the olive trees, vessels made of clay extracted from the ground by other slaves and decorated by other laborers.

Other simple terra-cotta figures show women kneading and baking bread. "A clay oven like a huge bowl was built up by hand in a convenient place. The usual fuel, dried grasses, was placed in around it and after the oven became heated and the fire had died down, the housewife set the flat loaves around the inside to bake"[15] The material practice of kneading and baking bread in a small oven informed philosophical, literary, and biological reflections. Ancient writers compared women's bodies, their wombs, to ovens.[16] Herodotus tells the story of the tyrant Periander and his dead wife, Melissa, who came to an oracle in a dream and proved that she was in fact Periander's wife by saying that he had put his loaves "in a cold oven." Herodotus says, "The messengers reported what they had heard [at the oracle], and Periander was convinced by the token of the cold oven and the loaves, because he had lain with her after she was dead" (5.92). The comic playwright Aristophanes mocks the scientists of his day by saying they "teach that the heavens are one vast oven placed around us, and that we're the cinders" (*The Clouds* 96–97). The visual evidence and the literary come together to provide a richer picture of ancient society than either would separately. Often the two sorts of evidence confirm one another or deepen the connections between literary and artisanal or artistic production.

❖ ❖ ❖

IN SOME cases, the literary evidence, or the cultural speculations built on literary evidence, are contradicted by material evidence. Michael Jameson, in his discussion of the Greek house, argues that literary evidence from Homer and beyond suggests that the hearth formed an important focus of life, a center for domestic existence and a crucial point for ritual in ancient Greek life.[17] The Amphidromia, for example, a ritual in which a father carried his ten-day-old child around the hearth, was used by Jean-Pierre Vernant to show the significance of worship of both the mobile god Hermes and the static goddess Hestia, goddess of the hearth, illuminating notions of space in Greek society (fig. 9).[18] Yet Jameson points out that archaeological evidence does not support the imagined centrality for the hearth in the ancient house, as one might expect from literary evidence, nor for the sorts of spatial differences one might expect concerning gender in this culture. For example: "few Classical houses appear to have had fixed hearths. . . . The significance of the household fire is not in doubt, only its centrality, circularity, and fixed character."[19]

In this case, archaeological evidence corrects assumptions based on

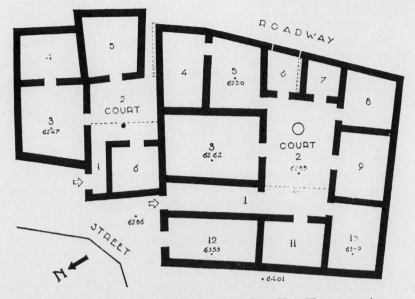

FIGURE 9. Athenian house plans. Fifth century BCE. From H. A. Thompson and
R. E. Wycherley, *The Athenian Agora* (Princeton, N.J.: American School of Classical
Studies, 1972), 14:176, fig. 41. Courtesy of the American School of Classical Studies
at Athens.

textual readings, and requires a further step in interpretation. Why is it
that the literary and textual evidence suggests one interpretation, and
the material evidence gleaned from archaeological labor another? Do
we simply not have enough domestic, everyday architecture to give a definitive sense of domestic space and its differentiations in this society?
Or is there some idealization, some representation of archaic ideas of
space that no longer corresponds to everyday life as lived in the fifth and
fourth centuries, that harkens back to earlier arrangements, aristocratic
houses, Homeric, heroic ideas of the differences between male and female, the ritual hearth and the ordinary space that surrounds it?

Jameson also discusses in detail the place of slaves in domestic space,
as revealed in the archaeological record:

Since only a few slaves were attached to any one household one should
suppose that they slept wherever they could lie down, female slaves with
or near the free women (this is implied by the arrangements made by the
cuckolded husband in Lysias 1). A graffito on the wall of a wretched cubby
hole in a house on Delos speaks nostalgically of the slave's homeland and
shows this was his corner. A slave was expected to answer a knock at the
door (Plato, *Protagoras* 314c) and a small room near the street door of

some houses has been thought to be a "porter's lodge." . . . [N]o particular arrangements were needed except in a few larger establishments with a greater number of slaves, none of which are represented in the archaeological remains. (104)[20]

Greek architecture seems rarely to have incorporated divisions of its space denoting differences of status. Gender is more strongly marked than status, or class, in the domestic architecture excavated up to this point.

> In general, the economic functions and living arrangements of slaves were not standardized; the architecture of the Greek house does not reflect the most important status distinction in the society, largely because, for any one family, slave-owning was on a small scale. The slave was a member of the household, the *oikos*, and was often referred to as an *oiketes*, even if the lowest in position. (ibid.)

Slaves have their place—that is, no place—in classical domestic space. Scholars disagree concerning the material evidence of slaves' origins. Ian Morris maintains that "in the one case in which we know we are excavating the homes of slaves, the material cultures of their homelands seem to have disappeared completely." He attributes the absence of evidence to the fact that "the material culture of the Athenian master class was unusually pervasive."[21] Yet James Davidson points to a building excavated in Athens's Ceramicus district, called "Building Z" by its excavators: "The women who inhabited these corridors were foreigners, almost certainly slaves, who left traces of their devotion to foreign goddesses in the form of little statuettes. These, together with the jewellery found on the site, suggest they had come from Thrace, Anatolia and Syria, the usual suppliers of slaves to Athens."[22]

Following the direction of archaeologists, we might look toward other intriguing aspects of ancient life, to be found not in the highest cultural forms but in the low, bawdy, raucous representations of Athenian comedy. Aristophanes has a radically different view of life in the city from the tragedians'; for example, in the *Acharnians* his character Dikaiopolis sits, waiting for the assembly to begin, wriggling in his seat like one of the spectators at the theater. He says:

> I am always the very first to come to Assembly and take my seat. Then, in my solitude, I sigh, I yawn, I stretch myself, I fart, I fiddle, scribble, pluck my beard, do sums, while I gaze off to the countryside and pine for peace, loathing the city and yearning for my own deme. (28–33)[23]

The beauties of the Attic countryside recalled by Sophocles in high lyric mode take on a radically different form here. Aristophanes records the everyday, and we find the quotidian embodied in ways that the museum and many idealizing narratives about ancient civilization do not often acknowledge. The actor speaks these lines, and we are connected with the ancient Greek's experience of his own body, its materiality, its functions. In a later obscene moment of this play, a character from Megara puts his daughters in a sack after dressing them as piglets in an obscene reference to female genitalia, and offers them for sale in Dikaiopolis's Athenian market (734–835): "the meat of these piggies is absolutely delicious when it's skewered on a spit" (795–6). Dikaiopolis buys the new slaves offered for consumption both literal and metaphorical.

❖ ❖ ❖

In his discussion of recent trends in archaeology, Morris urges:

> In abandoning what [one scholar] calls the "panoptic gaze" of the art historian, we fragment our perspective into the countless points of view of actors in the past—that is, we re-figure classical archaeology in the sense of treating material culture as something used by real people in pursuit of their social goals.[24]

Ancient objects, like attention to everyday life, can provide a material basis for a different connection with the dead; looking and touching produce different knowledges about ancient culture from those gained in reading a literary text from a medieval manuscript, edited first by a Renaissance editor and then a modern editor, printed and bound in a modern book that was translated by a modern poet.

But what can it mean to communicate passionately with the dead through ancient objects as Benjamin did in his dream? We see, but rarely touch, smell, or handle something that people now long dead saw, touched, smelled, handled, and used. When such opportunities do occur, they sometimes produce shock. In his history of the British Museum, Edward Miller tells the story of George Smith, who in the 1870s was working on clay tablets from Nineveh, tablets that seemed to confirm the flood story in the Old Testament: "On being handed the cleaned 'Deluge' tablet for which he had long been impatiently waiting . . . he read a few lines which confirmed his theories, shouted 'I am the first man to read that after more than two thousand years of oblivion.' Then, placing the tablet carefully on a table, he jumped up, rushed about the room in a state of excitement and, to the astonishment of all present, started to undress!"[25] Smith's ecstatic reaction to the ancient clay tablet reveals an impassioned and tactile engagement with the material remains of antiquity.

Yet how often do scholars imagine people of ancient times using objects, vases, holding them, mixing wine and water in them, ladling oil

FIGURE 10. Exekias, wine cup containing painting of Dionysos in his ship surrounded by dolphins. Close-up of Attic wine cup, 540 BCE. Staatliche Antikensammlung, Munich. Photograph copyright Erich Lessing/Art Resource, New York.

from them? Instead, Greek vases are usually treated as works of art, objects of high culture and connoisseurship.[26] In "Wine and the Wine-Dark Sea," an unusual and exemplary chapter in his book *The Aesthetics of the Greek Banquet*, François Lissarrague considers the pleasure derived from using these vases in demonstrating the analogies the Greeks drew between the sea and navigation, and wine and the banquet.[27] The drinker and the sailor alike relied on the "vessel." Lissarrague illustrates his point with a *krater*, a mixing bowl the neck of which was decorated with a frieze of boats; when the *krater* was filled with wine, the boats seemed to float on the wine-dark sea. "When the vase is full, the surface of the liquid is flush with the triremes, which seem to float on the wine in which they are reflected" (113). With another cup, as the drinker drank the sea-colored wine he revealed the god Dionysos reclining in his boat, and covering the masts with grape-vines (fig. 10). Imagining these vases in use transforms Lissarrague's reading of their images.

❖ ❖ ❖

WE ARE SOMETIMES so immersed in the practices and spectatorship of modern art that we forget that much of what we admire in ancient art figured differently in ancient societies than contemporary art does in our own. Modern art was made by individual named artists, often for purchase as commodified objects to be displayed in the homes of the wealthy, donated to museums to be placed on the walls or on pedestals, and admired by visitors to these spaces of acculturation. The mythification of the modern artist stands between the viewer and the representation. But ancient Greek statues were often representations of gods, figuring in the landscape of communal worship, festival, or domestic devotion; Greek vases were used for drinking, for containing perfumes or ashes, for mourning, for the pleasures of weeping and touching and tasting as well as seeing. And they were usually made and painted by unnamed artisans, slave and free. Although museum displays may inevitably have the effect of turning them into Art, encumbered with aesthetic, Romantic, and post-Romantic ideas of art and artist, in looking at and touching a Greek vase or a piece of Roman glass, or even imagining their manufacture in an ancient workshop, their place in an ancient household, still we encounter ancient, ordinary life. When we see objects from ancient tombs, we come into contact not just with stores of artifacts but also with the grief and ritual and bodily remains of the ancient dead.

Human history begins with rituals of burial. J. M. Roberts in his history of the world writes of "the primitive [Neanderthal] community in northern Iraq which went out one day to gather the masses of wild flowers and grasses which eventually lay under and surrounded the dead companion it wished so to honour."[28] Human beings mark and remember their dead, and when we forget the significance of funerary objects, we miss the opportunity to remember people, dead for centuries, who preceded us in human time. It is easy in museums, especially those devoted to high culture and to named artists and to the tribute of imperial adventures in such lands as Greece, to forget that others once lived among and used these things we now call art, and have since died, sometimes having used vases of ceramic and glass to commemorate or even hold the remains of their dead.

Ancient glass, not so imposing as the marble of the Parthenon, was nonetheless a special substance, expensive and rare. Yet it was made by human hands, and used by some in the course of everyday life. Greek glass was manufactured throughout the ancient Aegean, in Egypt, on the island of Cyprus, and at the great sanctuary of Zeus at Olympia in the Peloponnesus. Before glassblowing was invented, artisans slave and free used already-made ingots or canes of glass that they melted, fused, then sometimes zigzagged like cake batter.[29] Figure 11 shows early Greek

OBJECTS

FIGURE 11. Three vessels. Core-formed glass, Greece, sixth–fourth centuries BCE. Collection of The Newark Museum, gift of Mr. Eugene Schaefer, 1950. Photograph copyright The Newark Museum/Art Resource, New York.

glass, core-formed vessels, containers for oils or perfumes from the eastern Mediterranean.

Glassblowing was discovered in the first century BCE by some unknown adventurer. Hollow rods have been found in Jerusalem with slightly open ends; these rods were blown into, so that the shape of the glass they made still retains the mark of the breath of its long-dead maker. Lesley Stern, in her book on smoking, writes that smoke makes the shaman's breath visible.[30] Blown glass makes the breath, the outline of the breath visible, and preserves it, unlike the smoke, which dissipates. The Greeks talk about life as the *pneuma;* the spirit, the anima, the breath is the *psuche,* the soul. A living creature breathes. Blowing glass, the heat, the residues, damages the lungs; perhaps my passion, my attachment to ancient objects finds its beginnings in the fact that my great-grandfather was a Strasbourgeois glassblower.

Part of what makes ancient glass so beautiful is its age, the way in which the glass has mutated, become encrusted and iridescent, marked by the chemical transformations of centuries, taking light in an incredi-

56

bly complicated dappled, rich, layered pattern, so that the delicate glass seems to have infinite depth. I once touched some ancient glass, thanks to Mary Hart and Karol Wight of the Getty Museum. One vase was extraordinary because it seemed to have become iridescent only on the inside, so that an immense richness seemed to lie inside it, behind a curtain of glass. Looking down into the vessels, I thought about the oil, the perfume that they once contained. The skin of the container was to the touch almost as I had imagined it, but in some places slightly coarse, with a resistant tensile quality, the slightest pull. It had varied patches of iridescence, like encrustations on the surface, unpredictable in a once uniform surface. There was cobalt, gold veining, rougher bits, like excrescences on the skin, irregularities that appeared on the surface—col-

FIGURE 12. Group of ancient Greek glass objects: four small colored flasks, fifth century BCE–first century CE; ribbed cup, first century CE; mosaic cup, first century CE; bowl with foot, first century CE. Louvre, Paris. Photograph Hervé Lewandowski. Photograph copyright Réunion des Musées Nationaux/Art Resource, New York.

FIGURE 13. Bowl and bottle. Glass, Roman. Photograph copyright Erich Lessing/Art Resource, New York.

ors due, I was told, to the variable quality of the sand, to the minerals added to produce particular colors. Figures 12 and 13 show such ancient vessels, which have survived, intact, well more than a millennium beyond the life of their makers.

Antiquities are evidence of life before us. And they exist beyond modern aesthetic notions of the beautiful, which often assume a certain version of the classical, ideas of harmony, decorum, and balance that refer to the high cultures of Greek and Roman antiquity. Beyond the aesthetic, because we see not just the beautiful but also evidence of human history, of hands, labor, workers, artisans, and slaves. The objects of everyday life, signs of human beings who preceded us in life, in production and labor and use of things, create attachment. The objects of everyday life excite my fascination as a scholar, because they connect the present with the past. As objects, they have endured through centuries of human handling or loss, and embody that suffering and survival. They implicitly, tacitly record the labor and effort and even pain of long-dead ancient people, their passion and suffering, even while these people, free and slave, remain nameless and often invisible.

2   GREEKS IN THE MUSEUM

Museums became more and more central exactly in cultures touched most deeply by the factory system. The British Museum in London and the Metropolitan Museum in New York represent a new kind of institution. No longer did they provide a "visible history" of the culture itself: that is, a visual display of objects rich with symbolic, local significance. These institutions are instead storage areas for authenticity and uniqueness per se, for objects from any culture or period whatever that were "irreplaceable" or singular. Museums are counter-institutions to the factory within civilizations of mass production. As objects became more short-lived and geared to obsolescence, or rather to an ongoing series of inventions and adjustments that produced as one side effect obsolescence, the museum became more skilled at preservation, that is, at keeping selected things in a state that would never deteriorate or change.

—Philip Fisher, *Making and Effacing Art* (1991)

IN THIS chapter, I consider museums in order to bring together questions of the representation of antiquity in museums with the larger question of this book: the occlusion, the overdetermination of blind spots, the difficulty curators as well as scholars have had in placing slavery in relation to what else we know about ancient Greece, the disruptive power the slave body has in discourses concerning antiquity. I say "overdetermination," and I mean this in the sense in which Freud uses that term in writing about dreams.[1] We have a great deal of trouble seeing slaves and slavery in antiquity. Some people underestimate the importance of slavery and ignore it, simply noting it as one of many features of ancient life, or offering apologies for its presence. Others overestimate its importance, treating it as a "disembedded," "economic" feature of ancient life, to use Karl Polanyi's terms.[2] My desire throughout this book is to acknowledge the troubling presence of slavery, to set it within all else that we inherit from antiquity, to take account of its ubiquity, to remark upon its phenomenality as something we must see, allowing it to destabilize an idealizing or static portrait of the classical past.

59

Museums

One of the ways in which people gain a sense of ancient Greece is by visiting museums. What do these institutions teach their visitors about antiquity? Various attempts have been made recently to study museums, their histories, and their purposes.[3] We find various types of museums, among them such categories as the universal museum, containing all of human history; the art museum; and the ethnological or anthropological museum.[4] Other discussions of museums focus on their development from earlier cultural forms. Krzysztof Pomian offers a useful set of categories describing the formation of public museums as falling into four patterns.[5] The first, the traditional pattern, occurs where collecting and exhibiting to the public form part of the institution's normal activities. He gives as an example the treasure and treasury of the Church of Saint Mark's in Venice. (Others are the collections in the palaces of princes and kings, and those in teaching establishments like the University of Padova.) When a treasure-house is transformed into a museum, it loses its liturgical, ceremonial, decorative, or utilitarian role. A second pattern is the so-called revolutionary, in which a museum is founded by decree, absorbing works from diverse locations seized by the state and housing them in buildings unrelated to those works. The state assumes control of the objects, centralizing and modernizing their display; this pattern often results in the favoring of the capital over provincial towns. As Pomian says,

> this type of public museum formation was a direct result of the practices and ideology of the French Revolution, which the Napoleonic state inherited and which was profoundly influenced by Enlightenment thought, with its anticlerical, if not antireligious slant, and its belief in the benefits of a strong, philosophy-based power. (264)

Pomian points out that "the Anglo-Saxon world . . . contains no example whatsoever of this type" (265).

Pomian's third pattern he calls the "evergetic," and of this type there are many, especially in the United States. These are "private collections left to their founders' home towns, to the state or else to an educational or religious institution, so that the public may have access to them" (264). Usually such museums are donated by "industrialists, tradesmen, and financiers" (265). Although in Europe large national museums are the most important, in the United States the evergetic pattern prevails. Pomian cites the Smithsonian Institution, the National Gallery in Washington, and the Metropolitan Museum and the Museum of Modern Art in New York as examples of this category. A fourth type, the "commercial," is formed when "an institution either buys separately all the pieces intended to fill it or else purchases entire collections" (266). The British Museum, a so-called universal survey museum, "was founded around the collection purchased in 1753 from the executors of the will of Sir Hans Sloane for 20,000 pounds, after a ruling by the British parliament" (ibid.).

Collections of ancient Greek objects present certain complications for the idea of the museum that houses them. First of all, is it a historical, an anthropological, or an art historical collection? A historical collection can claim to present a relevant element of the possessors' own history; ancient Greece can be seen as a source, a point of origin even for European and Anglo-Saxon North American culture, so that any museum that provides a "universal survey," representations from all antecedent cultures, would of necessity present objects from the world of Greek antiquity. After the Gothic, medieval, Christian Catholic passages of European history, during the Renaissance, even in the Enlightenment, societies traced their genealogies back to the Greeks, or to stories told by the Greeks. Romans claimed descent from the Trojan Aeneas, or from the Greek Herakles; another legend connected the ancient Britons to a refugee from the Trojan War. As Salvatore Settis has shown, Italy was full of objects inherited from antiquity that were built into the fabric of churches, cemeteries, and houses;[6] still later, ancient objects were excavated and in part spurred the Renaissance, the newly born sense of historical distance, of temporality, of a passage from antiquity into feudalism and beyond. The universal survey museum contains references to the European past, and in a museum like the British Museum, that past was defined as Greek and Roman antiquity, a past of high civilization and awe-inspiring achievement, rather than the antiquity of the Britons themselves, scorned as barbaric, benighted, and provincial from the point of view of an ancient civilization centered on the Mediterranean. For a long time British antiquities were not shown in the British Museum; the historical emphasis lay almost exclusively on Greek and Roman antiquity.[7]

The narrative of origins was not necessarily an art historical narrative. Rather, ancient Greek and Roman civilization, home of art, poetry, and philosophy, formed the matrix for all that men of the Enlightenment sought to foster in their present. It was only later that art became the focus of the museum, and this shift produced a complicated and difficult passage for the exhibition of antiquities. For if the earliest collections of ancient objects had contained much of what might in these latter days be considered "art," there was also much that had very different functions and meanings in their original contexts, such objects as coins, ceramic vases, glass, mirrors, and other objects of everyday life. How were they to be presented as part of the narrative of origin for European, and especially for British, civilization? And how were the social relations of such societies, slave-holding, for instance, to be presented?

The curators of the British Museum had a long conflict over whether so-called primitive cultures should be represented within the universal survey. Artifacts from primitive cultures of the past, like Britain itself, and less developed cultures of the present, themselves sometimes subject to British rule, might be better suited to another kind of space, a museum devoted to earlier or more primitive cultures, a museum of anthropology, a museum of "mankind."[8] The position of Greek and Roman antiquity remains ambiguous in such a scheme, in which there is a division between earlier and more evolved cultures, because in certain aspects Greek and Roman societies were lower, more "primitive," less developed than the modern, and in other ways they were not—being seen as superior, exemplifying all that is best in human beings, in art, philosophy, and poetry.[9]

The problem of the universal survey museum becomes the problem of the art museum as well. If the justification for the placement of Greek and Roman antiquity at the source of European civilization remains its artistic and philosophical superiority, then the art of such a society is what must be shown, presented, valued, used as a model for didactic purposes, to be emulated in art of the present day. The anthropological museum, a subcategory of the universal survey museum, a historical museum, must therefore become an art museum. And what becomes of all the objects of everyday life in such a case, the loom weights and tools and furniture of daily life that remain, dug up from the soil of Greek and Italy and parts of the Roman Empire? If the relationship between the present and the ancient past is understood in terms of art, of styles to be imitated, within a progression from primitive, say, Cycladic representation through archaic art influenced by the Egyptians, to more naturalistic style culminating in the high classical, and if this narrative of progress becomes the significant one, then the anthropological ambition, and even the historical ambition, more broadly conceived, falls by the wayside. The idealizing narrative of evolution from and beyond the high classical culture of antiquity can only with difficulty accommodate a historical or anthropological perspective on ancient societies.

I look here at how different sorts of museums deal with this problem of representing, exhibiting, and producing antiquity, with particular attention to the question of everyday life and slavery. I take my cases from three of Pomian's four categories, leaving aside only the traditional pattern, that derived from institutions like the church, or academic collections. In fact, this model may be most appropriate for early modern and modern objects, since the primary example of such collections is the ecclesiastical one, the treasure and treasury of a great church that contains relics, reliquaries, altar pieces, and ritual objects such as chalices, gifts made to ecclesiastical functionaries, like those in the Musée de Cluny in Paris. I will consider an evergetic museum, the Getty Museum in Malibu; a commercial museum, the British Museum; and a "revolutionary" museum, the National Archaeological Museum of Athens.

The Getty Villa

The Getty Villa, opened in 1974, built as a replica of the Villa dei Papiri in Herculaneum, reflects the late billionaire J. Paul Getty's views about art:

> The difference between being a barbarian and a full-fledged member of a cultivated society is in the individual's attitude toward fine art. If he or she has a love of art, then he or she is not a barbarian. It's that simple, in my opinion. Tragically, fifty per cent of the people walking down any street can be classed as barbarians according to this criterion.[10]

The Getty Museum was from the beginning meant to be an "art museum," civilizing modern barbarians with an aesthetic mission. On the question of the shape the museum took, Getty writes:

> I have long been keenly interested in ancient Greek and Roman architecture. The beginnings of my interest can be traced back to my earliest visits to Italy and Greece, where I saw the crumbled and fragmentary remnants of the architectural marvels that these long-dead civilizations had produced. With the question of a new J. Paul Getty museum design before me, I decided to reproduce a Roman villa to house my collection.
>
> I thought it worthwhile to create one building in the Roman tradition. The Graeco-Roman buildings that remain to us have had hard usage during the last couple of thousand years. I suppose that 99.99 per cent of the buildings of Imperial Rome have disappeared. (283)

The villa was "unique and a work of art" (281); there may have been some sort of identification between Getty himself and what the first guidebook to the villa called the occupants of the original: "a patently wealthy and patrician Roman family" (284).

Among the works of J. P. Getty, besides the villa, are the autobiography *As I See It*, and *How to be Rich*, published by Playboy Press in 1966, which contains a chapter entitled "Fine Art: The Finest Investment" (220–32).[11] In the autobiography, Getty recalls visiting San Simeon, William Randolph Hearst's palace and the model for the Xanadu of Or-

OBJECTS

son Welles's film *Citizen Kane*. "I must admit that I do, on occasion, find some reason or other to compare myself with Hearst," he remarks (252). In the 1960s, Getty watched a BBC film about Hearst and San Simeon, and concluded that the newspaper magnate "lived like a Roman emperor." His rivalry may have had its effects on his decision to build the villa: "I suppose that in 1935 I was one-third as rich as Hearst and by 1950, I was twice as rich" (253). Writing of the house he inhabited in England, a Tudor "stately home" (224), he concludes: "When I compare Sutton Place with San Simeon I must admit that Sutton Place is a manor house and not a palace" (254). With a fascinating instinct for self-dramatization and immortality, Getty built a patrician villa for himself, a structure that its architects and builders strove to make historically accurate, unlike the hodgepodge of historical and cultural styles and artifacts that is San Simeon, Hearst's castle. In a certain sense, Getty's evergetic museum has aspects of what Carol Duncan calls "the donor memorial" as well; [12] she points out that although he never saw the villa, Getty is buried on a promontory near the museum: "It took over two years of legal work before Getty's body could be buried on the grounds of his palace museum. Guarded by television cameras, the actual grave site is not open to the public. Nevertheless, the very presence of Getty's remains on the grounds turns the museum into an explicit (if semi-secret) mausoleum" (82).

Duncan notes that as the visitor moves through the villa, in its old arrangement, from Roman imperial luxury to regal splendor to rococo intimacy, there is a historical aspect to the museum's arrangement. The process of turning barbarians into cultured individuals requires passage through its spaces, from archaic Greek objects through Hellenistic art to Roman portrait busts, and then, on the floor above, at least in its first incarnation, to later works of oil painting and the decorative arts. Yet throughout, the space imitates the Roman villa, the home of a Caesar such as Tiberius, at the seaside, and it is this reference to Roman antiquity that leaves the greatest impression, the long entrance garden with its colonnade punctuated by copies of ancient statues, the building itself with its atrium like that of the Roman villa. One is visiting a mock home, one in which the builder assimilates himself to the wealthy Roman, becomes the American equivalent of a Roman aristocrat. And in this atmosphere, antiquity becomes something to be put on like a garment.

If the ambition of the villa was to celebrate the wealth of Getty himself, to provide a donor memorial, to offer a tax break to the wealthy expatriate, it also was meant to convert barbarians to civilized persons, and it does so in part by familiarizing them with the domestic space of the ancient wealthy. The villa looks out to the sea, includes a central atrium

64

with a pond, and contains many diverse and richly decorated spaces, with extraordinary works of ancient art. The visitor is encouraged to imagine herself either as the "client" of the wealthy aristocrat, mimed by J. Paul Getty himself, a supplicant visitor in his home, or as a resident in the space herself, at home in the opulence of this fabulous setting, a simulacrum of an archaeological remnant miraculously brought back to life, reerected, with walls, elevators, and parking garage. The crumbling ruins of antiquity are made to live again, made clean, hygienic, and whole once more. It is a fascinating, brilliant conceit. However—and the point concerns the argument of this book—neither the building itself nor its didactic material ever alludes to the presence of slaves in ancient culture.

The villa is determinedly an art museum, eschewing anthropological intent. The visitor encounters masterpieces of archaic Greek art, of classical Greek vase painting, of Roman glass and portrait sculpture. The presence of slavery and slaves in antiquity is simply not acknowledged. There is no allusion to slaves as makers of works of art, or as represented in them, to the housing of slaves in ancient Roman villas, or to the actual dwelling arrangements of an ancient household, in the Getty villa. The collection focuses on artistic values, on beauty, and on our aesthetic inheritance from the past. The matter of the cultural coherence or incoherence of ancient life, or even the processes of daily life, barely register in the displays and exhibitions of this museum; the museum's project is one of civilizing barbarians through contact with the aesthetic values of the classical past; and ancient slaves, some barbarian themselves, are invisible.

The British Museum

The British Museum, a universal survey museum, an "encyclopedic" museum founded in the eighteenth century, is what Pomian calls a "commercial" museum, based on a collection bought by the state from the collector Hans Sloane. As Carol Duncan and Alan Wallach remind us:

> Today's universal survey museum might be compared to Roman displays of war trophies . . . the early Louvre deliberately evoked the Roman tradition of triumphal display: captured enemy arms were exhibited along with works of art, and cartloads of art pillaged from conquered nations arrived at the Louvre in triumphal processions designed to recall those of ancient Rome.[13]

The architecture of the British Museum cites the spatial rhetoric of ancient Roman architecture, with its Ionic columns, its pediment, its Pantheonlike rotunda, once the Reading Room, and its new Queen Eliz-

OBJECTS

abeth II Great Court. Visitors are meant to be struck with awe at the building's immensity, filled with reverence for all that it contains: the vast holdings of the imperial museum of the state that records past glories of Britain, its power to purchase, seize, and house for eternity the cultural legacy of other civilizations. The words "and let / Thy feet, millenniums hence, be set / In midst of knowledge," from Tennyson's "The Two Voices," have been inscribed at the entrance to the Great Court Concourse Gallery.

The possession of the treasures of other cultures authorizes the superiority and dominance of the possessor. Those no longer able to keep their patrimony, losing it through theft or sale, are revealed as weak, unworthy stewards of their cultural heritage; the possessor expresses domination through exhibition of the lost property of once-great civilizations now fallen on ruin, as we observe in the efforts of Britain to hold on to works of art in danger of passing into the hands of such newly wealthy institutions as the Getty Museum. This is, after all, *The* British Museum. And the heritage of antiquity still in large part belongs to Britain.[14] This museum contains massive holdings from Egypt, from Sumeria, from Assyria, and of course from Greece. The visitor negotiates the museum by means of a complex and labyrinthine set of paths. One entrance leads her into Asia; the front entrance gives into a great lobby; on the right is one of many museum shops, a crucial element of the museum-going experience in most of Europe and America at present. To the left the curators have exhibited early Greek objects, Cycladic and Mycenaean vases and artifacts, then the most valuable of vases, glass, and sculpture. Up a stairway one finds the frieze of the temple of Apollo Epikhthonios from Bassae, a temple built on a remote hill in Arcadia to commemorate Apollo's deliverance of its donors from a plague. The frieze surrounded the inside of the temple, unusually, and is exhibited at eye level within a special raised loft in this part of the museum; its panels may have been created by the sculptor of the Parthenon frieze, and so provide a preview both of the artist's work and of the placement of the greater frieze.[15]

If visitors take a slightly different path, they pass the Rosetta Stone (a trophy that passed into British hands via Napoleon, who took it from Egypt along with other objects from that country), and walk past vast Assyrian reliefs of winged dragons and the ritual anointing of emperors. Mary Beard discusses the information panels behind the Rosetta Stone:

[T]he account of the subsequent decipherment of hieroglyphs is told as the story of a dramatic race to be first with the solution, a story of international rivalry between the Englishman Thomas Young, and the Frenchman Jean-Francois Champollion. The hero here is, needless to say, Thomas Young.[16]

Even the exhibitions devoted to foreign, exotic cultures provide the opportunity for a nationalist narrative.

The passage through the halls also produces a historical narrative, one that sets earlier objects first, the more primitive before the more elaborate, with the high classical masterpieces bracketed between less impressive works. One passes through a great open hall exhibiting Hellenistic sculpture into an antechamber, then into the climactic hall housing the greatest treasure of the British Museum, the Parthenon frieze, most of which has been set just above the heads of visitors, around the edges of the Duveen Room, air-conditioned, skylighted, with what remains of the broken elements of the two Parthenon pediments under separate roofs at each end of the hall.[17] The greatness and importance of these treasures are signaled by their placement at the end of a narrative path; they are the culmination of Egyptian, Assyrian, and early Greek developments. Sculptured slabs and pediments and metopes are marked by their special treatment, the care with which they are maintained, and the vigilance of the guards who oversee them.

The Parthenon sculptures are the British equivalent of the Mona Lisa, which is protected by bulletproof glass in the Louvre. They were, as is well known, taken from Athens by Lord Elgin, who bought a firman from an underling of the Ottomans, permission "to remove any pieces of stone with inscriptions or figures thereon."[18] Elgin's men took from the Parthenon and other buildings "247 feet of the original 524 feet of the frieze, 14 of the 92 metopes, 17 pedimental figures, a Caryatid and column from the Erechtheum, four slabs of the frieze of the Temple of Victory, the statue of Dionysus from the monument of Thrasyllus and a number of Greek reliefs and fragments from Mycenae" (20). Elgin's workers literally sawed off most of the Parthenon frieze and carted it away to England.[19]

It is only upstairs, in a room more difficult of access, requiring a certain determination and passage past coins and money, through more Egyptian objects, Roman relics and vases, that one arrives at a place seemingly dedicated to the edification of the young, the room of "Life in Ancient Greece and Rome." This room eschews the aesthetic, art historical project of the lower floors, exhibition of the best that men have wrought, for a more purely historical, even anthropological purpose. And here one might expect some acknowledgment of the presence of slaves in the ancient world. Yet even here the vestiges of ancient slaves and slavery are few and far between. The vitrines composing the exhibit are divided into thirty-four categories, including such topics as "Marriage," "The Greek Drinking Party," and "Women." Only two of the thirty-four vitrines identify a representation of a slave; the first is the case entitled "Women," which contains a *hydria*, or water jar, labeled "courtesans and slave-women celebrate the festival of the Adonia."[20] The image on this vase shows a festival: women celebrating the god Adonis, said to be the god of prostitutes and of women of the lower classes, who lamented the death of Adonis, lover of Aphrodite, at the tusks of a wild boar, shown here with Pan, god of Arcadian wildness, and Eros, god of sexual desire.[21]

The only other image or object labeled as pertaining to slavery is a figurine representing an actor costumed as a runaway slave, in a context again referring to the pleasures of a religious festival, the celebration of Dionysos in the theater (fig. 14). What is missing is any reference to the selling of slaves, the buying of slaves, their punishment, slave quarters in the houses, slave garments, or slave labors. In works of art, slaves are usually recognizable by their rough haircuts, clothing differing from that of the free, and often smaller stature. Some of the objects in the exhibits probably do represent slaves, such as the amphora showing the harvest of olives (fig. 8). This object, though, figures in the vitrine called "Farming," and there is no reference to the fact that some of those laboring belonged to others, as there is no reference in the vitrine concerning "Potters and Carpenters" to the fact that those laboring to remove clay from the earth were probably slaves. In the drinking party scenes, slave boys form part of the furniture, erotic and servile, of the celebration, yet go unremarked.

This universal survey museum, encyclopedic, art historical, and historical at once, can barely acknowledge the presence of slaves in ancient society. I say this not to condemn the curators or even to find fault with the strategies of exhibition; it is nonetheless remarkable that the pressures to present Greek antiquity, to display its remains, provide information and situate it, somehow collude to suppress the ubiquity of slaves in ancient Athenian life. The desire both to possess and do justice to ancient Greek civilization, to offer it to visitors and to claim it as one's ancestry, perhaps makes it difficult to represent a crucial feature—if not of the high aesthetic domain of ancient civilization, certainly of life, daily life, everyday life in ancient Greece.

The National Archaeological Museum of Athens

Athens itself is a kind of museum, a treasury of buildings held within the urban fabric. The modern city consists mostly of postwar concrete construction, seeming ready to collapse at the first hint of an earthquake. The narrow and congested streets pass by storefronts with businesses and residences above them; constricted corridors of a rich street life;

FIGURE 14. Figurine of an actor. Terra cotta, Athens, ca. 350–325 BCE. Photograph copyright the Trustees of the British Museum.

bicycles and motorcycles and signs in Roman and Greek script; interior passages recalling a Near Eastern, Ottoman organization of space, with tiny courtyards set back from the street; commercial enterprises and cafes clustering around an alleyway.

Every so often, the visitor catches a glimpse of something else, another history, another kind of space: the city is punctuated by remnants, the shards of ancient Athenian life. Driving in from the airport, on a narrow, crowded street that stretches from Piraeus, past tire shops and lamp stores, endless tiny enterprises, one sees in the distance, above the city, the Akropolis and the Parthenon, seemingly floating on high. The Akropolis still dominates much of the city: the temple of Athena has had its back broken, yet is visible from below; next to it is the agora, with a reconstructed Stoa; across the garden is the Hephaisteion, the temple well preserved because it was once made into a Christian church. Across a busy street stand the huge columns and capitals of the temple of Zeus Olympieion; nearby is the reconstructed stadium, built for the first modern Olympics at the end of the nineteenth century.

The National Archaeological Museum itself, within Athens, is what Pomian would call a "revolutionary" museum. The citizens of the new Greece, free of the Ottoman yoke, founded this institution. Duncan and Wallach: "Because it belongs to the nation and therefore to all citizens, the museum helps foster the illusion of a classless society."[22] The National Museum in Athens offers a particular case of this pattern of museum foundation, since it celebrates the freedom of the modern Greeks from the empire of the Turks, who inhabited the space once occupied by the ancient Persians, defeated by the ancient Greeks and sent back to Asia. The modern Greeks take up the glories of ancient Greek civilization, the independence and democracy of ancient Athens, and offer them as the ancient history of their nation, in this museum effacing the intervening period of domination.[23]

In 1829, the first Archaeological Museum was founded on the island of Aigina, the temporary capital of the modern Greek state, established after a fierce war of independence. Then in 1835, all ecclesiastical objects were ordered removed from the so-called Theseion, actually a temple of Hephaistos converted into a Christian church, and the Theseion became the "Central Archaeological Museum." By 1836 the Theseion was full, and sculptures were kept in the library of Hadrian (to which the Aigina Museum's most important contents were transferred in 1837); after 1843 objects were stored in the Tower of the Winds, then moved to a room in the university, then to the building called the Varvakeion. Not until 1866 did construction begin on a new museum, designed by a German architect. A Greek from Petrograd paid for its construction. The building was filled with archaeological treasures, and an extension was built in 1925. When war began in 1940 the museum's holdings were reburied; archaeologists used the six months the Greek resistance held out in the Albanian mountains to bury the colossal Kouros of Sounion and other statues. After the war, as the author of the "Concise History of the National Museum" writes:

> The chief aim in the new arrangement of the galleries was that the visitor should feel a warm and close communion with the works of art and that his heart be open to the art of all phases of Greek cultural activity. In this respect it has been of great help that the treasures of the National Museum are not housed in an old, dark palace as is generally the case in European capitals, but rather in a neo-classical building of the late 19th century, comparatively simple in design, without ornaments on the walls and without multicoloured marble dadoes.[24]
>
> In many European Museums,—which originally consisted mainly of older private post-Renaissance collections—the ancient sculptures, restored and "beautified," as was the fashion, give a false idea of Greek art. In the way this art is presented in the National Museum, without any glamourization, not only does it serve pure knowledge but also broadens the intellect and intoxicates the spirit. (xviii)
>
> [E]ach artistic object (was) considered as an individual work but also as part of an organic historical evolution. (Ibid.)

This is a national museum, and an art museum. The visitor finds little mention of everyday life or of the presence of slaves in ancient Greek society here.

The direct axis into the museum leads the visitor to the gold objects recovered from Mycenae and other Mycenaean-era sites, the most spectacular of holdings of this museum. There are golden masks, rosettes, beaten-gold covers of babies' skeletons, gold cups, a dagger with an inlaid gold scene, gold signet rings, gold belts, gold diadems, gold scepters, and gold-foil diadems. Among the grave goods are golden models of everyday objects: a scales, a box, or *pyxis*, and other miniature vessels. These cases are labeled in Greek and in English, with lists of what they contain and the sites of their provenance; more detailed information is not given. Many tourists see only this room of the museum; most tour guides stand near the cases containing these treasures, and speak at some length about them, releasing their students to move on their own through the rest of the museum. Visitors seem rarely to enter the almost-deserted wings flanking this hall, with Neolithic, Early and Middle Bronze Age, and Cycladic remains.

The museum-goer must return to the foyer and only then enter the series of rooms containing a chronologically organized survey of Greek sculpture. The path of the visitor moves past archaic sculpture, maidens and youths, *korai* and *kouroi*, to a dramatic moment of punctuation in the last room on this side of the museum, the "Poseidon Room," housing the great Poseidon of Artemision (fig. 1). This statue is one of the few life-size or larger bronze figures remaining from antiquity, since most were destroyed or melted down in the intervening centuries. Those that survive have usually been found in shipwrecks; this Poseidon was found in 1926, probably taken by the Romans from a Greek temple, but as Semni Karouzou puts it, "the god of the sea took his revenge and sank the boat which was going to unload it in a Roman harbour."[25]

This statue, along with the golden treasures from Mycenae, are emblematic of the National Museum: precious metals, and the dynamism of the naked male body, mature and bearded, posed not for erotic contemplation or Apollonian devotion like the young men, or *kouroi*, but poised in action, in the hurling of the trident. This statue was previously thought by some to represent Zeus, father of the gods, throwing his thunderbolt. In any case, he is a fitting representative of a patriarchal genealogy, for a seafaring nation that traces its ancestry back to the Olympians. This magnificent figure, placed in the center of the room, draws all eyes; it is protected, like other climactic objects in other museums, by a glass barrier, and in this case a surrounding fence to prevent touch. The powerful statue has a rich, mottled skin—green, umber, pewter; a small penis intact; pubic hair in neat rows; a variegated rich surface; verdigris; thigh of orange, ochre, umber, gold, green, brown, gray, black; the translation into metal of mobile, living flesh.

It is not until room 18—the second room of classical grave stelae, placed in chronological sequence after the monumental sculpture from the archaic period and focused on aristocratic themes and on free retainers—that we find an image of a slave. In these later classical grave stelae, especially those erected over the graves of women, sculptors represented the deceased, sometimes with her children, sometimes also with a slave in attendance on the dead. Scholars differ about the significance of these representations.[26] In part the slaves' presence may be traced to an increasing interest and focus on everyday life in the later fifth century BCE, in many cultural domains. In Aristophanic comedy, as noted earlier, we find discussions of sex, food, and slaves, topics presented with a quotidian directness inconceivable in the genre of high tragedy; and in middle and new comedy, there are narratives of an almost realistic romantic nature. In part, our evidence may be due to the accidents of transmission, but through many sources, epigraphical, funereal, and forensic, we know more about everyday life in the later fifth and early fourth centuries than in earlier ones.

For example, on the very beautiful funeral stele of Hegeso, probably dating from about 410 BCE, a larger stele than earlier examples and produced during the Peloponnesian War, a period of much loss and grief in Athens, we see not just Hegeso but also a slave girl (figs. 15, 16).[27] Is this a marker of status, a woman with an attendant? Is it a sign of affection for a particular slave? The two women, balanced within the rectangular slab of the stele, face one another. The body of the slave girl exceeds the frame, a tiny temple suggested by the two columns in bas-relief on each side. Her body extends before and therefore outside this boundary, her breast profiled against the background of the scene. Hegeso sits in a chair, the lines of which break into and cradle the drapery of her elegant costume which, like other garments of this later period, clings more closely to the female body than does the drapery depicted in archaic sculpture. Her dress, her chair, her footstool, her jewel box, her jewel, her curls, caught in a fillet, all point to a certain luxury, as do the size and elegance of the stele itself.[28]

Hegeso wears the costume of a bride, and her name and patronymic are inscribed on the epistyle, the base of the stele's pediment. The stone's background was blue; the jewel she held in her hand painted gold. She takes it from a *pyxis*, a box, like the Mycenaean gold box exhibited elsewhere in the museum. The slave is represented as standing, holding the box and looking down at her mistress while Hegeso herself gazes pensively at the jewel. Nicholas Himmelmann comments on this image: "mistress and maid-servant are depicted with such an impression of atmospheric harmony, that the servant appears ethically and physically quite the equal in rank of her mistress, although she is designated as slave by her un-Greek, barbarian, sleeved costume."[29] The unnamed slave woman wears the so-called "barbarian sleeved chiton," a different garment from her mistress's, with long sleeves rather than the pinned drapery of the free woman. She also wears the *mitra*, or snood, covering her hair, itself a mark of noncitizen status; *hetairai*, or high-class prostitute-courtesans, are often depicted wearing this type of headgear (fig. 22).[30] This is a slave at work, serving her free mistress, a mistress who does not acknowledge her presence except to receive on her knee the box the slave holds with deference and sympathy. There may be mythic echoes of another bride, the goddess Persephone, or Kore, who lives for some part of the year in the underworld with the lord of the dead. Persephone is represented elsewhere in the museum with her mother, Demeter, and Triptolemos on the Eleusis stele, in the Poseidon Room.

We know nothing of the circumstances of Hegeso's life, except that she seems to have died young. Andrew Stewart comments: "Her maid stands quietly opposite her, with head cast down. She is dressed only in an ungirdled shift, a *chiton cheiridotos*, and of course is not named in the inscription. This forcibly reminds us that a slave girl is only a thing, an object to be used for work or sex, while her mistress is an Athenian lady, well-dressed, demure, and ravishingly beautiful: Pandora domesticated."[31]

What interests me most about this stele is its presentation in the mu-

FIGURE 15. Stele of Hegeso. Stone carving, ca. 410–400 BCE. Inv. #3624, National Archaeological Museum of Athens.

74

seum: its label, both in Greek and in English, calls the woman on the left a "servant," not a slave. Consistently, in these rooms containing grave monuments and other stelae, including finds from the shrine of Asklepios in Epidauros, slaves are called servants, or omitted altogether from the descriptions of the objects. In the artworks and other artifacts,

FIGURE 16. Gravestone of Hegeso from the Dipylon Cemetery, Athens. Nineteenth-century photography showing the stele in situ. Photograph copyright Alinari/Art Resource, New York.

slaves are sometimes partially obscured behind elements of architecture or furniture, often depicted as much smaller than the free persons in representations, clearly differing in stature yet distinctly present. But slaves do not figure in the explanatory material of the curators. Such figures are consistently called servants in English, in Greek *therapainida*, for a young "servant" holding a doll. It is not until a single grave stele of the mid-fourth century BCE (no. 873) that the word *doulos*, "slave" in the English text, is used.[32] Upstairs, in the circuit of rooms identical to the floor below, containing a chronological survey of masterpieces of Greek vase-making and -painting depicting many scenes of Dionysiac celebration, with slaves present pouring wine and in attendance at symposia, they are not acknowledged in the labels accompanying their display.[33]

An interesting feature of the current layout of the National Museum is a room devoted to antiquities of ancient Egypt, donated by a wealthy Greek who once lived in Alexandria and collected these objects. As Philip Fisher has written:

> Along with the "work of art" the museum displays and stabilizes the idea
> of a national culture, an identifiable *Geist*, or spirit, that can be illustrated
> by objects and set in contrast to other national cultures.[34]

Colonial nations like Britain display the spoils of empire, the trophies of their dominance, present or past, over others; the Greek display of Egyptian antiquities is a fascinating case. Are the Greeks acknowledging some genealogical connection with the Egyptians, in the sense of Martin Bernal's *Black Athena?*[35] Or are they indicating a position of superiority in relation to a Third-World culture that cannot retain dominion over the remnants of its own great past? This section of the Athens museum is the most carefully curated of all, with elegant glass cases and labels—not dusty pieces of paper in antiquated hands set within the vitrines but attached to the spacious cases themselves in printed black letters that describe in some detail the Egyptian objects within. The legend claims that their collection of Egyptian antiquities is "fourth in Europe"; geographically close as they are to Asia, to the new Turks, to Africa, the Greeks here stake a claim as Europeans by putting Africans on display.

An issue that surfaces powerfully in Athens is not Freud's "So all this really does exist, just as we learnt in school,"[36] but rather "So some of this really does *still* exist." Visiting Greece is always an experience of a certain melancholy at the recognition of so much loss. There is the perhaps inevitable erosion due to weather, human habitation, smog, and earthquakes. But there are also the signs of predation, of the weaknesses of a poor country unable to fend off the rapacious adventurers who destroyed and seized parts of Greek antiquity to decorate their own, at least temporarily dominant nations. The question of ownership of its national past is a vexed one for the Greeks. The issue of plunder surfaces not in the 1968 museum catalogue but in the 1998 version, reissued in the name of the same author, with a certain bitterness:

> Long before the pure souls of the philhellenes spurred them on to come to the Classical lands and sacrifice themselves in the cause of Greek freedom, many of their fellow countrymen had destroyed the ancient sites throughout the Greek world and Asia Minor, and had taken with them everything of beauty and value they found standing, or that was handed over to them by the unsuspecting villagers.[37]

Byron fought for Greek freedom, but Lord Elgin preceded him.[38] The question of Greek freedom, freedom from the Turks, emerges here, and suggests one reason for the significant silence concerning slavery that one reads in the exhibitions of the National Museum.

❖ ❖ ❖

THE GREEKS do not, perhaps choose not to, mount an anthropological and historical, as well as art historical, museum exhibiting their ancient past. They construct their nationality *variously*, sometimes in contrast with the Persian Empire, all of whose inhabitants were considered enslaved to the only free man, the emperor, in contrast with African neighbors eventually conquered by Greek-speaking Macedonians, and *implicitly*, as distinct from Asian, Ottoman conquerors of the more recent past. To call attention to the slaves of antiquity might erode the narrative of freedom, of continuity between past and present, to suggest hierarchy and the subordination of Greeks to Greeks. Questions of politics, membership in the European community, disavowal of Asian occupation in the past, the courting of tourists, all play a role in the choices made in museum display. The representation of nationality in the present depends in part on these differentiations from conditions of domination; in the contradictory play of forces determining museum representations, of traditions of scholarship, of display, of academic interest and political intervention, the National Museum may not embrace an anthropological or even historical interpretation and presentation of the ancient past over an aesthetic one, in part because such a version might cast a shadow over Hellenic claims to be the source of European and all Western civilization, embodying ideals of beauty, freedom, and philosophical inquiry inconsistent with the presence of slaves in everyday life.

77

FIGURE 17. Justus Engelhardt Kuhn, *Henry Darnall III*. Unsigned oil on canvas, circa 1710. The Maryland Historical Society, Baltimore, Maryland.

FIGURE 18. Detail of Justus Engelhardt Kuhn, *Henry Darnall III*. The Maryland Historical Society, Baltimore, Maryland.

Slavery in the Museum

To illustrate a provocative mode of exhibiting the history of slavery, calling into question its erasure in American and European museums, I offer a counterexample.[39] For an exhibit called "Mining the Museum" at the Maryland Historical Society, the contemporary African Caribbean American artist Fred Wilson was invited into the collections of the society, founded in 1844. He "mined" them, and made them his own.[40] In an earlier performance piece at the Whitney Museum, Wilson, asked "by the museum to give a tour to the staff and docents, . . . greeted them and arranged to meet them elsewhere in the museum. Changing into a guard's uniform, Wilson took up a post in the room where the group was waiting for the artist they had met just a few minutes earlier. He was suddenly invisible to them; the docents paced in the galleries anxiously looking for him, walking by him time and again" (10).

In the Baltimore exhibit, Wilson's work "mined" the history of slavery, its invisibility and its covert archaeology in the museum itself, in a variety of installations. The piece *Cabinet-making*, for example, installed a slave whipping post next to the elegant furniture of the slaves' masters. In his reframing of an oil painting, a portrait of "master with slave" (figs. 17, 18), Wilson called attention to both the presence and the diminution of a slave boy. His piece *Metalwork* (fig. 19) set up ornate, precious Baltimore repoussé silver next to iron slave shackles. As the American slave historian Ira Berlin writes in the exhibition's catalogue:

79

FIGURE 19. Fred Wilson, *Metalwork*. Silver vessels in the Baltimore repoussé style, 1830–80; Baltimore-made slave shackles, ca. 1793–1872. From Fred Wilson, *Mining the Museum, An Installation*, edited by Lisa G. Corrin (New York: New Press, 1994). Copyright © 1994. Reprinted by permission of The New Press.

> Even a cursory exploration of the history of the silver vessels and the iron shackle suggests the multiple ways in which the lives of people—black and white—were joined together, for who made these artifacts, who purchased them, who tended them, who paid for them, who used them?— masters, slaves, and servants; white, black, and red; free and slave. The fine silver vessels are as much artifacts of the African-American experience as they are of the European-American one, and the shackle is as much a part of the European-American story as it is a part of the African-American one. (44–45)

Wilson's is a dramatic, provocative, atopic, and discontinuous use of the historical resources of a conventional museum, staging, framing, and calling attention to both the presence and the erasure of slavery in American representations of the past.

❖ ❖ ❖

THE FORGETTING of ancient Greek slaves serves as a support for various cultural fictions, including the story of modern Greek nationalism, the narrative of Anglo-Saxon descent from the Hellenic past, and the fantasies of a modern would-be aristocrat. The absence of slaves and slavery in the exhibition of classical Greek antiquity, in three very different museums in different national settings having very different histories and formations, suggests to me that the forgetting or disavowal of ancient slavery has been inevitable, structurally necessary to representations of ancient Greek high culture and the civilizing project in the active acculturation of modern museum-going populations. Acknowledging the labor, sale, and presence of slaves in classical antiquity would disrupt certain narratives of Western civilization, and the privileged status of the Greeks as exemplars and as origin.

But the slaves are, of course, not absent; their troubling presence, even unacknowledged, persists. It is in the name of disturbing the complacent invocation of Greek antiquity that I cite these cases. I do not mean to advocate the simple addition of slavery to the museum in the name of a full, or fuller, representation of antiquity. Slavery should disturb, be inassimilable, disrupt the seamless narratives of lineage, in institutions that record descent from the high culture of the past. It should lead us to call into question filial pieties, the many forms of disavowal in exhibition and in scholarship, to make connections among contemporary societies, and the Greek, British, and American histories of slaveholding, the multiple genealogies of slavery.

3   DILADOS

3   DILDOS

Hermogenes: "Any name which you give, in my opinion, is the right
one, and if you change that and give another, the new name is as correct as the old—we frequently change the names of our slaves, and
the newly imposed name is as good as the old. For there is no name
given to anything by nature; all is convention and habit of the users."

—Plato, *Cratylus* 384d

IN THIS CHAPTER, I consider further ways in which
slaves have been rendered invisible in modern practices of representing
antiquity. The question of slavery here intersects with that of sexuality,
another vexed issue for the presentation of ancient society to modern
audiences. In most of the museums of the world, including those discussed in the previous two chapters, there is an occlusion of the presence
of slaves in antiquity and, in addition, of the vital erotic life of ancient
peoples: their myriad and various representations of sexual intercourse;
of the *phallos*, a sacred object; and of the *phallos*'s double, the dildo. The
suppression of slaves meets the suppression of sexuality in modernity's
deployment of and phantasmic investment in a certain idea of antiquity
as a lost golden age of freedom and philosophical detachment. Even in
the relatively new subdiscipline of the history of sexuality, work in classics has focused on women and on homoeroticism; slaves, disturbingly
ubiquitous as available sexual partners, have been effaced. How are we
to understand the ubiquity of slaves in antiquity, and their consequent
informing of ancient sexualities?

Can we even speak of "sexuality" when discussing antiquity? This
question implicates the work of Michel Foucault, especially the second
volume of his history of sexuality, *The Use of Pleasure*, which has met
with much ambivalence from the discipline of classical studies.[1] A passionate debate has arisen concerning the value of his arguments concerning the Greeks. Misunderstandings have resulted from this work,
which is multifaceted and part of a much longer and unrealized project.
In keeping with the positivist orientation alluded to earlier, many clas-

sicists tend to focus on problematic details of Foucault's work on the Greeks, which stands at the very beginning of a projected long narrative concerning what might be considered "world-historical" issues in the genealogy of Western ideas about pleasure.

Foucault's perspective on antiquity was influenced by Hegel's notions of the evolution of the subject, even though Foucault himself would have disavowed the progressive aspects of such influence. Foucault looked to the philosophical and prescriptive strain of discourses in Greek culture for traces of the beginnings of a philosophical subject. His gaze was directed toward the influential Platonic project of asceticism and cultivation of the self, which involves in its historical development a turn away from politics and the *polis*, as Hegel argues. This strain produces post-Platonic Stoicism, for example, and has its effects on new, Roman notions of the body and marriage and on Christian theological developments, which Foucault began to describe in *The Care of the Self*.[2] Foucault's work, although limited in certain respects, does shed light on this important strain of discourse in ancient culture. Some scholarly readers' dismissal of this work, because of a reduced body of evidence upon which his findings depend, leads them also to reject or ignore important insights about historicity and cultural difference that are compatible with the most valuable insights on classical culture of our era, those of the Parisian school.[3]

For some, Foucault seems to deny that there *is* sexuality in antiquity, and they go so far as to suggest that following his arguments might lead one to conclude there was no sex at all in the ancient world. The point is that the sexual universe we inhabit—defined as it is by the sexologists of the nineteenth century, by Freud and Lacan, by liberationist movements of the later twentieth century, by transgressive bodies of the twenty-first —cannot be mapped unproblematically onto antiquity and the activities and codes of meaning we see in the ancient world in relation to the acts we call sexual. The debate has sometimes centered on the question of the existence of "homosexuality" in antiquity, but in fact is rooted in the question of the historicity of sexuality itself as a category. A healthy dose of estrangement and of historicism might enable a perspective on how the ancient world is not just commonsensically the same as our own, in the domain of sex as in many others, and significantly includes the ubiquity of slaves, who figure prominently in that domain, although they have until recently been remarkably absent from the nascent field of the history of sexuality in antiquity, including the work of Foucault.[4]

In this chapter, I look at how taking slaves into account might affect the subdiscipline of the history of sexuality in classical studies. At the beginning of *Les Mots et les choses*, published in 1966, Foucault cites a text he claims was from Borges, an entry from "a certain Chinese encyclopedia": "'animals are divided into: (a) belonging to the Emperor, (b) embalmed, (c) tame, (d) suckling pigs, (e) sirens, (f) fabulous, (g) stray dogs, (h) included in the present classification, (i) frenzied, (j) innumerable, (k) drawn with a very fine camelhair brush, (l) et cetera, (m) having just broken the water pitcher, (n) that from a long way off look like flies.'" [5] Foucault recalls "the laughter that shattered . . . all the familiar landmarks of my thought—*our* thought, the thought that bears the stamp of our age and our geography—breaking up all the ordered surfaces and all the planes with which we are accustomed to tame the wild profusion of existing things." He remarks of this list: "What is impossible is not the propinquity of the things listed, but the very site on which their propinquity would be possible" (xvi). The laughter of Foucault, Borges's orientalism, that attribution of the fantastic taxonomy to the Chinese, might serve once and for all to erode confidence in and to estrange our own taxonomies, and to argue most persuasively that not only in fiction but also in history it is possible to think that the conceptual world we now inhabit has not always existed, that culture has been organized otherwise elsewhere. The very categories of sexuality and pornography have to be put into question when we look at such a distant culture as that of ancient Greece. And here, as elsewhere, the overlooked presence of slaves contributes to a mapping of difference.

I would like to juxtapose that Foucauldian-Borgesian catalogue with one from Aristophanes. In a passage preserved in Pollux's *Onomasticon*, supposedly from the *Thesmophoriazusae* of Aristophanes, recording all kinds of women's ornaments and equipment, we find a male actor performing the role of a woman pronouncing a list:

> xuron, katoptron, psalida, keroten, litron,
> prokomion, ukhthoibous, mitras, anademata,
> egkhousan, olethron ton bathun, psimuthion,
> muron, kiserin, strophi', opisthosphendonen,
> kalumma, phukos, periderai', hupogrammata,
> truphokalasirin, elleboron, kekruphalon,
> dzom'ampekhonon, truphema, paruphes, xustida,
> khitona, barathron, egkuklon, kommotrion.

Like a Platonic interlocutor, her companion asks for more: *eita ti;*

> diopas, dialithon, plastra, molokhion, botrus,
> khlidona, peronas, amphideas, hormous, pedas,
> sphragidas, haluseis, daktulious, kataplasmata,
> pompholugas, apodesmous, olisbous, sardia,
> hupoderidas, helikteras . . .

Some of these items are still mysterious and as yet undeciphered. Here is nonetheless the translation of John Maxwell Edmonds:

> Here's razor, mirror, scissors, wax-salve, soda
> A false front, trimmings, hair-ribbons, bandeaux,
> Alkanet, "sudden death," some face-powder,
> Some scent, a pumice-stone, breastbands, a hair-bag,
> A veil, some rouge, two necklaces, some eye-paint,
> Peignoir, some hellebore, a hair-net, girdle,
> Shawl, woollie, bordered wrapper, velvet gown,
> Camisole, "death-pit," tippet, curling-tongs—

The series continues:

> Earrings, a pendant, more earrings—a lot,
> Pins, necklet, armlet, bangles, carcanets,
> Anklets, seals, chains, rings, plasters, bandelettes,
> "Bubbles," carnelians, baubons, more earrings . . .
>> [This last line reads, literally, "bubbles (whatever they are), breast-bands, dildos (*olisbous*)," carnelians, i.e., Sardian stones"]
>> (Aristophanes frag. 321 = 320 K = 332 Austin)[6]

Clement of Alexandria also cites, most disapprovingly, some of this list, calling it *ton gynaikeion kosmon*, "women's ornament, or dress." This well-equipped Athenian woman was massively, comically fortified with apparatus, and the dildo figured in her panoply. The list also contains a *kekruphalon* (l.6), "hair-net" and punningly, "secret phallus," and *sphragides* (1.12), "seals or gem-rings," possibly dildos as well, according to Jeffrey Henderson.[7] Of course this is comedy, a comic catalogue, with these items seeded in among the jewels for comic effect; but they nonetheless figure prominently in this catalogue of women's appliances, in this site of promiscuous juxtaposition.

Greek vases often bore representations of the *olisbos*, or dildo, sometimes indistinguishable from the *phallos*, a mimetic representation of the detached and erect penis used in rituals. Vases show dildos hanging on the walls above prostitutes, *pornai* or *hetairai*, being deployed in scenes of group sex, and in scenes of solitary female masturbation. One vase shows a woman using two dildos simultaneously (fig. 22). In another (fig. 20), a vase painter pictured a woman watering a bed of *phalloi/olisboi*; scholars disagree about whether this scene depicts a hopeful future user of the dildo crop, or a woman keeping the ceramic products of a potter from drying out. Another vase (fig. 21) shows a woman carrying off a giant *phallos/olisbos* as large as she is; is this a scene from ritual, as some scholars claim, or a figure for female sexual insatiability? The matter of the visual representation of the dildo has been usefully taken up by scholars, including Eva Keuls and François Lissarrague.[8]

FIGURE 20. Detail of a vase by the Hasselmann Painter, ca. 430–420 BCE. Photograph copyright the Trustees of the British Museum.

❖ ❖ ❖

THE OBJECT in question is, in English, the *dildo*, a word always associated now with what we call sexuality, sexual practices, sex. The *Oxford English Dictionary* classifies the word as "obsolete," describing it as a word of obscure origin, once used in the refrains of ballads. It is "also a name of the penis or phallus, or a figure thereof; the lingam of Hindoo worship." Ben Jonson used the word in 1610 in the *Alchemist:*

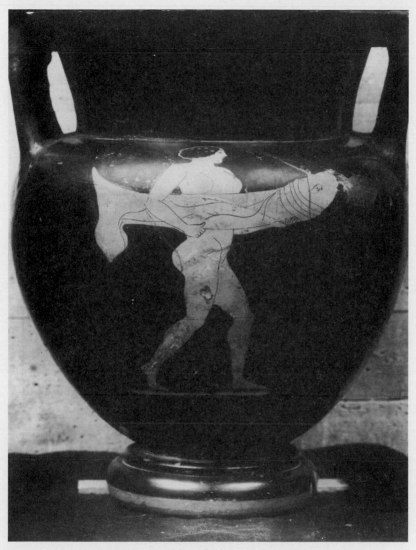

FIGURE 21. *Krater* by the Pan Painter, woman carrying a giant phallus. Second quarter of the fifth century BCE. Staatliche Museen zu Berlin—Preussischer Kulturbesitz, Antikensammlung/bpk.

> Here I find . . .
> The seeling fill'd with poesies of the candle:
> And Madame, with a Dildo, writ o' the walls.
>
> (v.iii)

Also in the seventeenth century, in an account of East India, a certain Fryer describes an Oriental scene: "Under the Banyan Tree, an Altar with a Dildo in the middle being erected, they offer Rice." In the semantic network into which it falls in English, *dildo* was a disparaging nickname for men or boys, with a slightly obscene connotation; was once associated with nonsense rhymes, with questionable females, and with the sexual practices of exotic others. In Jonson's hand, the dildo seems to take on the connotations of suspect sexual acts, in a cultural situation in which sexuality as a category is just emerging—perhaps still the world in which the appropriate category is not in fact sexuality, that product of nineteenth-century scientism, but rather sodomy, or another word connected with the confessional, with illegal acts of various sorts, not yet scrutinized in the coherent pseudoscientific work of such sexologists as Kraft-Ebbing and Freud.[9]

If one is open to the possibility that sexuality as such does not yet exist in the seventeenth century in England, then what does it mean to match this word *dildo* with its Greek "equivalents," the word listed alongside it in that very arbitrary catalogue we call a dictionary? Or, better, if we make a concordance, what are all the usages of this word in classical texts; what does a reading of the collected examples of this word yield? The standard Greek-English dictionary of Liddell, Scott, and Jones (hereinafter LSG) gives a definition of *olisbos* only in Latin—*penis coriaceus*—characteristically deferring the dangerously obscene meaning, "leather penis," with a linguistic displacement into another "dead" language.[10]

Our own contemporary, postmodern sense of these particular objects figures in two discourses. We live in a world in which the dildo is a literalization of the Freudian fetish, a figuring of the phallus, that nonexistent thing that conceals or protects the viewer from the castration of the mother which Freud describes as "fact" in his 1927 essay "Fetishism."[11] We understand the dildo in light of discourses about pleasure or drives or needs, in a post-Freudian, post-Lacanian syntax in which the dildo serves as a pathological substitute, as a fetish, as a simulacrum of the penis. Or we understand the dildo as figuring in liberatory sexual practices, representing the refusal of rigid gender identities, signifying a celebration of multiple postmodern sexualities, within the context of gay and lesbian and sex-affirmative feminist discourse.

One can offer an interpretation, a reading of the dildo within ancient

Greek society, that remains within a network of purely sexual or sexo-logical meanings. If the meaning of ancient sexual practices depends on one's location in the act of penetration, as David Halperin has argued, then women cannot be imagined by men to have sex unless penetration occurs.[12] In keeping with the metaphors of plow and of stilus, so common in decorous literary representations of sexual intercourse, the Greek male imagination can only conceive of women's masturbation or sex play with a substitute phallus, the *olisbos*.[13] Sexual acts performed between women, or female masturbation, cannot take place in the absence of dildos; and there are multiple examples of dildos being used by men with women in art, and by women alone, on the vases used by the Greeks for drinking parties, *symposia*, and Dionysiac celebration. A line of reading consistent with a certain feminist perspective would imply a critique of the phallocentric politics of representation of this object in ancient art and text. One might even imagine an interpretation that argued for ancient women's seizure of the dildo as an appropriation of the penis, the *phallos*, the feminist hijacking or compensatory provision of this all-important instrument of penetration. A hermeneutic, historicist model here, one that recognizes our situation in a Freudian, sexualized universe, one in which our truth, our secret, has come to be understood as our sexual nature, might be more productive.

The encrypted dictionaries and writings on ancient sexuality have the effect of reproducing this hiddenness and latency in describing the sexual practices of antiquity, deftly concealing them from students, from scholars who must labor, must know Latin if they are to read the obscene in Greek, so that there is an artificially produced "sexuality," a forbidden, obscene zone of our knowledge of ancient Greece. Jeffrey Henderson's *Maculate Muse: Obscene Language in Attic Comedy*, for example, an elaborate exploration of Greek comic diction with obscene English equivalents, a lexicon for the obscene comedies of Aristophanes, supplements the more decorous or repressed entries of the dictionary.[14] Not until 1975 was such information compiled and made available in one text for the English-speaking Aristophanes readers, who had previously been confronted with the evasive tactics of Liddell, Scott, and Jones, and with euphemism and bowdlerization even in such texts as the Loeb editions, which commit themselves to the task of printing Greek (and Latin) texts and English translations on facing pages, but which sometimes offer a translation not in English but in the other of the ancient languages when confronted with ancient obscenity.

My argument is that when we look at the taxonomy connected with the *olisbos*/dildo, just one of the objects we associate exclusively with the restricted domain of sexuality, in ancient Greece we find not our familiar organization of sex, sexual practices, sexology, sexuality, but a very different set of things to think. What is the web, the cultural and semantic field, the syntax in which the dildo figures in ancient discourses? I will look at some other texts in which the dildo appears, neither to treat them exhaustively, nor to read them from the perspective of modernist feminism, but rather to try to sort out another taxonomy, a cultural field in which we might situate the *olisbos*, one that implicates the slave and slavery. This will be an unfamiliar taxonomy to those for whom the object figures only within the field of sexology and sexuality, within a limited social-scientific study of private life, within the post-Enlightenment creation of the private sphere described by Jürgen Habermas.[15]

Olisbos

Sappho's fragment 99a was discovered on a third-century CE papyrus, and is thought by some scholars to be the work of Alcaeus rather than Sappho. It reads, fragmentarily, in David Campbell's translation:

> . . . after a short (time?) . . . descendants of Polyanax . . . strike the strings . . . receiving the *'olisbos'* . . . kindly . . . quivers . . . [16]

The phrase I am interested in here is tentatively recorded as "*olisb' dokois<i>*"; the participial adjective *olisb . dokoisi* seems to agree with *khordaisi*, strings. There is a vigorous debate concerning the meaning of *olisbos* here, one that reveals the difficulties of situation within the elite institution of classical scholarship, which has been both repelled and fascinated by ancient sexual practices, producing an unnerved and self-conscious discourse about them.

Denys Page remarks in his *Sappho and Alcaeus*, à propos of the scandal of Sappho's sexual desire for young women:

> To the . . . question—so often propounded, so seldom considered without prejudice—whether evidence for practice as well as inclination is to be found in the fragments of Sappho's poetry a negative answer must be returned.[17]

In a subsequent note, after the discovery of the Oxyrhynchus fragment xxi, attributed to Sappho and listed as fragment 99a in her corpus, Page adds that he "had written that there is no reliable evidence in the fragments of Sappho for any impropriety in the conduct of herself or her companions. This remains true as stated in that form" (144 n. 1). (Yet he has been made uneasy.) Such a remark resembles that of a translator of Sappho who once made a distinction between the "inversion" of the poet, in light of evident desire, and the absence of evidence for "perversion," activity driven by such desire. Such scholars evidently mean to compliment the poet and rescue her from those who might think her improper, a pervert, and show the degree to which modern ideas about sexuality, desire, and judgment colored and obscured classical scholarship about ancient sexual activity well into the twentieth century.[18] About fragment 99a, Page continues, "Sappho used in her poetry a word of quite unusual coarseness, referring to practices about which silence is almost universally maintained." He goes on to detail his view about the reading of the manuscript, laboring to show that the word at the beginning of column 1.5 need not be construed as *olisbos*, "dildo," but concluding finally: "The answer is that it is practically certain that *olisb-* is what was written" (145).

M. L. West resists not the textual reading of *olisbo-* but rather the translation of it as "dildo," arguing that the word must be a synonym for *plektron*, the instrument used for striking the lyre.[19] As Giuseppe Giangrande later writes about this strategy, "the only way to preserve a puritanical vision of Sappho was to dream up a new meaning for *olisbos*."[20] This metaphorical understanding of the *olisbos*, as *plektron*, "pick," or "bow," for the playing of a musical instrument, protects Sappho from the allegations of "unusual coarseness," either in invective or in some more benign view of the use of the *olisbos*.

Giangrande, on the other hand, insists that *olisbos* always means *aidoion dermatinon*, "leather private part." He maintains that if *olisbodokoisi* is the reading here, and if it agrees with *khordaisi*, this is an example of "adjectival enallage," that is, the substitution of one grammatical form for another. The rhetorical figure *enallage*, adduced by Giangrande to account for the transfer of the epithet from the person to the thing, is a kind of characterizing displacement, in which all that the *olisbos*-receiving person touches takes on the qualities of *olisbos*-reception. "[T]he *khordai* of the instrument used by the player . . . are called *olisbodokoisi* because the player herself was *olisbodokos*" (250). Giangrande retreats into a macaronic flurry, employing the German *Notbehelf* to amplify his sense, and also resorting to Latin; in disagreement with K. J. Dover, who believes the *olisbos* was used exclusively for solitary female masturbation, he writes that the device "was used whenever the replacement of a real *mentula* was needed." Giangrande concludes that the word "leaves us in no doubt as to what Sappho and her companions were up to, and confirms the ancient view that Sappho was a *tribas*" (250). That is to say, as LSJ define the term, "a woman who practises unnatural vice with herself or with other women," a "rubber," from *tribo*, "rub."[21] Giangrande, in the scholarly debate that ensues, insists that *olisbos* always and everywhere means "dildo."

He also discovers dildos in Callimachus's 38th Epigram, in which Simon the prostitute, abandoning her trade, dedicates her apparel and her apparatuses to Aphrodite; he argues that the disputed wickerworks of her dedication are in fact *olisboi* as well.[22]

If Sappho sings of sexual acts, satisfaction of desire on soft beds, of desire for girls, the *olisbos* in her work can be located as well in another semantic field, that of objects with which one performs tasks, produces pleasure, musical or sexual, and adorns oneself. There may after all be some analogy posed or suggested between the playing of the lyre with the *plektron*, the plucking or striking of the strings, and the sexual activity of striking or rubbing with the dildo—the connection of the *olisbos* with the *plektron* implicit but present, even if it may have been exaggerated in order puritanically to deny the use of the word *olisbos* in a sexual context in Sappho's verse. This semantic nexus is intriguing, since we find a possible connection between two "instruments," tools, devices to produce a certain result, rather than a connection through discourses of sexuality per se. The dildo might then be understood as an instrument and even eventually as a commodity, a product of artisanal labor, just as much as an element of possible invective, or as a figure in erotic discourse.

This fragment follows Sappho 98, which describes a *poikilan mitran*, a decorated headband which the poet laments she cannot obtain for Kleis. Campbell notes that "S. may be saying that luxuries (reminders of happy days in Mytilene) are not obtainable, now that she is in exile."[23] The yearning for absent luxuries is a theme that recurs in other passages I want to discuss, in which objects, especially luxury items, associated with beauty, erotic pleasure, and feminine finery cease to be available and become the objects of frustrated desire.

Elsewhere in the fifth-century comedies of Aristophanes, we again find the *olisbos*, here a commodity difficult to put one's hand on. In Aristophanes' *Lysistrata*, the character Kalonike complains about the absence of men—husbands or seducers—saying:

> Even lovers have vanished without a trace. Ever since the Milesians revolted from us, I haven't even seen a six-inch dildo, which might have been a consolation, however small.[24]

> [all'oude moikhou kataleleiptai phepsalux
> ex hou gar hemas proudosan Milesioi,
> ouk eidon oud'olisbon oktodaktulon,
> hos en an hemin skutine 'pikouria.]

> (107–10)

The *skutine'pikouria*, "leather helper," is a joke, a play on the proverbial
sukine epikouria, "a support made of fig wood," that is, illusory help. She
clearly thinks a dildo, at least a dildo of this size, an "eight-finger" model
six inches or so, would be relatively useless. Here Sappho's theme of the
scarcity of the luxury commodity from Asia Minor recurs; the dildo,
fabricated in Miletus, is nowhere to be found now that the Athenians are
at odds with the Milesians, and the women must act, setting in motion
their sex strike. Later in the play we find another complaint about the
inadequacy of the imitation penis; Lysistrata has explained her plan to
deny the men of Greece their sexual satisfaction, and the women explore
alternative possibilities for their own pleasure. Lysistrata orders the
Greek women, if their husbands ignore them, to "skin the skinned dog,"
said by Henderson to refer to masturbation with a dildo, with possible
reference to the depilated pubis of Greek women.[25] In the next line
Kalonike complains:

phluaria taut' esti ta memimemena.
[Facsimiles are nothing but poppycock.] (158–59)

The women of Aristophanes, while recognizing that the well-equipped
woman possesses the dildo, prefer the real thing.[26]

There is a distinction to be drawn between the *phallos* of comedy and
the *olisbos* or dildo. Henderson says that "the ordinary comic phallus was
of course not erect, but . . . made of leather, pendant, red, uniformly
thick."[27] Special *phalloi* were used in comedy performances when erec-
tions were called for. The use of the *phallos* as part of the comic costume
has its affinities with ritual uses of the detached phallus, which was "sac-
rificed": for example, thrown in the form of cakes into troughs in the rite
of the Thesmophoria, erected as apotropaic sign at Apollo's shrine at
Delos, and carried in Dionysiac processions. The phallos synecdochi-
cally embodies potency, fertility, and masculinity. Athenaeus cites Se-
mos on the *phallophoroi*, "phallus-bearers," who are known to carry the
simulacrum of the male member, erect, on poles and to perform songs
in honor of Dionysos (xiv.621–22). Athenaeus also (xv.676f), intriguingly
and fleetingly mentions *narkissous olisbous*, "narcissus-dildoes," whatever
they might be. Ritual uses of the *phallos* approach the limit of the *phallos*
worn in comedy, which may be the point of intersection between the sacred, Dionysiac *phallos* and the mimesis of a body part used for sexual
pleasure, the *olisbos*/dildo.

Another comic passage, Cratinus's fragment 316, recorded by Photius in the *Lexicon*, glosses the word *misete*, meaning "lecherous," and
connects the *olisbos* with a whole set of metaphors used in tragedy and

elsewhere in comedy to connote sexual intercourse, representing the woman's body as a field to be plowed, a tablet to be inscribed, an oven to be heated and filled.[28] Photius cites Cratinus: "misetai de gynaikes olisboisin khresontai"; [And lecherous womankind will the *olisbos* use]. Nauck suggested that this was a parody of the oracle in Herodotus 8.96, "and devotees of Aphrodite Colias (i.e. courtesans) will cook with (the wood of) oars." Edmonds comments:

> [F]or, as Herodotus tells us, it was on the promontory where stood this Aphrodite's temple that wreckage of the battle of Salamis was washed up; this oracle would be on everybody's lips in 480–79 and perhaps remembered in the autumn of 433 after the battle of Sybota, which Athens and Corcyra considered they had won over courtesan-loving Corinth.[29]

Here the dildo, rather than taking over the function of plow or stilus, serves like oars, used as firewood to heat the ovens that are women's bodies.

The sixth mime of Herodas centers on a dildo, a finely crafted red model. In this text, in a genre frequently disdained by scholarship focused on high culture, Metro, visiting her friend Koritto, first complains about the laziness of slaves. She then asks Koritto: "lissomai se, me pseusei / phile Korittoi, tis kot'en o soi rapsas / ten kokkinon baubona" [Please tell me the truth, dear Koritto, who stitched you the scarlet *baubon?*] (fig. 22)[30] Note the convention of omitting to translate the obscene word *baubon*, or dildo. Koritto is shocked that Metro has seen the *baubon*; she had loaned it to Eubule, who gave it to Nossis, who showed it to Metro, who wants to have one made for herself. Koritto finally reveals that a certain Kerdon made it. Metro recalls that there are two Kerdons, one of whom "couldn't stitch a plectrum for a lyre" (6.51). A third Kerdon made this *baubon*, and Koritto marvels at his craftsmanship: "in workmanship he is a true Koan, you would think you saw not Kerdon's handiwork, but Athena's" (6.65–68). In fact, the maker had made two:

> [A]t first glance my eyes swelled out of my head; I may tell you,—we are alone—,they [*ta balli'*] were firmer than the real article, and not only that, but as soft as sleep, and the laces are more like wool than leather; a kinder cobbler to a woman you could not possibly find. (6.69–73)

This mime, replete with the language of rubbing and grinding, ends with a sly warning against *ornithokleptai*, "bird-thieves" (6.102); the editor notes solemnly, "the most anxious care cannot protect poultry against depredation."

FIGURE 22. Myson, painting of naked woman with *olisboi*. Vase, terra cotta, fifth century BCE. Museo Archeologico Regionale, Syracuse. Photograph copyright the Trustees of the British Museum.

The word *ballia*, used of the pair of dildos, may be related to the word *phallos*. *Baubon*, on the other hand, used in the earlier passage here as well as in the catalogue of women's accessories in the first Aristophanes fragment cited, has not been satisfactorily accounted for. It may be derived from the verb *baubao*, "sleep," "lull to sleep"; this etymology would be supported by Koritto's admiring observation that the *ballia* are *he malakotes hupnos*, "the softest sleep," "the softness sleep." However, some scholars have connected this name for the *olisbos* with Baubo, who in the cult of Eleusis, the Eleusinian mysteries, causes the mourning Demeter to burst into laughter, pulling up her dress to expose her genitals; Baubo who is represented in a series of remarkable figurines from Priene (fig. 23). Maurice Olender, in his important essay on Baubo, describes these statuettes:

> [T]he disproportionately large head sits directly on top of the legs, blending into and replacing the hips of the atrophied body. The huge face is broad and frontal, with a nose and with two large eyes in the position of

FIGURE 23. "Baubo" figurine from Priene. Terra cotta, ca. 200 BCE. Staatliche Museen zu Berlin—Preussischer Kulturbesitz, Antikensammlung/bpk.

the breasts. Below the mouth, and corresponding to the dimple in the chin, is a representation of a woman's genitals.[31]

Olender explores the possibility that Baubo, the feminine, is the personification of the vulva, corresponding to the *baubon*, like Priapos, the incarnation of the *phallos*. Koritto's toy, the sought-after dildo, product of artisanal labor, may have mythological resonance, connections with the very early myth and cult of Demeter at Eleusis.

❖ ❖ ❖

WHAT, THEN, can we say about the *olisbos*, the dildo, in Greek antiquity? I would place it in a complex, various, heterogeneous set of overlapping cultural networks that resemble very little our sexological fixing of this same object as fetish or as toy. The dildo in ancient Greece is, although rarely visible in displays in museums,

1. part of women's apparatus of seduction.
2. like the plow or stylus—i.e., a tool for cultivation or inscription, or like the firewood that warms the womb, a woman's oven, an instrument for working on women's bodies.
3. an instrument of pleasure—for sounding the lyre, for causing women's bodies to resound in pleasure—to their praise or blame.
4. an artifact, one artisanal object among others, the product of skilled labor.
5. a commodity—often exotic, a luxury item from the East.
6. a *baubon*—a tranquilizer, or a figuration in the masculine of the mythological character Baubo.

Representations of the dildo/*olisbos* do not appear in the public spaces of most museums with collections of ancient objects, and, like slaves, seem invisible to the modern gaze. I want to conclude this chapter by arguing that the *olisbos* intersects with slavery in another way: that it is also necessary to locate the *olisbos* within the context of slavery, in a cultural series that begins with inanimate tools; passes to tools that are imitations of the animate; passes then to those bodies that are, in Aristotle's phrase (*Politics* 1253b), "animate tools," the bodies of slaves; and ends with fully human bodies, the bodies of the free. Aristotle says:

> if every tool could perform its own work when ordered, or by seeing what to do in advance. . . .
> if shuttles wove and plectrums played harps of themselves [*ta plektra ekitharizen*] . . . , masters would have no need of slaves. (1254a)

Here Sappho's *olisbos*, imagined as a plectrum, recurs in a new context. Such is a recurrent phantasy, in this slave culture, of a world where things might behave like slaves, where inanimate tools would work as do the animate.

The following passage, a fragment from a comic writer of the mid-fifth century BCE, Krates, preserved in the writings of Athenaeus, belongs in a utopian, postslavery imaginary. It comes from a comedy called *Animals*, or *Beasts*, in which the animals rise up and refuse to be eaten by men; there follows an exchange in what might be thought of as a low utopia, in which the object world, the lifeless, soulless world of things, is imagined as coming to life:

> Then there shall be no one who may own a slave or a slave girl, but each
> man, each old man, shall have to serve himself?
> By no means: for I am going to make everything walk about on its own.
> How is that going to help?
> Each object will come to him when he calls for it. Put yourself down next
> to me, table. . . . Get kneading, my sweet little kneading trough. Fill
> up, jug. Where's the cup got to? Go and get yourself washed. Cake,
> come along over here. The pot ought to empty out the cabbages. Get
> moving, fish:—"but I'm not yet toasted on the other side!" Then why
> don't you turn yourself over—and cover yourself with oil and salt.
> (Athenaeus, *Deiphnosophistai* 267e–f)

Athenaeus cites other passages from other comic writers, who similarly describe the gratifyingly automatic arrival of food and drink.[32] In a world without slaves, the imaginable, utopian alternative to slave labor is not work by the free but labor performed by inanimate objects themselves.

In an especially revealing fragment from the comic *adespota*, fragments not assigned to particular authors but possibly also from the second *Thesmophoriazusai*, women again complain of sexual frustration, and mention again the dildo, that leathern commodity from Miletus:

> [A. Are our respective husbands to go on]
>   Treating us badly?
> B. *I* think not, for one.
>   If we've got sense we shall think out a plan
>   To turn the tables on them.
> A. If we can.
> B. Listen [and learn.] What's the [kid] thing (*to skutinon*) they say
>   The women play with at [Miletus], eh?
> A. Why Trash by Nonsense [out of] Naughtiness;
>   Reproach and Ridicule—that's all. With this
>   It's just like wind-eggs—[there's no] chick [inside it.
>   Your plan's a wish, no more, and if you tried it
>   Like a fool, you'd only make things worse].
> B. Still, though,
>   I'm *told* it's like the genuine [thing. (*homoion posthio*) (i.e., "dick,"
>   "cock")]

A. I know,
   As moon to sun—looks like but gives no heat.
B. It *can't* do that.
A. Well things being thus, [I'm beat.]
   Let's—(*tois therapoisi koinos[aimetha / to pragma*)
   Whisper secretly the *pi*—(*to pi*) [for *peos*, cock] [33]

The Greek *tois koinosaimetha to pragma* might better be understood to mean "if we, should we communicate, share the plan, the plot, the 'thing,'" in other words, "have sex with the servants," which Edmonds, bowdlerizing as he does throughout, translates as "suppose the servants came to hear." [34] As they allegedly did in the history of Sparta, slaves were positioned to serve as substitute sexual partners when husbands or lovers were absent, when dildos did not satisfy, at least in the fevered, libidinous imagination of a comic female character. In Aristophanes' extant *Thesmophoriazusai*, Euripides' kinsman, disguised as a woman at a women's festival, gives voice to this very fear, in his list of Euripides' omissions concerning women's crimes: "Nor how we get banged by the slaves and mule grooms if we haven't got anyone else, he doesn't talk about that" (491–92). [35] In the comic fragment cited earlier, an imagined dildo figures in a graduated series of things and objects, in which slaves and their bodies find their place in the list of commodities at the disposal of the free.

The seventh mime of Herodas describes a trip to the workshop of Kerdon the shoemaker, who displays his fine handiwork to Metro and a friend, including a list of sixteen special types of shoes. The fifth centers on the unfaithful slave-lover of Bitinna, who jealously orders him flogged, then tattooed. The slave is an unruly commodity who might choose unacceptable sexual partners and enrage his mistress; the ideal world of static, inanimate objects like shoes remains more manageable. The *olisbos*/dildo, unlike the sacred or ritual *phallos*, can be understood to figure within this cultural domain, to occur in a series of objects, object-subjects, devices for satisfying women. In a world inhabited by slaves, such commodities figure differently.

We might think again about sexuality and slavery and their intersections, about those ancient human beings who were not human in the same way as citizens or the free, who dwelt on a borderline between humans and things. There are in the ancient world some human beings without status, without standing, some bodies that are things, that blend gradually into the landscape of animals and of inanimate objects, that have property value without consciousness, without subjectivity, or whose subjectivity and consciousness represent a threat to mastery. The rhetorical representation of slaves as dildo-like sex toys works to fix them in a hierarchy of objects, not persons. Such an unfamiliar categorization of human beings and objects is polemically inscribed into ancient Greek ways of thinking about politics, others, bodies and mastery, material existence, sexual acts, and the objects of the material world. The dildo, a representation, a simulacrum of a human body part, is for the Greeks not a fetish, a veil for the castration of the female, nor a toy. Rather, it is an inanimate imitation of a part of an animate human body, in a world in which there are various kinds of bodies, those human bodies that must be tools, those human bodies that are free and master others, in sex as in all forms of activity.

What we find in the ancient dildo—invisible like slaves in modern museums, with their displays of works of high art—is not the postpsychoanalytic, queer domain of postmodern sexuality, nor a pathologized fetish of phallocracy, but rather an object at the crossing of many different networks of meaning and performance. We cannot see the ancient *olisbos* if we are bound by our own restriction of such objects to the domain of perverse or liberatory sexuality. There certainly are representations of sexual practices in antiquity, not often available for viewing in museums. They must be mapped otherwise, not simply and unproblematically identified with the objects of our own contemporary landscape, not limited to our projections of our own sexual meanings, defined by categories of perversion or queerness, but rather taking on distinct meanings in a world informed by the opposition between slave and free.

4   THE SLAVE BODY

> Ah tortoises, I envy you your shells! It was good and brainy of you
> to roof your backs with tile and so cover your sides. Me, I've been
> bruised within an inch of my life by a walking stick! [ego d'apolola
> stidzomenos bakteria]
>
> —Aristophanes, *The Wasps* 1292–96

MANY PRESENTATIONS of antiquity in museums
occlude, forget, or overlook the slave body, which interferes with or
interrupts the surfaces of messages about an idealized past, contaminating not in a moral sense but in the way that textual scholars use
the term to discuss the corruption of texts in their transmission. How
might the slave's body be recognized were it to appear and be acknowledged in commentary? Nicholas Himmelmann points out the great variety of representations of slaves on objects from antiquity, including
"wet-nurses, pedagogues, negroes, weapons-bearers, grooms, charcoal-
haulers, camel-drovers, serving-women, *hetairai*, symposium-boys, ac-
robats, flute-girls, dancers, sacrificial victims, athlete-youths, potters'
apprentices, travelling-companions, forge-workers, shepherds, miners."
He argues that two different sorts of images of slaves emerge from these
many representations: one an idealized type of representation, used in
art when the "larger connections with the aristocratic-heroic represen-
tational world were intended,"[1] the other based on what were thought
to be "slavish" physical characteristics.

Archaic artists presented the attendants of heroic warriors and gods as
beautiful, like the legendary characters of the past, and in an aristocratic
perspective, idealizing the objects of representation. Nonaristocratic
figures rarely appear in art of this period, according to Himmelmann:
"The heroic idealism of archaic art allows us to understand that the representation of slaves had no role to play in it, although social reality was
already considerably determined by slavery" (33). In periods when artists desired to emphasize the humanity of slaves, they were rendered
more sympathetically, marked only by dress rather than by size or gro-

tesque difference from the free. When slaves are shown as attendants of the idealized free, they are often idealized; when they are shown alone, they bear slavish characteristics so that they can be identified as slaves. In later material culture, artists or artisans, some of whom may have been slaves themselves, often represented slaves as smaller than free persons, crouching, with bent posture, with characteristic, often roughly cut hairstyles, and nude or wearing animal skins. Such representations in art formed part of a polemical discourse concerning slavery, especially toward the end of the fifth century. Slaves were presented as caricatures, as grotesques, with potbellies, during periods when slavery was tendentiously represented as natural, or by artists who intervened in the debates on the side of natural slavery: "Crouching on the ground labels the slave more a naïve, human, immature creature of nature, which means that he is a slave by his very nature" (35).

The iconography of the representation of slaves in material culture has received some attention from archaeologists and art historians, even though it is often forgotten, effaced, or suppressed in museum exhibition of the remains of Greek antiquity. How does the slave body, as an object, appear in texts? In the ancient world there were few first-person, subjective accounts by slaves or former slaves about their condition. We have the oblique, often cryptic testimony of such writers as the fabulist Aesop, allegedly a freed slave; the Roman playwright Terence and Epictetus the philosopher, freed slaves; or the poet Horace, whose father was a freedman of Rome. But a poem such as Horace's ode 1.39, addressed to a slave, called *puer*, "boy," does not tell us a great deal about the experience of slaves themselves. What we do have is the testimony of free persons about the slave bodies that surrounded them. There is a great deal of evidence from these sources about slave bodies as ubiquitous and serviceable, as remarkable in their difference from those of the free, as sexually desirable and available, as marked by their condition of servitude, as difficult to manage, as unwieldy, treacherous, conspiratorial bodies threatening the safety and the realization of the projects of the free. Slave bodies, like that of the tattooed slave of the Aeschines scholiast discussed in the introduction, could remind free persons of their own vulnerability to enslavement. And it may even be possible to find, in the representations of slaves and slave bodies in antiquity, free persons' imagination of traces of resistance, of a refusal of complete objectification by slaves themselves.

Although it rarely surfaces directly, free persons may have sensed the danger of having subjected persons living in such close proximity in their houses and farms. Such stories as that of Aristodemus survive: in the Greek colony at Cumae, in southern Italy, Aristodemus seized power as tyrant in 504/5 BCE. He persuaded the city's slaves to murder their masters; their reward was wives, daughters, and property. The boys of the citizen households were spared, sent into the countryside to work, and brought up as girls. When they came of age, they nonetheless rose up and drove out the tyrant, demonstrating their essence, their "nature" as free men.[2] Polemically, rhetorically, perhaps to allay fears concerning such resistance and to inculcate subjection, ancient authors do from time to time present the often occulted, subjected bodies of slaves.

Bound and Beaten

There are various traces in texts of these disciplined yet unruly bodies. The slave body was, for one thing, described frequently as fettered, bound, beaten, always vulnerable to beatings and to whipping, with refinements. The Athenian, a character in Plato's *Laws*, reminds his interlocutor concerning slaves:

> Some distrust the whole class and make their servants threefold—nay, a hundredfold—slaves at heart by the scourge and the lash, as though they were dealing with so many wild beasts. (6.777a)[3]

Later the Athenian proposes a law mandating that if a slave intervenes when a man strikes one of his relatives, perhaps risking death, he should be freed; if the slave does not intervene, he "shall suffer a hundred lashes with the scourge, to be administered by the commissioners of the market" (9. 881b).

The slave body was always susceptible to such discipline by public or private masters. The premise of Aristophanes' *Knights* is that a new slave with a barbarian name, Paphlagon, has assumed domination over Mr. Demos, the "people," and effects beatings for the slaves already present in Demos's household: "he's been getting the homebred servants beat nonstop" (5). These later complain that the new slave, a figure for the demagogue Cleon, whips them if they don't bribe him, and "if we don't, the master will pound on us till we shit out eight times as much" (69–70). The Hermes of Aristophanes' *Peace*, enlisting helpers to dig up Peace herself, says: "If anyone refuses to help because he wants to be a general, or is a slave getting ready to run away [*automolein*] . . . " and Trygaios completes his thought: "—let him be stretched on the rack and flogged!" (450–52)[4] (Peace, when she's finally unearthed, smells of all good things, including thrush meat, ivy, and "a drunken slave girl" [537].) Also in *The Peace*, the chorus boasts of Aristophanes that he, unlike other comic writers, stopped writing stereotypical roles for slaves who ran away, or got a beating just so a fellow slave could mock: "could it be that the lash has stormed your flanks in great strength and defoliated your rear?" (746–47)

Whipped

Herodotus tells the story of the Scythians' slaves, blinded by their masters, who slept with free women and had children with them. When the free Scythians returned from war, this new generation fought them successfully for a time, until one of the returning soldiers pointed out: "When they saw us armed, they naturally felt that they were as good as we are, and were meeting us on equal terms; but when they see us coming with whips instead, they will remember they are slaves" (Herodotus 4.3).[5] The slaves, slavish by nature, flee at the sight of the masters' whips. Proof of the enslavement of all his subjects to the Persian emperor was that Xerxes' troops passed over the Hellespont under the whips (7.54). In Aristophanes' *Knights*, the slave is addressed as "rogue," *mastigia*, that is, someone who needs whipping (1228). In Lysias 1, a murder trial, her master threatens a slave girl with whipping before she betrays her mistress: "choose as you please between two things,—either to be whipped and thrown into a mill, never to have any rest from miseries of that sort, or else to speak out the whole truth" (18). In a possible allusion to the judgment of slaves after death, Sokrates in Plato's *Gorgias* describes the arrival of various bodies before Rhadamanthus, judge of Asians in the underworld:

> [I]f anyone had been a sturdy rogue [*mastigias*], and bore traces of his stripes in scars on his body, either from the whip or from other wounds, while yet alive, then after death too his body has these marks visible upon it. (524c)[6]

Such signs of slavery can be metaphorical; even the Great King, the emperor of Persia, can bear such marks on his soul, "striped all over with the scourge [*diamemastigomenen*], and a mass of wounds" (524e)

Sexually Vulnerable

The slave body was sexually available, especially to males of the master class; the male slave was positioned provisionally, perhaps phantasmally, rhetorically, at least in comedy, as a slightly higher form of dildo for the women of the master class. In one of the mimes of Herodas, mentioned in chapter 3, a mistress jealously threatens to have her male slave tied up, beaten, and tattooed or branded because he has slept with another woman (Herodas, *Mime* V). The slave body, one of the instruments of sexual pleasure of the ancient city, conditions the sexual existence of the free. In Aristophanes' *Acharnians*, the hero Dikaiopolis sings a hymn to Phales, the personification of the phallus, celebrating his separate peace with the Spartans:

> Yes, it's far more pleasant, Phales, Phales,
> To catch a budding maid with pilfered wood—
> Strymodorus' Thratta from the Rocky Bottom—
> And grab her waist, lift her up, throw her down
> And take her cherry.
>
> (*Acharnians* 271–75)

This maid bears a slave name, Thratta, signifying Thracian origins; the verb *katagigartisai*, translated as "take her cherry," has violent connotations, meaning "take out the kernel," "pit." The prize from the "Sausage-Seller," given to Demos at the festive end of *The Knights*, is "a split-bottom chair and a well hung boy [*paid*] to carry it for you. And if you ever get the urge, use the boy as your split bottom too" (1385–86).[7]

Tortured

The slave body was also tortured, or vulnerable to torture.[8] An interesting case, much cited and involving a freed slave, features an accusation by Apollodorus against Neaera that was once attributed to Demosthenes.[9] It is in this legal oration that the oft-cited remark is found: "Mistresses [*hetairas*] we keep for the sake of pleasure, concubines [*pallakas*] for the daily care of our persons, but wives [*gunaikas*] to bear us legitimate children and to be faithful guardians of our households" (*Against Neaera* 122). Apollodorus claims that Neaera, an alien, is living illegally with an Athenian citizen as his wife. He accuses Neaera, once a slave, of having been sold as a prostitute, buying her way out of slavery, marrying, and then pretending to be an Athenian citizen with the result that her daughter, illegally married to an Athenian, went so far as to perform the sacrosanct sexual rites of the *hieros gamos*, the sacred marriage, in the worship of Dionysos. In Apollodorus's voice, pseudo-Demosthenes sets Neaera's body, in a sort of personification, against the laws, the *nomoi*, of Athens: "consider that the laws and Neaera here are contending in a suit regarding the life which she has led" (115). The speaker expresses outrage that Neaera's slave body, which has prostituted itself, would come so close to the secret, sacred heart of the city. He rouses himself into a frenzy of condemnation:

> [A]re you then shamefully and recklessly to let off unpunished a woman
> who has openly played the harlot throughout the whole of Greece, who

treats the city with outrage and the gods with impiety . . . ? Where has this woman not prostituted herself? To what place has she not gone in quest of her daily wage . . . ? Does she not serve all the lusts of those who deal with her? (107–8)

He asks the citizen jurors, all male, to imagine what the women of their households would think about their verdicts, women who are wives and daughters of citizens, respectable women. And then the speaker recalls how he offered to torture the slaves of Neaera to prove his case:

I proposed that he [Neaera's husband] deliver up for the torture the women-servants Thratta and Coccaline, who remained loyally with Neaera when she came to Stephanus from Megara, and those whom she purchased subsequently, while living with him, Xennis and Drosis. (120)

In a conventional move, he also offers to pay for any injuries suffered by these slaves if they are damaged during the torture. Neaera herself, once a slave but now free, has slipped beyond the torturer's reach, having used her sexual powers to obtain her freedom.[10]

Another law court speech, written by Lysias, *Against Simon* (Lysias 2), recounts an Athenian citizen's attempt to keep a Plataean boy, *meirakion*, from his rival, Simon, who raided his house, attacked him in the street, and with his friends tried to grab the boy, and then indicted the speaker for wounding him. We conclude that the boy was a slave because, although from Plataea, whose citizens were exempt from torture, the speaker says of him: "I came utterly unprepared, without calling to my aid either friends or servants or anybody at all, save only this child [*to paidion*], who would have been unable to support me, but was capable of giving information under torture upon any crime [*basanidzomenon*] that I might commit" (2.33). It is the beloved object's torturability that marks him as a slave.

Tattooed

The scars of beatings and whippings that marked the slave body until death were not the only marks that set apart the bodies of the unfree. As noted earlier, the slave body carried tattoos or brands, like that of Histiaios's messenger in Herodotus, who after he communicated his message to Aristagoras bore the tattooed marks on his scalp for the rest of his life, a unerasable tablet with an obsolete set of signs. C. P. Jones argues that tattooing had several functions in antiquity: "self-decoration," associated with the less advanced barbarians, "religious," associated with the East, and "punitive" functions: "this came to the Greek from the

Persians."[11] In Aristophanes' lost comedy *The Babylonians*, someone says: "Samos, not Babylon! what a lettered lot" [*hos polugrammatos*] (Edmonds fr. 64). Literally, "how very lettered"; ancient scholars explained this moment variously. Aristophanes is ridiculing branded slaves, some say because the Athenians branded Samian prisoners of war in 439 BCE with an owl, the sign of Athena that appeared on Athenian coins; and the Samians in retaliation branded enslaved Athenians with the *samaina*, a sort of bireme, a ship first built by the Samian tyrant Polycrates.[12] Plutarch, in his life of Pericles, says this tattoo or brand was "a warship with a turned-up beak, like a boar's snout, but . . . broader than a trireme, with a paunch-like hull" (26). In his life of Nicias he writes that the Sicilians sold their Athenian captives as slaves, bearing the tattoo of a figure of a horse on their forehead (29). The slave body, then, could be distinguished from other bodies by these signs of possession, elaborate tattoos or brands.[13]

Tattoos mark the slave as distinct, and connect slaves with barbarian peoples like the Thracians, whose women are shown in art as wearing marks on their arms and legs. Herodotus says that Thracians "consider tattooing a mark of high birth, the lack of it a mark of low birth" (6.5). After a storm destroyed the bridge the Persian emperor Xerxes had attempted to build over the Hellespont from Persia on his way to invade the Greek cities of the mainland, he sought to punish the strait as he would a slave:

> Xerxes was very angry when he learned of the disaster, and gave orders that the Hellespont should receive three hundred lashes and have a pair of fetters thrown into it. I have heard before now that he also sent people to brand it with hot irons. (7.35)[14]

Commanding that those who had built the bridges be decapitated, Xerxes—who considered himself the sea's master, the sea his slave, like all else in the world—also ordered those whipping the sea to remind it that he was master. Some of the Thebans who surrendered to the Persians as they invaded Greece through Thermopylae were killed; "all the rest were branded by Xerxes' orders with the royal mark, beginning with Leontiades their commander" (7.233).

Herodotus also refers to *stigmata hiera*, "sacred punctures, or tattoos," marks of possession worn by temple slaves; he describes a temple dedicated to Herakles at the Canopic mouth of the Nile: "If a runaway slave takes refuge in this shrine and allows the sacred marks, which are the sign of his submission to the service of the god, to be set upon his body, his master, no matter who he is, cannot lay hands on him" (2.113).

The Greeks associated tattooing with barbarians, and then, with those barbarians among them, their chattel slaves. In Aristophanes' *Lysistrata*, a fire begins, and the members of the chorus say of trying to fill their pitchers at the well, to quench the flames, that they were "fighting the elbows of housemaids and branded slaves [*doulaisin /stigmatiais*]" (331). These marks on some persons constituted part of the visual landscape of the ancient city and its households. Attic vase paintings show Thracian women, "usually slaves," according to Jones, "with marks usually placed on the leg or the arm and consisting of designs such as spirals around the wrist or animal figures such as deer." [15] In Aristophanes, such sightings of slave tattoos abound. In *The Birds*, a utopian fantasy of escape from the city, of a world upside down, the chorus leader, addressing the audience, calls on them, recruiting slaves to run away and join the birds:

> all things shameful here, for people controlled by custom, are admirable among us birds. Say by custom it's shameful here to hit your father; up there it's admirable for someone to rush his father, hit him, and say "Put up your spur if you mean to fight!" And if you happen to be a runaway slave with a branded forehead [*drapetes estigmenos*], with us you'll be called a dappled francolin . . . if you're a slave and a Carian like Execestides, join us and generate some forefeathers, and proper kinfolk will materialize. (755–65)

Being a slave, a Carian, runaway and tattooed is as shameful as beating one's father; and in the fantasy realm of the birds, slave genealogy can be revised retrospectively, in a probable allusion to contemporary Athenian practices, an impure mixing distressing to someone like Aristophanes. In *The Frogs*, Pluto, sending Aeschylus up from the underworld, calls others, guilty officials, down: "And branded and fettered [*stixas kai sympodisas*] the slaves shall go / With the vilest rascal in all the town, Adeimantus . . . down, / Down, down to the darkness below" (1511–14). Menander's Demeas, in the *Samia*, threatens to tattoo Parmeno (106–9). Plato, in the *Laws*, says: "if anyone is caught committing sacrilege, if he be a slave or a stranger, let his offence be written on his face and his hands" (854d). Bion of Borysthenes said of his father, a freed slave, that he had "not a face, but a narrative [*suggraphen*] on his face, the mark of his master's harshness." [16]

Aristotle says, in a passage from a biological text that implicitly has bearing on the debates concerning whether slaves are slaves by nature or convention:

> Children are born which resemble their parents in respect not only of congenital characteristics but also of acquired ones; for instance, there

have been cases of children which have had the outline of a scar in the same places where their parents had scars, and there was a case at Chalcedon of a man who was branded on his arm, and the same letter, though somewhat confused and indistinct, appeared marked on his child. (*Generation of Animals* 721b32)[17]

If a slave bears marks of tattooing or branding, his children may inherit them as well as his status as a possession. Tattoos associated with religious subjection, punishment, and barbaric origins were for the Greeks not adornments but signs of otherness, of the strangeness of slaves and of their status as possessions, producing a difference when the slave body, unmarked, was alarmingly similar to that of a free person.[18]

Ubiquitous

The slave body was tattooed, beaten, threatened with torture, and also ubiquitous, almost invisible to the master class yet simultaneously imagined to be always listening; in *The Frogs* Aristophanes depicts two slaves celebrating the mischief they can do because they surround their masters:

> Aeacus: I'm entranced
> When I can curse my lord behind his back
> Xanthias: How about grumbling, when you have felt the stick,
> And scurry out of doors?
> Aeacus: That's jolly too
> Xanthias: How about prying? . . . And what of overhearing
> Your master's secrets?
> Aeacus: What? I'm mad with joy.
> Xanthias: And blabbing them abroad?
> Aeacus: O heaven and earth!
> When I do that, I can't contain myself [*ka'kmiainomai*].
> (745–53)[19]

The Greek *ka'kmiainomai* means "I pollute myself," "I have an orgasm"; as Jeffrey Henderson puts it, the slaves mean "ejaculate happily," the sanitized, long-standard translation, "I can't contain myself," offering another example of the sexual as well as social censorship classical scholarship has imposed on the objects of its study.[20]

❖ ❖ ❖

To READ the bodies of slaves and their place in ancient history is not simply to engage in an empirical listing of these among many other features of the representation of social existence. We need to understand the structuring ubiquity of slaves in ancient society. In the Greek imagination even the golden age—the age of Kronos, before civilization, before agriculture—included slaves. Fantasies of overwhelming abundance and the lack of labor still conceive of slaves as inevitably part of the landscape of the time before history. Athenaeus cites the comic writer Telecleides' *Amphictyons;* the speaker may be Kronos himself:

> I will, then, tell of the life of old which I provided for mortals. First there was peace over all, like water over the hands. The earth produced no terror and no disease; on the other hand, things needful came of their own accord. Every torrent flowed with wine, barley-cakes strove with wheat-loaves for men's lips, beseeching that they be swallowed if men loved the whitest. Fishes would come to the house and bake themselves, then serve themselves on the tables. A river of broth, whirling hot slices of meat, would flow by the couches; conduits full of piquant sauces for the meat were close at hand for the asking, so that there was plenty for moistening a mouthful and swallowing it tender. On dishes there would be honey-cakes all sprinkled with spices, and roast thrushes served up with milk-cakes were flying into the gullet. The flat-cakes jostled each other at the jaws and set up a racket, the slaves would shoot dice with slices of paunch and tid-bits. (6.268b–d)[21]

Even in a world of automata, with self-propelled inanimate objects, in the golden age before time and labor slaves, well-fed, were there; the poet imagines freedom from labor for the free, but not a world without slaves.[22] For these ancient thinkers, slaves were so much a part of the landscape, of the space even of prehistory, that even, or perhaps especially, a utopia could not lack its servile population. The comic utopian fantasy of Aristophanes' *Ecclesiazusae* requires that slaves do the work once done by poor citizens so that all citizens can live in leisure, and that female slaves sleep only with their male counterparts, dressed in slave mode, with their "piggies," their "cunts," slavishly depilated (651–52, 724). The poet uses the word *katonaken* for slave dress, referring to "a coarse frock with a border of sheepskin" (LSJ); the slave women are thus "plucked," depilated "slavishly." Although slavery is a crucial, structuring presence and metaphor in Aristophanes' comedies, as I will argue in the next chapter, it appears often to be invisible or incidental to scholarly readers. Just as the obscenity of ancient comedy has often been expurgated for schoolboys, women, and other susceptible types, so slavery is written out of the translations and the commentary on them; B. B. Rogers translated this line: "In servile fashion, snipped and trimmed to match," expurgating the obscenity and toning down the allusion to the slave body.[23]

Murder

I conclude this chapter with a text by the orator Antiphon, a speech that may have been delivered in a trial for murder by poisoning, in which a slave body acts as an instrument to carry out the will of a free woman. One of the parties involved in the case is the *pallake*, the slave "mistress" or concubine of a certain Philoneos, who desired to place her in a brothel. The opponents of the speaker, his half-brothers and their mother, are on trial for murder; the mother allegedly convinced this slave concubine of Philoneos to give him what she claimed was a love potion in order that the slave might regain his affections. The speaker calls his stepmother "Clytemnestra" in one reading of the text, a reference to myth and tragedy, to the terrifying and vengeful wife of Agamemnon, who hacked her husband to death in his bath. The speaker in this case describes the administering of the philter to Philoneos and to the speaker's own father:

> After supper was over, the two naturally set about pouring libations and sprinkling some frankincense to secure the favour of heaven, as the one was offering sacrifice to Zeus Ctesius and entertaining the other, and his companion was supping with a friend and on the point of putting out to sea. But Philoneos' mistress, who poured the wine for the libation, while they offered their prayers—prayers never to be answered, gentlemen— poured in the poison with it. Thinking it a happy inspiration, she gave Philoneos the larger draught; she imagined perhaps that if she gave him more, Philoneos would love her the more: for only when the mischief was done did she see that my stepmother had tricked her. She gave our father a smaller draught. So they poured their libation, and, grasping their own slayer, drained their last drink on earth. Philoneos expired instantly; and my father was seized with an illness which resulted in his death twenty days later. In atonement, the subordinate who carried out the deed has been punished as she deserved, although the crime in no sense originated from her: she was broken on the wheel and handed over to the executioner. (1.18–20)

It is possible that this speech is only an exercise, like Antiphon's *Tetralogies*, designed to teach others how to plead in court. It seems more likely that this is an actual legal case, in which the prosecution relies on the claim that the defense has refused to allow its family slaves to be questioned under torture, and that this unwillingness proves the family's guilt. The most interesting feature of the case in this context is that, if these accusations are accurate, the "mistress," or slave woman, was the instrument (the tool, as it were, to use Aristotle's term), the *organon* of the stepmother's will. Her slave body enacted the poisoning for the free woman, and she paid the price for murder, having been tortured on the wheel and executed. The "Clytemnestra," the stepmother referred to by the speaker, acted through the unfree body of the other. We may discern here, leaking through a hegemonic account of the discipline, torture, and execution of the slave woman, traces of ingenious resistance, her choice for homicide and death over prostitution, refusing the fate of Demosthenes' Neara or Aristophanes' slave girl Dardanis in *The Wasps*, discussed in chapter 5.

There are many moments at which the free encounter and describe, even narrativize the slave body, producing difference, establishing distinctions, seeking often to close down interrogation of the boundary between slave and free. The slave body does more than occupy space in ancient culture. It cannot be acknowledged, set on the margins, and then dismissed from further discussion of the literary or rhetorical merits of a text, or simply listed in a social-scientific account of the ancient economy. The slave body informs all the physical, spatial, sexual and social relations of ancient society, disturbingly persistent, potentially unruly, and ubiquitous.

❖ ❖ ❖

IN AN ESSAY in *The New Yorker*, Patricia Williams quotes a conversation she had with someone she called her "best white friend":

> "Just think about it," I say. "The human drama is compact enough so that when my mother was little she knew women who had been slaves, including a couple of runaways. Cinderellas who had burned their masters' beds and then fled for their lives. It doesn't take too much, even across the ages, to read between those lines. Women who invented their own endings, even when they didn't get to live happily or very long thereafter."[24]

Cinderellas, like Clytemnestras, can be dangerous presences in the house.

Americans' own fear or shame or rage about slavery, the repression of our own history, can lead to blind spots, to denial, to projection and transference onto ancient culture, to suturing in our accounts of ancient society, to lacunae and omissions and denial. The presence of slavery affects every aspect of ancient culture. We cannot say simply, "Of course, slavery existed in the ancient world," and then proceed to navigate our accounts of ancient society around this fact. Simply reading ancient comedy, framing it with our situation in American history, changes one's sense of the valence of the comedy, of the jokes at slaves' expense, of the jokes the actors make in the person of slaves: "Ah, tortoises, I envy you your shells" (*The Wasps* 1292). The humor shifts, and those comic ancient slaves—defamiliarized—become both victims of cruelty and potential agents of disruption, resistance, and subversion.

Scholars of our own day, women and men writing about slavery and racism and the law and African-American history, have called attention to these crucial features of American history. The United States of America was until the mid-nineteenth century a slave-owning society—not very long ago for those who study ancient history. Of course slavery still exists in some places in the world, and it has been a feature of human history for much longer than has abolition. Conservatives might prefer that we not dwell on or even acknowledge this feature of Western civilization—have complained, for example, that it is overemphasized in the curriculum drawn by American historians for high-school teaching—and wish to return to Western civilization's idealized origin in ancient Greece.[25] But it is time to come to terms with the ways in which American slavery and its aftermath have formed and deformed all our knowledges, including that of the ancient world, producing blind spots, suppression of certain kinds of bodies and presence, and even an unconscious acceptance and replication of the strategies of distinction in ancient texts.

II TEXTS

5 SLAVERY AS METAPHOR, SLAVERY AND FREEDOM

Socrates: What do you think will happen to you if you kiss a handsome boy? Won't you immediately become a slave, lose your freedom, spend lots of money on harmful pleasures, have very little leisure to cultivate what is truly noble, and be forced to pursue what only a madman would pursue?

—Xenophon, *Recollections of Socrates* 1.3.11

AMERICAN anxieties about slavery, its historical existence, its mark on the present of American society, have affected our understanding of classical antiquity. How can we best consider this problem of historiography in classical studies? Fredric Jameson has discussed representations of the ancient world, those characterized by claims of identity and those characterized by difference. The first, the scholarship of identity, finds in antiquity the ideal of classical beauty, Pericles, and the Parthenon, a lost utopia that has become in the modern era the possession of what he calls the "English aristocratic oligarchy as it persists as a privileged enclave." He draws a contrast between this historiography of identity and that of an alternative Greece, "something savage or barbaric, . . . a culture of masks and death, ritual ecstasies, slavery, scapegoating, phallocratic homosexuality, an utterly non- or anticlassical culture."[1] Another historiographical possibility Jameson identifies is the listing of the empirical facts of the ancient world in a catalogue of features of ancient life, a practice of which classicists are sometimes guilty. Such practices are, as Ian Morris notes, what Moses Finley calls the "'tell all you know about X' school of historiography":

Empiricist studies tend to foreground details at the expense of formal argument and methodological exposition, drawing attention to the richness, variety, and irreducible uniqueness of individuals, institutions, and states in the ancient world. Although these critiques are valuable, they tend to be undertheorized.[2]

Such history can be what Jameson calls "the sheer mechanical and meaningless succession of facts . . . (where History . . . is just 'one damned thing after another')."[3]

All these varieties of classical scholarship coexist; American history and our situation within it have had their defining effects on our view of the ancient world, and structure our relationship to classical antiquity, producing cathexes, fetishization, defenses, and disavowals. The psychoanalytic notions of denial or disavowal, adduced by Freud in his disturbance of memory on the Akropolis, and projection illuminate these practices. To recall, Laplanche and Pontalis define *disavowal* as "a mode of defense which consists in the subject's refusing to recognize the reality of a traumatic perception."[4] In *projection*, they write:

> The subject perceives his surroundings and responds according to his own interests, aptitudes, habits, long-standing or transient emotional states, expectations. (350)

To extend these concepts beyond the individual psyche and the analytic situation is to read them metaphorically or allegorically, to deploy them in trying to understand a history of modern English and especially American scholarship on the question of ancient slavery, to see the effects on scholars of their own recognition of identity or difference in the ancient world. In relation to the question of slavery, we might say some scholars do not see slavery, they deny or disavow; some scholars see only slavery, they project. Projection casts outside of oneself an unwelcome feature of psychic life, and in this case involves forgetting that America itself was recently a slave culture, and that we live with the traces and residues of slavery and racism in the present.

All classicists have experienced the deployment of these strategies of managing the past. We have read accounts that make it difficult to see the slave body, accounts that ignore its presence, denying slavery's existence and importance, or that condemn the Greeks for inhumanity, projecting evil onto ancient society without interpreting its internal logic, accounts that simply list slavery among other features of ancient life, or that present the Greeks as benign and benevolent slaveholders. Glenn R. Morrow wrote, for example, in a classic study first published in 1939 and reissued in 1976: "The condition of the slaves at Athens seems to have been an exceedingly happy one. We know from many sources that the Athenians treated their slaves, whether from humanity or from shrewd considerations of policy, with considerable leniency, or as Plato would doubtless regard it, with extreme laxness."[5]

I argue in this chapter that we can only look at ancient history, and the bodies of ancient slaves, through our situation in our own country's history, one that includes slavery; and the history of scholarship *about* ancient slavery must be part of what we see. We can read strategies of projection, of disavowal, or even of empiricist trivialization as part of *our* history, our history of ancient history, as we read the absence or presence of the ancient slave body, its materiality that occupies space precisely at a blind spot of American culture. In both discussions of the political rhetoric of the classical period and its reflections in ancient comedy, slavery itself, as a fact of the everyday life of the ancient Athenians, can slip from notice.

Aristophanes and the Discourse of Slavery

The comic playwright Aristophanes, whose plays offer a vivid and extreme portrait of everyday life in ancient Athens, frequently depicts slaves, as noted in chapter 4. Paul Cartledge lists all the slaves who populate these comedies, including the only female slave with a speaking role, the attendant of Persephone in *Frogs:* "the attendant of Lamakhos in *Acharnians;* the three slaves of Demos in *Knights* (the Paphlagonian, i.e. Kleon, and the two identified in antiquity as surrogates for Demosthenes and Nikias); Sosias and Xanthias, slaves of Bdelykleon, in *Wasps;* the anonymous slaves of Trygaios, Lamakhos and Kleonymos, and Kudoimos ('Uproar') slave of the War god in *Peace;* the slaves of Tereus the hoopoe in *Birds*, of Kinesias in *Lysistrata* and of Agathon in *Thesmophoriazusae;* Xanthias slave of Dionysos and Aiakos slave of Pluto in *Frogs;* and finally . . . Karion slave of Khremylos in *Plutus.*" [6] I survey here some of the ways in which slavery, metaphorical and literal, saturates just one of Aristophanes' comedies, *The Wasps*, a play about the law courts of Athens, and also consider how difficult it has been for scholarship to acknowledge slavery here.

The Wasps begins with the slaves of one particular household watching their master's father on the roof of his house. As they recall the beatings they habitually receive on their ribs they console themselves with wine, as devotees of the alien, Phrygian Bacchus, Sabazius, who is popular with slaves (3–10). The two slaves explain the circumstances of the comedy to the audience. Their owner, the household's master, son of a devoted juror, seeks to contain his unruly father, who yearns to run off to the courts for jury duty. His slaves guard the old man. A chorus of Athenian jurors in the form of wasps appears, seeking to free their fellow juror from the protection of his guards, and ordering the slaves to release him. The chorus leader, enraged, exclaims: "I do declare you'll envy turtles their shells!" (428–29) [7] The old man commands his fellows, the wasp-jurors, to fly up the slaves' asses *(eis ton prokton auton)*, and their younger master threatens more slaves, named Midas and Phrygian, as well: "Hold on to him and don't turn him over to anybody. Otherwise, it's thick leg irons for you and no lunch" (434–35). The chorus of wasps reminds the audience how the old man once cared most tenderly for these very slaves, dressing them in the rough clothing of the unfree:

> These two forcibly manhandle their former master, completely forgetting all the jackets and tunics he used to buy them, and the caps, and how in wintertime he saw to their feet so they wouldn't always be frozen. But in their eyes there's no respect at all for their former footwear. (442–47)

The father, seized by the vigilant slave, reminds him of the time he was caught stealing grapes, and provides an affectionate vignette of their former relationship:

> You still won't let me go, you vile animal [*o kakiston therion*]? Even when you recall the time I caught you stealing grapes, marched you to the olive tree, and did a right manly [*andrikos*] job flaying you raw, so that everyone envied you? But you were apparently ungrateful. (448–51)

Such is the humor of the masters.

The son, firm in his opposition to the so-called "demagogue" Cleon and the law courts is accused of tyrannical sympathies. The crux of the son's argument against the father's addiction to the courts is an analogy he draws with slavery:[8]

> You're unaware that you've been enslaved. (517)
> [alla douleuon lelethas]

He sees the father's dependence on the jury system as a form of enslavement to the politicians of Athens who abuse the poorer citizens of the *polis*, thereby depriving them of their freedom and status as free men, as those who should exercise power over others, who master. The metaphor of slavery here structures Aristophanes' implicit critique of Athenian politics.

The father denies utterly being a slave: "stop talking about slavery. I'm master of everyone" (517–18). He delivers a long and eloquent speech on the joys of jury service: "Look what kind of advantages you're locking me out of and holding me back from, the ones you said you'd demonstrate were really slavery [*douleian*] and drudgery" (601–2). He reminds his son that the topic was "how I'm a slave" (653), and demands a response, that the son spell out the father's alleged slavery *(douleian)* (681). In an elaborate parody of rhetorical argument, the son retorts that the father's pay is negligible, a *megale douleia* (682), "a great enslavement"; that he is subjected absolutely to the power of the court; and, what is worse, feminized, that is, powerless like slaves and women, mastered by the effeminate masters of the city:

> They want to keep you poor, and I'll tell you the reason: so you'll recognize your trainer, and whenever he whistles at you to attack one of his enemies, you'll leap on that man like a savage . . . you traipse around for your employer like olive pickers! (703–12)

As a juror, the father behaves just as do the slaves of his son, the master; as a dog does.

This exchange, central to the drama of *The Wasps*, centers on the issue of slavery and its crucial status in defining the citizen of Athens and his freedom. If the cultural labor of these comedies proceeds in part through an ongoing process of definition through opposition, the practices of Aristophanes are especially complex. The free man must pose himself against the slave, the citizen body against the city's many, atomized slaves. And slavery itself must be considered the status and place of the other, not-Athenian, foreign, other Greek, dependent, dressed differently, speaking differently, worshipping other gods. Aristophanes never locates himself unequivocally on one side or the other of a struggle between "elite" and "middling" tendencies in the city.[9] His sympathies seem to lie with the citizen farmer, but in *The Wasps*, in the struggle between the deluded juryman father and his affected *nouveau riche* son, there is no heroic character but rather a riotous, free-floating critique of citizen enslavement to demagoguery, and of the climbing, striving pretenses of a would-be aristocrat. If both father and son are ridiculous, both are vulnerable to charges of enslavement and dependence.

The father is in the course of this exchange convinced by his son's arguments describing his humiliation, horrified at the notion that he himself is treated like a slave in the law courts, and convinced to act out his membership in the class of masters by staying home and conducting a trial of the household's actual slaves (766). Candidates for prosecution include the Thracian girl, a slave who scorched a pot (828). The members of the household eventually try the household's cheese-stealing dog, a figure for the Athenian general Laches, with mock testimony from the cooking implements; and the play moves into a choral phase with related reflections on Athenian politics, the manly stingers of the citizen soldiers of the Persian Wars, and the city's decline. The old man, rejuvenated, has gone off to a symposium. He returns, accompanied by a speech from one of the slaves recalling the earliest lines of the play, lamenting the sore ribs of the beaten slave as well as the chorus's boast that they would make the slave Xanthias bless turtles for their hard shells (429). Here the chorus leader calls the slave "boy," *pai*, even though he's old, because he's been beaten, that is, because he's a slave (the joke is a pun on the verb *paio*, "beat"). And Xanthias describes the father's rehabilitation as a free citizen, recounting how the old man youthfully beat him, the slave, all the while crying *"pai pai,"* "boy, boy" (1307).

The free old man, father and ex-juror, appears, drunk and lurching, with a flute girl in tow from the symposium who he says was about to *lesbiein*, "lesbiate," fellate, the symposiasts (1346). She bears a slave name, Dardanis, denoting a woman from Dardania, the Troad, in Asia Minor. The old man says she owes her escape from the symposium to his cock, *to peei todi*. Calling her his "piglet," another obscene reference, he promises that when his son dies, he will free her and make her his concubine:

ego s', epeidan houmos huios apothane,
lusamenos hexo pallaken, o khoirion.
[I promise that, as soon as my son dies, I'll buy your freedom and keep you as a concubine, my little pussy.] (1352–53)

When his son reproaches him for stealing the girl from the party, the old man claims that she is not in fact a girl but a thing, a torch. In a passage I have discussed elsewhere, they refer to the girl's body in language that recalls that earlier speech by a male slave, in which he called himself *stidzomenos*, "tattooed" by a stick or staff.[10] The father obscenely claims she is a torch, saying she is *estigmenen*, "punctured." Then a baking girl appears, accusing the father of having riotously overturned her wares. He insults her with a reference to Aesop, the freed slave, the author to whom the fables are attributed (1405), discussed in chapter 8.

The fable as a genre has a crucial intertextual relationship to the whole of Aristophanes' *Wasps*: the two slaves at the very beginning of the play recount their dreams, which involve animals and resemble Aesopian fables; they also prefigure the later dream interpretation text of Artemidorus, another body of work that illuminates master-slave relations in ancient society. In *The Wasps*, the first dream concerns an eagle, a figure for the famous Cleonymus, coward and glutton; the second portrays a flock of sheep holding an assembly on the Pnyx, like the Athenians themselves (15–53). A whale, like the despised politician Cleon, is cutting up fat, *demos*, a pun for *demos*, "the people." The slaves in the comedy are like Aesop himself, presenting allegories, beast fables for their audience, and acting out the centrality of slavery in this culture. Their presence, and the references throughout this play to slavery, are not incidental, and cannot be understood as just one item of the one-damned-thing-after-another sort, a trivial feature of everyday life in antiquity. Slavery founds representation here.

The last reference to a fable, a Sybaritic tale, concerns an inexperienced driver who fell out of a chariot and broke his head; it concludes with the moral "let each practice the craft he knows" (1431), in a sentiment echoed by the antidemocratic Plato. Here the motto might stand for Aristophanes' plot in this comedy, urging that the father stay home from the jury, that the son, "Hatecleon," stop trying to pretend to be an aristocrat, and that they resume their lives as householders of the old Athenian stamp. Before the ultimate crab dance, which sends the play off in celebration, the chorus opines: "it's hard for anyone to depart / from his normal and natural character [*phuseos*]" (1456). The father might aspire to a life of greater luxury, as we see in the end, but his wild, lecherous ways are too natural, and he ends spinning around like a top. The play affirms what it defines as nature, not only character but also the difference between slave and free. The wild old man cannot become a refined and sophisticated aristocrat, nor can he remain enslaved.

Scholarship, Aristophanes, and Slavery

Scholars who discuss the comedies of Aristophanes, who have contributed immensely to our understanding of these plays, consider with varying degrees of interest the place of slavery in *The Wasps*, but focus more on literary and psychological aspects of the comedy than on a perspective that connects social history with cultural phenomena. For example, *The Wasps* begins with a dialogue between two slaves, Sosias and Xanthias, in which the pain of beating figures prominently, yet for one critic the slaves in this scene provide a "preliminary catharsis," preparing the audience for the greater cathartic, healing experience of the comedy as a whole:

> Aristophanes is warming to larger political themes, and he is entertaining the audience by putting them in a happy and receptive mood.[11]

The fact that the speech is delivered by slaves and features violent corporal punishment is barely commented upon. There follows in this critic's text a long excursus on his own dreams and their interpretation, in the service of the claim that *The Wasps* is like a dream, with a healing effect on the audience, to be psychoanalytically interpreted by the modern critic. Another scholar discusses the play in terms of "reverse *ephebeia*"; in the course of the comedy Philocleon, the jury-obsessed father, regresses to youth, "with a new and frequently emphasised status as a 'young man,' richly characterised by such symbols of chaos and marginality as the sea and animals."[12] Cedric Whitman points out that

the equivocation on the word "rule" permits the most elegant dramatiza-
tion of the dilemma . . . of the individual psyche in the complex imperial
society of late fifth-century Athens, the dilemma which induced Antiphon
and other sophistic thinkers to reject, or all but reject, social institutions
entirely.[13]

As Whitman puts it, Philocleon wants to rule "the self as Zeus," while
his son sees the Athenian empire ruling, receiving tribute, controlling
the jurors with three obols a day. Bdelycleon's solution to the problem
might be a retreat to self-mastery, the "quadri-thematics of austerity"
discussed by Michel Foucault in *The Use of Pleasure*. The matter of slavery does not figure prominently in Whitman's analysis.

Critics focus on various aspects of this play, often without considering slavery except as comic relief. K. J. Dover, exceptionally, who does
acknowledge the role of slaves in *The Wasps*, observes:

> Probably the humour of the (last) scene, unlikely to be appreciated (and
> not deserving appreciation) by the modern reader or spectator lies en-
> tirely in the bullying and threatening of slaves by tipsy citizens and in the
> exaggerated manifestations of fear on the part of slaves.[14]

Literary critics of Aristophanic comedy, if they do discuss slaves, tend to
focus on their place in the drama as characters, as individuals among the
dramatis personae, with a modernist emphasis on individuality or a generic interest in stock characters.[15] My argument rests on the structuring ubiquity of the fact and metaphor of slavery for the play, which
grounds Bdelycleon's critique of Athenian politics.

David Konstan, who has written a powerful book about Greek comedy, one of the few that consider the politics and ideology of Aristophanes, does take into account the issues of hierarchy and of slavery in *The
Wasps*:

> The collapse of the class distinction between Philocleon and his fellow ju-
> rors reflects the ideological solidarity among citizens of all classes in Ath-
> ens as against slaves or resident aliens, who did not have the right to own
> property in land.

He points to the dependent condition of the slave, like that of the child,
and concludes with the observation that there is "class conflict within
the citizen body of the Athenians."[16] I agree with his assumption that for
masters to exist, there must be slaves; part of the ideological labor of this
play is to reinforce the division between slave and free. Konstan's observation stands out in the scholarship on the play for its discussion of slaves,
rare in the scholarly commentary, which focuses usually on literary or
textual questions. The issue of slavery, taken for granted by the playwright and the audience, ancient and modern, plays a more prominent

role in the comedy than most critics acknowledge, both as a crucial metaphor and in reference to the everyday life of its characters and audience.

Slavery and Freedom in Political Rhetoric

To juxtapose the topicality and quotidian reference of ancient comedy with the high rhetoric of the ancient historians and orators is to break an implicit rule of classical scholarship, one that insists on the discreteness of genres. Philologists and literary scholars of antiquity tend to develop expertise in such fields as archaic poetry, tragedy, or comedy, or perhaps, in a broader definition of a subdiscipline, in drama, both comic and tragic. The promiscuous mixing of history with forensic rhetoric, of tragedy with mime, violates disciplinary order and decorum. Yet, of course, a citizen of ancient Athens might very well have heard orations in the assembly, speeches in the law courts, and the lines of ancient comedy all uttered within a day's or a week's time. To juxtapose political rhetoric with comedy, to contaminate the metaphor of political slavery with its use in comedy, and with the reference to the presence of actual slaves in ancient households, is to refuse disciplinary demands, and is to place the awkward, ugly, brutalized slave body in the midst of the most elevated of classical situations.

The opposition between slavery and freedom extends beyond such literary scenes as the comic complaints of Aristophanes' slaves, or the eventual enslavement of a tragic heroine like Andromakhe, discussed in chapter 6, to define, for example, the Greeks' resistance to the Persians in the Persian Wars of the early fifth century BCE. It constitutes a crucial element in the rhetorical and ideological apparatus of many texts of the classical period; yet scholarship tends to focus on the incipient political theory of these histories, on the allegorical or metaphorical use of terms for slavery, without taking into account the haunting presence of slaves in the households and public life of the ancient city. Herodotus's text recounting the events of war is saturated with references to the freedom of the Greeks, the necessity of preserving this freedom in the face of Persian despotism, and the potential enslavement of all the peoples of the empire to the Persian emperor. See, for example, his account of free Spartans visiting a Persian who urges them to come to some accommodation with the emperor:

> "Hydarnes," came the answer, "the advice you give us does not spring from a full knowledge of the situation. You know one half of what is involved, but not the other half. You understand well enough what slavery is [*to men doulos einai*], but freedom [*eleutheries*] you have never experienced, so you do not know if it tastes sweet or bitter. If you ever did come

to experience it, you would advise us to fight for it not with spears only, but with axes too." (7.135 [Burn-Selincourt])

The great conflict between Asia and Europe is posed as a struggle between slavery and freedom: Europe metaphorically marked as free, Asia as enslaved. The Greeks as a people, united in opposition to the Asians, fight for what they understand as freedom, against enslavement, against incorporation into an empire in which only the emperor is free. Plutarch recalls in his life of Aristides how the Greeks, having beaten the Persians in the battle of Plataea, celebrated their victory in the name of Eleutheria, "freedom":

> After this at a general assembly of the Greeks Aristides moved a resolution that delegates and religious representatives from all the Greek states should meet every year at Plataea, and that every four years the Eleutheria, or festival games in honour of freedom, should be celebrated. . . . [N]o slave is allowed to play any part in the ceremony, since the men who are being honoured gave their lives for freedom. (*Aristides* 21)[17]

Literal and metaphorical slavery are inextricable here, as the struggle for Greek freedom was understood both as the preservation of a way of life, and as a escape from the fate of literal enslavement.

In Thucydides' later history of the Peloponnesian War, the author records how the Athenians, after having voted to kill all the adult citizens of the rebel city of Mytilene and to enslave *(andrapodisai)* the women and children, changed their minds and sent a second ship after the first, which had been dispatched to execute and enslave the inhabitants (3.36–49), to countermand its orders. The very language of the debate about this decision reveals the profound implications of the opposition between slavery and freedom in the rhetoric of the classical period. The orator arguing for execution and enslavement of the Mytileneans, Cleon, scornfully calls those Athenians who wish to rescind the order "slaves": "You are adepts not only at being deceived by novel proposals but also at refusing to follow approved advice, slaves [*douloi*] as you are of each new paradox and scorners of what is familiar" (3.38). The accusation moves by echoing what is at stake in the debate: Cleon insists that the assembly must either kill and enslave the Mytileneans, or recognize that they themselves are born slaves to rhetoric. Thucydides, like almost all extant classical writers, takes an aristocratic, antidemocratic position on the events of the day, and the opposition between slavery and freedom figures prominently both in the rhetoric of the political figures of the classical democracy and in the implicit judgment made on them by the author. Thucydides had described the Athenians' acquisition of their empire, between the Persian and Peloponnesian Wars, as enslavement of other cities:

> First, then, under the leadership of Cimon son of Miltiades, they (the Athenians) took by siege Eion on the Strymon, which the Persians held, and enslaved [*endrapodisan*] its inhabitants; then they enslaved Scyros, the island in the Aegean inhabited by Dolopians, and colonised it themselves. (1.98)

He calls the domination of Athens over its empire slavery. And when the Athenians invade Sicily and are roundly defeated at Syracuse, Thucydides sets up their military effort in the same language:

> [I]ndeed they looked like nothing else than a city in secret flight after a siege, and that no small city. . . . [I]t so fell out that in place of having come to enslave [*doulosomenous*] others, they were now going away in fear lest they might rather themselves suffer this. (7.75)

Fears of such enslavement, literal or metaphorical, persist in the discourse of war in the classical age. The Sicilian opponent of the Athenians argues:

> [T]he Athenians came against this country in the first place for the enslavement [*katadoulosei*] of Sicily, and after that, if they should be successful, for that of the Peloponnesus also and the rest of Hellas. (7.66)

> [T]hey came against our land to enslave [*doulosomenoi*] it, and, if they had succeeded in that, would have inflicted upon our men all that is most painful, upon our women and children the worst indignities, and upon the city as a whole the most shameful of appellations. (7.68)

The dynamic oscillation between enslaving and being enslaved echoes throughout Thucydides' text, and seems more pressing than the more static opposition between slaves and free persons and the abstract categories of slavery and freedom, defining other explorations of this issue.

Thucydides describes Pericles as using this vocabulary as well, urging his fellow citizens to pursue their war: "the spirit is cowed [*douloi*] by that which is sudden and unexpected and happens contrary to all calculation" (2.61). Nonetheless, he says, they must carry on: "freedom [*eleutherian*], if we hold fast to it and preserve it, will easily restore these losses" (2.62). He elaborates further, in this same speech, on what is at stake in war, suggesting that Thucydides, speaking through Pericles, set himself against Herodotus's formulation (and his own)[18] concerning the earlier struggle. The Peloponnesian War, unlike the Persian Wars, which was said to be fought between east and west to avoid enslavement, is rather a struggle for the maintenance of empire:

> Nor must you think that you are fighting for the simple issue of slavery or
> freedom [*douleias ant'eleutherias*]; on the contrary, loss of empire is also in-
> volved and danger from the hatred incurred in your sway. (2.63)

In this war of Greek against Greek, the stakes have changed. Yet in another incident, later in the Peloponnesian War, the Athenians notori-
ously did carry out punishment on the inhabitants of the island of Melos, one of the Cyclades: they "slew all the adult males whom they had
taken and made slaves [*endrapodisan*] of the women and children" (5.116).

This language recurs constantly in political rhetoric and in the representations of political debates by historians of the time, manipulating
the fears and anxieties of the free Greeks by threatening them with the
status of their chattels, who were insistently, troublingly present—tattooed, bearing the scars of beatings and whippings, sexually vulnerable
—among the furnishings of everyday life. The historians both call attention to the promiscuous use of this metaphor in the mouth of such a
demagogue as Cleon, and use the opposition themselves to define the
significance of the great military clashes of Persians versus Greeks, and
Spartans versus Athenians.

The dread of enslavement, literal or metaphorical, remains one of the
most potent of tropes in the rhetoric of this culture, and it affects both
public discourse and private life.[19] Such events as the Melian debacle,
anticipated in fear, enacted against other Greeks, remained a feature of
the warfare of the classical period and ought to temper our reading of
ancient comedy, of the high classical literary or dramatic texts that represent such moments as the enslavement of the Trojan women, set in the
remote past of the Trojan War—just as the archaeology of the ancient
house (discussed in chapter 1), with its erasure of the origins of slaves,
ought to condition our readings of all ancient texts. Yet, although the
opposition between slavery and freedom, between slaves and free persons saturates the political discourse of historians in this period, it is often omitted from discussion of literary texts. Slavery becomes the province of modern historians and political theorists, who treat it in their
own way, using disciplinary techniques that isolate it from a wider cultural perspective.

❖ ❖ ❖

IN THE *Nicomachean Ethics*, discussing friendship, Aristotle says:

> [W]here there is nothing in common between ruler and ruled, there can
> be no friendship between them either, any more than there can be justice.
> It is like the relation between a craftsman and his tool, or between the soul
> and the body or between master and slave: all these instruments it is true

are benefited by the persons who use them, but there can be no friendship, nor justice, towards inanimate things; indeed not even towards a
horse or an ox, nor yet towards a slave as slave. For master and slave have
nothing in common: a slave is a living tool *[empsukhon organon]*, just as a
tool is an inanimate slave *[apsukhos doulos]*. (8.11.6 [1161b])[20]

Compare the similar formulation in the *Eudemian Ethics:* "The body is
the soul's tool born with it, a slave is as it were a member [*morion*] or tool
of his master, a tool is a sort of inanimate slave" (1241b).[21] This is an especially significant intervention in a presumed debate, since the philosopher locates the slave between the animate master and the inanimate
tool, discerning a spectrum of bodies where the slave's body is both a part
of the master and his instrument. A slave has a body, is a body, distinguished from other tools by its animation but set apart by its incapacity
for purpose, for happiness, and for deliberation. Such an articulation of
the difference between master and slave, its assertion, affirmation, assumption, as part of ideological labor about kinds of human beings, figure prominently in ancient comedy and history as in other forms of ancient writing. Scholarly idealizations of the invention of democracy and
freedom, of comic, festive, healing laughter tend to disregard this cultural labor done by ancient comedy, its crucial elaboration in textual and
theatrical representation of the defining and structuring institution of
slavery in ancient life.

In the body of works still extant from Greek antiquity, there are many
texts, including old comedy and history, where the line dividing slave
from free is continually redrawn, reinforced, and reinscribed. Such efforts point to the fundamental project of maintaining the distinction between slave and free, between slavery and freedom, and to the anxiety
produced by slippage, erasure, and fraying of this difference.[22] Textual
labor underlining difference often escapes the notice of modern critics
and readers, yet it is an active, constant process, with every writer whose
work has come down to us engaging in it with varying degrees of commitment to this distinction. Aristophanes, the comic genius, mocks all
sorts of practices, persons, ways of life, and ideologies in his comedies.
Yet he is also engaged in discourses about slavery, in which slaves figure
not just as comic relief, as the low characters who engage most particularly in obscenity and scatology, who exhibit the comic characteristics of
bibulousness, cowardice, and dishonesty; slavery in his texts is naturalized, made a crucial feature in the differentiation of kinds of beings. The
juxtaposition of historians' rhetoric concerning metaphorical slavery
and freedom with such comic moments affects our readings of both
kinds of texts.

The ubiquity of slaves may be seen to produce a differentiated landscape in the physical space of the ancient city, and for comic play-wrights, legal writers, historians, philosophers, and political thinkers, one in which certain persons, the slaves, beaten and demeaned, inevitably serve as foils for others. Slavery itself becomes the other for the ideology of the free citizen, through which he defines himself for himself as a member of a community of the free, who must vigilantly protect themselves from any threat to the freedom that defines them against inhabitants of other landscapes, those of cities ruled by demagogues, tyrants, or the barbarians of other lands. Comedy and history participate, along with other genres, textual and material, in the exploration and production of difference inside the *polis* and its households.

6   THE WOMAN ENSLAVED

I was setting my hair
in the soft folds of the net,
gazing at the endless night
deep in the golden mirror,
preparing myself for bed,
when tumult broke the air

. . . .

Dressed only in a gown,
like a girl of Sparta,
I left the bed of love
and prayed to Artemis.
But no answer came.
I saw my husband lying dead,
and they took me over sea.
Backward I looked at Troy,
but the ship sped on
and Ilium slipped away,
and I was dumb with grief.[1]

—Chorus member in Euripides, *Hecuba* 923–41

THE QUOTIDIAN details of this scene, the quiet rou-
tines of the wife readying herself for bed, gazing in the mirror, are shattered by the shouts of the Greeks who have invaded Troy in their
wooden horse.[2] This free woman's life changes forever in this instant in
which her freedom is lost. A married woman whose life includes the
pleasures of Aphrodite, she turns in her fear to the virgin goddess Artemis, like an unmarried girl, hoping to ward off the sexual enslavement of
the woman who becomes a prize of war. The intimacy of Euripides'
lines—the setting of the hair, the mirror, the marital bed—bring the
catastrophe to life. Each member of the chorus, singing as part of the
collective entity, calls to mind the individual tragedy of every woman
whose city falls, and who becomes a slave in that instant, never again
to enjoy the pleasures of luxury, of golden mirrors, of conjugal eros.[3]

Euripides' chorus from *Hecuba* conjures up a disturbing, haunting moment, one that seems to capture the day of enslavement for ancient women, so many of whom were indeed slaves. How are we to interpret such moments in Greek tragedy, lines in which actors, men dressed as women, present themselves as characters in remote historical dramas and speak of slavery?[4] Literary scholars often represent the theme of enslavement as generic catastrophe, a precipitant of dramatic action, appropriate to the high genre of tragedy, rather than connecting slaves, in the chorus or as characters in the drama, with the slaves inhabiting ancient households, or with the possibility of enslavement in war in the classical period.[5]

These are moments of great dramatic power, and yet I want to consider their characters not as persons in any simple sense but rather as embodied moments in the discourses about slavery in the classical period. I will put aside the issues associated with our identification with these representations as "characters." Not only are they usually women characters played by male actors on the stage, but the very ideas of self, of character, of identity, need to be interrogated historically lest we transfer onto these words on the page some modern notions of selfhood, depth, interiority, or unconscious. These words belong to the set of discursive remnants about the question of slavery, and as tragic texts they raise particularly difficult questions about their relationship to their first audience, the citizens of classical Athens.

In this chapter I consider the recurrent representation of women enslaved in classical Greek culture. How do the figures of women and slaves intersect?[6] Are there forms of unfreedom peculiar to women, who probably made up the preponderance of the slave population in the ancient city, where many houses contained resident domestic female slaves? Female slaves in ancient texts appear as early as the maidservants in the house of Odysseus in Homer's *Odyssey*, women hanged for their sexual collusion with the suitors of Odysseus's waiting wife, Penelope. Prominent here are not just the slaves, the *doulai*, those women born to slavery in classical culture, but especially those women enslaved, those whom the text represents as in the process of becoming slaves, *andrapoda*, women who have been free and who are made the possessions of others in the temporal sequence of the text. Thucydides makes this distinction, for example, when he writes of "ta andrapoda panta, kai doula kai eleuthera" [all the captives, both bond and free] (7.28).

The women enslaved in Greek tragedy are not only figures for those slaves who surrounded the free in the everyday life of the classical city, who were ubiquitous in every life, cooking, feeding, nursing, cleaning, laboring, and sexually serving their masters. The anonymous enslaved women of tragic choruses can call up emotions of grief and pity, as do the *personae*, the named participants in these dramas. But their statuses differ radically. All the enslaved characters in high drama may evoke sympathy from the free, rather than the unease or indifference that in comedy, for example, seems most often to characterize master-slave relations involving *douloi*, slaves born to slavery. In tragedy, the *personae* emerge more fully than do the anonymous members of the chorus; these women's aristocratic status, their role as victims of conquest in war, set them apart from the barbarian and even Greek slaves who shared homes and labor with the free Greek citizens of the classical democracy. Moreover, these texts allow anxiety about enslavement to enter public discourse while distancing it from male citizens by displacing it onto characters remote from them in time, in their class situation, and in gender. These texts allow for reflection, even mourning, concerning the overt or shadowed topic of unfreedom while protecting the viewer from explicit identification with suffering.

I will look here at some Homeric passages, at a scene from Herodotus's *Histories*, and finally at some classical tragedies in which women have just been enslaved because their husbands and brothers and fathers have been defeated in war; in another tragedy a noble Greek man has served as a slave. The earlier Homeric texts represented the situation of slaves differently. It may be that an aristocratic culture, like that of the Homeric world, could better tolerate the pathos of the fictional slave in epic who had once been free, even noble, while democratic culture, in which slavery took very different forms, had correspondingly different ideological practices in relation to the question of enslavement, projecting it backwards in time in dramatic representations, for example, especially to the legendary epoch of the Trojan War.[7] Such an estrangement in time, a dis-placement, allows for a changed relationship to the potential for enslavement that haunts all of ancient society. Representations of enslavement in classical tragedy may awaken anxieties about slavery, about the presence of slaves in the midst of the free, but they may also attempt to contain these anxieties by confining them to the archaic, legendary world of gods and heroes; Euripides' fallen queen Hecuba, for example, once wife of Troy's king Priam, exhibits resources of pride and violence that the socially dead slaves of the classical city seem incapable of mustering.

Homer's Slaves

The Homeric epics provide the narrative matrix for many classical tragedies. In the *Iliad*, it seems likely that the women won as prizes of war, especially Chryseis and Briseis, become "slaves," if we can call them that, when they fall into the hands of the victorious warriors Agamemnon and Achilles.[8] The entire first book of this epic is taken up with the dispute over possession of these women. The poem begins with a plague cast by Apollo on the Greek armies, sent at the request of the priest Chryses, who wants his daughter returned. She is now owned by Agamemnon, who won her as a prize, a *geras*, and claims to prefer her to his wife Clytemnestra (113). She is returned to her father, but Agamemnon demands as a replacement Achilles' prize, his *geras*, the girl Briseis, who leaves Achilles "unwilling" [*aekous'*] (348). Enraged by this seizure, Achilles recalls how the heroes were awarded these women: "We went against Thebe, the sacred city of Eetion, / and the city we sacked, and carried everything back to this place, / and the sons of the Achaians made a fair distribution / and for Atreus' son they chose out Chryseis of the fair cheeks" (1.366–69).[9] Agamemnon's original prize, the girl Chryseis, is carried back to her father. These women are prisoners of war, prizes, possessions of the victors. Are they slaves? The status of women, slaves and wives, in this society has excited vigorous debate. Most women seem to have only a relative freedom, since even noble wives were often valued like possessions of their husbands.[10] Although the queen Arete in the *Odyssey* has powers of her own and a certain autonomy, if aristocratic women were exchanged for dynastic purposes, as Jean-Pierre Vernant argued, to bind clans together, many wives seem to partake of the status of valuable commodities.[11]

Certainly, the female inhabitants of Troy in the *Iliad* fear the conquest of their city, for some the repetition of earlier losses. Andromakhe, wife of the Trojan hero Hektor, saw her city, Thebe, fall to Achilles, who killed her father and sold, or "ransomed," her mother.[12] Hektor, anticipating defeat, voices apprehension for Andromakhe in a famous speech in the sixth book of the *Iliad*:

> It is not so much the pain to come of the Trojans
> that troubles me, not even of Priam the king nor Hekabe,
> not the thought of my brothers who in their numbers and valour
> shall drop in the dust under the hands of men who hate them,
> as troubles me the thought of you, when some bronze-armoured
> Achaian leads you off, taking away your day of liberty [*eleutheron emar*],
> in tears; and in Argos you must work at the loom of another,
> all unwilling, but strong will be the necessity upon you;
> and some day seeing you shedding tears a man will say of you:
> "This is the wife of Hektor, who was ever the bravest fighter
> of the Trojans, breakers of horses, in the days when they fought about
>   Ilion."

So will one speak of you; and for you it will be yet a fresh grief,
to be widowed of such a man who could fight off the day of your slavery
 [*doulion emar*].
But may I be dead and the piled earth hide me under before I
hear you crying and know by this that they drag you captive.

(6.450–65)

The significance of this moment resounds after Hektor's death; his sense
of care, of responsibility for his wife's freedom, his fears for her as the
sexual possession of another, all cast a shadow over the individual warrior's death in the *Iliad*. The poem poses vividly here the contrast between freedom and slavery; the women of the defeated city will work in
the houses of the victors. Hektor does not mention the sexual duties of
an enslaved woman, but perhaps alludes to them in his phrase *kratere
anagke*, "strong necessity."

What is the temporal dimension of this opposition, the "day" of freedom, the "day" of slavery? The phrase "day of slavery" specifies the moment at which the free woman, wife of the prince of the city, loses her
freedom, like the night recalled by the women in the chorus of Euripides' *Hecuba*. The day when she enters into servitude can be pinpointed
as the day the city falls. But what is the "day of freedom"? The Homeric
texts use the word *emar*, "day," to refer to a state or condition as well as
to day as opposed to night. Hektor again uses the word *emar*, "day," in a
vaunting speech to Patroklos as he kills him:

Patroklos, you thought perhaps of devastating our city,
of stripping from the Trojan women the day of their liberty [*eleutheron
 emar*]
and dragging them off in ships to the beloved land of your fathers . . .
I . . . beat from them
the day of necessity [*emar anagkaion*].

(16.830–36)

The expression marks the particularity of a Homeric idea of time: if there
is a day of slavery, of fate, of necessity, associated with death, as in *nelees
emar*, "pitiless day" (16.484), such an expression calls up Orlando Patterson's description of slavery as "social death."[13] On the day of enslavement, as on the day of death, one's identity dies. And retrospectively, from the perspective of enslavement, one gazes at the day of
freedom, life preceding the day when freedom was last experienced, the
condition of freedom extending up to that fateful day of loss.

The *Odyssey* takes place not on the battlefield but on the Mediterranean Sea, its shores and islands, and in the homes of its various characters, where slaves appear as servants, often as ancient retainers of noble

families.[14] The swineherd Eumaios, a slave faithful to Odysseus back on
Ithaka, tells the story of his kidnapping from the island of Syria as a child,
son of a king, bought eventually from Phoenician pirates by Laertes, father of Odysseus (*Odyssey* 15.403–84).[15] The slave women of the *Odyssey*
serve as maids in the house of Odysseus. Homer recounts the story of
Eurykleia, the faithful slave maid, nurse of both Odysseus and his son
Telemakhos, early in the poem:

> She was the daughter of Ops the son of Peisenor,
> and Laertes had bought her long ago with his own possessions
> when she was still in her first youth, and gave twenty oxen for her,
> and he favored her in his house as much as his own devoted
> wife, but never slept with her, for fear of his wife's anger.
>
> (1.429–33)

Eurykleia, washing the disguised Odysseus's feet, recognizes him, keeps
his secret, and offers to give him the names of those women who serve
in the house and have betrayed him with the suitors. Later, she de-
nounces them: "You have fifty serving women here in your palace, / and
these have I taught to work at their own tasks, the carding / of wool, and
how to endure their own slavery [*doulosunen*]. Of these / fifty, twelve in
all have taken to immorality" (22.421–24).[16] These women clear away
the bodies and blood and mess of Odysseus's massacre of the suitors.
Then, refusing them a "clean" death by the sword, Telemakhos hangs
the unfaithful slave women:

> taking the cable of a dark-prowed ship,
> (he) fastened it to the tall pillar, and fetched it about the round-house;
> and like thrushes, who spread their wings, or pigeons, who have
> flown into a snare set up for them in a thicket, trying
> to find a resting place, but the sleep given them was hateful;
> so their heads were all in a line, and each had her neck caught
> fast in a noose, so that their death would be most pitiful.
> They struggled with their feet for a little, not for very long.
>
> (22.465–73)

The simile compares these women, perhaps once relatively free like birds,
although ironically still slaves, to snared thrushes in a hateful bed.[17] In
the context of the poem, and the fictional society of Homer, the maidservants deserve their punishment, and the pathos of the last lines has
limited range. The reader may feel pity for these slave women, taught by
Eurykleia to endure their slavery, but the aristocratic ethics of the poem
require servile devotion and fidelity. The maids, unlike Odysseus's wife

Penelope, betrayed him shamelessly and pay the price of a humiliating execution, condemned to this fate by their infidelity and their unfreedom.

Classical Slaves

Hektor's speech to Andromakhe in the *Iliad* expresses an early elaboration of a fundamental opposition of ancient Greek culture, freedom/
slavery, mapped onto sexual difference. How does this opposition affect
the representations of women enslaved in the texts of the fifth century,
texts produced after the victory of the Greeks over the Persians at the
beginning of the century? The historian Herodotus offers a story of a
woman enslaved that seems to mediate between the women of Homer
and the queens of Greek tragedy:

> After the rout at Plataea, a woman, who had made her escape from the
> Persians, came into the Greek lines. She was a captive of the Persian Pha-
> randates, the son of Teaspis; and when she realized that the Persian army
> was done for and that the Greeks were winning the day, she dressed her-
> self and her maids in the finest things she possessed, loaded herself with
> gold ornaments, and, getting down from her covered waggon, made her
> way to the Spartans while the work of slaughter was still in progress. . . .
> "O King of Sparta," she cried, clasping his knees in supplication, "save me,
> I beg you, from the slavery [*doulosunes*] which awaits the prisoner of war! . . .
> That Persian took me by force and made his concubine."
> "You need not be afraid," Pausanias replied; "as a suppliant you are safe
> —and still more so, if you are indeed the daughter of Hegetorides of Cos,
> for he is bound to me by closer ties of friendship than anyone else in those
> parts." With these words he put her in charge of the Spartan magistrates
> who happened to be on the spot, and afterwards sent her, at her own wish,
> to Aegina. (9.74–76)[18]

There are echoes of a certain Helen here, the woman who sees which
way the wind is blowing, and knows how to ally herself with the victors.
Yet this woman establishes in the historical record the possibility of enslavement in war that continues to shadow the Greek imagination, and
also exhibits a class privilege, with her wealth and aristocratic connections: the guest-friendship, or *xenia*, that bound aristocratic families
across city-states.[19] Because of her father's ties with the victor, she escapes the ordinary fate of women in captured cities. She is neither ransomed nor enslaved; the network of privileged families produces connections that transcend *polis* affiliations. And the unnamed woman, who
had been the concubine of a Persian, nonetheless is treated with courtesy according to her previous station. Such a story, though perhaps

apocryphal, suggests that the ordinary fates of ordinary people enslaved, their presence among the free, may have had little direct impact on the lives of the relatively wealthy free Greeks who enjoyed the privileges of citizenship in the classical city, and may have served the rhetorical purpose of allaying fears about humiliation and enslavement. As matter for ideology, for meditation on the potential fates of the conquered in war, for maintaining the fragile boundary between slave and free, and as a site for the exploration of unacknowledged anxieties about the possibilities of enslavement, the tragedies of ancient Athens return again and again to the theme of the women of Troy and their enslavement.

Tragic Slaves

The story of the fall of Troy, the slaughter of its heroes, and the captivity and enslavement of its women provide the narrative elements for many Greek tragedies of the classical period. I want to look at several scenes from these dramas and others, including one representing a male temple slave, Ion, to consider the ways in which the figure of a woman enslaved in war has meaning in the historical context of Athenian tragedy. Such a method goes against the grain of reading individual tragedies, or even the corpus of a particular tragedian, as a literary entity; such techniques have yielded much of great interest at the hands of gifted philologists. My interest concerns less the individual characters, plays, even corpora of individual writers or the status of tragedy as a genre of masterpieces in the history of the West, and more the ways in which these discourses fit within a larger set of discourses about slavery.

Given that the audiences know well the epic narratives of Homer, the episodes of women enslaved in these tales, how does the translation of these figures from the past into dramatic contexts work? How does the episode recounted by Herodotus of the unnamed daughter of Hegetorides of Cos help us situate these representations on stage of women enslaved? My argument will be that capture, rape, enslavement, and ransom for the rich were possibilities constantly present in Greek warfare and piracy, but that the representations of women from the heroic age enslaved on the tragic stage touched on more than the cultural anxieties, experienced surely by both free men and women, that the women's sexual purity would be violated, and that they might fall into the hands of their enemies.

In the context of the democratic Athenian *polis*, tragic representation draws on a complicated set of meanings. They include allusion to a legendary, Homeric past of epic, to the archaic age, dominated by aristocrats who traced their descent from the heroes and the gods, to the past of the Trojan and Persian Wars, and to the contemporary political negotiations of the *polis* itself in the middle and late fifth century. The anxiety occasioned by warfare itself may of course affect the prevalence of the theme of enslavement in the classical texts. Women enslaved predominate in many tragedies, where they are depicted, rather than their men about to be killed in battle; the tragedians were perhaps attempting to come to terms with fears of death in battle, so likely for young warriors in a city-state almost constantly in a state of war. And the representation of these women can also be interpreted as a way of confronting the aristocratic past, the anxiety E. R. Dodds sees in classical culture, where the authors of classical democracy fear the wrath of their gods and their aristocratic fathers for having abandoned the more hierarchical order of the past.[20] The queens and princesses of Troy can stand as figures for aristocracy hobbled by democratic reforms, imagined to be full of wrath and desire for vengeance, like Priam's queen Hecuba, who takes a terrible revenge on her enemies. The women of tragedy, their parts played by male actors, speak to other issues in addition to the fear of enslavement in war that must have haunted the free in this period. The historians and other writers of the classical period used the language of slavery, as discussed earlier, as an almost technical political language, deploying it as a metaphor to invoke possibilities of domination and submission of one city-state in its relations with another, or even of the *demos*, the people, in their relations with individual powerful politicians. These forms of political language provide a context for the presentation of enslaved characters onstage, offering rich possibilities of allegory.

The Athenian playwright Phrynichus had written an early tragedy about the fall of Miletus in 494 BCE, one of the events of the Persian War, in which the Asian city had fallen and its men were killed, its women enslaved. The performance of the tragedy so affected the Athenians that they fined the playwright for "reminding them of a disaster which touched them so closely [*hos anamnesanta oikeia kaka*], and they forbade anybody ever to put the play on the stage again" (Herodotus 6.21). Such a comment suggests that the Athenians may have felt pity for their fellow Ionians, the Milesians, but also that they feared that they themselves might suffer a similar fate. Afterwards, the tragedians were compelled to represent their stories in the form of mythic and heroic narratives inherited from the past. And this formal constraint produced the conditions for allegorical representation.

The tragic poets allude frequently to slavery both metaphorical and literal. In the *Persians*, first performed in 472, Aeschylus staged the relatively recent Persian Wars as an encounter between slavery and freedom. The Persian warriors "threaten to yoke / In servitude [*zugon doulion*]

Hellas" (50), the Greeks "slaves [*douloi*] to none, nor are they subject" (242). The battle cry of the Greeks depends on resistance to slavery: "Free [*eleutheroute*] your fathers' land, / Free your sons, your wives, the sanctuaries" (403–4). Xerxes had tried to make the Hellespont his slave [*doulon*], to yoke the waters (745), and failed to yoke and enslave the Greeks; the tragedy ends with lamentation for his losses.

Aeschylus's trilogy the *Oresteia*, first performed in 458, begins with the tragedy *Agamemnon*, representing the return of the Greek victor to his home, Argos, and his wife, Clytemnestra. He brings a captive, once priestess and princess Cassandra, daughter of Priam, dead king of Troy.[21] The text insists on her status as a slave (950ff., 1035–38, 1040–46, 1226, 1322). Cassandra steps onto the tragic stage, princess and priestess of Apollo, given the power to prophesy because she once was possessed by the oracular divinity.[22] As a literary invention, she sings her magnificent, archaic, inspired arias as a refugee princess, as a possessed priestess of the god, and her enslavement and vulnerability have pathos because of her tragic fall. Clytemnestra had earlier reminded her that Herakles himself was once a slave (1040–41); later, as her husband and his slave lie dead, she calls Cassandra Agamemnon's *aikhmalotos*, his "spear-captive" (1440). As Cassandra exits, she reminds the audience that she, once Apollo's royal lover, is now a victim, a slave, and calls for vengeance for "one simple slave [*doules*] who died, a small thing, lightly killed" (1326). The once-powerful women of the preclassical age, like Clytemnestra herself, killed by her own son, suffer defeat and are incorporated into the mythic base of the classical city, like the Furies buried in its foundation. Aeschylus implicates Cassandra in a historical network of allusions, where her femaleness registers her status as a sign for defeated Troy, and association with her marks Agamemnon as contaminated, feminized, and weak, the victim of his murderous and tyrannical wife.

Laura McClure, in *Spoken like a Woman*, suggests that the female characters played by male actors in Athenian drama use deceptive, persuasive language onstage, and that there is an almost allegorical feature to these representations, that such depictions refer not only to the dangers of women speaking in the public sphere but also to rhetoric itself.[23] That is, as rhetoric becomes an important aspect of speech in the democratic Athenian assembly, as men of less than aristocratic stature begin to speak, trained rhetorically, offering persuasive speech to the assembled citizens, conservative fears of demagoguery and rhetoric produce their effects in classical tragedy and comedy. Rhetoric, represented rhetorically as a feminized discourse associated with the traditionally deceptive powers of women's speech, woven by such traditional figures as Helen, Circe, and Calypso, is deployed on the stage by *personae* like Aeschylus's Clytemnestra and Euripides' Phaidra. Although McClure is concerned with the gender implications of such representations, she also points to the ways in which women signify allegorically as rhetoric and its dangers:

> Skillful rhetoricians are portrayed in Attic New Comedy and elsewhere as possessing a powerful means of subverting the normative social order and blurring class lines: thus speakers of low birth may gain power over aristocrats, thereby jeopardizing, from the standpoint of the elite, the stability of political and social hierarchy. Women, because they stand largely outside the discursive spheres controlled by men in classical Athens, and because of their long-standing association with deception in the literary tradition, provide the perfect vehicle for conveying this contemporary political crisis. (28)

Something similar occurs with the enslaved women of the stage, whose parts are performed by men and who stand not only for the fears of the enslavement of the city's women but also for the political allegory of enslavement of the city itself, and for the lessening of power experienced by aristocrats, traditionally the most powerful figures in the city, whose domination of politics has lessened with the rise of rhetorically skilled commoners in the assembly.

Such an interpretation as McClure's encourages readers to treat the women characters of tragedy and comedy not as persons, focusing on their moral life, their psychology, their motivations as human beings like ourselves, as much classical scholarship still does, but rather to see their representation differently, as representation, often allegorical, allowing for conflict and contradiction presented through the binary categories of gender. In this case, the tragic poet presents through women characters anxiety about defeat in war, and about the declining political power of the elite. The displacement of slavery onto women protects the male audience from identification but allows for consideration of such issues as military conquest and political defeat, death in battle, and enslavement.[24] Cassandra, the princess enslaved, calls up fears of loss of status and freedom, anxieties about slaughter at the hands of one's enemy, rather than expressing a personality, even one person with moral choices, rather than reflecting the everyday situation of slaves who served the free Greeks in their houses, on their farms, in their mines.

Women newly enslaved appear as characters or as chorus members in many other classical tragedies, including the second play of Aeschylus's *Oresteia* trilogy, the *Libation Bearers*, in which the chorus consists of women enslaved, who lament at the very beginning: "as for me: gods have forced on my city / resisted fate. From our fathers' houses / they led us here, to take the lot of slaves. / And mine it is to wrench my will, and consent / to their commands, right or wrong, / to beat down my edged hate" (76–81). In Sophocles' *Trachiniae*, the entry of a new woman, captured by Herakles, precipitates disaster for his household and himself; Deianeira, Herakles' wife, in order to win him back from his new bride, smears his cloak with what she believes is a love philter, in fact a terrible poison that brings him to death.[25] Deianeira's nurse is a slave, like many in tragedy (53: *gnomaisi doulais*; 62–63: *gune doule*), who advises her free mistress. When Herakles returns from battle, like Agamemnon, he brings with him new slaves, newly captured women. His subordinate Lichas reports not only that Herakles has been victorious; he also recounts the story of Herakles' own enslavement to queen Omphale:

> [M]ost of this time he was kept in Lydia,
> and, as he himself declares he was not free
> but a bought slave [*empoletheis*]. (One should not hesitate, lady,
> to tell a tale where it is seen Zeus did the work.)
> He was sold [*pratheis*] to Omphale, the foreign queen,
> and served her a full year, as he says himself,
> and was so stung by this disgrace he had to bear
> that he set himself an oath and swore that he
> would live to see the author of his suffering,
> along with wife and child, all in slavery [*doulosein*].
>
> (247–57)

The man Herakles, eventually deified after death, suffered slavery himself; unlike the women enslaved in Greek tragedy, he endured his period of servitude, according to some accounts dressed as a woman, that is to say feminized by his status as a slave, and then resumed his position as hero, as enslaver himself.[26] After his time in the court of Omphale, when he became once again "pure," *hagnos*, having endured a slavery imposed by Zeus for killing through guile, Herakles returns, enslaves the inhabitants of his enemy's city, and brings back its women to his home, where his wife Deianeira waits.

In the drama, she approaches the captives, now facing a life of slavery (*doulon bion*, 302), with pity. Iole, daughter of the king, Herakles' slave, never speaks, but a messenger tells Deianeira that Herakles conquered the city of Oechalia because he fell in love with Iole, and that he has brought her with him not to be a slave (*doulen*, 377). Deianeira, fearing displacement as Herakles' wife, resolves to win him back.

> [H]ere I have taken on a girl—no,
> I can think that no longer—a married woman, as
> a ship's master takes on cargo, goods that outrage my heart.
> So now the two of us lie under the one sheet
> waiting for his embrace.
>
> (536–40)

This woman enslaved because of eros lies as a threat to Herakles' wife; her attempt to administer a remedy that will guarantee his love results in his death, and her own suicide. The foreign woman, slave and bride, enters the domestic space, the marriage bed itself, and wreaks havoc without speaking. As he lies dying, Herakles gives her to his son Hyllus to marry.

Zeus, who had brought slavery upon Herakles, brings the enslaved daughter of Herakles' enemy into his own house to perpetuate the family of Herakles. The mention of the marital bed evokes the domestic life of the contemporary audience, and the sexual availability and threat represented by slaves in the house. Yet once again, the enslaved of tragedy seem not only to exemplify the actual slaves who inhabited the houses and beds of classical societies but also provide occasions for reflections on other questions of power, domination, and conquest. If Herakles' own story is contaminated by the episode of slavery to Omphale, as one of his ordeals, he emerges from this servitude to conquer again. And the woman he enslaves becomes a posthumous daughter-in-law, preserved as the aristocratic prize she is by assimilation into his bloodline and family.

The Slaves of Euripides

My discussion of Euripidean tragedy begins with a moment of opacity in the text of Euripides' *Suppliant Women*. In the course of asking for assistance in retrieving the Argive dead from the battleground of Thebes, another mythic battle zone, Adrastos, king of Argos, addresses these lines to Theseus, king of Athens:

> The sight of poverty is well for wealth;
> The poor should gaze with envy on the rich,
> To learn the love of goods; untroubled men
> Are well advised to look at wretchedness.
> The poet bringing songs into the world
> Should work in joy. If this is not his mood,
> He cannot—being inwardly distressed—
> Give pleasure outwardly. That stands to reason.
>
> (176–83)

He then rather awkwardly resumes his speech to Theseus. This strange little fragment, buried in a speech about supplication, argues for a reciprocal gaze of rich and poor. The wealthy should look at the poor, the poor should learn acquisitiveness from observing the rich. And again, returning to the wealthy, the prosperous, the fortunate, the poet urges a gaze on wretchedness and poverty. This is an anacolouthon, a rhetorical figure, a non sequitur, at the level of thought as opposed to the sentence. It stands weirdly in the midst of plot and action and exposition of the situation at the temple of Demeter at Eleusis, near Athens, the location of the tragedy. Scholars have struggled over how to place and interpret these lines. Are they interpolated, drawn in mysteriously by a scribe or editor to an inappropriate spot in the developing plot of Euripides' play? The Chicago translator remarks: "Lines 176–83 present some difficulty. It is likely that the poet is here defending himself against charges that he broke the decorum of tragedy by presenting paupers and slaves as serious personages."[27]

The question of whether these lines "belong" here or not will remain unanswered, even if another manuscript of Euripides' tragedy appeared. We will never have the definitive, accurate, perfect version of this play; it has traveled to us over too many centuries, through too many vicissitudes of performance, papyrus, hands. Its anomalousness, its lack of fit with what surrounds it, its very atopia, its eccentricity, its out-of-placeness here makes it a sort of manifesto for Euripides' tragic practice. Whether it was written by the tragedian himself or another, written to be spoken here or elsewhere, to be understood as the language of the tragedian or of a character, it calls attention to the eccentricity of Euripides. And to the unusual habits of his drama, which allowed space and time for representations absent from other tragedies, for slaves, male and female, who speak and act in new ways. And this rocky beginning of The *Suppliant Women*, with its speeches that miss each other, that contain inassimilable parts, that break into disjunctive sections, exemplifies a complex, heterogeneous set of discourses about slavery in the hands of this playwright, and reveals once again that "the Greeks" did not have a consistent position on slaves and slavery. Even those works that end up grouped around the name Euripides contain irreconcilable differences about the beings called slaves.

The distinction between those born to slavery and those enslaved is crucial to exploration of the representation of slaves on the Greek stage, and is especially relevant to the slaves of Euripidean tragedy. Slaves born in the house, servants, nurses, attendants, rarely speak; Phaidra's nurse in Euripides' *Hippolytus* may be an exception, like Medea's nurse, who is called by the *paidagogos* "palaion oikon ktema despoines emes," [ancient possession of my mistress' house] (49), and thus is clearly a slave. These are characters born to servility. The nurse in the *Hippolytus* uses the sophisticated, dangerously amoral discourse of the sophists to persuade Phaidra to approach her son-in-law sexually; her place in the drama concerns not just slavery but the inappropriateness of listening to such base

arguments as hers and those in the city who were seen to be eroding traditional morality. She figures not as the subject of a tragic fall from freedom and status but as the voice of low pragmatism and opportunism.

In Euripides' *Hecuba*, Polyxena, the noble, beautiful daughter of Priam
and Hecuba, a princess of the blood, a noble, vulnerable, gloriously ide-
alistic child, chooses her own death when enslaved.[28] Like many a young,
virginal Euripidean heroine, she seems to die in vain, acting nobly for
ideals transmitted by cynical, manipulative characters unworthy of her
sacrifice.[29] The former queen, Hecuba, an old woman now enslaved herself, has none of her nobility and idealism. She has, rather, the prophetic
power of the Pythian priestess at Delphi, who conveyed the oracular wisdom of Apollo; she has the violent, vengeful bloodymindedness of the
Furies.[30]

The year in which the *Hecuba* was first performed was a grim and
mournful time for Athens. The Peloponnesian War was in full flood,
and the Athenians witnessed and committed acts of barbarity that may
have shaken their confidence in the democracy for which the earlier
tragic playwright Aeschylus had had such great and ambivalent hopes. In
the *Oresteia* he had caused the doglike Furies who tracked the matricide
Orestes to be transformed into the benevolent Eumenides, the blessed
ones. Buried beneath the Akropolis, they were to watch over the city. In
the *Hecuba*, Euripides shows us the potential for the woman, this creature at the margin of civilization, to revert to bestiality under the pressure of loss, grief, and rage. The enslaved Hecuba's mutilation of the
body of her onetime ally Polymestor is the act of woman becoming dog,
the act of a savage creature. In its embodiment on the tragic stage, Hecuba's story is not an abstract dissertation on the nature of justice, the
nature of vengeance; it is about the dangerously unstable figures at the
boundaries of civilization. Surrounded by loss, a captive, a slave, having witnessed the collapse of everything that gave her life coherence,
everything about which to be vigilant, the woman regresses to animal existence. The character Hecuba is a noblewoman who becomes a
slave, who ends her days as a dog: Polymestor, her enemy, who betrays
her and is punished with blindness and the murder of his children, at the
end of the play predicts her end: "I foretell that you . . . shall drown at
sea. You shall climb to the masthead and fall. . . . You shall climb the mast
of your own free will . . . changed to a dog, a bitch with blazing eyes"
(1259–65). Hecuba's enslavement, her social death, begins the process
of metamorphosis.

Even for the ancient audience, accustomed as it may have been to stories of bodily transformation, this story is a scandal. Human beings can

sometimes be mythically transmuted into gods; Herakles, for example, a human being, lives both in the underworld with the human dead and above, on Mount Olympus, because of his extraordinary accomplishments on earth. But for a human woman to become a dog is shocking, a paradigm of violent change, like that from freedom to slavery. And this play moves toward that end, as a sort of *telos*, an accomplishment of Hecuba's history and her destiny, her crossing the boundary of humanness into bestiality. This is not trivial, not incidental, not something beyond the scope of the play, a perfunctory ending to the story of the heroine Hecuba. She is moving toward a canine state throughout the play, becoming an animal, a despised animal, as she recognizes her status, her powerlessness as a slave, and plots vengeance against those who have injured her.

A Digression on Dogs

Some Greek dogs are noble creatures, waiting faithfully for their masters, guarding their masters' possessions. The loyal Argos, dog of Odysseus, waits twenty years after his departure for the Trojan War, and expires at Odysseus's feet as the hero, his master, returns. Dogs can be loyal, faithful, protective, and true to their masters. But there are more sinister dimensions to the dog: the Theban Actaeon, out hunting with his dogs, unluckily comes upon the virgin goddess Artemis bathing. Angered at having been seen naked by a mortal man, she turns him into a stag, his own dogs mistake him for their prey, tear him to pieces, and kill him. Dogs were famously carnivorous carrion eaters; one of the great horrors that haunts Greek epic and tragedy is the fear of being eaten by dogs after death. Priam, husband of Hecuba, speaks of this in a famous speech in the *Iliad*, lamenting the loss of his children:

> And myself last of all, my dogs in front of my doorway
> will rip me raw, after some man with stroke of the sharp bronze
> spear, or with spearcast, has torn the life out of my body;
> those dogs I raised in my halls to be at my table, to guard my
> gates, who will lap my blood in the savagery of their anger
> and then lie down in my courts.
> . . . .
> when an old man is dead and down, and the dogs mutilate
> the grey head and the grey beard and the parts that are secret,
> this, for all sad mortality, is the sight most pitiful.

$$(22.66-76)$$

Dogs are faithful companions to men in life, live with them in promiscuity, and share their food. But when a man is vulnerable, or dead, an object himself, the dog turns on him, shows that he is not cognizant of a difference between comrade and prey, violates the boundaries of master and animal, and eats human flesh.[31] The poet Hesiod describes the doglike mind of Pandora, the first woman; in a famous misogynist poem, the lyricist Semonides writes of the various kinds of women, comparing them to beasts, "One from a bitch, and good-for-nothing like her mother" (frags. 7, 12). Antigone fears that her unburied brother will be devoured, and Creon orders that his corpse be "chewed up by birds and dogs and violated" (225). After Antigone is captured trying to prevent this desecration, the altars of the city smoke, contaminated by the waste of the corpse, bringing disaster on Thebes. The seer Teiresias informs Creon: "our altars and our sacrificial hearths / are filled with the carrion meat of birds and dogs, / torn from the flesh of Oedipus' poor son" (1073–75). The ubiquitous dogs powerfully resemble slaves: obedient to a degree, yet always ready to turn on and devour their masters in their weakness.

Women, like slaves and dogs, stand both inside and outside of human space, human community, and Euripides shows in the *Hecuba* that under the pressure of war and catastrophe, slavery, loss, and grief, women, at some frontier between human beings and the other, between human beings and animals, break down. Hecuba exemplifies a latent tendency among this dangerously unstable element of the human community, as her enslavement precipitates a series of violent reprisals against her enemies. Just so, the slaves of the city, ubiquitous and obedient to the commands of the masters in the audience, like faithful and obedient dogs, threaten the bodily security and integrity of the free. The displacement of anxiety onto dogs, which recurs in other classical texts associating slaves with these animals, registers the degree to which the comfort of the free with mastery masks a fear of these companions, animal and human.

Slavery is central to the first half of Euripides' tragedy *Andromache*. The character Andromache announces her situation as a slave in the first speech of the play: after her husband's death, and the murder of her son by the Greeks as they plundered Troy:

I—free as I pleased in homes of leisure
Till then—was clapped in servitude, shipped to Greece
As booty for Neoptolemus, wild islander,
His tidbit from the total spoil of Troy.

(12–15)

These words recall Hektor's pained imagination of her future in the *Iliad*. After Andromache bore him a son, Neoptolemus married Hermione, who remains childless and accuses the slave of making her infertile.

147

Andromache's confidante is another slave woman, unnamed, who serves her, remembering that Andromache was once her free mistress. Andromache addresses her as "Dearest of sister-slaves (for that's our story) to one your mistress once, though sadly fallen" (64–65). This woman expresses bitterness and resignation about her fate: "What's my life, that I should care / What happens now? A slave's life, and a woman's" (89–90). And Andromache herself is a slave to her rival, unwilling: "only a slave, *her* slave—one who oppresses me so" (114).

The portrait of Andromache in this play differs from the immediacy of enslavement experienced by Hecuba in the eponymous tragedy; there Hecuba is in a state of shock, in some liminal third space between Troy and the place of her enslavement (as Zeitlin points out), in transition between her roles as queen and as slave. Andromache represents a woman, a princess now experienced in slavery, closer to those slave women who have lived all their lives as the possessions and servants of others. She recalls her past life of freedom, the losses of husband and son, but her reality has become her situation as slave in a new house in Thessaly, where the local women express sympathy for her fate, but remind us that she is a slave (136). Unlike this chorus, Hermione, wife of Neoptolemus, addresses her with contempt and rage: "You! you common slave! you soldiers' winnings!" (155) Andromache recalls that her children will be slaves because born from a slave mother (200). She remembers that when free, she, unlike Hermione, tolerated her husband's other sexual liaisons, even nursed his bastard children (224), while Hermione only rails at her, accuses her of barbarian, Asian sorcery, and sends her father, Menelaus, to threaten the child with death, asserting further that he has the right to command his son-in-law's slaves (374, 585). Peleus, father of Achilles, grandfather of Neoptolemus, comes to her rescue:

> I'll loosen these tightly tangled cords.
> You blackguard, look at her mutilated hands!
> What did you think you were roping? Bulls? Or lions?
>
> (718–20)

The slave woman is bound, treated with brutality. Then, because of her aristocratic bearing, her status as former queen, as mother of Neoptolemus's son, she is freed from the violence to which ordinary slaves were subjected. Such treatment distinguishes her from the slaves of the spectators' environment, reminding them of her past and of her nobility, still recognized by Peleus. Could such a moment produce empathy for the ordinary slaves of domestic life, an opening in the allegedly universal acceptance of slavery as a fact of everyday life? Or does it underline the difference, the distance between this princess of Troy and the slave women of the audience's households, born in slavery or sold by pirates and slave traders? It is at this point in this strange tragedy that Andromache leaves the stage, midperformance, never to return.

Euripides returns again and again to the theme of women enslaved. The chorus of the *Helen* consists of Greek captive women. He set *The Trojan Women*, first performed in 415, the year of the disastrous Athenian expedition to Sicily, just after the fall of Troy, when the women and children have been seized and made captive. Poseidon speaks the prologue of the play, describing its landscape: "Scamander's valley echoes to the wail of slaves, / the captive women given to their masters now . . . / while all the women of Troy yet unassigned are here / . . . chosen to wait / the will of princes, and among them Tyndareus' child / Helen of Sparta, named—with right—a captive slave [*aikhmalotos*]" (28–35). This tragedy ends with Hecuba's words: "O / shaking, tremulous limbs, / this is the way. Forward: / into the slave's life [*douleion hameran biou*]" (1328–30). Another juxtaposition, perhaps transgressive in terms of the generic integrity of scholarship on Greek tragedy, might here adduce Thucydides' description of the defeated and captive Athenians and their allies in Sicily:

> The Syracusans treated the men in the quarries harshly during the first stage. For since there were many in a deep and narrow space, the sun and the suffocating heat were still distressing them at first, and the contrasting cold autumnal nights that ensued weakened their condition by the change, and since they had to do everything in the same space because of close confines, and furthermore the corpses were piled together on one another, dead from wounds and because of the change and so forth, there were unbearable smells, and at the same time they were afflicted with hunger and thirst (for eight months they gave each a cup of water and two cups of food a day), and of all the other miseries men thrust into such a place were likely to suffer there was not one that they did not encounter. For up to seventy days, the whole group lived like this; then, except for the Athenians and whatever Sikeliots or Italiots had joined them, they sold them all.[32]

In tragedy, women take the place of men.

Prisoners of war made up part of the slave population. Religious institutions like the Apollo shrine at Delphi also owned slaves. Slaves comprise the chorus of the *Phoenician Women*; entering the stage, they sing of their place of origin and their place as slaves to Apollo:

> I came, I left the wave of Tyre
> the island of Phoenicia,
> as prize for Loxias, slave to Phoebus' house
>
> . . . .
>
> Chosen most beautiful of my town,

an offering to Apollo . . .
I might, like the golden statue-girls,
have served Phoebus by now.
But Castalia's water is waiting still
to wet my hair for his service.

(202–25)

War in Thebes prevents these women, related by blood to the Thebans, from serving in Delphi, but as slaves dedicated to the god they observe the episodes of the tragedy, the terrible aftermath of Oedipus's life. And they recall the temple slaves of the classical world; the Locrians, for instance, sent two girls to the Athena temple at Ilion supposedly to expiate the crime of Ajax, son of Oileus, who had tried to rape Cassandra, according to an early third-century inscription.[33]

Euripides' tragedy *Ion* depicts the ancestor of the Athenian tribe as himself a temple slave in service to the god Apollo in Delphi. The young man, a foundling, discovers his parentage in the course of the play. Ion enters the scene, describing his duties at the temple: "I will be a slave to Phoebus [*Phoiboi douleuso*]," euphemistically translated as "I will bend to the labors / Of my devotion" (182), a formulation which obscures the degree of servitude of the play's protagonist. The *ekphrasis*, or description, of the temple facade early in the tragedy significantly describes the temporary servitude of Herakles, one of whose ordeals, as we recall from Sophocles' *Trachiniae*, was to be sold and to spend a year enslaved to the Lydian queen Omphale.[34] When broached by Creusa, wife of Athens's king, who visits the shrine, Ion declares: "I am what I am called, Apollo's slave [*doulos*]" (309). Creusa asks if he is a votive gift (*anathema*) of a city, or sold by someone (310); the slave women, the members of the chorus of Euripides' *Phoenician Women*, sent to Delphi, were votives. He responds that he does not know, only that he is called Apollo's. The early encounters of the play convince him that he is the son of Xuthus, husband of Creusa, and he reacts: "I am not a slave then [ekpepheugamen to doulon]" (555). He errs, though, in his belief concerning descent from Xuthus, and fears that the Athenians, and his father's wife, will reject him as a stranger: "For when a stranger comes into a city / Of pure blood, though in name a citizen, / His mouth remains a slave [to ge stoma / doulon pepatai]: he has no right / Of speech [*parrhesian*" (673–75). The chorus in this play too consists of slave women; Creusa addresses them: "You women, faithful servants of my loom and shuttle [*douleuma piston*]" (748). The neuter collective noun here, like *to doulon*, used elsewhere, communicates the mistress's sense of impersonality, the lack of discrimination among a group of slaves. But she comes to believe

that her husband secretly had a child by a slave ("doula lektra numpheu-
sas lathra") in Delphi, and that she must accept his offspring into their
household (819, 838).

An old man, a slave, Creusa's advisor, promises to help her kill the
child. Ironically, he argues for his own value, proven by his loyalty to
her, even as he conspires to kill the child he thinks is a slave, because its
slavish presence will shame Creusa:

> Worst shame of all is that he should bring into
> Your house a cipher, motherless, the child
> Of some slave woman [ametor', anarithmeton, ek doules tinos /
>   gynaikos]
>
> . . . .
>
> Now I will help you kill the son:
> Visit the place where he prepares the feast,
> To pay the debt I owe my masters, thus,
> To live or die. A slave bears only this
> Disgrace: the name. In every other way
> An honest slave is equal to the free.
>
> (836–56)

Ancient and modern writers who cite this speech as evidence for Euripides' sympathy toward slaves may disregard its ironic burden. Arguing
for the goodness of a good slave, himself, the speaker simultaneously
plots to kill the contemptible offspring of a slave, contemptible precisely
because he is the worthless child of "some slave woman." Euripides' representation of the slave may be intended to call up in the audience a
sense of the contradictory ideologies concerning status and value: Could
a slave be a good man?

The child is spared poisoning when one of the servants utters a word
of evil omen, and Ion pours out the poisoned drink onto the ground to
be drunk by a bird, which dies an anguished death (1205). The old man
reveals Creusa's complicity, and she is condemned to death, until a
priestess's revelations prove Ion to be the son of Creusa and her divine
lover, Apollo—no longer a slave, but origin of the tribe of the Ionians.
This aspect of the *Ion*, with the concealed birth of the hero, son of a god
and a queen, prefigures the plots of late comedy, Roman comedy, and
the Greek romances, with their narratives of Freud's "family romance":
the child's imagination of a nobler origin, his belonging to a higher class,
to more aristocratic parents, than those who care for him.[35] Such a narrative would not console the slaves of the city, who probably did not attend the tragic performances, but rather speaks to the Athenian myths
of autochthonous and divine origin, which ideologically justified prac-

tices of exclusion and empire. The tragedy reveals the lowly slave, tending the temple at Delphi, as the product of divine and mortal union. Few actual, ordinary slaves, participants in the everyday life of the city of Athens, could hope for such revelations and such rescue.

In the cases of Sophocles' Herakles and Euripides' Ion, men enslaved, they pass from the status of servitude into freedom, and even sovereignty. It is as if the playwrights split the troubling and problematic issue of slavery in two, and treat men and women enslaved differently. Male characters escape their condition; women pass from aristocratic freedom into slavery and remain slaves through the plays' duration. The anxiety about slavery can be managed thus; it is a condition that befalls women, who are vulnerable, prey to the aggression of strangers. It is also a condition that can befall states, represented thus allegorically in the convenient and ready-to-hand language describing some persons present in everyday life. Neither political, nor metaphorical, nor literal slavery can be tolerated by the free citizen. But the aristocratic women of legend, like the goddesses of the pantheon, powerful females, can be relegated in spectacle to positions of servitude, their dominant status temporally removed to the past, to the archaic world of Troy.

The tragedians allegorize troubling contemporary realities, displaced through dramatic representation, through gender difference, through temporal distancing, through the class differences between democratic citizenry and ancient aristocracy. Even though tragic performances call up anxiety, grief, and mourning in their exploration of past and present, in the presence of the Athenian audience for whom tragedy was first produced, the routine enslavement of barbarian captive women, of exposed children, of the children of slaves, of Athenians themselves, captured in war, was only obliquely called into question by such dramatic spectacles.

7   THE SLAVE PLATO

Anecdote brings things closer to us in space, allows them to enter into our lives. Anecdote represents the extreme opposite of history—which demands an "empathy" that renders everything abstract. Empathy amounts to the same thing as reading newspapers. The true method of making things present is: to imagine them in our own space (and not to imagine ourselves in their space). Only anecdote can move us in this direction.[1]

—Walter Benjamin

Philosophers Enslaved

THE FOLLOWING anecdote concerning the philosopher Plato appears in various ancient sources. Like Sokrates and Diogenes, they say, Plato was once a slave. This element of his biography rarely figures in philosophical Platonic scholarship focused on the dialogues themselves, Plato as slave inassimilable into philosophy's myths of origin. Yet the Athenian philosopher made several voyages to Sicily, according to the stories, first to see the island and "the craters," then to visit Dionysius, tyrant of Syracuse. According to Diogenes Laertius, biographer of the philosophers, Dionysius forced Plato to "become intimate" with him, and Plato accused Dionysius in their intimacy of talking like a tyrant. Dionysius wanted to do away with him, to kill him, but was dissuaded. Diogenes Laertius relates, in an anecdotal narrative:

[H]e indeed did not go so far but handed him over to Pollis the Lacedae-monian, who had just then arrived on an embassy, with orders to sell him into slavery. And Pollis took him to Aegina and there offered him for sale [*epiprasken*]. . . .
    Anniceris the Cyrenaic happened to be present and purchased him for twenty minae—according to others the sum was thirty minae—and dispatched him to Athens to his friends, who immediately remitted the money. But Anniceris declined it, saying that the Athenians were not the only people worthy of the privilege of providing for Plato. Others assert

that Dion sent the money and that Anniceris would not take it, but bought for Plato the little garden which is in the Academy. Pollis, however, is stated to have been defeated by Chabrias and afterwards to have been drowned at Helice [in the tidal wave that sank 10 Spartan triremes in the earthquake of 372], his treatment of the philosopher having provoked the wrath of heaven (Favorinus). (19–21)

The earliest preserved account of this sale is in the first-century BCE *Index Herculanensis;* in that fragmentary text, Dionysius, enraged at Plato's *parrhesia,* his "freespokenness," is said to have handed Plato over to Lacedaemonian merchants. This fragmentary text contains an account of conditions on Aegina, according to the biographies the birthplace of Plato. In this version of the story, Plato was sold incognito to a poor man *(peneti),* and he later rewarded his purchaser with a payment of oil. When Aristotle discusses chance in the *Physics* (2.8.199B 20), he says: "The stranger came by chance [*apo tukhes*] and when he had ransomed him he departed." Philoponus says this remark alludes to the sale of Plato;[2] if he is accurate, the allusion suggests that the anecdote of Plato's enslavement came early in the biographical tradition. Plutarch in his life of Dion (5.5–6) says Dionysius instructed the Spartan Pollis to kill or sell Plato, but does not describe the sale; in another text (*De tranq. an.* 471f), Plutarch concurs that Dionysius had Plato sold in Aegina. Plato's savior is said elsewhere to be the Libyan named Anniceris, who ransomed him and set him free, refusing reimbursement, or who took the money from Dion to purchase the garden in the Academy for Plato. Anniceris was a non-Greek, not a student of Plato, who was later rebuked by Plato for reckless chariot driving. Diodorus Siculus says Dionysius had Plato sold in the *Syracusan* slave market, in Sicily itself. Diogenes the cynic, himself once sold as a slave (according to his biographers), adds insultingly, with reference to Plato's later voyages to Sicily, that Plato, like a dog, went back to those who had sold him (Aelian V. h. 14.33).[3] The association between slaves and dogs, mentioned earlier, recurs.

The point is not whether the enslavement and sale of the philosopher really occurred. Alice Riginos believes the story may be part of anti-Platonic discourse, originating among those philosophical tendencies hostile to Plato and the Academy. But she adds: "While it may well be that the sale is the invention of the hostile tradition, the report that Plato was a slave becomes a commonplace not only in his biographical tradition but in other authors as well who treat of the philosopher/slave motif or of sudden reversals in fortune which reduced prominent figures to slavery" (89). Historians of philosophy told more anecdotes of the enslavement of other philosophers. There is an account of Sokrates having been a slave: "Duris makes him out to have been a slave [*douleusai*] and to have been employed on stone-work, and the draped figures of the Graces on the Acropolis have by some been attributed to him" (Diogenes Laertius 19). Sokrates' student Phaedo was also said once to have been a slave; Sokrates "made Crito ransom Phaedo who, having been taken prisoner in the war, was kept in degrading slavery, and so won him for philosophy" (31).

In the later philosophical tradition, the enslavement of the philosopher becomes a commonplace. Diogenes the Cynic (404–323 BCE), son of a banker, went into exile because his father, entrusted with the money of the city-state of Sinope, adulterated the coinage; some accounts say Diogenes himself debased the coins. In exile in Athens, he attended Plato's lectures but denounced them as a waste of time (*katatriben*).[4] The Cynic Menippus wrote a *Sale of Diogenes*; when captured and put up for sale, asked what he could do, Diogenes replied: "Govern men." He instructed the crier to ask if anyone wanted to buy a master and when told he couldn't sit while being sold, he retorted that whatever position fishes are in, they still find purchasers. Xeniades bought him, and was told: "You must obey me . . . although I am a slave; for if a physician or a steersman were in slavery, he would be obeyed" (29–30). Eubulus too wrote a *Sale of Diogenes*; here the philosopher is reported to have trained the sons of Xeniades, encouraging athletic training and wrestling school to heighten their coloring and keep them in good condition. Diogenes was said to have grown old as a slave in Xeniades' house, and to have been buried by his sons. When Plato styled him a dog (*kuon*), the animal from which the name Cynic, *kunikos*, is derived, his response was "Quite true, for I come back again and again to those who have sold me" (40). He was reported to have pissed on people who were throwing him bones like a dog. Another version of the story of Diogenes' sale goes as follows:

> [W]hen he was sold as a slave he endured it most nobly. For on a voyage to Aegina he was captured by pirates under the command of Scirpalus (Harpalus, Cicero N.D. iii.34.83), conveyed to Crete and exposed for sale. When the auctioneer asked in what he was proficient, he replied, "In ruling men." Thereupon he pointed to a certain Corinthian with a fine purple border to his robe, the man named Xeniades above-mentioned, and said, "Sell me to this man; he needs a master." Thus Xeniades came to buy him, and took him to Corinth and set him over his own children and entrusted his whole household to him. And he administered it in all respects in such a manner that Xeniades used to go about saying, "A good genius [*daimon*] has entered my house." (74)

When friends wanted to ransom him, Diogenes called them simpletons, for, he said, "lions are not the slaves of those who feed them, but rather those who feed them are at the mercy of the lions: for fear is the mark of the slave, whereas wild beasts make men afraid of them" (75).

In these stories reported about him after his death, Diogenes demonstrates a relationship to slavery typical of post-Platonic philosophy, teaching that "bad men obey [*douleuein*] their lusts as slaves obey their masters" (66). Diogenes' life exemplifies self-mastery, and a lack of interest in social status that becomes a defining characteristic of the philosopher, the wise man. His life exhibits *atopia*, out-of-placeness; he is the philosopher enslaved, the wise man serving another, but his status as the property of another cannot affect his wisdom. It was said that he did the works of Demeter and Aphrodite *en to meso*, "in the middle" (69), that is, eating and masturbating in public space, refusing the norms and conventions of spatial distinctions. "If to breakfast be not absurd [*atopon*] . . . , then it is not absurd to breakfast in the market-place" (69), he said, using the spatial metaphor in *atopon* (from "out of place") to slide from "extraordinary" to "eccentric" or "out of place," to "disgusting," condemning what he saw as senseless propriety.

The philosopher-slave lived on, imperturbable; Epictetus, the Stoic philosopher of the first and second centuries CE, had been a slave. The later, second-century CE Cynic writer Lucian wrote a mocking text called *The Sale of Lives*, in which he lampooned various philosophical schools.[5] The scene is a slave auction, in which the founders or exemplars of the schools are put up for sale. In this dialogue the buyer asks "Chrysippos," a figure for Stoicism, if he is unhappy to be sold and a slave (*doulos*). Chrysippos replies: "Not at all, for these things are not in our control, and all that is not in our control is immaterial" (21).[6] The *atopia*, the eccentricity, the absurdity of these philosopher-slaves make them appropriate figures for slaves in the idealized accounts of Greek civilization. The most exalted thinker of the Western tradition, Plato of Athens, appears not just as an aristocratic Athenian engaged in philosophical conversation with peers but also, paradoxically, inassimilably, as the basest of men, a commodity sold in the marketplace.

❖ ❖ ❖

DO THE ANECDOTES of Plato's and Diogenes' enslavement make them, in Benjamin's sense, "more present"? The narratives, as part of a network of meanings in antiquity, might be interpreted as a symptom of envy; popular culture brings low the pretentious and the great. The anecdote concerning Plato may figure in the post-Platonic philosophical schools as a narrative about philosophical invulnerability, or the imperturbability that is *ataraxia*, which leads through the Stoics to Christianity.[7] And the anecdote about Plato's enslavement may respond to or draw on or extend some potential in the dialogues themselves, especially, I will argue, in Plato's *Meno*. The amount of the ransom paid by Plato's purchaser on Aegina, Plato's birthplace, corresponds to the amount reported in the *Apology* (38b) to have been offered by Sokrates' friends in lieu of his execution in Athens in 399 BCE. Sokrates could not convince the Athenian jury that it should award him free meals for life for his alleged crimes, nor did they accept his payment of a fine, the fine which would have ransomed, and purchased his life. Instead he drank hemlock, ending his life with the words: "Crito, we ought to offer a cock to Asclepius" (*Phaedo* 118a), a sacrifice to the god for his salvation from the sickness that is life, for pleasure after pain, the soul's freedom from the fetters of the body.[8]

Plato's *Meno*

Scholars usually consider the *Meno* an early dialogue of Plato, written in about 386–85.[9] The dramatic date is probably 402 BCE, that is, three years before Sokrates' execution by the city-state of the Athenians. In the course of the dialogue, the Thessalian aristocrat Meno, on a visit to Athens, asks Sokrates if *arete*, "excellence," can be taught. They converse first about the nature of excellence, and reach no conclusion. Sokrates argues that the soul of human beings is immortal, and that therefore he and Meno can try to recollect what their souls once knew, the truth about the nature of virtue. To demonstrate that one can bring to mind what the soul knew before birth, he leads one of Meno's slaves through a problem in geometry.[10] Sokrates argues further that although knowledge can be recollected, *arete* is not knowledge and cannot be taught. Excellent men do not leave behind them excellent sons; there are no teachers of excellence. Anytus (later one of the prosecutors of Sokrates in his trial) enters, shows that he cannot distinguish between a philosopher and a sophist, threatens Sokrates, and departs. Sokrates concludes that if any man could know what excellence is and could teach it, he would be as different from other men as Teiresias is a solid reality among the shades in the underworld.

In the philosophical tradition, the *Meno* has often been treated as one of the aporetic dialogues, in the course of which Sokrates and his interlocutors discover through philosophical conversation that they are ignorant, that they cannot proceed.[11] For scholars committed to a certain dating and sequence of the dialogues, it is noteworthy as a text in which Plato introduces the doctrine of *anamnesis*, of recollection, which later, it is argued, figures in the so-called theory of the forms.[12] Philosophical essays on the dialogue usually address the matter of recollection, or the nature of the mathematical problem first posed by Sokrates.[13] Marcus Giaquinto reveals the customary philosophical lack of interest in rhetorical and ideological issues in the dialogues: "I follow custom in writing as though the text were a faithful record of an actual exchange, for brevity's sake."[14] But rather than reading the dialogue solely within the history of philosophy, of the Platonic corpus, within the developmental theses about the stages in the theory of recollection and the theory of forms, the terrain of most philosophical readings of this text, if we consider this dialogue, read aslant, from another place, it belongs as well among the ancient Greek discourses about slavery, discourses that include Diogenes Laertius's anecdote about the enslavement of Plato, Aristotle's treatises on politics, the beast fables of the freed slave Aesop, Xenophon's text on "economics," or household management, Aristophanes' comedies, Herodotean history, and Athenian tragedy.

The metaphorical texture of the dialogue raises questions that implicate questions of slavery, calling attention to its participants' freedom of motion, to their commitment to engagement in dialogue, and to mortality and immortality, an issue that further brings into question the nature of the soul of human beings, slave and free. In one of the dialogue's salient metaphors, Meno, overwhelmed by argument, compares Sokrates to a variety of paralyzing stingray, a *narke*; the word is connected etymologically to the verb *narkao*, "to grow stiff or numb," and to *narkissos*, the narcotic flower:

> [b]oth in your appearance and in other respects you are extremely like the flat torpedo sea-fish; for it benumbs anyone who approaches and touches it, and something of the sort is what I find you have done to me now. For in truth I feel my soul and my tongue quite benumbed. (80bc)

Not just a gadfly, an insect that stings, excites, and irritates his interlocutors, Sokrates is like a ray delivering an electric shock, leaving its victim immobilized. The comparison touches on the themes of motion and stasis present here and elsewhere in the Platonic corpus. Sokrates, for example, excites remark in the *Crito* for his stasis, his unwillingness to leave Athens. The good citizen stays put, unlike the traveler Plato. Sokrates, when given a choice between exile and hemlock, chose execution by the citizens of Athens, having never left the city except for his military service. He voices his critics' objections:

> You would not have been so exceptionally reluctant to cross the borders of your country if you had not been exceptionally attached to it. You have never left the city to attend a festival or for any other purpose, except on some military expedition. You have never traveled abroad as other people

do, and you have never felt the impulse to acquaint yourself with another country or constitution.

. . . You could not have absented yourself from the city less if you had been lame or blind or decrepit in some other way. (*Crito*, 52b–53a)

In the *Meno*, the reciprocity of the paralysis inflicted by the stingray compels attention. Sokrates says flirtatiously that handsome people like the game of comparisons. He does not, yet he adds, "As for me, if the torpedo is torpid itself while causing others to be torpid, I am like it, but not otherwise" (53a). He shares the condition of paralysis that Meno accuses him of inflicting on others. Both players in the dialogue, both interlocutors, are paralyzed by their *aporia*, caught up too in the leisure that enables their conversation.

All the participants in this dialogue are marked by possibilities of mobility and stasis. Sokrates is explaining to Meno why knowledge is superior to right opinion, and Meno does not understand:

Socrates: It is because you have not observed with attention the images of Daedalus. But perhaps there are none in your country.
. . . if they are not fastened up they run away and escape [*drapeteuei*]; but, if fastened, they stay where they are.

· ·

To possess one of [Daedalus'] works which is let loose does not count for much in value; it will not stay with you any more than a runaway slave: but when fastened up it is worth a great deal, for his productions are very fine things. And to what am I referring in all this? To true opinions.

For these, so long as they stay with us, are a fine possession, and effect all that is good; but they do not care to stay for long, and run away [*drapetousin*] out of the human soul, and thus are of no great value until one makes them fast [*desei*] with causal reasoning. (97de)

Opinions run off like escaping slaves, unless they are bound down with fetters; knowledge must be bound, held down, fastened by reasoning.[15] Opinions are like works of art are like runaway slaves, all better off bound and fettered.

Fixity of the citizen, the interlocutor, the fettered slave, the bound statue of Daedalus, of knowledge—all these are superior to wandering opinion and to the wandering and capricious aristocrat Meno, whose name puns on "remaining," "staying"; who was, at least according to his portrait in Xenophon's *Anabasis*, a greedy and unscrupulous, deeply unphilosophical man. Meno served as a general in the mercenary troop that fought with Cyrus in Persia, a campaign recorded in detail by Xenophon. Captured along with the other generals after Cyrus's death, he escaped execution with the rest, perhaps because he betrayed his fellow

Greeks to the Persians. He is said to have lived a year longer, treated as a criminal, and then to have died. Xenophon says of him:

> Menon the Thessalian made it perfectly clear that his dominant ambition was to get rich. . . . He thought that the shortest cut to the satisfaction of his ambitions was by means of perjury and lying and deceit. . . . Menon took pride in his ability to deceive, in his fabrications and falsehoods, and in sneering at his friends. He always looked upon a person who had scruples as being only half educated. (*Anabasis* 2.6)

If Xenophon's portrait has any merit, Meno failed to benefit from his dialectical contact with Sokrates. Pseudoeducated by Gorgias the rhetorician, he came from far-off Thessaly, went off again to Persia, and perhaps became a traitor, at the least meeting an unfortunate and unheroic end. If Plato's first audience knew this account of the future of Sokrates' partner in dialogue, then the significance of not only his failure to grasp the philosophical issues at hand but also the imagery of the stingray stung, the statues running off like disobedient, unbound slaves, has its negative bearing on the proper, fixed life of someone committed to philosophical inquiry.

One of the rhetorical, political purposes of the *Meno* may be to argue against Sokrates' responsibility for the bad ends of certain of his followers: the oligarch Critias and the charismatic, frequently fleeing, profligate Alcibiades. This responsibility is implied in the charges that led the city to condemn and execute Sokrates, who tries to engage both Anytus and Meno in dialogue, with both efforts ending badly—in fact Anytus played a central role in bringing about that execution. Sokrates' failure here to teach either of them may be intended to demonstrate his innocence of the charge of corrupting the young, and in particular exposes Anytus's crime against philosophy.

If we imagine the whole of the Platonic corpus to be mourning-work, a great monument to the memory of Sokrates, then this dialogue must stand among those that refer most directly to Plato's loss. The reference to Teiresias at the end of the *Meno* signifies within this mourning. Sokrates has been conversing with the unworthy Meno, with an ignorant slave boy, with the malicious and ultimately destructive Anytus. At the end, after he and Meno have acknowledged their state of *aporia*, he refers to the man who would have a true knowledge of virtue, a real understanding of it, a statesman who could make a statesman of another man.

> And if there should be any such, he might fairly be said to be among the living what Homer says Teiresias was among the dead—"He alone has comprehension; the rest are flitting shades." [oios pepnutai ton en Haidou, hai de skiai aissousi] [*Od.* 10.494] (*Meno* 100a)

The dramatic character Sokrates is a powerful and evocative image. Among all the dead, only Teiresias has substance. So in life and in Plato's text, Sokrates has a vividness and solidity, an understanding that renders all those around him, all those in dialogue with him, shadowy, flickering shades. The image is complex, because at the time Plato writes, it is Sokrates who is dead, who may be in the land of Hades, understanding; but even in life, as Sokrates himself says, such a one has a more vivid existence than any other man. The verb *pepnuma*, cited by Plato and thus by Sokrates, used by Homer in the first instance, derives from the verb *pneo*, "breathe," "live"; it means "to have breath or soul," and metaphorically "to be wise, discreet, and prudent." Teiresias alone lives among the flitting shades, as Sokrates alone lives among his partners in conversation, still lives in the fiction of the text, will not flee like the fabricated statues of Daedalus, who will run if they can, like slaves who want to be free.

In the philosophical literature, as I have said, scholars have focused principally on the question of *anamnesis* in the dialogue, on the introduction of the notion of recollection. Yet the *Meno* also reveals the place of slaves in everyday life in this society. When Sokrates wants to try out his ideas, he turns to a slave, part of the landscape, the furnishings of his world, just as he talks about a *kline*, a couch, when thinking about the relationship among the ideas, physical things, and representations of those things in the *Republic* (10.596b–598a). Slaves are everywhere, ubiquitous, and appear elsewhere in the dialogues as apparatus, furnishings of everyday life. Plato frames the conversation making up the body of the dialogue called the *Theaetetus* with an exchange between Euclides and Terpsion in which they recall this conversation of years before, written down by Euclides. He orders his slave: "Well, boy, take the book and read" (143c). The boy reads, aloud, for his free audience.

In the dialogue *Meno*, the only one in which a slave speaks for himself, Meno has many attendants, many slaves, and Sokrates' partner in geometry, nameless, is one of them. If scholars are correct in identifying the site of this dialogue as a gymnasium, which would account for the presence of Meno's attendants, for the earth or sand in which to inscribe geometric figures, then there may be a haze of eroticism over these scenes. Sokrates flirts with Meno, telling him how handsome he is, how vulnerable he, Sokrates, is to the beauty of others; the slave too may in the context of the gymnasium partake of the sexual availability of slaves to free men in this city. The ubiquity of slaves is made clear by Sokrates' settling on this "boy," presumably and confessedly ignorant of geometry, for his experiment, perhaps ultimately designed as a proof of the immortality of the soul.

What interests me most here is the invisibility of the slave and his slave status to modern readers of the *Meno*. As noted earlier, this term of address which Sokrates directs to the slave, *pais*, means "boy," but it is also what the Greeks usually called a slave, and does not necessarily suggest that the slave is a child or an adolescent. Scholarly articles usually overlook him as one of the *dramatis personae*. Who, then, is the fourth participant in this dialogue, the *pais*? R. S. Bluck remarks that the slave "merely represents someone who is completely uneducated." According to J. E. Thomas, "Fritzsche contends that the Slave-boy is not a character, but an abstraction, a typical blank mind." Jane Day says of the slave that "his function is to be colourless." In an especially striking phrase, one that records the implicit desire of some philosophical scholarship to disregard any social or historical context for the dialogues, Julius Moravscik says: "We can represent the slave-boy as a geometry learning device." [16]

But of course the intriguing thing about this *pais*, this "boy," is that he has a soul, and the capacity to recollect, to reason, and to gain knowledge. In fact, the rhetoric of the Platonic text encourages reflection on stasis and mobility, mutations of status, birth into one condition and migration into another. In its reference to Teiresias among the shades, in its evocation of Sokrates' death, we are reminded of the soul's sojourn in the underworld, and perhaps even of the possibility of rebirth developed elsewhere, for example in the *Phaedo* (81a–82b). The image of Daedalus's moving statues recalls slavery and flight, and suggests the reverse: passage from freedom into slavery, from capture or sale into bondage. The *Meno* reminds us to see this slave as in possession of a soul like any other human being's, as capable of reasoning and deduction, as a fit interlocutor for Sokrates, as a human being who will live and die.

Plato's dramatic representation of this slave must be set against the arguments of Aristotle in particular, arguments that have a long history, arguments that were deployed for centuries to justify the survival of slavery in the Old and New Worlds. In the *Politics*, in a passage recently discussed by Peter Garnsey, Aristotle says that every animal has a body and a soul. [17] But he specifies the difference between slave and free in the following terms:

> [H]e is by nature a slave who is capable of belonging to another (and that is why he does so belong), and who participates in reason so far as to apprehend it but not to possess it. (*Politics* 1254b)

The slave is essentially different from the free person, lacking powers of reasoning or, as Eugene Garver has argued, *thumos*, in the sense of "spirit," or "courage": "What is missing is not the ability to formulate and follow reasons, but the ability to have reasons as one's own."[18]

Sokrates, in the *Meno*, appears not to share this view about the slave's capacity for reasoning, for having reasons. He emphasizes for Meno, after describing the boy paralyzed by the stingray's questioning (84b), that the slave answered only with opinions that were his own:

Socrates: And at this moment those opinions have just been stirred up in him, like a dream; but if he were repeatedly asked these same questions in a variety of forms, you know he will have in the end as exact an understanding of them as anyone.
Meno: So it seems.
Socrates: Without anyone having taught him, and only through questions put to him, he will understand, recovering the knowledge out of himself?
Meno: Yes.
Socrates: And is not this recovery of knowledge, in himself and by himself, recollection? (85c–d)

Sokrates' slave does possess reason, and can achieve understanding. Plato's discourse on slavery includes not just what he says about slavery as an institution in the *Republic*, the *Laws*, and elsewhere; we must also take into account the extent to which, in the *Meno*, he emphasizes the slave's status as a human being, dramatizes the presence of this slave who is seen to learn and move toward understanding and knowledge. The slave of the *Meno*, fixed as he is, has more aptitude for learning and philosophy than either of the free men, Meno or Anytus.[19] Slave status does not exclude a human being from philosophy.

It is currently fashionable to see Aristotle as the man of Heideggerian *phronesis*, as a progressive thinker, the pragmatist, even the materialist, someone who thought things we can think with him in considering problems, even ethical problems, for example, of the present day. Martha Nussbaum writes, "We have discovered that we do live in the world that Aristotle describes."[20] And Bernard Williams: "As opposed to Plato, who is manifestly and professedly offensive to liberal and democratic opinion, Aristotle can be seen as expressing a more generous and accommodating humanism, and there is a strong motivation to find a centre to that outlook that will push to one side his less congenial opinions."[21] Plato, on the other hand, is branded with the label "metaphysician," source of the move beyond the world we inhabit to an imaginary utopia of phallogocentric presence.[22] Yet I think in this case Plato must be seen as imagining human capacities more generously than Aristotle, who in passing theorizes natural slavery, who establishes the terms of discourse that dominate the debates of antiquity and the Middle Ages, even into the proslavery arguments of the antebellum South.

Of this slave, Sokrates says:

> And must he not have either once acquired or always had the knowledge he now has?
>
> Meno: Yes.
>
> Socrates: Now if he always had it, he was always in a state of knowing [*epistemon*]; and if he acquired it at some time, he could not have acquired it in this life. . . . Now can anyone have taught him all this? You ought surely to know, especially as he was born and bred in your house.
>
> . . . .
>
> And if he did not acquire them in this present life, is it not obvious at once that he had them and learnt them during some other time?
>
> . . . .
>
> And this must have been the time when he was not a human being? [*anthropos*]
>
> Meno: Yes.
>
> Socrates: So if in both of these periods—when he was and was not a human being—he has had true opinions in him which have only to be awakened by questioning to become knowledge, his soul must have had this cognisance throughout all time? For clearly he has always either been or not been a human being.
>
> Meno: Evidently.
>
> Socrates: And if the truth of all things that are is always in our soul, then the soul must be immortal. (85d–86b)

The slave, born and bred in a Greek-speaking household, remains a slave, but his soul is immortal, intermittently housed in a human being, and capable of understanding. And the fact that in this last remark Sokrates uses the first-person-plural pronoun *(hemin)*, speaking of "our" soul, argues for a status shared between him and the *pais*, the slave.

There are other such moments. In the *Phaedo*, in a passage cited earlier, Sokrates argues that human beings must not commit suicide because they are, as it were, the possessions, the slaves of the gods. He imagines himself as a slave, a thing, a possession, and places Cebes in the place of the master, the god. Elsewhere in this same dialogue, just before the discussion about refusing to commit suicide, Sokrates explains that, practicing a popular art, he has been putting into verse the fables of Aesop, Aesop the legendary inventor of the fable, Aesop the freed slave. Phaedrus, the Roman author whose collection of fables is the first extant one we possess, later explained the genre of the fable as a hermetic, cryptic discourse of slaves:

> Now I will explain why the type of thing called fable was invented. The slave, being liable to punishment for any offence, since he dared not say

outright what he wished to say, projected his personal sentiments into fables and eluded censure under the guise of jesting with made-up stories. (3, prologue 33–37)

His allusion to Aesop and the versification of one of the fables precedes Sokrates' saying "I shall be going today," referring to his drinking of the hemlock—possibly an allusion to the death of Aesop, killed as a sort of scapegoat by the angry citizens of Delphi, who accused him falsely of theft. Sokrates is about to become the victim of angry citizens of Athens.

There is, to my mind, little exploration of a possible sympathy or empathy, some "feeling with" the nameless slave of the *Meno*, on Sokrates' or on Plato's part. Such an attitude would be anachronistic, foreign to Greek ways of thinking about identity. The Greek free man's relations with others—slaves, women, barbarians—occur in a constant negotiation of differentiation and hierarchy, which precedes by millennia the historical development of sentiment, sympathy, and identification we see in later moments of the Western tradition. Yet in these dramatic dialogues and in other texts, narratives, and anecdotes concerning the lives of the philosophers in antiquity, there is a cultural recognition of the universal possibility of enslavement, some conception of an interchangeability in Platonic philosophy between slave and free, an equation of Meno and the slave, of Sokrates himself and the slave, of Plato and slaves. Because of Plato's myths about transmigration of souls, speculation that souls are rewarded or punished after evaluation of their conduct in one life by rebirth in a nobler or baser soul, the philosopher stands in a different place from Aristotle's on the question of slavery. For Aristotle, the condition of slavery is essential and absolute, and the weight of his analysis of slavery falls on its fundamental status as an institution, and further, less centrally, on differentiating definitively between slave and free. Plato, on the other hand, sees the slave here as born into his condition, but not as essentially slavish, not set for all time within the body of a slave, not possessing an eternally slavish soul.[23] Rather, his emphasis is on the immortality of all souls, their previous history of having glimpsed true knowledge once upon a time, and their power to recover, to remember, what they once knew.

Plato in America

The Platonic scholar Gregory Vlastos, in an early and influential essay, wrote about the centrality of the metaphor of slavery to all of Plato's doctrines, and then to a certain extent withdrew this claim. In "Slavery in Plato's Thought," first published in 1941 in *Philosophical Review*, Vlastos argued for slavery as a central, controlling metaphor for Plato's thinking. In his political theory, Vlastos noted that "Plato idealized the institution of slavery, the contract theorists the institution of democracy. Their conflicting idealism mirrored the real contradiction in Athenian society: a free political community that rested on a slave economy."[24] He read slavery in Plato's cosmology: "Plato attacks Ionian physics not only on philosophical, but also on political grounds; so that both the political and the cosmological associations of slavery came into play in his polemic. The issue is the very existence of a philosophy which conceives of the government of the state and the government of the world as analogous to the government of the slave" (158). Vlastos concluded that

> his [Plato's] views about slavery, state, man and the world all illustrate a single hierarchic pattern, and . . . the key to the pattern is in his idea of *logos* with all the implications of a dualist epistemology. The slave lacks *logos;* so does the multitude in the state, the body in man and material necessity in the universe. Let to itself each of these would be disorderly and vicious in the sense of that untranslatably Greek word, *hybris*. Order is imposed upon them by a benevolent superior: master, guardian, mind, demiurge. Each of these rules [*arkhein*] in his own domain. The common title to authority is the possession of *logos*. In such an intellectual scheme slavery is "natural": in perfect harmony with one's notions about the nature of the world and of man. (161–62)

In a postscript written in 1959 for M. I. Finley's *Slavery in Classical Antiquity*—published in 1960, almost twenty years after the first publication of his own essay—Vlastos's sweeping claims about slavery, and the Marxizing language of "contradiction," are disavowed; Vlastos asserts that the statements in his essay are not false, yet "a few may leave a wrong impression on the reader's mind." (162) Responding to criticism, and undoubtedly affected by the postwar climate of the United States in the Eisenhower fifties, he recants: "I would gladly confess [*sic*] that there are many, and equally important aspects of Plato's thought which this metaphor does not illuminate. I would not wish to suggest that slavery is *the* key to Plato's philosophy." I find Vlastos's earlier arguments persuasive, and his recantation illuminating, as an example of the chilling effects of political context on scholarly judgment.

Vlastos's description of the centrality of the concept of slavery in Plato's thought does not elaborate on the differences between Plato's and Aristotle's thinking. Slavery for both ancient philosophers may be natural, yet Plato acknowledges the ephemerality of freedom as well as of slavery, and the mutability of both conditions, within the context of his arguments for the soul and its immortality. For Aristotle, as I will argue in chapter 9, the emphasis lies on the secular, quotidian management of slaves and slavery, and the issue of potential enslavement of the free recedes rhetorically.

❖ ❖ ❖

THE ANECDOTES about ancient philosophers and these dialogues, read against the grain of the philosophical tradition and its developmental model, can bring ancient slavery closer to us in space, break through a narrative of progress, of the serial inevitability of linear history. As Benjamin wrote in 1937,

> disquiet . . . marks the beginning of any critique of history worthy to be called dialectical, which must renounce a calm, contemplative attitude towards its subject to become aware of the critical constellation in which precisely this fragment of the past is found with precisely this present.[25]

Readings of ancient texts and of ancient society should continue to be disquieted by the question of slavery, which has produced unease, anger, guilt, accusations, apology, defenses, and consistently fascinating engagement and concomitant disavowals by classical scholars in relation to the present, the recent past, and antiquity.

The implicit evaluation made by some readers of Plato might be rethought, especially in light of the racializing essentialism of modern American discourse on slavery. Of course Plato accepts slavery, never questions the institution of slavery, sees it as a fundamental structure, uses it as a metaphor for the relationship between gods and human beings, between one part of the soul and another. Yet there is a fluidity, a slippage imagined between slave and free that would violate the rigid barrier between them erected later by Aristotle and reified in terms of race in New World slavery.

Juxtaposed against the proximity of the ancient anecdotes, Plato and Diogenes entering our space in chains, one might set the bad repetition of American proslavery discourse. George Fitzhugh, discussed in the introduction, offered a critique of nineteenth-century capitalism that stressed its inhumanity to its laborers, painting a Dickensian portrait of the plight of workers in England and in the capitalist, slave-free North of his contemporary America:

> And now Equality [his name for the Northern nonslave economy] where are thy monuments? . . . perhaps, it is an echo from some grand, gloomy, and monotonous factory, where pallid children work fourteen hours a day, and go home at night to sleep in damp cellars. It may be too, this cellar contains aged parents too old to work, and cast off by their employer to die.[26]

Fitzhugh was one of the few advocates of slavery who argued for the enslavement of whites as well as blacks in antebellum America.

> How can we contend that white slavery is wrong, whilst all the great body of free laborers are starving; and slaves, white or black, throughout the world, are enjoying comfort?[27]

He cites with approval an article by "a philanthropist" from *Jerrold's Magazine:*

> [S]lavery and content, and liberty and discontent, are natural results of each other. Applying this, then, to the toil-worn, half-fed, pauperized population of England, I found that the only way to permanently and efficiently remedy the complicated evils, would be to ENSLAVE the whole of the people of England who have not property. (155)

Fitzhugh saw slavery both as a restoration, a repetition of the heroic past of Western civilization, and as a refuge for those who had become helpless victims in the new capitalism.

Saidiya Hartman, on the other hand, in *Scenes of Subjection: Terror, Slavery and Self-Making in Nineteenth-Century America,* analyzes a moment of empathic identification between free man and slave experienced by the abolitionist John Rankin in 1837. Rankin, observing daily life in the South, indulged himself extravagantly in a masochistic fantasy of being himself a slave, beaten along with his wife and children: "[E]very indignant principle of my blood was excited to the highest degree."[28] The modern critic Hartman, writing in 1997, argued that "if this violence can become palpable and indignation can be fully aroused only through the masochistic fantasy, then it becomes clear that empathy is double-edged, for in making the other's suffering one's own, this suffering is occluded by the other's obliteration" (19). What may disturb a reader most in this scene is the phantasmic usurpation and appropriation of the black slave's suffering by the white abolitionist. Yet our indignation relies more on the chasm separating African American from white man than on the chasm separating slave and free.[29] The history of American racialized slavery has produced an equation of slavery with color difference, and made it difficult for black and white people to empathize and sympathize across the line of color, across the line that separated freedom from slavery in this country. White Americans can rely on their privileged history to protect them for coming to terms with the legacy of American slavery, since slavery is something that happened to other people, not their problem, not part of their past. Yet, of course, the history of slavery in America affects everyone, including scholars of the classical past.

❖ ❖ ❖

MY INTENTION in studying ancient slavery is neither to express indignation nor to identify with ancient slaves but rather to see antiquity and modernity otherwise, and to wonder if studying ancient slavery can illuminate how race and slavery have cohered in this nation's past and in the national imaginary, how even critiques of the appropriative power of empathy can remain locked into an essentializing paradigm of racial difference. We inherit a set of racial categories, and few can imagine themselves placed elsewhere in its mapping of difference. The study of ancient slavery might interrupt and disquiet the essentialized differences of American history, the mapping of slavery onto race in the New World. Classicists live in societies that until recently numbered slaves among their population. A critical relationship to our own history, and then to the ancient world, its abrupt, anecdotal, unassimilable proximity, might enable new readings of antiquity, and a reading of antiquity *against* modernity, a critique of the present that illuminates class and racisms now.

8   AESOP THE FABULIST

Historicism presents an eternal image of the past, historical materialism a specific and unique engagement with it. . . . The task of historical materialism is to set to work an engagement with history original [*ursprunglich*] to every new present. It has recourse to a consciousness of the present that shatters the continuum of history. . . . It is the dialectical construction which distinguishes that which is our original concern with historical engagement from the patchwork findings of actuality.

—Walter Benjamin, "Theses on History" (1940)

THE TONDO, the painted interior of a drinking cup now in the Museo Gregoriano in Rome, appears to represent Aesop and a fox (fig. 24).[1] The fox sits on the right, poised on a rock, a protruding crag; his haunches are pressed up against the border of the round, decorated interior of the cup. He sits well back on the rock, which has a small concavity at its back to accommodate his buttocks, and his feet touch the rock near its front. The fox's back curves with the rounded edge of the decoration, bordered by a maeander pattern that echoes the round shape of the vase. The mouth of the fox stands open, above a snout pointed directly at his interlocutor. His ears are pricked, and his left paw is pressed down in an emphatic gesture. He raises his right paw, seeming to command the attention of his audience. He has an audience of one, the very much larger figure of a man, seated to his left.

The man has a huge, disproportionate head, several times the size of the fox's entire body. He looks up, gazing far above the fox toward the roof formed by the painted circle in the cup's interior. He has a beard, indicated roughly, a mustache, and wrinkles on his balding forehead. His cloak surrounds a body far smaller than one proportioned to match his head, with lumps of shoulder and no discernible arms. He holds a staff, perhaps a crutch, which emerges from his lap like a sort of phallus and almost reaches the triangular, pointed lower part of his beard. He too sits on a crag, one obscured by his rather slender buttocks, looking barely substantial enough to support his immense head. His feet extend below the picture's surface, vanishing outside the frame.[2] It is all quite hilarious.

Figure 24. Aesop cup, interior. Museo Gregoriano, Rome. Photograph courtesy of the Vatican Museums.

Is this in fact the mute fabulist, Aesop the slave, the teller of tales, getting his material from the horse's mouth? He looks like an early ethnographer interviewing a native, a *histor* like Herodotus examining a witness, consulting an oracle. Who would know better the culture of the foxes than a fox?[3] The humor of the cup arises from the contrast between the great size of the deformed human being, especially his enormous head, typical of caricatures, and the tiny body of his interlocutor, as well as from the dumb intensity of the human being, who attentively listens, seemingly recording the discourse of Mr. Fox as he helpfully, generously holds forth about something he knows well, carrying on like an experienced, skilled *rhetor* or storyteller.

The *ainos*, the fable or story, was traditionally told in the golden age. Babrius, the Roman versifier of the fables, reminds his readers that in the golden age animals had the same *phone*, the same speech, as human beings, and this stage of history is mentioned in the *Life of Aesop* as well. When Aesop was on Samos, the Samians wanted to give him up to Croesus:

> Aesop came forward and said, "Men of Samos, I agree and would be content to die at the feet of the king, but I want to tell you a story that I wish you would have engraved on my tombstone when I'm dead. When animals talked the same language [*homophona*] as men, the wolves and the sheep started a war with one another . . . "[4]

The story involves only wolves, sheep, and dogs, no human beings; a wolf appears before the sheep and talks "like a politician" [*hos demegoros*]. Like an example in Aristotle's *Rhetoric*, this fable alludes to performances before the people. The dogs bark, protect the sheep from the wolves, and when the sheep give up the dogs, foolishly thinking they themselves will be spared, they are left without protectors.

Fables often appear to take place in this epoch, the time when animals had the same *phone* as human beings. Even if the events of a fable take place in the world of animals, without human presence, animals speak the language of humans, which is recorded in the fable; and they all speak the same language among themselves, so that dogs can communicate without difficulty with wolves and sheep. If a god or a human being is present, part of the fable narrative, that god or human being communicates effortlessly, in the same language, with all the animals of whatever species. The tondo of the cup from the Vatican, then, records a scene from that imagined time, when the fox, telling his tale, expresses himself to Aesop without the need of translator or translation. As Gregory Nagy points out, Aesop himself, once upon a time, was without voice, without *phone*, until he received the gift of speech from Isis.[5] Aesop is an outsider, likened to a thing, an animal, a dog. In his biography he is called *kunokephalon* (11), "dog-headed"; such an epithet connects Aesop with Diogenes; the dog, *kuon*; his Cynics, *kunikoi*; and with slaves. And the slave status of Aesop, the element of his biography that describes him as once a slave, later a freedman, often troubles scholarship concerning the fable itself. Is it the voice of the people, or is the fable's source irrelevant to its function in the ritual and religious life of the ancient cities? Scholars of the fable sometimes argue either that all the meaning of the fable resides in Aesop's low status, that the fable is protest from below, or that Aesop's enslavement is irrelevant to the fable's significance among ancient and modern genres.

Aesop the Slave

Aesop the fabulist, according to the stories, had been a slave. Herodotus reports on him while recounting the history of Rhodopis, a famous courtesan who worked in Egypt, supposedly erected a pyramid, and was set free to prostitute herself by the brother of the poet Sappho, Kharaxos:

> She was a Thracian by birth, slave to Iadmon, son of Hephaestopolis, a Samian, and fellow-slave [*sundoulos*] of Aesopus the story-teller [*tou logopoiou*]. For he also was owned by Iadmon; of which the chiefest proof is that when the Delphians, obeying an oracle, issued many proclamations inviting whosoever would to undertake atonement for the killing of Aesopus, none would accept it but another Iadmon, grandson of the first. Thus was Aesopus too shown to be the slave of Iadmon. (Herodotus 2.134)[6]

The story of Rhodopis continues to be intertwined with that of Aesop. Herodotus says that Xanthos of Samos, later reported to be the owner of Aesop, brought her to Egypt.

The *Life of Aesop*, mentioned earlier, a narrative of uncertain date, with early and later elements, begins as follows:

> The fabulist Aesop, the great benefactor of mankind, was by chance a slave but by origin a Phrygian of Phrygia, of loathsome aspect, worthless as a servant, potbellied, misshapen of head, snub-nosed, swarthy, dwarfish, bandy-legged, short-armed, squint-eyed, liver-lipped—a portentous monstrosity. In addition to this, he had a defect more serious than his unsightliness in being speechless, for he was dumb and could not talk. (31)

The ingenious Aesop nonetheless proves to his master that he is innocent of a charge of eating figs by vomiting up water and forcing his fellow slaves, in fact guilty of the crime, to do the same. He subsequently encounters a priestess of the goddess Isis (a sign of the late, possibly Egyptian setting for this part of the biography), and the goddess gives him the power of speech as a reward for her care. His master sees his speaking as an ominous portent, and has him sold. The slave dealer thinks him an unlikely prospect, saying: "This must be the trumpeter in the battle of the cranes. Is he a turnip or a man? If he didn't have a voice, I would have said he was a pot or a jar for food or a goose egg" (37).

The reference to the battle of the cranes seems to allude to a fable well known to the readers of this life; the author sets the origin of the fable anterior to the career of Aesop the storyteller, and thus confirms what scholars believe, that the fable predates the fabulist, going back perhaps to Sumerian traditions, arriving in Greece perhaps in the eighth century. The stories associated with the name of Aesop seem to have gathered around him in the fifth century BCE: "It is in the second half of the fifth century that we begin to hear of Aesop," notes M. L. West. "Once given this starting-point, the Greek instinct to attach anonymous compositions or achievements to any appropriate individual ensured that Aesop would attract fables."[7] West believes that there was a written text, a book, of fables attributed to Aesop in the classical period; the life of Aesop we have today has its beginnings in this earlier, classical source.

Scholarship and the Politics of the Fable

Much of the scholarly work on the fable in antiquity has been concerned with locating and cataloguing the vast array of stories found in many different literary and popular texts.[8] Other scholars have focused on the question of the ties between the Aesopian fable and other, especially "Oriental" traditions. Still others have focused on the place of the fable in archaic poetry, especially poetry of praise and blame, and on the ritual aspects of the life of Aesop.[9] Those scholars who have tried to assess the political significance of the fable have often argued that Aesop represents a carnivalesque, Bakhtinian trickster character, one who temporarily turns the world upside down, or that he speaks for the underclass, the poor and the weak, in a populist oral mode. Aesop's status as a freedman, as a former slave, is significant only for this latter group of commentators, and only ambiguously.

Much of the important scholarship on the fable has been produced by European scholars interested in popular culture and its survival into the present. Antonio La Penna's long discussion of the ancient fable contains much of interest.[10] He argues that it offers a deeply pessimistic view of the world. His essay is framed by a claim for utilitarianism and secular reason, proceeding from the humble classes of antiquity, who are in his view free from the prejudices of high culture, of the philosophical tradition, or of devotion to the Olympian gods. La Penna points out that the story of the life of Aesop shows his distance both from traditional religious organization (at Delphi, for example) and from the institution of philosophy (in contrast with his master, the philosopher Xanthos) (528). Thus, he argues, the ancient fables reflect their origin in the culture of the masses.

La Penna's characterization of the import of the fables is quite convincing; their listener or reader is encouraged to accept his position in the world, to avoid attempting change or revolution, to avoid pretentious ambitions to achieve a higher status, and so on. The animals of fable who make such attempts are laughed at, ridiculed by the other animals of the narratives, or simply worsen their situations. Yet I would not conclude, as La Penna does, that the body of fables necessarily represents popular culture, a current of pessimism and reason that can be traced back to slaves, to the humble, poor, and oppressed of the ancient world.[11] The legacy and import of the fable tradition are more ambiguous, suggesting both a view from below and a conservative ethos of essentialism.

Stefano Jedrkiewicz contests the view of Marxist scholars who claim Aesop for the proletariat.[12] In a chapter entitled "Schiavitù e contestazione" (199–205), he argues that if Aesop is proletarian, so is Apollo, since the god himself labored to build the walls of Laomedon. The image of Aesop as "the cultural champion of the humble against the ideology of the powerful is not a constant of the tradition" (203). Such an image, he argues, is introduced for particular ends at a given moment: "It is not demonstrable that the 'plebs' would see in Aesop the incarnation of their mentality and in the fabulous a form of alternative 'culture.' In the second place, Aesop as the exponent of the 'mentality of the subaltern classes' is a personal invention of Phaedrus" (ibid.). Jedrkiewicz connects Aesop's status as a slave with another tradition: the true matrix of Aesopian slavery is "philosophical," and Aesop's contestation is elaborated in high culture (207). Modern readers must recognize, in Jedrkiewicz's view, the diversity and alterity of Aesop. He is bivalent, moving between high and low, an "over-turner" [*rovesciatore*], both a stranger and an insider, inside and outside Greek culture. Jedrkiewicz concludes, with a reference to the Roman god Janus, of the two faces: Aesop is a "paradoxical" figure, exemplifying learned ignorance; he is an "indefatigable mediator between the rational and the absurd" (443), "una figura di alterità e paradosso" (444).

Francisco Adrados, the author of a magisterial work on the fable, emphasizes ritual connections in his account.[13] In discussing the text on the life of Aesop, he argues:

> [W]hen Aesop is bought by Xanthus, he has the appearance of the saviour god who arrives, guaranteeing food and sexual life, intimately related to the cycle of fecundity in nature. He has the ugly appearance of the ancient *pharmakos*, but is somebody described as a "demon" [*daimonion*] on account of his victories and his riddles; he is also described as *katharma*, an "impure object," like the *pharmakoi*, but he triumphs over his master and describe [sic] as *huperkatharma*, "more impure still." (280)

Aesop's adventures are connected with ritual *agones*, with the carnival: "the fable is the popular equivalent of the myth, the result of a split that created this sort of comic myth" (281). In Adrados's view, the fable's Oriental origins, depicting the wise advisor counseling the king, converged with original Greek elements to produce the paradigmatic Aesopian narrative: "There is a Greek Aesop underlying the Oriental character that merged with him" (284). Adrados sees an iambic, carnival, ritual Aesop, who, eventually, through the perspective of cynicism, achieves his critical distance on human culture: "Only through the work of the Cynics was the synthesis of the legend of Aesop with Oriental and Greek wisdom literature and with the theme of the journey achieved, allowing a satirical view of all strata of society" (665). The Cynics "add a touch of realism, of *parrhesia* and populism to the solemn figure of the sage" (ibid.).

Annabel Patterson, in her work on the fable in English literature, makes a claim for the subversive or at least "alternative" power of the fable tradition. She writes: "It is my hope . . . to recover (the Aesopian tradition) definitively as an alternative to the Platonic tradition, with its strong elitist basis."[14] Patterson usefully discusses the legacy of Aesop, and points to the ways in which Bakhtin's work illuminates the fable:

> For Aesop works a world marked by acts of excretion and in which body parts, especially those which Bakhtin called "the lower bodily stratum," are symbolic of human relations. The Life anticipated Bakhtin (whose own conceptions were shaped by a repressive culture) in seeing the "material bodily principle" as a populist form; the "grotesque realism" that makes the body and its functions unforgettable is also a political statement. (25)

Patterson shows how the beast fable evolved in early modern English literature as a populist voice or as the voice of an aristocracy silenced.

I am especially interested in the political valence of the fable; scholarship has tended to argue concerning this point that, as Annabel Patterson puts it, the Aesopian fable offers an alternative to the elitist tradition of Platonism. Others suggest that the fables represent an encrypted source of popular knowledge, concealed from the elite through its animal allegory. Such arguments emphasize a timeless, an ahistorical Aesop. I am more concerned with the social and political implications of the status of Aesop as slave and freedman than with his status as a paradigmatic scapegoat figure; the fable is more likely to be a hegemonic genre, especially in versions that depict an *agon*, a contest between two opponents, in which their relative value is established, rather than the voice of the poor, the people, the silenced majority of ancient society. In these fables, the species of animals correspond to kinds of human beings, so that there are natural aristocrats like the lion, natural slaves like the ants. The clever fox, like a slave, can maneuver in this universe, but his nature remains fixed, defined by birth as vulpine.[15]

Moreover, the fable form is implicated in arguments about slavery.[16] The view that slavery is natural for some fits well with elite arguments concerning the proper and natural domination and administration of the state, and the hegemony of the elite. The fable, with the fixed essences of different animal species, subtly supports arguments that blood should determine one's place in the city. Although Aesop was freed from slavery, his biography serves almost as a homeopathic gesture, a counter-effect that allows the fable itself to support hierarchy, both slavery and aristocracy, through narratives that in their form may present a victorious, sly fox, but that rely on essence. The essence of the fox is that he must be clever, since he will always retain his species' nature. Gregory Nagy argues, "The gaps that are bridged in his ainoi between animals and men and gods are bridged in the course of his *Life*."[17] But in fact, others, in everyday life, Aesop's audience, aristocrats, citizens, metics, and slaves, rarely bridge the gaps established among kinds in ancient societies, and his life story may serve as a counterexample for the fixity of kinds that the fables illustrate.

Although it is possible that some of the fable narratives derive from popular strata, the messages the fables convey are much more consistent with an antidemocratic, antityrannical, aristocratic strain in political culture, at least in the archaic and classical Greek worlds. Putting the arguments of the fable into the mouth of Aesop, an ex-slave, displaces the source of the stories. The fable constitutes a means for the elite strain in public debate to disguise itself and pose as populism, a sort of cynical, skeptical, playful recognition of the inevitabilities of social hierarchy, injustice, and hypocrisy.[18] Two famous fables:

> When the hares addressed a public meeting and claimed that all should have fair shares, the lions answered: "A good speech, Hairy-Feet, but it lacks claws and teeth such as we have."

> A vixen sneered at a lioness because she never bore more than one cub. "Only one," she replied, "but a lion."[19]

Fables sometimes illustrate the cleverness of the fox, and even allow for the possibility that the ferocious nature of the lion can be eroded through age and time. Yet they nonetheless stress the essential difference of fox and hare from lion. It has been argued that fables allow human readers to identify different aspects of themselves with different characteristics from the animal world.[20] On the other hand, accompanying and sometimes even overriding such slippage and fluidity is a different message, one of essentialism. The final import of such fables is that slaves, like all others in the *polis*, must know their place. They can, through the use of intelligence, wit, and cunning, evade the worst consequences of their station, but unlike Aesop, they cannot escape their nature, as finally attached to them as is the fox's coat to his back.

Comedy and the Fables

The telling of fables in many environments in classical texts calls on their association with Aesop the slave and freedman, and introduces ideas of natural difference. Ancient comedy had strong links with the traditions of the fable. Nagy suggests that the Archilochean *iambos*, blame poetry, may have evolved into "its newer form resembling comedy."[21] The choruses of Aristophanes' works, after whom the plays are often named by others, have their affinities with the fables in which animals speak like human beings; the beast fable, stories of animals interacting, serves as a matrix for old comedy as a whole. There are several moments in Aristophanic comedy in which the figure of Aesop is invoked.[22] Aristophanes alludes to Aesop in his comedy *The Birds* (651–53); Peisthetairos claims that the birds were once sovereigns of men and gods, citing Aesop as authority:[23]

> You're naturally ignorant and uninquisitive, and you haven't thumbed [*pepatekas*] your Aesop. He says in his fable that the Lark was the first of all birds to be born, before Earth; and then her father died of a disease, but there being no earth, he'd lain out for four days and she was at a loss what to do, until in desperation she buried her father in her own head. (*The Birds* 471–76)

The joke plays on the name of one of the demes of Attica, Kephale, "head." Also in this play, where the chorus is made up of singing, dancing birds, Peisthetairos refers to Aesop's fable of the fox and the eagle (651–53), fearing that he, wingless, will fare as badly in the land of the birds as did the fox when the eagle ate its cubs.

One of Aesop's last fables, told to the Delphians as they are about to execute him, is the story in which a dung beetle loaded with dung forces Zeus himself to break the eggs of the beetle's enemy, an eagle; this fable is alluded to several times in the course of Aristophanes' comedies. In *Lysistrata*, the women's chorus says that "she" will be to the eagle giving birth a dung beetle–midwife (*kantharos maieusomai*), that is, that she will destroy the offspring of her opponents. The line suggests that these women consider themselves another species, an enemy species, of the old men, as different from them as the dung beetle is from the eagle. The hero of Aristophanes' *Peace*, Trygaios, flies to the gods on the back of a dung beetle, who dominates the play's first scene. He is an ideal mount, since he feeds on his rider's excrement, and as we know from Aesop's fable, has been to visit Zeus before: "In Aesop's fables it's the only winged thing I could find that ever reached the gods" (129–30), says

Trygaios. There is much hilarity about this dung beetle: the need to refrain from defecation on the earth below, so the beetle will not be tempted back to land; the contentment of the beetle among the gods, where he will find the plastic, well-worked dung of Ganymede to his satisfaction, molded by the pederastic attentions of Zeus (724).

In the hands of Aristophanes the figures of animals, as choruses, inhabit the everyday life of the city, and bring the scatological, earthy, rural life of the citizen-farmer-soldier to life. Aristophanes also uses the fable as a genre internal to his comedies, deploying them as popular knowledge, and in a certain sense reinforcing his conservative arguments about kinds. As Philokleon, the father of *The Wasps*, has betrayed his free nature, becoming a slave to Cleon and the law courts, so the son tried to move up in the social hierarchy and live as a symposiastic aristocrat, both men failing to recognize their proper place in the world of the *polis*.

The figure of Aesop stalks Aristophanes' *Wasps*, a rich source for our understanding of ancient slavery. The accused in a legal case is said to tell Aesopian jokes (566–67); tales of a cat and a mouse are said not be appropriate in nouveau riche company (1182–85), although Aesopian or Sybaritic tales are useful for shrugging off injuries inflicted on others while drunk (1256–61). Philokleon uses the verb *alopekizdein*, "to behave like a fox, to play the fox," literally "to fox," at 1241.[24] After Philokleon returns from his symposium, drunk and disorderly, there is a flurry of allusions to Aesop.[25] He has a fight with a woman baker, and takes on the voice of Aesop to chastise her:

> When Aesop was walking home from dinner one evening, a bold and tipsy bitch [*kuon*] started barking at him. And he said, "Bitch, bitch, if you'd trade that nasty tongue of yours for some flour, I think you'd be showing some sense." (*The Wasps* 1401–5)

Philokleon is putting into practice his son's instructions about soothing the injured party with an Aesopian joke, but this retort only enrages the woman further, because she thinks he is mocking her, laughing at her because she works for a living. Having offended another accuser, he tries to fend him off with a "Sybaritic" fable, mentioned earlier, the moral of which is "Let each practice the craft he knows" (1431). The tag has interesting echoes in Plato's doctrines, his teaching that democracy is a ruinous form of government because every man and no expert practices the art of government. Allusions to Aesop strengthen the rhetorical naturalization and hierarchy of kinds.

The incident is capped by a speaking jug: "Lovekleon: 'Once upon a time in Sybaris a woman broke her pot.' Accuser: 'Witness, take note.' Lovekleon: 'So this pot told its companion to be a witness'" (1435–40). The demagogic speech that deploys the rhetoric of the fable emerges here, in this mock trial scene, in this play aimed at the law courts of Athens. The father Philokleon, slave to the law courts and to the demagogue Kleon, in his son's view, reverts to the fabulizing practices of the law courts and the popular assembly at the end. The ventriloquism of the talking jug, or the imagination of a time when not only animals but also things could speak in human language, recalls the utopian, prehistoric, golden-age fantasies of later comedy, in which food flies into the mouth of the diner, as well as the automata of the earliest of poems, the *Iliad*, where Hephaistos commands his servants to do his will.

The fable of the eagle and the dung beetle finds mention here as well, at the end, the climax of Aristophanes' *Wasps*. Philokleon stands accused by various characters, the baking girl, and another complainant, and his son announces that he is about to carry him inside for his own good. Philokleon or, as Jeffrey Henderson calls him, "Lovecleon," retorts:

> One time the Delphians accused Aesop—
> Loathecleon: I'm not interested!
> Lovecleon: —of stealing a bowl from the god. He told them how once
>   upon a time the beetle—
> Loathecleon: Damn, you'll be the death of me with these beetles of yours!
>   (1446–48)

The mention of Aesop's dung beetle, a stalling tactic with hints of excremental revenge, is the last straw, and Philokleon, like Aesop himself, is silenced. The play ends with the "cock-like" Phrunikos, and the mad, wild whirling dance of the sons of Karkinos the "crab."

For Aristophanes, the allusions to Aesop and his beasts bring a dimension of the popular into his plays, consonant with the obscenity and the everyday-life elements of his comedy. Yet Aristophanes also offers a critique of the present, of the new, set against the backdrop of the old ways, which he both mocks and demonstrates his allegiance to. Even though Sokrates is ridiculed in Aristophanes' *Clouds*, there is a certain consistency between the comic playwright's views and those of Plato, an antidemocratic, antidemagogic strain, exemplified in the notion that the cobbler should stick to his last. Aesopian allusions reinforce this view— that wasps are waspish, foxes vulpine, and that men like Philokleon and his son Bdelukleon do best when they maintain their essence. For Aristophanes, the essentialism of the beast fable implicitly, formally underlines the naturalization and essentializing of human kinds.

Aesop and Sokrates

Once again, the practice of Plato in relation to these questions of essence, here expressed in terms of Aesop and slavery, differs from the norm. The deployment of Aesopian themes and allusions in the Platonic corpus offers a popular, rhetorical version of many of the arguments Sokrates and his fellows develop in a more elaborate and logical form in the dialogues. Sokrates, ugly, a man of the people, and known for his wisdom, seems in some contexts to resemble Aesop himself, and such a resemblance speaks to the complex relationship Plato delineates between slavery and freedom elsewhere in his texts. In the *Republic*, Plato's Adeimantos refers to the fox of fable in his discussion of whether one should live virtuously, justly:

> For a front and show I must draw about myself a shadow outline of virtue but trail behind me the fox of the most sage Archilochus, shifty and bent on gain. (365c)

This fox exemplifies the true self of the unjust man, who conceals his nature; Adeimantos's is the realism of the citizens of the democracy as depicted by Plato, the corrupt facade of virtue displayed for the benefit of others. The real democrat is as self-interested and devious as the fox.

In Plato's work, as noted in chapter 7, freedom and slavery are not seen as absolute conditions but depend on each other, and may replace each other in the course of a soul's mortal passages. Plato seems to use the mention of Aesop as a figure for the release from slavery, which is for him bound up with the theme of the merely relative freedom possible in material existence. In the *Phaedo*, Sokrates mentions Aesop several times in a favorable light, awakening the theme of the freed slave. While waiting for his execution, he has been practicing and cultivating the arts, obeying the command of a dream, and has written a hymn in honor of Apollo.

> When I had finished my hymn, I reflected that a poet, if he is to be worthy of the name, ought to work on imaginative themes [*muthous*], not descriptive ones [*logous*], and I was not good at inventing stories [*muthologikos*]. So I availed myself of some of Aesop's fables which were ready to hand and familiar to me, and I versified the first of them that suggested themselves. You can tell Evenus this, Cebes, and bid him farewell from me, and tell him, if he is wise, to follow me as quickly as I can. I shall be going [*apeimi*] today, it seems; those are my country's orders. (61b)

In Greek the discussion of *muthos* and *logos* sets up a tension between fiction and reason that is immediately eroded by Sokrates' naming himself mythologue, a term that incorporates both elements of the distinction.[26] This passage may suggest the last scene recalled in the *Symposium*, in which the narrator reports: "Socrates was forcing them to admit that the same man might be capable of writing both comedy and tragedy—that the tragic poet might be a comedian as well" (223cd). The same man might be capable of *logos* and *muthos*, of reason and story; the philosopher might be a fabulist, even a slave.

Just before the exchange in the *Phaedo* about versifying the fables of Aesop, Sokrates invents a *mythos*, a story, that seems very un-Aesopian, uncharacteristic of the animal tales attributed to the Phrygian ex-slave. After dismissing his wife, Xanthippe, after having his chains removed, after receiving the news that he is to die on that day, that the boat sent to Delos in honor of Apollo had returned, and the city was free to execute him, Sokrates sets out the link between pleasure and pain in the form of a fable:

> Some of Crito's servants led her away crying hysterically. Socrates sat up on the bed and drew up his leg and massaged it, saying as he did so, What a queer [*atopon*] thing it is , my friends, this sensation which is popularly called pleasure! It is remarkable how closely it is connected with its conventional opposite, pain. They will never come to a man both at once, but if you pursue one of them and catch it, you are nearly always compelled to have the other as well; they are like two bodies attached to the same head. I am sure that if Aesop had thought of it he would have made up a fable [*muthon*] about them, something like this—the god wanted to stop their continual quarreling, and when he found that it was impossible, he fastened their heads together; so wherever one of them appears, the other is sure to follow after. (60b–c)

This *muthos* has little in common with the fables we inherit gathered under the name of Aesop, fables about foxes and hares and tortoises. Even the Aesopian fables told by Aristotle are characteristically inhabited by conversing animals, and in Aristophanes the fables called Aesopian have the qualities we recognize from their later translation or collection.[27] In contrast, Sokrates' Aesopian fable is a Platonic myth, resembling in particular the story Aristophanes tells in the *Symposium*, of the three globular beings each divided in two by Zeus and forever after in search of their lost other halves (189d–193d). In the *Phaedo*, the creature is like a conjoined twin, a being with two heads, a mixture of pleasure and pain.[28] Perhaps Sokrates' command to Crito to sacrifice a cock after his death might be linked to his fable, which connects pleasure and pain: pleasure and pain are linked like slavery and freedom. The human soul, fettered and enslaved to the body, will be freed by death as Aesop the slave was freed to tell his stories.

Aristotle as Fabulist

Aristotle's discussion of fables characterizes them as common knowledge, accepted truths, evoking the most conventional of opinions, including acceptance of an absolute hierarchical difference among kinds of human beings, and therefore useful for argument. He locates the fable in the field of rhetoric; the fable is a mode of persuasion, especially attractive in popular situations in which the audience has not been trained in the analysis of logical proofs. In the *Rhetoric*, he advocates the use of fables, called *logoi*, in his discussion of proofs. Among proofs are examples; among examples things that happened before, as well as invented examples; among the latter *parabole* (comparison) and *logoi* (stories or fables), "such as those of Aesop and the Libyan":

> A fable [*logos*], to give an example, is that of Stesichorus concerning Phalaris, or that of Aesop on behalf of the demagogue. For Stesichorus, when the people of Himera had chosen Phalaris dictator and were on the point of giving him a body-guard, after many arguments related a fable to them: "A horse was in sole occupation of a meadow. A stag having come and done much damage to the pasture, the horse, wishing to avenge himself on the stag, asked a man whether he could help him to punish the stag. The man consented, on condition that the horse submitted to the bit and allowed him to mount him javelins in hand. The horse agreed to the terms and the man mounted him, but instead of obtaining vengeance on the stag, the horse from that time became the man's slave [*edouleusen*]. So then," said he, "do you take care lest, in your desire to avenge yourself on the enemy, you be treated like the horse. You already have the bit, since you have chosen a dictator [*strategon autokratora*]; if you give him a body-guard and allow him to mount you, you will at once be the slaves [*douleusete*] of Phalaris." (1393 b 5–6)

This story explicitly connects the fable of Stesichorus with a metaphorical form of slavery, like that deployed by the ancient historians and rhetoricians, and warns the free citizens, like horses, not to enter willingly into slavery, to maintain their place in the hierarchy, better suffering the depredations of the staglike enemy than subjecting themselves to a master. The fable recalls a story told by Herodotus describing the ascension to power of the Athenian tyrant Peisistratos, who wounded himself and his mules, asked for a bodyguard from the people, and obtained a guard that seized the Akropolis and made Peisistratos ruler (1.59). Phalaris similarly subdued and dominated the people of Himera, and was later notorious for commissioning a brazen bull with which to torture his enemies, then putting the maker in it as the bull's first victim.

This fable is somewhat unusual in that it involves interaction between the human and the animal world. Often the setting of fables concerns no human beings at all; the animals live amongst themselves without the intervention of men or gods. This fable crosses a line, that border between animal and human, and suggests that slavery is an ever-present possibility, a status analogous to that of the domesticated animal. Yet implicit in the fable world is a lost utopian autonomy of the animals. Aristotle's ventriloquism of Stesichorus uses the diction of slavery, the enslavement of the animal by the human, to illustrate the irreversibility of the rider's domination of the horse. Once the animal falls under the control of the superior technology of the man, his bridle, he is lost.

The fable posits a difference of kinds among the animals. The horse, associated often with aristocratic ways of life in the classical city, inhabits the meadow, an enclosed space, but is vulnerable to the depredations of the stag. The stag, a wild creature, equipped with sharp hooves and antlers, possesses weapons that can damage the tranquility of the horse. The *demos*, threatened from outside by what seems like wild domination, is like the horse: rather than tolerating such losses as an inevitable fact of nature, it might instead choose the greater of two evils; the bodyguard, like a bridle, the tool that will seal their domination, will force them into slavery, a slavery ironically of their own choosing. Stesichorus, poet and storyteller, stands outside the narrative as advisor, using the rhetorical device of the fable as a monitory allegory. The fable ambiguously refers to essence, the differing kinds of animals made analogous to differences between *demos* and dictator; yet slavery can intervene and change the relationship between these kinds, forever subordinating *demos* to dictator. The ordinary struggle among animal species is encoded as natural; the enslavement of free men borders on the unnatural, like the intrusion of man into the animal world, upsetting its order.

Aristotle offers another example of a fable, this one involving Aesop himself:

Aesop, when defending at Samos a demagogue who was being tried for his life, related the following anecdote. "A fox, while crossing a river, was driven into a ravine. Being unable to get out, she was for a long time in sore distress, and a number of dog-fleas clung to her skin. A hedgehog, wandering about, saw her and, moved with compassion, asked her if he should remove the fleas. The fox refused and when the hedgehog asked the reason, she answered: 'They are already full of me and draw little blood; but if you take them away, others will come that are hungry and will drain what remains to me.' You in like manner, O Samians, will suffer no more harm from this man, for he is wealthy; but if you put him to death, others will come who are poor, who will steal and squander your public funds." (1393b6–1394a7)

This fable is remarkable for its cynicism. In the legal context, Aesop makes an argument similar to that of Stesichorus in the political. Both fables point to the advantage of the lesser of two evils. The fox prefers the enemy that she knows, those fleas accustomed to preying on her, to those untried. The characters in this fable occur together in another fable, attributed to Archilochus, in which the poet says that the fox knows many things, the hedgehog one, one big one.[29] Here the hedgehog moves beyond his unitary practice, the curling up in a ball and projecting his spines to protect himself, to offer assistance to his presumed erstwhile enemy, the fox, who is, with his many tricks, baffled by the one big trick of the hedgehog. This generous hedgehog is rebuffed by the fox with his familiar fleas.

Both these fables are told in political contexts, although the second has a secondary legal setting, in which the demagogue is on trial, being defended by the former slave, Aesop. In both cases an issue is set before the people, the *demos*; in both cases they are to decide the fate of a single man who stands out from the crowd, a tyrant or a demagogue. In both cases the speaker is named: in the first case as the ally of the people against the tyrant, in the second as the defender of the demagogue against the people. Stesichorus the poet stands above the crowd, reminding them of certain home truths about animals and men. In the reversal of the second fable, the single demagogue on trial is likened to a multitude, while the fleas that besiege the single fox resemble the plural *demos*, the city of Samians. Aesop the ugly slave or freedman is presumably beneath the status of the free citizens of Samos, yet his cleverness and eloquence provide a context for his didactic account, urging the familiar torment of the satiated demagogue-fleas.

What are the political connotations of these stories in Aristotle's view? After telling these two fables, he says: "Fables are suited for public speaking" [*eisi d'hoi logoi demegorikoi*] (Cf. Plato, *Gorgias* 482e). They have the advantage over historical events, for comparison, in that they can be invented by the speaker. And it is easier, he says, for one who studies philosophy to see the likeness. The superior man, the man who deploys rhetoric to persuade others, can, like Aesop, invent stories to sway his listeners, who are easily moved. Such stories reify species difference and press a conservative politics, a resistance to change.

Aristotle also refers to the use of the fable in his discussion of the institution of ostracism in the *Politics;* he calls attention to the possibility of men outstanding in virtue occurring in the polity, too few, or just one, not enough to make up a state on their own, like a "god among men." It is impossible to legislate for such persons, "for probably they would say what in the story of Antisthenes the lions said when the hares made speeches in the assembly and demanded that all should have equality. 'Where are your claws and teeth?'" (*Politics* 3.8 1284a) This too is a conservative use of the fable, enforcing an elite view of natural difference, the essential, species superiority, and the rule of force, of the stronger over the weak. While the *Rhetoric*'s fables urge no change, a policy of "better-the-devil-you-know," this fable reveals the necessity for such an attitude, exposing the naturally predatory nature of superior or dominant creations like the lion and the tyrant. Such "proofs," suitable for moving the masses, are consistent with an aristocratic, antidemocratic, antityrannical perspective. The fact that Aristotle places one of these fables in the mouth of Aesop does not make them "popular," or even derived ultimately from the oral culture of the oppressed. Their form evokes reaction from the ordinary listener, but their import finally serves the interests of the conservative philosophical tradition.

❖ ❖ ❖

IT IS POSSIBLE to read the fables ahistorically and typologically, as offering an exercise in defining universal kinds of human character. M. T. W. Arnheim states this bluntly: "The use of animals instead of people was undoubtedly intended to facilitate the representation of easily recognisable human character-types . . . once a wolf, always a wolf."[30] Like some other writers on Aesop's fables, Arnheim assumes an author, a subject, a consistent point of view in the collection attributed to Aesop: after pointing out an inconsistency between two of the collected stories, the author writes that "this does not of course mean that Aesop is in any way inconsistent in his views" (10). But there is no "author" Aesop; rather, the stories themselves stand for him. And in the fables there are types of beings, some lupine, some leonine. One of the extant fables extends this essentialism, revealing the political valence of typology:

> At the direction of Zeus, Prometheus fashioned men and beasts. But when Zeus saw that there were more of the dumb animals, he ordered him to destroy some of the beasts and make them over into men. When he did as he was told, it turned out that the ones who had not been fashioned as men from the start had human form but were bestial in spirit. (240)[31]

This fable would seem to confirm Aristotle's argument, discussed in chapter 9, for the existence of natural slavery, of a population of bestial natural slaves, born to serve free men. Rather than some universal psychologizing or characterological typology, in antiquity the naturalization of difference—especially in this genre, attributed to the former slave Aesop—bears on questions of status, class, and the difference between slave and free. The fable calls up the question of slavery, naturalizes hierarchy, and attributes essential differences to the species of animals in its narratives and, by extension, to classes of human beings. Just as the wolf is always a wolf, so the aristocrat is always an aristocrat; just as the tortoise is always a tortoise, so the slave, unlike the exceptional Aesop, is born, lives, and dies a slave, naturally, essentially servile as the fox is vulpine. Unlike Babe the sheep-herding pig, the hero of a recent movie, an animal fable in its own right, ancient fabulous animals enact their species being without deviation.

Uncle Remus

The American example of the beast fable offers an intriguing analogue with the ancient tradition of fables as tales told by slaves or freed slaves. Joel Chandler Harris, a favorite of Teddy Roosevelt, wrote down the canonical American animal fables, ventriloquized in the mouth of the ex-slave Uncle Remus. The old black man tells his stories to a young white boy, stories of Brer Fox and Brer Rabbit, and of the victories of the clever rabbit over his stronger antagonists. Alice Walker recalls seeing the Disney film *Song of the South*, which represents the Uncle Remus stories in animated form, which she calls "vastly alienating."[32] Dialect and garbled forms of high diction mark Harris's texts, tales that, as Walker and others point out, appropriate the oral and popular culture of the black antebellum and Reconstruction South. Florence Baer has shown that many of the animal tales of Uncle Remus can be traced back to Africa.[33]

The stories themselves, collected from slaves and former slaves by the white journalist Harris, contain elements of folklore from Africa preserved by African and African American storytellers over centuries. What is most interesting about the Uncle Remus stories in the context of the Aesopian tradition is that once again, fables are associated with a freed slave narrator. The framing of the Uncle Remus stories sets the ex-slave firmly in place as the teller of the tales. He speaks to the young white boy as a sort of oracle, offering moral lessons, continually stressing the survival and resilience of Brer Rabbit in the face of persecution and humiliation by other animals. In *Legends of the Old Plantation*, for example, the story formally entitled "Uncle Remus Initiates the Little Boy" ends with the voice of the ex-slave: "wid dat Brer Rabbit gallop off home. En Brer Fox ain't never kotch 'im yit, en w'at's mo', honey, he ain't gwineter."[34] In "Mr. Rabbit Nibbles Up the Butter," in which Brer Possum burns to death for consuming the common store, a crime actually committed by Brer Rabbit, who "scrape it clean en lick it dry, en den he go back ter wuk lookin' mo' samer dan a nigger w'at de patter-rollers bin had holt un" (100), Uncle Remus concludes: "In dis worril, lots er fokes is gotter suffer fer udder fokes sins. Look like hit's mighty on-wrong; but hit's des dat away" (102).

Anthropologist James Scott cites slave pilfering as an example of what he calls a "hidden transcript": "discourse that takes place 'offstage,' beyond direct observation by powerholders."[35] "Publicly . . . the master's definition of *theft* prevailed. We know enough, however, to surmise that, behind the scenes, theft was seen as simply taking back the product of one's labor. We also know that the semiclandestine culture of the slaves encouraged and celebrated theft from the masters and morally reproved any slave who would dare expose such a theft" (188). Joel Chandler Harris exhibits a paternalism and condescension toward Remus, who accepts the injustice of misdirected punishment for theft. Wayne Mixon argues in Harris's defense that in the course of the publication of the stories, which appeared in several volumes at the end of the nineteenth century, Harris became less and less optimistic about his project of reconciliation between black and white in the South: "As Remus develops in his role as a teller of animal legends, his relationship with the white world becomes increasingly problematic."[36]

Scholars who work on the Uncle Remus tales may argue about the political affiliations of Harris. But once again, what interests me most is their telling by a freed slave, and their beast fable form, which once again is essentializing, reifying the difference between black and white Americans through the analogy with animal species. Just as Brer Fox is always a fox, and Brer Rabbit always a rabbit, so there is a formal analogy between the species of animals and the different kinds of people, African American and white American. Species retain their specificity, interact, but do not mix. The tales may elicit enjoyment of the cleverness and survival of the rabbit, and of his subversive genius. But in the world of the Jim Crow code, the form of the fables stresses the discrete nature of species; embedded in their telling is a message of absolute, natural difference. Different species do not reproductively mix. And so it is in the ancient fables that sustain an essential grading of kinds of beasts, separation and a claim concerning the natural superiority of humankind over all the beasts. Rather than a discourse of subversion, the fable seems to be a discourse of resignation, of the fertile possibilities inherent in negotiation by the lower orders among themselves and with their betters, but with kinds kept always separate, lacking a discourse of intercourse, mixture, or metamorphosis. While Aesop and Uncle Remus, framers of the tales, may be freed, the various creatures of the fables cannot change their nature. The fox may be clever, but he will never be a lion. Finally, the fable naturalizes hierarchy, and Aesop the freedman, ethnographer of the fox, records for his audience the inevitability of degree.

9   ON ARISTOTLE

Or, The Political Theory of Possessive Mastery

Socrates: "[W]ho would care to have a man in his house who wants to do no work and has a weakness for high living? But now let us see how masters treat such servants [*oiketais*]. Do they not starve them to keep them from immorality, lock up the stores to stop their stealing, clap fetters on them so that they can't run away, and beat the laziness out of them with whips?"

—Xenophon, *Memorabilia* 2.1.16

"Antisthenes," Socrates said, "have friends like servants their own values? For one servant, I suppose, may be worth two minas, another less than half a mina, another five minas, another no less than ten. Nicias, son of Niceratus, is said to have given a whole talent for a manager of his silver-mine. So I am led to inquire whether friends too may not differ in value." (2.5.2)

IN THIS chapter, I argue that a perspective informed by modern "racial" slavery, a slavery based on color difference, affects readings of Aristotle's work on politics and slavery. The African slaves of modernity stand between us and the ancient text, interfering with the analysis and interpretation of Aristotle's work. Some scholars' will both to justify and somehow to redeem the experience of slavery for Africans and African Americans has resulted in a focus on the issue of natural slavery in Aristotle's work. So-called natural slavery is in fact a relatively minor issue in his political theory, overshadowed by the ancient philosopher's rhetorical positioning of slavery as the foundation of human social relations. In other discussions of the issue of personhood in ancient philosophy, also implicating Aristotle, slaves become invisible. Aristotle offers an argument on natural slavery almost in passing, in the course of describing the good life, the potential for happiness in the life of a free man, the only person who mattered in antiquity: a life realized through marriage, politics, mastery, and the possession of goods, including slaves, the results of the will to possess, the art or science of acquisition.

Malcolm Bull argues that Aristotle is the source of both a multiple and a unitary view of the self, and that there are advantages to be had in a conception of the self as multiple, in a multiplicity that he attributes theoretically to models dependent on slavery, on divided slave consciousness.[1] In his critique of the work of Charles Taylor and Alasdair MacIntyre, he suggests that both philosophers rely on a unitary conception of self, and that such a description excludes many human subjects. Using Aristotle's work in the *Politics*, which distinguishes between the actual and the natural slave, Bull suggests that it is the unitary soul of the master that takes the place of the soul in the *natural* slave, governing the slave's body as the master's soul rules his own body. In his view, Aristotle suggests that only a slave by nature, not governed by his own soul, is available so to be governed by a master; if the enslaved person ruled his own body with his own soul, there would be no place for the soul of the master in the slave's body.

Bull goes on to connect Aristotle's argument about the allegedly multiple soul of the slave in ancient Greek thought to the master-slave dialectic in Hegel, arguing that Hegel is influenced not only by notions of animal magnetism, in which the soul of the magnetizer enters the body and cohabits with the soul of the somnambulist, but also that the microcosm-macrocosm analogy found in Aristotle, concerning the parallel between governance of an individual's body by his soul and the governance of a natural slave's body by the master's soul, leads Hegel to posit a complex interpersonal interaction, resembling an intrapersonal coming to consciousness. The master and slave interact, the slave realizes himself through labor and comes to recognize not only his own self-consciousness but eventually that of the master as well. Such a recognition frees him.

This process of emancipation provides a model for the coming to consciousness within the individual, who similarly has a dual consciousness, eventually recognizing his own self-consciousness, then coming to a recognition of universal self-consciousness. Bull further traces this lineage, from Aristotle's double-souled creature, through Hegel, to W. E. B. DuBois's description of postemancipation consciousness in African Americans, the double consciousness, the veil that defines the psychic existence of what he calls the negro.[2] These three thinkers provide examples of a multiple self, all three based on slave consciousness, which Bull wants to celebrate for its emancipatory potential in contrast with the unitary self valued by Taylor and MacIntyre. Bull contrasts the portraits of the divided consciousness exemplified in the slave with another line, which he also traces from Aristotle, who argues in *De Anima*, a very different text from the *Politics*, for an ultimately unitary soul. This lineage passes through Nietzsche, who in Bull's view celebrates a unified, aristocratic, masterful self, like the self of Taylor and MacIntyre.

Problems arise with Bull's description of Aristotle, problems that illuminate the interested readings modern thinkers make of ancient society and slavery's place in it. The elaborate attempts to clarify Aristotle's theory as resting on the clear conceptualization of "natural slavery" betray a very different set of interests and passions from those of ancient Greece. For proslavery thinkers of modernity, the notion of natural slaves allows for a racial discrimination between the naturally slavish and the naturally free, mapped on the difference between black Africans and their white masters. For thinkers like DuBois and Bull, recuperating a positive moment in the experience of modern slavery, focus on natural slavery similarly depends on the racist opposition of modern slavery, not a matter of interest for ancient theory.

Aristotle's account is far more complex and contradictory than Bull allows. As Peter Garnsey, in his recent *Ideas of Slavery from Aristotle to Augustine*, writes, "Natural slavery as presented by Aristotle is a battered shipwreck of a theory."[3] In fact, there is no coherent, consistent justification for natural slavery in Aristotle's work. Natural slaves are intermittently deficient in reason, in deliberative powers, fuzzily indistinguishable from animals (111). The idea of the natural slave appears only in the *Politics:*

> The union of natural [*phusei*] ruler and natural subject for the sake of security (for one that can foresee with his mind is naturally ruler and naturally master, and one that can do these things with his body is subject and naturally a slave . . .) (*Politics* 1252a)

> One who is a human being belonging by nature [*phuseis*] not to himself but to another is by nature a slave . . . in some cases things are marked out from the moment of birth to rule or to be ruled. (1254a)

> All men that differ as widely as the soul does from the body and the human being from the lower animal . . . these are by nature [*phusei*] slaves, for whom to be governed by this kind of authority is advantageous. (1254b)

The discussion of "natural" slaves is scattered, relatively incoherent, and dispersed in Aristotle's reasoning about slaves and free men. Garnsey points out the inconsistencies between the *Politics* and Aristotle's ethical treatises, and concludes that his views about natural slavery constitute a response to some contemporary exchange about the possibly conventional nature of slavery: "Natural slave theory offered ideological support to slaveowners rather than prescriptions for or descriptions of actual master/slave relationships."[4] But if we take Aristotle's discussion of *Politics* as a whole, masters and slaves constitute a fundamental pairing, and a trope that justifies other forms of inequality, while the issue of natural slavery, of whether some persons are "natural slaves," is discussed only briefly.

What I am interested in here is the blind spot of many theorists of slavery, who do not discuss the naturalized will to acquire and to own another human being, to extend one's own soul to the body of another, to govern the body of another as one's own. Such an acquisitive drive is something that the ancient philosopher Aristotle takes for granted but which is rarely acknowledged in readings of his texts. There was of course a simple economic benefit in owning a slave. Slaves in antiquity were relatively expensive and valuable property. Although subject to unfortunate depreciation if acquired at a certain point in their life cycles, they were in economic terms decidedly worth owning. Orlando Patterson adds, in *Slavery and Social Death*, that "it is not unreasonable to speculate that slaves did more than help in meeting material needs, they also satisfied a psychological need to dominate."[5] Even such a psychologizing account, however, is foreign to the ancient world; the terms by which a life was evaluated as satisfactory or happy did not involve such psychological needs as domination per se. Aristotle assumes the naturalness of relations of *ruling* in all human institutions. The psyche of the free slave owner did not "need" to dominate another human being; a happy man exercised the arts of ruling, and of acquiring and possessing what he ruled.

In his important book *Personality in Greek Epic, Tragedy and Philosophy*, Christopher Gill argues for a historical difference marking modern ideas of the person and those we encounter in the texts of ancient Greece.[6] His argument rests on the contrast between the modern "subjective-individualist" conception of the person and the ancient Greek "objective-participant" conception (11). Modern readers may be more familiar with the individualist notions governing our own personhood, notions that seem to flow from the personhood described by C. P. MacPherson: being conscious of oneself as an "I," "grounding one's moral life by a specially individual stance," disinterested moral rationality based on abstraction from attachments and emotions, acting autonomously in establishing moral principles for oneself, possessing a unique personal identity (11). Gill calls attention to contrasting features of the ancient model: action on the basis of reasons, ethical life expressed in engagement with an interpersonal role, in debate about such participation, psycho-ethical life conceived as a dialogue between parts of the psyche, realization of humanness through rule by reason, depending on interactive and reflective discourse, reason as reflective understanding of participation in other forms of being, animal and divine.

One element of these latter definitions struck me particularly. Gill, striving for gender balance or neutrality in proper feminist mode, uses the masculine and feminine personal pronouns interchangeably in his text: "I use she/he and her/him indifferently as indefinite personal pronouns, even when summarizing authors (ancient or modern) who use only masculine forms for this purpose. When translating ancient authors, I retain their practice of using masculine forms for this purpose" (9 n. 26).[7] He clarifies his view of the "objective-participant" conception in the fourth of five "themes":

4. To be human is to be capable, in principle again, of becoming fully "reason-ruled." But the extent to which any given human being is able to develop in this way depends on the extent to which she is able to participate effectively in these types of interactive and reflective discourse. (12)

This is an important move, one in which the modern scholar, informed by feminism, properly wants to avoid sexist language in discussing the matters at hand. Yet it seems to me that it in fact calls attention to a crucial historical difference not really taken account of in Gill's distinctions between modern and ancient persons. That is, women do not speak for themselves in philosophical discourses in antiquity. Are they seen as capable of participating "effectively in these types of interactive and reflective discourse"? Are women persons, to use Gill's term?

Helene Foley has written of how women characters in Greek tragedy have moral and ethical lives, of how they conduct themselves as human beings, make arguments, make choices based on ethical principles.[8] Yet women characters, played by male actors in roles written by male tragedians, may represent not so much the personhood of women as such but rather a gendered, allegorical archaism even within the studied archaism of the narratives of Greek tragedy itself. If Antigone, as I have argued elsewhere, represents not women per se but woman as a sign of aristocratic culture, kinship, and the valorization of blood and family over political culture, then the representation of her ethical life is not that of a person but rather a move in a field of discourses in which Sophocles is making an enunciation of a certain kind.[9]

But my stronger argument concerns not women, and the question of whether they as human beings can be seen to have a share in the "objective-participant" conception of personhood in Greek antiquity, but whether their exclusion from this description might point to another category, that of slaves, which included women and men, girls and boys. Slaves are certainly human beings (*anthropoi*) in the view of theorists in ancient culture. Yet are they persons? And if not, who does count as a person in this culture, and what are the ideological and social relations that isolate him as the only "person"?

I want to consider this question in relation to Aristotle's *Politics*, and the ways in which he formulates his ideas about households, families, and polities.[10] Gill's model points to crucial differences between us and the Greeks. No one would, I think, want to argue in favor of adopting the ancient model, although it does seem to have some affinities with the sort of moral reasoning that theorists like Carol Gilligan attribute to women in our culture, in contrast with that of men. However, like Foucault, like Aristotle and Plato and other ancient writers, Gill assumes that ancient and modern persons are those privileged and philosophical human beings who have the opportunity to participate in dialogue, have access to modes of reasoning based on dialogue, and a reflective relationship to their own existence. In a culture that excludes women and slaves from participation in political life, in philosophical conversation, in the leisure of dialogue allowing for the cultivation of a ruling and reasoning self, and that furthermore defines as persons only those beings who do share in these practices, can we say that women and slaves, while human beings, are persons? [11]

Gill disregards a central feature of Greek poetic and social and philosophical reflection on the idea of personhood: only the free male Greek citizen is a person in this world, and his own "participant-objectivist" conception of the person describes only such a being.[12] Gill's view helps me to articulate an argument made before and elsewhere, that persons in antiquity are not all the human beings around, that persons as such may not even exist, since they seem to be an effect of what Gill calls the "subjectivist-individualist" conception. He wants to argue for normative concepts, for rational, ethical consideration about human interactions, and not to take for granted the idea of the person at all, arguing for a comparative study of the person in different cultural settings, not accepting the notion of a person but rather of "normative concepts" in ancient thought.

Which is it? Are there always persons, given by nature but defined differently? Or are persons the effect of subjective individualism? For example, "the objective-participant and subjective-individualist conceptions of the person are offered here not as general categories to be applied across human cultures, but for a different, and more limited, purpose." [13] Earlier Gill explains that "the concept of 'person' [in modern philosophy] belongs to the class of normative concepts which are taken to be grounded on facts of nature and, by being so grounded, to be able to legitimate, supplement, or revise, conventional ethical norms. I also

think that Greek philosophical ideas about normative concepts can rea-
sonably be put in this same general class, and that, to this degree, we have
the basis of comparison between the two kinds of concepts" (403). In any
case, to my mind there is a discourse about power, mastery, gender, and
slavery that is masked by this discussion. The "objective-participant"
person is not just considering objective notions of the ethical, the good
life, not just participating in discussion about these matters with his
peers; he is also master of slaves, husband of his wife, father of his children, head of his household, and therefore in possession of or ruling
others who are not candidates for personhood in this extended sense.
The feminist gesture of using the feminine pronoun covers up this implicit situation of power, and justifies Foucault's discussion, in *The Use of
Pleasure*, of a philosophical self or person defined by its relationships to
diet, household and wife, boys, and eros.[14] Gill is in fact also effacing the
exclusion of these others from participation in personhood, but nonetheless describing the social circumstances of the invention of the philosophical, objective, participant person, who acquires and owns slaves,
naturally. What I will argue is that most ancient philosophical thinking
takes for granted the existence and rightness of slavery, makes assumptions about personhood based on it, and defines some human beings,
slaves, as outside its terms.

Aristotle's *Politics* is his most sustained text on life in a Greek *polis*.[15]
It is my hypothesis that the person, the human being defined in the objective-participant conception so well described by Gill, is in fact always
the master to the slave, always the husband to the wife, and that it is in
fact possession of slave and of wife that characterizes the personhood of
a person in this culture and distinguishes him from other human beings
who can never achieve this status. From the very beginning of the *Politics*, Aristotle focuses not on the single human being but rather on the
first couplings *(koinoniai)* that human beings form:

> The first coupling together of persons [*syndyazesthai*] then to which ne-
> cessity gives rise is that between those who are unable to exist without one
> another, namely the union of female and male for the continuance of the
> species . . . , and the union of natural ruler and natural subject for the sake
> of security (for one that can foresee with his mind is naturally ruler and
> naturally master, and one that can do these things with his body is sub-
> ject and naturally a slave; so that master and slave have the same interest).
> (1252a4)

The primary associations of human existence, then, are heterosexual
union and the master-slave relationship; Aristotle begins not with the
individual but with these "couplings," these pairings. There is no dis-

cussion of the individual as the smallest unit; human beings are always already in relation and association with one another. And their relations are always already about ruling and being ruled.

In his discussion of the household, the *oikos*, the next highest unit, part of the village, then the *polis*, Aristotle also claims that the *polis* is "prior in nature to the household and to each of us individually" (1253a), because a whole is necessarily prior to its part. Gill's arguments about personhood as objective-participant are supported here, although in fact the very notion of personhood seems overly subjective, since what the ancient thinker contends is that *polis* and association precede the individual, who is not theorized within this system:

> The state is also prior by nature to the individual [*hekastos*]; for if each individual when separate is not self-sufficient, he must be related to the whole state as other parts are to their whole, while a man who is incapable of entering into partnership, or who is so self-sufficing that he has no need to do so, is no part of a state, so that he must be either a lower animal or a god. (1253a)

A being, understood as such, in isolation, is not a human being but rather bestial or divine, slave or god like Aristophanes' Xanthias and Dionysus in *The Frogs*. There is no prior human individual, only associations that include human beings. And the master-slave association is one of the two most basic associations, in Aristotle's view.

The *polis* precedes the household; the household "in its perfect form consists of slaves and freemen" (1253b).

> The investigation of everything should begin with its smallest parts, and the primary and smallest parts of the household are master and slave, husband and wife, father and children. (1253b)

In this analytic moment, the master-slave association has assumed priority over the association of husband and wife for the purposes of reproduction. Also worthy of note is the fact that in these three relationships, there is the one person who participates in all three, one man who is simultaneously master, husband, and father, while his partners in these three relationships differ. There are certain ambiguities for the master-husband-father inherent in the household with slaves, since the master can be the partner of a slave for purposes of pleasure or reproduction, and since the offspring of an association between master and female slave will yield children, children who are not only the master's children but also his slaves.

At another moment in the *Politics*, Aristotle reviews the importance of the master-slave relationship. He is discussing the state, the *polis*, and the fact that it consists of unlike persons:

> [J]ust as an animal (to take this example first) consists of soul and body, and a soul of reason and appetite, and a household of husband and wife and [ownership involves] master and slave, in the same manner a state consists of all these persons. (1276b–1277a)

The paradigm master and slave, set last in this list, seems the fundamental one, emphatic in its placement, sealing the inevitability of the rest. These relationships, all hierarchical, are naturalized by the obvious pairing of master and slave. And of course the extension of this duality, into the opposition of soul and body, within the soul of reason and appetite, in the household between husband and wife, is modeled by the fact, the existence of slavery.[16] Just as it is proper for the master to rule the slave, so soul must rule body, reason must rule appetite, husband rule wife.

> [T]he soul by nature contains a part that rules and a part that is ruled, to which we assign different virtues, that is, the virtue of the rational and of the irrational. It is clear then that the case is the same also with the other instances of ruler and ruled. For the free rules the slave, the male the female, and the man the child in a different way. (*Politics* 1260a)

Slavery founds, grounds, justifies, and legitimizes all the relationships of domination that define social existence and even the proper governance of the internal relations of the soul.

The master possesses the *arkhe despotike*, the authority of the master. He exercises this authority over the work of the household, knowing not how to execute that work but rather how to command and use it. The slaves know how to perform menial tasks, and there are several kinds of slave, among them handicraftsmen (*khernetes*) (1277ab). Aristotle points out that before "extreme democracy" developed, manual laborers—because, presumably, they were like such slaves—were not admitted to state office. Men fit for citizenship ought not to learn such tasks, "for then it ceases to be a case of the one party being master and the other slave" (1277b). The *polis* properly purifies itself of those tracing their ancestry back to slaves and freedmen (1278a). Discussing various forms of rule (*arkhe*), Aristotle begins with the rule of the master over the slave, and only then extends his discussion to other forms of authority:

> The authority of a master over a slave [*he despoteia*], although in truth when both master and slave are designed by nature for their positions, their interests are the same, nevertheless governs in the greater degree with a view to the interest of the master, but incidentally with a view to

that of the slave, for if the slave deteriorates the position of the master cannot be saved from injury. (1278b)

Aristotle makes this characteristic move again and again; as he discusses politics, the proper situation of the *zoon politikon* who is the free Greek man, he begins with the master-slave relationship, moves to the husband and wife relationship, or to the soul/body, reason/appetite dualism, always grounding exposition in the inevitability of the master/slave dominance, as if it justified, explained, and illustrated the logic of what he proceeds to discuss. Here he goes from slave to wife and children to the state, arguing that constitutions ought to provide for the common interest of ruler and ruled, rather than serving only the advantage of the ruler. His is a sort of synecdochic logic, a justification of various relationships through the deployment of this grounding one. The master-slave relationship is part of the household, and the household is part of the state; the logic of the one founds the logic of the larger community. Rule is justified by the naturalness of slavery; rhetorically, slavery, or rather *despoteia* (mastery), is a kind of proof, a shorthand that explains and accounts for other forms of governance.

Echoing remarks he makes in the *Nicomachean Ethics* about the impossibility of slaves achieving happiness (1177a), Aristotle denies that slaves could constitute a state:

> [I]f . . . the state was formed not for the sake of life only but rather for the good life (for otherwise a collection of slaves or of lower animals would be a state [*polis*]), but as it is, it is not a state, because slaves and animals have no share in well-being or in purposive life. (*Politics* 1280a)

> [A] state consisting entirely of poor men would not be a state, any more than one consisting of slaves. (1283a)

Nor, one might assume, could there be a state, a *polis*, a "city," consisting only of freemen, only of masters, or indeed only of husbands without wives, although interestingly enough, the master-slave relationship appears more frequently than that of husband and wife. Is it because the master-slave relationship must be rhetorically naturalized with more effort than that of the heterosexual reproductive union? Or is it even more inevitable, more "natural," than the marital heterosexual dyad, in a world which of course includes many other sorts of relationships, the *eromenos/erastes* dyad of ancient pederasty, for example?

The city, the *polis*, the "state," must consist of these relationships of ruler and ruled, of varieties of domination and possession; difference constitutes the state, differences of power, of rulership, the presence of both ruler and ruled, owner and owned, whether the ruler is the master, the monarch or the *demos*, the people. A homogeneous state cannot be; partnerships are founded not on equality but on inequality of power, and it is this that is most fundamental in Aristotle's notion of *Politics:* "A collection of persons all alike does not constitute a state" (1261a). (And: "components which are to make up a unity must differ in kind" [ibid.].) The crucial point is that there be difference, difference in kind, difference in power, rule, and subordination, and therefore hierarchy. For Aristotle democracy is not government by equals, but rather a deviant, corrupt *politeia*, where the *demos* governs for its own advantage, for the advantage of the poor. To justify his argument he recounts the fable cited earlier, in which the lions say to hares calling for equality: "Where are your claws and teeth?" (1284a) The essentializing and naturalizing of species difference in the fable finds its echo in the political theory of hierarchy, ruling, and possession.

In discussing the proper forms of constitutions, Aristotle clarifies what he means by democracy, a deviation from the constitutional form, the *politeia*. He continues by listing the parts of the state, the *polis*, which consists of households, and of "classes," or groups (*genos*) (1291a), including farmers, manual laborers, and defenders of the state:

> no less indispensable than the others if the people are not to become the slaves of those who come against them; for surely it is quite out of the question that it should be proper to give the name of state to a community that is by nature a slave, for a state is self-sufficient, but that which is a slave is not self-sufficient. (1291a)

Metaphorical slavehood can be extended to the *polis* itself, the city-state, or state as a whole; a state can be slavish "by nature" [*phusei*], and thus Aristotle echoes the discourses on slavery and unfreedom of the fifth-century historians. Kings have at times been awarded with sovereignty because they benefited their cities, "some having prevented their enslavement in war, for instance Codrus, others having set them free, for instance Cyrus" (1310b). Such states would presumably not be slavish by nature, but are seen as having escaped an undeserved slavery, on the analogy with a nobleman in war. Citizens resist the further slavery that may come in a divergent or perverted monarchy, a tyranny: "it is from [notables in a tyranny] that counter-movements actually spring, some of them wishing themselves to rule, and others not to be slaves" (1311a). Safety for the tyranny involves, among other things, forcing the people to be visible, to hang around the palace gates, since thus "they would get into a habit of being humble from always acting in a servile way [i.e., slavishly, *aiei douleuontes*]" (1313b). Aristotle also claims that women and slaves are well disposed to tyrannies (and democracies); these things are favorable to tyranny: "dominance of women in the homes, in order that they may carry abroad reports against the men, and lack of discipline among the slaves, for the same reason; for slaves and women do not plot against tyrants" (1313b).

In his discussion of magistracies, Aristotle lists the offices of governance of women and children in the wealthier of states but points out that these are not popular offices, "for the poor having no slaves [*dia ten adoulian*] are forced to employ their women and children as servants" (1322b). Thus the happiness, liberty, and capacity of the poor man to participate in civic life are limited by his poverty, by his slavelessness; in his description of individual as well as collective, civic happiness, Aristotle requires means as well as virtue. Some people define civic happiness as the despotic, masterly *(despotikon)* control over one's neighbors (1324b). Aristotle argues that such control should only be exercised over those of one's neighbors who are suited for it, "just as it is not right to hunt human beings for food or sacrifice, but only the game suitable for this purpose, that is, such wild creatures as are good to eat" (1324b).

In specifying the ideal state, Aristotle points out that it contains others besides the citizens, those who are a "portion of the state": "States are doubtless bound to contain a large number of slaves and resident aliens and foreigners" (1326a). Those who count, who are part of the body of the state, are the free, the citizens, who provide for its self-sufficiency. As to the population, the Hellenic character is set in comparison to both the European and the Asian. The Europeans are "full of spirit but somewhat deficient in intelligence and skill"; they remain free but lack political organization and the ability to rule their neighbors. "The peoples of Asia on the other hand are intelligent and skilful in temperament, but lack spirit, so that they are in continuous subjection and slavery" (1327b). The Greeks, happily, geographically in the middle (as indeed what people is not?), are also characterologically middling, possessing both spirit and intelligence, therefore free and capable of ruling all others. Citing Archilochus, Aristotle reminds us that it is from spirit *(thumos)* that both freedom and the ruling principle derive; Greeks are not content merely to be free, they also spiritedly rule others.

In his account of the soul, Aristotle again has recourse to the language of rulership, language that recalls his account of the relationship between master and slave in the household at the very beginning of the *Politics*:

> The soul is divided into two parts, of which one is in itself possessed of reason [*logou*], while the other is not rational in itself but capable of obeying reason. (1333a)

Compare this to the passage early on in this treatise:

[H]e is by nature a slave who is capable of belonging to another . . . and who participates in reason [*logon*] so far as to apprehend but not to possess it. (1254b)

The soul is like a household, its rational part like the master, its obedient part like the slave. The rational part of the soul is superior, and should dominate. Even within the soul's rational part there is a division between the theoretical and the practical reason, both necessary for life, but the lesser subordinated and harnessed for the benefit of the greater (1333a25). Even in this finer set of discriminations we find the echo of slavery; slaves are necessary, useful, and necessarily and usefully directed by the higher, rational master.

As to education, Aristotle argues that the great importance of military training derives from its connections with slavery:

The proper object of practising military training [*askesin*] is not in order that men may enslave those who do not deserve slavery, but in order that first they may themselves avoid becoming enslaved to others; then so that they may seek suzerainty [*hegemonian*] for the benefit of the subject people, but not for the sake of world-wide despotism; and thirdly to hold despotic power over those who deserve to be slaves. (1333b–1334a)

Education is haunted by the possibility of slavery, avoiding it for oneself, imposing it on those who reveal themselves, by defeat, as slavish. The military enterprises of the Greeks rise and fall on these possibilities, not on defense of territory per se, but in order that one's people not be enslaved to others who invade, that one rightly rule those who need rule.

Aristotle repeats his call for leisure, the leisure of the individual and the state:

I[I]t is proper for the state to be temperate, brave and enduring; since, as the proverb goes, there is no leisure for slaves [*ou skhole doulois*], but people unable to face danger bravely are the slaves of their assailants. (1334a)

War is fought for the sake of peace, business conducted for the sake of leisure. The alternative is slavery, a defeat in war or life without leisure. Education must be toward peace and leisure; children must associate as little as possible with slaves (1336a): "Even at this age (before seven) they may acquire a taint of illiberality [*aneleutherian*] from what they hear and see" (1336b). As a further sign of the necessity to police the boundary between slave and free, rhetorically as well as politically, Aristotle is concerned that children not be exposed to indecent talk:

[A]nybody found saying or doing any of the things prohibited, if he is of free station but not yet promoted to reclining at the public meals, must be punished with marks of dishonour and with beating, and an older offender

> must be punished with marks of dishonour degrading to a free man [*atimi-ais aneleutherois*], because of his slavish behavior [*andrapododias*]. (1336b)

This is an especially revealing passage in light of the earlier remarks about ruling and being ruled. The younger free man will be treated like a slave, beaten and dishonored, if he has not yet attained manhood. An older offender too, who behaves like a slave, will be treated like a slave. In order that children grow up without slavish ideas or behaviors, they must be shielded from slaves themselves, and those free persons who behave slavishly before them must be punished as slaves would be.

Aristotle does not discuss the raising of slave children, nor of those children, slave in status, who are the children of the master. Free children should learn not all the useful arts but only the "liberal" arts, the arts of the free, as opposed to the unfree *(aneleutheron)* (1337b). The same practices can seem both "liberal" or menial and slavish *(thetikon kai doulikon)*, depending on whether one pursues them for oneself or one's friends (that is, liberally), or for others (that is, slavishly) (1337b). Music *(mousike)* is a form of "liberal" education, neither necessary nor useful, rather "as a pastime in leisure," proper for free men *(eleutheron)* (1338a). "To seek for utility everywhere is entirely unsuited to men that are great-souled and free," Aristotle maintains (1338a). The very rhythms of music are classified with regard to whether they are more vulgar or more liberal, more free *(eleutherioteras)* (1340b). Some music is enjoyed even by the lower animals, "as well as a multitude of slaves and children" (1341a). The *Politics* ends with this discussion of music, and its role in educating free men for their task of ruling.[17] I conclude: the central trope is *arkhein/arkhesthai*, to rule and to be ruled; a fundamental paradigm, naturalized and essentialized, deployed at the level of *psykhe*, the soul; the *oikos*, the household; the *polis*, the city; the *ethnos*, the kind, is the unequal relationship between master and slave, possessor and possession.

Not only in his political treatises but even in logical texts, slavery informs Aristotle's thinking, where his rhetoric constantly works to naturalize slavery and to establish it as fundamental. In the *Categories*, he discusses the slave in the section on Relation *(pros ti)*; "we call a thing relative, when it is said to be such as it is from its being of some other thing or, if not, from its being related to something in some other way" (6a).

> All relatives have their correlatives. "Slave" means the slave of a master, and "master," in turn, implies slave. (6b)

> Correlatives are commonly held to come into existence together. . . .The existence of a master involves the existence also of a slave. If a slave exists, then must a master. And so in all similar cases. Moreover, this holds of them also: to cancel one cancels the other. (7b15–20)

Slaves and masters are defined relationally: masters must rule, slavery is good for slaves and good for masters, and serves as the basis for human society and the happiness of free men. Theirs is an existence founded on the acquisition and ownership of other, slavish human beings.

The work of Aristotle constitutes a continuous rhetorical project concerning the inevitability of slavery and the natural will to possess slaves, superior to other material goods. In the *Politics*, he says:

> The art of acquiring [*ktetike*] slaves is different both from their ownership and their direction—that is, the just [*dikaia*] acquiring of slaves, being like a sort of warfare or hunting. (1255b)

> The art of war is a natural [*kata phusin*] art of acquisition [*ktetike*], for the art of acquisition includes hunting, an art which we ought to practise against wild beasts, and against men who, though intended by nature to be governed, will not submit; for war of such a kind is naturally just. (1256b20–25)

Part of human happiness, the realization of human potential, acting in the good life, is engaging in the acquisition and possession of human beings, among other goods. The free male, the citizen, the only subject who counts for Aristotle, must exercise his faculties, his powers, and in so doing acquire and possess other human beings. The term Aristotle uses is *ktesis* (1256a), or *ktetike tekhne*, the art of possession and acquisition, which he describes as different and separate from *oikonomike*, or household management, which is rather the use of what is acquired and possessed. Aristotle takes for granted the will to acquire and possess. Further, he makes a distinction between that acquisition of slaves, especially in war, *ktetike*, and "wealth-getting," the bad *khrematistike*: "All men engaged in wealth-getting [*hoi khrematizomenoi*] try to increase their money to an unlimited amount" (1257b). He makes a distinction, familiar to us, between use value and exchange value, calling the desire for the second "acquisitiveness" [*khrematistike*], and arguing that it is unnatural: "the branch connected with exchange [*metabletikes*] is justly discredited [for it is not in accordance with nature, but involves men's taking things from one another]" [1258b]. We see here a continuation of elitist assumptions about the ignobility of monetary exchange.

As Leslie Kurke points out concerning a struggle in the archaic period over the social meanings of coinage, "By providing a standard against which all goods and services can be measured, money symbolically makes all labor comparable and thereby constitutes a more egalitarian order opposed to ranked spheres of goods and services . . . coinage represents a civic, egalitarian challenge to the structures of elite authority—a challenge that does not go unrecognized or unopposed."[18] In the earlier period, aristocrats' claims to privilege had rested on their naturalized possession of land, as in the Athenian and Theban myths of autochthony. The conservative antidemocratic views of Aristotle in the fourth century BCE urge rather the naturalness of slave acquisition and ownership, and contrast it with the baser practices associated with money and of "wealth-getting," *khrematistike*.

❖ ❖ ❖

C. B. MACPHERSON, in *The Political Theory of Possessive Individualism*, defines what he calls "original seventeenth century individualism":

> Its possessive quality is found in its conception of the individual as essentially the proprietor of his own person or capacities, owing nothing to society for them. The individual was seen neither as a moral whole, nor as part of a larger social whole, but as an owner of himself. The relation of ownership, having become for more and more men the critically important relation determining their actual freedom and actual prospect of realizing their full potentialities, was read back into the nature of the individual. The individual, it was thought, is free inasmuch as he is proprietor of his person and capacities. The human essence is freedom from dependence on the wills of others, and freedom is a function of possession. Society becomes a lot of free equal individuals related to each other as proprietors of their own capacities and of what they have acquired by their exercise. Society consists of relations of exchange between proprietors. Political society becomes a calculated device for the protection of this property and for the maintenance of an orderly relation of exchange.[19]

These "possessive assumptions" "correspond substantially to the actual relations of a market society" (4). Hobbes reads market relations "back into the very nature of man" (268); "a possessive market society is a series of competitive and invasive relations between all men, regardless of class; it puts every man on his own" (269). In the ancient mode, the equivalent, the only "man" is the master of slaves, someone defined by his mastery over and ownership of other human beings, and by his will to acquire slaves.

Ancient Greek society valued the military and cynegetic powers of free men, and saw the exercise of these powers as part of the good life. Aristotle is interested in describing the household, the acts, the arts and sciences of the good and useful and happy man, the man in the *polis*. Some modern scholars, like Michel Foucault and Christopher Gill, see only the free man, the master, that person. The focus on the issue of natural slavery in other modern readings of Aristotle occludes and misrepresents the ways in which slavery was taken for granted in ancient societies, anachronistically overlaying the racialization of slavery onto the institution in antiquity. Paradoxically, such readings can end by insisting on the theoretical benefits that slavery grants to ideas of the self.

There is something in Nietzsche's critique of what he calls "slave morality" that speaks to the current climate, in which politics is often grounded in a hierarchy of oppressions, in the states of injury described by Wendy Brown,[20] in which the valorization of suffering derives perhaps from the same Christian humanism that produced the distortions of Aristotle and of classical culture, urging "racial" slavery for the benefit of the pagans. A humanistic focus on the victims, the enslaved, racially distinguished, imaginarily seeks to come to terms with the great wrong of slavery by citing the theoretical benefits it bestows in the production of a concept of multiple selves. Ancient theory in the hands of Aristotle rather worked to produce masters as the only visible selves. For Aristotle, the only significant persons, sites of happiness, philosophical reflection, and useful political engagement, were free Greek male citizens, who naturally and inevitably acquired, possessed, and ruled other human beings, and by doing so became persons. The crucial understanding to be communicated to Aristotle's listeners and readers concerns not "natural slavery," the natural slavishness of some human beings, but rather the primacy of the master, and the absolute naturalness of slavery itself.

IRATE GREEK MASTERS
AND THEIR SLAVES
The Politics of Anger

A slave's head is never erect but always bent, his neck crooked. For just
as the squill does not produce roses or hyacinths, so no slave-woman
ever produces a free-spirited child.

—Theognis 535–38

THIS CHAPTER marks the distance between moder-
nity and antiquity: the troublesome figure of an angry African American
slave recasts Athenian mockery of a tragic slave. Ancient scenes of anger
between masters and slaves, as well as the earliest psychological analysis
of emotions such as anger, work rhetorically to maintain the difference
between slave and free men. I frame this final chapter with the distinction drawn by Jacques Rancière between *the police* and *politics*, defined in
idiosyncratic and illuminating terms:

The police . . . is first an order of bodies that defines the allocation of ways
of doing, ways of being, and ways of saying, and sees that those bodies are
assigned by name to a particular place and task; it is an order of the visible
and the sayable that sees that a particular activity is visible and another is
not, that this speech is understood as discourse and another as noise. . . .
Policing is not so much the disciplining of bodies as a rule governing their
appearing, a configuration of occupations and the properties of the spaces
where these occupations are distributed.[1]

Rancière defines *politics* as "an extremely determined activity antagonis-
tic to policing: whatever breaks with the tangible configuration whereby
parties and parts or lack of them are defined by a presupposition that, by
definition, has no place in that configuration. . . . This break is manifest
in a series of actions that reconfigure the space where parties, parts, or
lack of parts have been defined" (30).

As an illustration of *politics*, I give you a scene set very far from ancient Greece and Rome, a scene of anger from antebellum North Amer-

ica. This moment comes from one of the versions of the autobiography of Frederick Douglass, introduced by Douglass's chiastic, rhetorically dynamic remark: "You have seen how a man was made a slave; you shall see how a slave was made a man."[2] He had been sent to a man named Covey, whom he calls a "nigger-breaker" (88), a man employed to "break," or train, young slaves. Douglass stubbornly refused to be broken, and Covey came after him with a rope:

> Mr. Covey seemed now to think he had me, and could do what he pleased; but at this moment—from whence came the spirit I don't know—I resolved to fight; and, suiting my action to the resolution, I seized Covey hard by the throat; and as I did so, I rose. He held on to me, and I to him. My resistance was so entirely unexpected, that Covey seemed taken all aback. He trembled like a leaf. (103)

The two men fought for two hours; Douglass drew blood, Covey could not. The scene, he says, changed Douglass's life:

> The whole six months afterwards, that I spent with Mr. Covey, he never laid the weight of his finger upon me in anger. He would occasionally say, he didn't want to get hold of me again. "No," thought I, "you need not; for you will come off worse than you did before."
>
> This battle with Mr. Covey was the turning-point in my career as a slave. It rekindled the few expiring embers of freedom, and revived within me a sense of my own manhood. (104)

Paul Gilroy, in *The Black Atlantic*, proposes that

> we read a section of Douglass' narrative as an alternative to Hegel: a supplement if not exactly a trans-coding of his account of the struggle between lord and bondsman. In a rich account of the bitter trial of strength with Edward Covey, the slave breaker to whom he has been sent, Douglass can be read as if he is systematically reworking the encounter between master and slave in a striking manner which inverts Hegel's own allegorical scheme. It is the slave rather than the master who emerges from Douglass' account possessed of "consciousness that exists for itself," while his master becomes the representative of a "consciousness that is repressed within itself."[3]

I cite the scene from Douglass's autobiography not because I think it easy or even productive to draw analogies between ancient slavery and the slavery of modern America. In fact, I want to point to the very great distance and *difference* between this representation of anger, the anger of a slave at the sustained attempt to tame him, and the scenes of anger between masters and slaves in Greek antiquity. What does this difference reveal about representations of subjectivity in these two very different historical situations?

Rather than projecting Hegel's categories or Gilroy's, however accurate a reading of Hegel's, anachronistically back onto the situation of masters and slaves in antiquity, I will in this chapter explore the scene of anger between Greek master and slave, its representations in some ancient genres, precisely because such a coming to consciousness, on the part especially of the slave, seems literally inconceivable within the horizon of possibilities in Greek antiquity. The ancient situation of anger between master and slave was not an occasion for recognition, consciousness, or emancipation. Rather, it affirmed the isolation of the free man, his philosophical task of mastering himself, and his power. And the discourses on one of the principal emotions identified first in classical Greece—anger, literary and philosophical—constitute not just the beginnings of the mapping of the passions but also part of the ongoing, dynamic discourses concerning slavery, the ideological policing of the boundary between slave and free, as they consistently attribute anger solely to the free person and represent the slave solely as the target of that anger.[4]

To set Frederick Douglass first in this chapter is to defamiliarize the classicist's experience of encountering representations of slaves in ancient texts. It is more difficult to accept the indigenous, internal view of ancient slavery, one in which slaves are foils, literary devices, comic relief, or unfaithful objects subject to execution, after hearing the voice of a modern slave, after hearing a slave speak, encountering the ways in which the coming to consciousness, the literacy, the polemical subjectivity of a nineteenth-century slave, call into question the naturalized passivity in the representations of slaves we encounter in ancient texts.

There are many scenes of anger between free men and those other human beings whom they possess, their slaves, in ancient Greek texts. It would be fascinating to trace the trajectory of such representations, to produce a chronological series, to discuss generic differences among epic, tragedy, comedy, and philosophical dialogue, for example. I restrict myself to a few such scenes, leaving aside such tempting examples as Odysseus's rage at his household maidservants, whom he observes going off to sleep with Penelope's suitors: "anger took him like a wave [*orineto thumos*] to leap / into their midst and kill them, every one [*hekaste*]" (xx, 10); he is compared to a "bitch, facing an unknown man," who "stands over / her callow puppies, and growls and rages to fight" (xx, 14–15). These maids suffer the fate of hanging, as noted earlier, Telemakhos unwilling to grant them the killing by the sword he would give an animal; they have cleaned up the mess of the suitors' slaughter and then die slaves' deaths, distinct in their lack of chastity from Penelope herself.[5]

Other related scenes presented to listeners', readers', audiences' view include such moments as the exchanges between master and slaves in *The Wasps*, master Dionysos and slave Xanthias in *The Frogs*. But these slaves do not manifest anger, even when beaten; Aristophanes' slaves are figures of fun, never of a coming to consciousness, never expressing anger toward their masters. Of course, the genre is comedy, but rather than stopping there in the explanation of the phenomena, I would look rather to the fact that slaves are often represented in comedy, less frequently in tragedy, and never in autobiographies like Douglass's, a genre foreign to the period. The two slaves named Xanthias, "Blondie," although perhaps irritable, never in their comic interchanges with masters, divine or not, achieve a state of rage; their pleasures lie in complaining behind their masters' backs. Other Aristophanic slaves exhibit similar tendencies. The slaves of *The Peace* begin the play kneading dung for a dung beetle, a job they find objectionable: "There's no job more wretched than kneading food to serve to a beetle. A pig or a dog will simply gobble up any shit that falls, but this conceited thing puts on airs and won't deign to eat anything that I don't spend the whole day mashing and serve kneaded into a ball, as for a lady" (22–28).[6] Finding themselves in such ridiculous circumstances, Greek comic slaves aren't angry, could never arrive at "self-consciousness." Is this a rhetorical technique for shielding free men from slaves' rage, for imagining a world of obedient living tools? In the imagination of the free comic writer and the free audience, slaves enjoy grousing about their masters behind their backs, knead beetle dung, and receive beatings with relative equanimity, certainly with humor, without anger.

Euripides' *Orestes* contains a bizarre scene, especially bizarre when read juxtaposed against the aforementioned scene from Frederick Douglass's autobiography. In this sometimes comic tragedy, Orestes himself confronts a Phrygian slave of Helen, the queen whom he has just attempted to murder.[7] This scene has attracted much critical interest. There are two principal questions internal to philological investigation: Is this passage authentic, or is it an interpolation? What is the place of this seemingly comic scene in a tragedy?[8] The first question is a purely textual query concerning the original Euripidean lines; the second, a generic question. These matters are not without interest, and have led to fruitful speculations of a literary and critical nature about the character of Orestes. Is he mad? Is his character consistent throughout the tragedy? But these are not my questions here. The fact that the scene early on was imbedded in the canonical Euripides text seems more significant than whether it emerges from some authentic intention of the "author" Euripides.[9] The generic question is more interesting, especially because it touches the discourses concerning slavery in antiquity. Why is it that scenes between masters and slaves figure in comedy, why are they comic, why does the representation of slaves appear often in comedy while rare in tragedy? And what is this scene in the *Orestes* doing here? I mean "doing" not in the sense of furthering the development of the character of Orestes, or the depiction of his madness or its abeyance, but rather, what kind of cultural labor is it doing here? How does it work in the discourses about slavery that form part of the ideological fabric of this society?

The play concerns the events taking place in the palace of Agamemnon, days after Clytemnestra's children Orestes and Elektra have murdered her. Orestes decides to murder Clytemnestra's sister Helen as well. The scene in question begins with the entry of Helen's Phrygian slave onto the floor of the theater. He sings a song about what he saw as Orestes and his companion Pylades invaded the palace, terrifying the Asian slaves of Helen and attempting to carry out their murderous plot against her. It is unclear whether she is dead or alive at this point in the drama. The Phrygian's song is marked by various grammatical peculiarities and seems to allude to the new music of Timotheus, who composed a similar song in his almost contemporary dithyramb, *Persians*, a fragment of which remains.[10] The slave may represent contemporary Persia itself, an object of mockery in allegorical form.

The stichomythia between Orestes and the Phrygian follows this song, and displays the hero in a state of rage:

Orestes: Where is that coward slave
   who ran from my sword inside?
Phrygian: I bow down, yessir.
   I kiss the ground, lord. Is Eastern custom, yes.
O.: This is Argos, fool, not Troy.
P.: But anywhere
   wise man wants to live, not die.
O.: And those screams of yours?
   Admit it: you were shouting to Menelaus for help.
P.: Oh no, nosir. Not I. For you I was screaming.
   You needed help.
O.: Did Helen deserve to die?
P.: Oh, yessir. Three times cut madam's throat,
   and I not object.
O.: This is cowardly flattery.
   You don't believe it.
P.: Oh sir, I believe, sure.
   Helen ruin Hellas, yes, kill Trojans too.
O.: Swear you're telling me the truth or I'll kill you.

P.: Oh, oh! By life I swear—if life can have mebbe?

O.: Were all the Trojans as terrified by cold steel
as you?

P.: Ooh, please, please, not so close!
All shiny bloody!

O.: What are you afraid of, fool?
Is it some Gorgon's head to turn you into stone [*petros*]?

P.: Not stone, corpse [*nekros*], yes. But this Gorgon thing
I do not know.

O.: What, nothing but a slave
and afraid to die? Death might end your suffering.

P.: Slave man, free man, everybody like to live.

O.: Well spoken. Your wit [*sunesis*] saves you. Now get inside.

P.: You will not kill me?

O.: I spare you.

P.: Oh, thank you, thank you.

O.: Go, or I'll change my mind.

P.: I no thank you for that.

O.: Fool, did you think I'd dirty my sword on your neck? Neither man
nor woman—who could want your life? (*Orestes* 1506–27)[11]

The translation by Arrowsmith adopts a sort of pidgin English to communicate the awkward syntax of these disputed lines, thought by some, as I have said, to be interpolated, since they resemble too much scenes from that other genre, comedy.

Part of the effect of this scene, especially as it figures in the discourses of slavery (of which more later), is the dissonance between a Homeric, epic representation of a Trojan, even a Trojan slave, and the supposed syntax of foreign, "barbarian" slaves in the everyday life of the Athenian audience of the fifth century BCE, for whom jokes about Phryx, Xanthias, Manes, refer to members of their own households, naming them by their places of origin, or by allusion to physical characteristics that mark them as different from their Greek masters. The presentation of such a comic figure, and the topos of anger between master and slave, produces not only a generic but also a historical dissonance. This slave is especially "other," simultaneously Homeric and contemporary, marked by historical indifference as well as linguistic otherness. Euripides' "tragicomedy" is not just a mixing of high and low, of grandeur and mockery; it also serves to undermine the majesty of the Homeric, epic, legendary past of the heroes.[12] This play, in which a hero of the epic cycle reveals himself as sick, mad, inconsistent, incapable even of following the plot assigned to him by myth, incorporates this weird moment of rage of a free man toward a slave not his own.

This is a peculiar prefiguration of the master-slave, lord-bondsman moment in Hegel's *Phenomenology*, where death is at issue; here the tragic is contaminated by the comic, the philosophical, and the rhetorical. Supposedly, the slave's statement of his position, his vulnerability, moves Orestes, in the rhetorical perfection of his expression of the sentiment that no one wants to die, even the slave who has nothing to lose. The translator, exaggerating the barbarism of the barbarian, gives us: "Slave man, free man, everybody like to live" (1519). The Greek is "pas aner, k'an doulos e tis, hedetai to phos horon" [every man, even if he be a slave, takes pleasure in seeing the light]. We are far from Hegel, whose bondsman risks death; from Marx, whose proletarian has nothing to lose; from Frederick Douglass, who is willing, though a slave, to risk his life and express his rage and fight his master.

Orestes, tragic hero, contemptuously encounters Phrygian, comic slave, suggesting that the slave is a eunuch, or at least feminized by his slave condition. He angrily faults him for oriental deference, requiring that he claim indifference to the fates of his mistress, Helen, and her husband, Menelaus, and even that he applaud Orestes' attempt to kill Helen. Orestes accuses him of cowardice as well, asking him to denounce Helen as the cause for Trojan deaths as well as Greeks'. Mocking the slave's fears as he brandishes his bloody sword, he suggests that the slave would be better off dead. Then, somehow, he decides to spare the slave's life, perhaps because of his own lack of will or the form of the appeal, perhaps because of theatrical decorum, which requires both that murder not be committed on the tragic stage, and that bloody violence occur nowhere in comedy. Whether Orestes is angry or not, whether he is mocking the slave and pretending anger—he can be angry, and the slave cannot.

Is there some moment of recognition here on the part of Orestes of the common humanity of free man and slave, Greek and barbarian? Is this moment a trace, a vestige of philosophical debates about the humanity of all men? In any case, the character Orestes does not acknowledge his own moment of compassion or mercy, does not ask for recognition for himself as a humanist. He excuses his sparing of the slave by saying that he would not want to be stained by such blood, barbarian Phrygian blood, from a creature neither man nor woman, feminized because a slave, fearful, a eunuch.[13] His rage does not abate, in his view, because of recognition that passes between the two interlocutors in this scene; rather, he came with sword drawn to silence the slave's screams, and he succeeded in his aim without killing him and contaminating his weapon with unworthy blood.

This scene of anger between master and slave is "atopic," atypical,

weird, and disturbing. The slave is too comic, too barbarian, too obsequious, and too undignified for tragedy. He enters from another world,
an almost Aristophanic universe, ludicrous here, a Phrygian without the
dignity of a Homeric Trojan, to grovel and submit to the petty tantrum
of the tragic Orestes. This scene signifies that anger between master and
slave is unnervingly comic, even an element of everyday life, and, most
significantly, flows from master toward slave. To the citizens of the democratic *polis*, such representation of the cowardice and obsequiousness of
slaves may be entertaining, even amusing, certainly reassuring if free
men feared the resistance, mutiny, and potential violence of a surrounding, ubiquitous slave population. In any case, the scene opens up the
possibility of a shared humanity, a shared mortality, a philosophical possibility perhaps adduced in this period, only to shut it down immediately
through the reaction of a pathetic hero. The encounter, with anger passing only from free man toward slave, finally affirms the boundary between slave and free in this world lavishly furnished with slaves.

The rage of Orestes diminishes the free man; he is himself contaminated by the comic aura of this encounter, made ludicrous and cowardly
by his bullying of the slave. The very sentiment of the slave, who expresses his desire to live, threatens to unsettle and tip the valences of this
encounter. However, we cannot find a reciprocal anger in this slave.
The focus is on Orestes, tragic, legendary hero, a free man even in the
unsettling, unsettled world of Euripides. Karen Bassi argues in *Acting
Like Men* that

> dramatic performance calls forth a normative social subject defined both
> by his innate Greekness and by his irrefutable masculinity (which for all
> intents and purposes are the same thing). Another way of putting the
> matter is to say that the alternative possibility, negatively embodied in the
> performances of Oedipus or Pisistratus or Dionysus, is the necessary pre-
> condition for defining that normative subject.[14]

In this scene in the *Orestes*, neither the slave nor the hero is admirable or
"normative"; yet one is constituted as free, Greek, masculine through
his anger, while the other is not.

The recognition in the scene is that of mortality, mutual mortality,
the common vulnerability of human beings to death, and their desire to
survive. Orestes recognizes the desire to live, since the play in fact begins with his own sentence to death, which motivates the subsequent
events and the plot he hatches to kill Helen. Yet even when the slave expresses a common human desire for survival, he cannot display anger,
exhibiting only fear, compliance, and a groveling deference. A moment
of risk comes for Orestes in the encounter with the slave, in which there

is the possibility of confirmation of all the worst one could imagine of a fallen hero, someone who comes to exemplify late fifth-century Euripidean bitterness, exhaustion, and cynicism about the Homeric world and its gods and heroes, and the celebration of war. If at the end of the fifth century intellectuals, sophists, the disillusioned in general, have little confidence in the *polis*, its gods, its democracy, its myths of foundation and origin, then a Euripidean hero who kills an obsequious, spineless slave onstage would offer a culminating example of cultural exhaustion. That this hero forebears, if even for the sake of not soiling his sword, perhaps points forward to another cultural matrix, the world of philosophical subjects in which self-control, self-mastery within empire eventually become more important than the former social hierarchy, in which living as a philosophical slave is said to be a better condition than to be juridically free but enslaved to one's passions. How does the situation of anger directed at a slave present itself in the earlier philosophical literature, in the classical period of Greece?

I will look here at just two moments, one from the documentation about the life of Plato, one from Aristotle's mapping of the emotions, to see how anger figures further in the delineation of kinds, drawing the line between slave and free. If we think of anger as a way not of expressing what is inside a modern, psychological self, that container of innerness, of private subjectivity, and instead think of it as a kind of policing, a way of maintaining domination, of power over others, if we understand it as unidirectional, the anger coming from the master toward the slave, but never expressed, never expressible in Greek antiquity at least by slaves, then we can understand the discourse of anger—including its location in a new philosophical typology of the emotions and passions—differently, and anger's function in discourses of slavery differently as well.

Of course, the language of slavery, as noted earlier, plays an important role in political language of the classical Greek period; it is used metaphorically to describe and allude to many forms of domination: the Greeks resist the Persians because they see conquest as enslavement of all Hellas, because all Persians are enslaved to the emperor. In *The Wasps*, Bdelykleon argues that Philokleon is enslaved to the jury system, that such a situation of domination must be intolerable. And such discourses, including that on anger, omnipresent as they are, naturalize and familiarize slavery, so that the inevitability of a slave presence is not questioned, so that each individual resists falling into metaphorical and literal slavery precisely because slavery is naturalized, and if one were to be enslaved to anything or anyone, such subjection would be natural and fatal to free selfhood.

Diogenes Laertius repeats the following anecdote in his life of Plato:

One day, when Xenocrates had come in, Plato asked him to chastise his slave, since he was unable to do it himself because he was in a passion [*dio to orgisthai*]. Further, it is alleged that he said to one of his slaves, "I would have given you a flogging, had I not been in a passion [*orgizomen*]." (*Plato*, 3.38)[15]

The truly free man, both juridically free and free of enslavement to the passions, the philosopher, does not act in anger against his slaves, and masters himself so that he can flog them dispassionately. Peter Brown writes of late antiquity:

To beat a slave in a fit of rage was condemned. This was not because of any very acute sense that an act of inhumanity against a fellow human being had been committed, but because the outburst represented a collapse of the harmonious image of the self of the wellborn man, and had caused him to behave in a manner as uncontrolled as a slave.[16]

Plato, here as elsewhere, serves as a model for the philosophical schools.

Aristotle uses a compelling figure when he discusses anger *(thumos)* in the *Nicomachean Ethics:*

The trouble about anger would seem to be that, while it does to some extent listen to reason, it does not hear it aright. It is like an over-hasty slave who scuttles out of a room before he has heard the whole of his instructions, which he then proceeds to bungle. (1149a25–28)

That is, anger *is* a slave; a slave is like anger, anger which is an agent, a possession that does not always obey the free person properly, which ought, in its bungled performance of its instructions, to be the object of anger, which is like a slave, and so on ad infinitum. In this view of a metaphorically divided self, the language of slavery again proves useful in delineating the master's existence. His very emotions are likened to slaves, which ought to obey, if he has properly mastered himself. Control of his feelings, his *pathe*, mirrors control of his human possessions.

The *Rhetoric* of Aristotle contains the first important, systematic discussion of the *pathe*, or emotions, in Greek philosophical writing. Aristotle considers anger in relation to the project of the *Rhetoric*, the production of persuasive speech for deliberative, forensic, and epideictic occasions. Anger can be usefully excited in the speaker's audience, making it better disposed to the speaker's views. The philosopher provides the first map of the emotions, and his analysis of anger explains that men are angry when pained, opposed, or troubled. Inevitably, Aristotle accompanies this seminal discussion of anger *(orge)* with the issue of the management of slaves:[17]

> [F]inding as it were satisfaction in the pain the offenders feel at what they have done, men cease to be angry. Evidence of this may be seen in the punishment of slaves; for we punish more severely those who contradict us and deny their offence, but cease to be angry with those who admit that they are justly punished. The reason is that to deny what is evident is disrespect, and disrespect is slight and contempt; anyhow, we show no respect for those for whom we entertain a profound contempt. Men also are mild towards those who humble themselves before them and do not contradict them, for they seem to recognize that they are inferior; now, those who are inferior are afraid, and no one who is afraid slights another. (1380a5–6)

Anger emerges in relationships of striving and competition with equals, with rivals, where it is reciprocated, but also unilaterally, in representations, literary and philosophical, in which masters are constructed through their anger at slaves, and through which relations of superiority and inferiority, rule and deference, are continually established.

❖ ❖ ❖

IT IS POSSIBLE to posit anger as a universal human attribute, a psychological constant, present in all human beings; a map of the passions might include it, deducing its existence in the soul, or in the chemistry of the human body, from its familiar appearance in Western culture.[18] Or one might argue that all Western psychologies, descended from the description of the passions in Aristotle's *Rhetoric*, are merely dialectal variations on the Greeks' mapping of emotions or passions, that to generalize to all humans one would have to compare non-Western cultures and judge whether "anger" as we know it exists throughout human societies. It seems significant that the anger of Frederick Douglass is unimaginable within the horizon of ancient Greek *polis* society—rage expressed from such a location cannot be represented. The emotions themselves emerge historically, bound up in social relations.

Policing and ordering labor is performed by the mapping of the passions, especially in the Greek texts; there anger exists between equals, between rivals, and is thus reserved for the free members of the social hierarchy. The very categorization of the emotions serves to produce "an order of the visible and the sayable that sees that a particular activity is visible and another is not, that this speech is understood as discourse and another as noise."[19] The anger of free men defines them as free, as agents of anger, with the choice of expressing it or not, orders them in a hierarchy where although the tragic hero can recognize the mortality of the slave, the anger of the free man is the only form of anger visible, sayable, and stageable.

At the moment of abolition of slavery in the nineteenth century, after centuries of the slow development of the Enlightenment emotions of empathy and sympathy, the scene between the slave breaker and his victim stimulates rage and violence in return, and can be written, published, and read. In contrast, the ancient representations of anger help to perpetuate a social order, an order based not just on flogging, on coercion, on juridical torture, on implicit and explicit violence, but even on these earliest mappings and descriptions of emotion, and on the invisibility of slaves in such mapping—except as the targets of free men's rage.

EPILOGUE
Material World

IN A STRANGE prefiguration of the display of family, household, and household goods depicted in *Material World*, a collection of twentieth-century photographs, the fifth-century BCE comic playwright Aristophanes staged a similar moment in his comedy *The Women at the Assembly*, the *Ecclesiazousae*. The conceit of the play is that the women of Athens, disguised as men, have seized control of the assembly and approved various measures, to ensure among other things that the older women receive sexual attentions and are not overlooked for the sake of younger women, especially slaves. Allusions to slavish depilation and compulsory sex between slaves aside, the comedy also represents the women as demanding a sort of communism among citizens. All labor will in the utopian future be performed by slaves (651).

The scheme is presented as a solution to the problem that some are rich, some poor, that one man should have many slaves, another not one (593). Praxagora, the assembly's leader, seeks to abolish private property: "First, I'll provide / That the silver, and land, and whatever beside / Each man shall possess, shall be common and free, One fund for the public; then out of it we / Will feed and maintain you, like housekeepers true, / Dispensing, and sparing, and caring for you" (596–600). The assembled women approve this radical plan, and Praxagora goes to the *agora* to receive all their goods as the citizens bring them in. And it is here that we see "the material world" of the Greek citizen, a world of *things* which includes not just inanimate objects, the apparatus of the household, but also human beings. They are brought by Chremes, who commands his possessions:

> My sweet bran-winnower, come you sweetly here.
> March out the first of my household goods,
> Powdered and trim, like some young basket-bearer.
> Aye many a sack of mine you've bolted down.
> Now where's the chair-girl. Come along, dear pot,
> (Wow, but you're black: scarce blacker had you chanced

> To boil the dye Lysicrates employs)
> And stand by her. Come hither, tiring-maid;
> And pitcher-bearer, bear your pitcher here.
>
> (730–39)

The scene combines allusions to the comedies, cited earlier, in which the playwrights imagined a world without slaves, in which food cooks itself and flies directly into the master's mouth, and a scene from Athenian festival ritual, in which various participants carried baskets, chairs, pots of water, and dishes. The possessions of the household are presented by such ritualistic presenters, but they also move themselves, as does the personified "dear pot," the *khutra* of line 735.[1] The "bran-winnower," "rubbed," "painted," has performed sexual acts for the speaker; *thulakos*, the word translated here as "sack," suggests *thulake*, scrotum, "balls." The list of goods, incongruously for us, includes a "tiring-maid," a dresser or a beauty-shop worker, *kommotria*, and a pitcher bearer among the "chattels," the household goods, or *skeuaria*, listed by this householder.

The line between things and persons blurs in this Aristophanic moment in a scene that includes obscenity and the casual confusion of animate and inanimate goods. Slaves, often troubling or difficult to see for modern and postmodern readers living in postslave economies, formed an inextricable part of the fabric of everyday life in classical Athens. They worked to produce the food people ate; they labored in factories; they mined the silver that first made Athens wealthy. Slaves cooked and wove and sewed the garments people wore. They had sex with their owners and with those who paid them. They policed the city. They ran away when conditions in the city permitted. The slave presence in classical Athens informed classical experience.

The idea of slavery produced its concomitant, freedom, another idea with literal and metaphorical implications. For a few radical thinkers— accessible only in fragments, in moments in Euripides' tragedies and in the reactions of conservatives like Aristotle—slaves may have perhaps come to represent an unnatural exclusion, and the possibility of universality, of a humankind. Slaves helped philosophy to define the body first as a possession, a thing attached to the soul. Their bodies in the eyes of some were inevitably, essentially different, marking them off from the free. Slavery shaped ideas of bodies and spaces, public and private, alien and familiar, high and low. Slaves were ubiquitous, furnishings of the world, invisible and essential, taken for granted as instruments of labor and of pleasure. They were human beings yet not rulers, not citizens, objects with senses, possessions that spoke. Slaves were outsiders who inhabited the innermost spaces of the city and the house, who knew secrets and truths yet could not testify in Athenian law courts, who invisibly sustained and enabled the life of the first democracy. The presence of ancient slaves has left its mark on the West, in its moment of legal, philosophical, literary, and artistic beginnings; yet they have often remained disturbingly unseen, disavowed, and invisible.

✢ NOTES

Preface

1. Peter Menzel, *Material World: A Global Family Portrait* (San Francisco: Sierra Club Books, 1994).
2. See Kevin Bales, *Disposable People: New Slavery in the Global Economy* (Berkeley and Los Angeles: University of California Press, 2000). Bales estimates the number of slaves in the world in 2000 at 27 million (p. 8).

Introduction

1. Herodotus, *The Histories*, rev. A. R. Burn and trans. A. de Selincourt (Harmondsworth, England: Penguin Books, 1972), 5.35 (pp. 352–53) [translation modified]; subsequent references are to this edition and translation unless otherwise noted. This story is repeated by Aeneas Tacticus in his advice on secret messages (31.28–29).
2. Page duBois, *Sowing the Body: Psychoanalysis and Ancient Representations of Women* (Chicago: University of Chicago Press, 1988).
3. On slave tattoos, see C. P. Jones, "Stigma and Taboo," in *Written on the Body: The Tattoo in European and American History*, ed. Jane Caplan (Princeton, N.J.: Princeton University Press, 2000), 1–16. I discuss slave tattooing further in chapter 4. On another "branded" slave, see Mark Munn, *The School of History: Athens in the Age of Socrates* (Berkeley and Los Angeles: University of California Press, 2000), 216.
4. Throughout this book I will refer to "slaves." However, the English word covers a more complicated semantic field in Greek, with various words translated as "slave" into English. These include *doulos; andrapodon,* "human stock," a word formed in the neuter gender, perhaps signifying "captive," some "thing" taken in war and sold, a man-footed thing, like a *tetrapodon,* a four-footed beast; *pais,* which also means "child," used to address a slave of any age; and *oiketes,* household slave. This culture in which slaves were ubiquitous employed many words referring to the unfree persons who surrounded the free, with subtle distinctions made among them. Benveniste argues that the Indo-European words for slaves, like the word *slave* itself in English, refer to foreigners, those outside the community, and that the ancient word *doulos,* found in Mycenaean texts as *do-e-ro,* may have been taken very early from a non-Indo-European language of the Aegean basin. "The geographical distribution of proper names in *doulo-,*

which suggests an Asianic origin" (292), makes it probable that the word comes from Asia Minor. In Benveniste's view, the slave is designated by a foreign word because the slave is necessarily a stranger. Emile Benveniste, "The Slave and the Stranger," in *Indo-European Language and Society*, trans. Elizabeth Palmer, Miami Linguistics Series, no. 12 (Coral Gables, Fla.: University of Miami Press, 1973), 289–94. But Greeks themselves were enslaved by other Greeks, and even Athenians by Athenians until Solon made this illegal in the sixth century BCE. See also P. Vidal-Naquet, "Les esclaves grecs étaient-ils une classe?" in *Travail et esclavage en Grèce ancienne*, by Jean-Pierre Vernant and Pierre Vidal-Naquet, 83–93 (Paris: Ed. Complexe, 1988). The English-language version of this reading is Vidal-Naquet, "Were the Greek Slaves a Class?" in *The Black Hunter: Forms of Thought and Forms of Society in the Greek World*, trans. A. Szegedy-Maszak (Baltimore: Johns Hopkins University Press, 1986), 159–67.

5. Aeschines, *The Speeches of Aeschines*, trans. C. D. Adams, Loeb Classical Library Series (Cambridge, Mass.: Harvard University Press, 1919), 2.178, 3.171; subsequent references are to this translation unless otherwise noted. Aeschines says that, because of his impure lineage, Demosthenes was not born a citizen, nor was he kin of the Athenians. Moreover, "he has not one member of his body left unsold *(apraton)*" (2.23).

6. Ibid., 2.79.

7. Aeschines' insults against Demosthenes include calling him a *kinaidos*, a passive partner in male-male sex—translated as "unclean in his body," even in the part from which his voice issues (ibid., 2.88)—and a bastard according to Athenian law, which by this time required purely Athenian ancestors (2.93). The speech also contains the customary offer of slave torture, which is refused by Demosthenes (2.127). See Page duBois, *Torture and Truth* (New York: Routledge, 1991).

8. M. R. Dilts, ed., *Scholia in Aeschinem* (Stuttgart: Teubner, 1992), 75. (170a: "estigmenos automolos: epeide hoi fugades ton doulon estidzonto to metopon, ho estin epegraphonto katekhe me; pheugo" [mgVxLi].) See also 170b; cited in Jones, "Stigma and Taboo," 148.

9. See W. V. Harris, *Ancient Literacy* (Cambridge, Mass.: Harvard University Press, 1989); and Rosalind Thomas, *Literacy and Orality in Ancient Greece* (Cambridge: Cambridge University Press, 1992).

10. See B. Knox, "Silent Reading in Antiquity," *Greek, Roman and Byzantine Studies* 9 (1968): 421–35; M. Burzachechi, "Oggetti parlanti nelle epigrafi greche," *Epigraphica* 24 (1962): 3–54; Jesper Svenbro, *Phrasikleia: l'anthropologie de la lecture en Grèce ancienne* (Paris: La Découverte, 1988).

11. See Svenbro, *Phrasikleia*, on the tattooed body of the free Epimenides: "La vraie metempsycose: Lycurge, Numa et le cadavre tatoué d'Epimenide," 137–60. He argues that the reading of the tattooed cadaver of Epimenides constitutes a reanimation, a reincarnation of the dead man. See also D. Steiner, *The Tyrant's Writ: Myths and Images of Writing in Ancient Greece* (Princeton, N.J.: Princeton University Press, 1994), esp. "Inscribing the Body," 154–59.

12. "Slavery was never made, but instead was continually remade, for power

—no matter how great—was never absolute, but always contingent." Ira Berlin, *Many Thousands Gone: The First Two Centuries of Slavery in North America* (Cambridge, Mass.: Harvard University Press, Belknap Press, 1998), 3.

13. Sokrates in Xenophon's *Memorabilia:* "Magnificence and freedom, lowliness and slavery, temperance and prudence, insolence and vulgarity, are apparent in the face and bearing of a man." (10.5). Xenophon, *Recollections of Socrates,* trans. A. Benjamin (New York: Macmillan, 1965).

14. Just as there is a complex semantic field referring to unfree persons in Greek antiquity, so there is also a wide spectrum of statuses *among* unfree persons. Some slaves were individual chattel slaves, the privately held property of individuals. Others belonged to the *polis,* the "city-state," as did some mine slaves and the Thracian archers who served as police in ancient Athens. The Spartans, who had conquered the neighboring peoples of Laconia and Messenia, enslaved them *as* communities; these unfree people were called *helots,* sometimes translated by analogy as "serfs." Among other such peoples were the *penestai* of Thrace and the Mariandyni of Sicilian Heraclea, unfree "slaves" who lived apart in separate communities and were collectively the property of their masters' city-states. See Moses I. Finley, "Between Slavery and Freedom," *Comparative Studies in Society and History* 6 (1964): 233–49; Yvon Garlan, *Slavery in Ancient Greece,* rev. ed., trans. Janet Lloyd (Ithaca, N.Y.: Cornell University Press, 1988); G. E. M. de Sainte-Croix, *Class Struggle in the Ancient Greek World from the Archaic Age to the Arab Conquests* (Ithaca, N.Y.: Cornell University Press, 1981). For bibliography on slavery, see N. Brockmeyer, *Antike Sklaverei* (Darmstadt: Wissenschaftliche Buchgesellschaft, 1979); and J. Vogt and H. Bellen, eds., *Bibliographie zur antiken Sklaverei,* rev. by E. Hermann and N. Brockmeyer (Bochum: N. Brockmeyer, 1983).

15. Moses I. Finley, *Ancient Slavery and Modern Ideology* (New York: Viking, 1980), 65.

16. Or to minimize slavery's importance: "In its historical context, an ancient world in which slavery was universal and authoritarian rule by royal dynasties or aristocratic elites the political norm, Athenian democracy was nothing less than a miracle." B. Knox, *Backing Into the Future: The Classical Tradition and Its Renewal* (New York: Norton, 1994), 150. There are vigorous debates about the relative numbers of slaves in ancient Greek society; see the summary in M. Dillon and L. Garland, *Ancient Greece: Social and Historical Documents from Archaic Times to the Death of Socrates (c. 800–399 BC)* (London: Routledge, 1994), 322. Paul Cartledge has concluded that "between 450 and 320 BC about 80,000–100,000 slaves of all kinds were active in Attica at any one time (out of a total population of perhaps a quarter of a million)." *The Oxford Classical Dictionary,* 3d ed., ed. Simon Hornblower and Antony Spawforth (Oxford: Oxford University Press, 1996), 1415, s.v. "slavery." Ian Morris says: "There cannot have been fewer than 30,000 slaves in fifth-century Athens, and probably no more than 100,000. Slaves made up 10–30 percent of the population." Ian Morris, *Archaeology as Cultural History: Words and Things in Iron Age Greece* (Oxford: Blackwell, 2000), 152.

17. See Tracey Rihll, "The Origin and Establishment of Ancient Greek

Slavery," in *Serfdom and Slavery: Studies in Legal Bondage*, ed. M. L. Bush (London: Longman, 1996), 89–111.

18. On slavery, in a vast bibliography, see especially D. B. Davis, *The Problem of Slavery in Western Culture* (Ithaca, N.Y: Cornell University Press, 1966); and Orlando Patterson, *Slavery and Social Death: A Comparative Study* (Cambridge, Mass.: Harvard University Press, 1982). Patterson discusses the role of religion, especially sale to the Apollo cult, in reconciling the Greeks' slaves to what he calls the "social death" of slavery (66–68). See also Igor Kopytoff, "The Cultural Biography of Things: Commoditization as a Process," in *The Social Life of Things: Commodities in Cultural Perspective*, ed. Arjun Appadurai (Cambridge: Cambridge University Press, 1986), 64–91.

19. Sigmund Freud, "A Disturbance of Memory on the Acropolis" (1936), in *Standard Edition of the Complete Psychological Works*, trans. J. Strachey (London: Hogarth Press, 1953, 1973), 22:239–51; extract is from pp. 240–41.

20. See I. Morris, *Archaeology as Cultural History*, 3–76.

21. Christopher Stray, *Classics Transformed: Schools, Universities and Society in England, 1830–1960* (Oxford: Clarendon Press, 1998).

22. See, for example, Orlando Patterson, *Freedom*, vol. 1, *Freedom in the Making of Western Culture* (New York: Basic Books, 1991). Patterson cites favorably the work of Kurt A. Raaflaub, *Die Entdeckung der Freiheit* (Munich: Beck, 1985), and Max Pohlenz, *Freedom in Greek Life and Thought: The History of an Ideal*, trans. C. Rofmark (Dordrecht: D. Reidel, 1966).

23. J. Laplanche and J.-B. Pontalis, *The Language of Psychoanalysis*, tr. D. Nicholson-Smith (New York: Norton, 1973).

24. See David Halperin, *One Hundred Years of Homosexuality and Other Essays on Greek Love* (New York: Routledge, 1990); John J. Winkler, *The Constraints of Desire: The Anthropology of Sex and Gender in Ancient Greece* (New York: Routledge, 1990); Ralph Hexter and Daniel Selden, eds., *Innovations of Antiquity* (New York: Routledge, 1992); James I. Porter, *The Invention of Dionysus: An Essay on the Birth of Tragedy* (Stanford, Calif.: Stanford University Press, 2000).

25. Rey Chow, *Writing Diaspora: Tactics of Intervention in Contemporary Cultural Studies* (Bloomington: Indiana University Press, 1993), 3–4.

26. See Page duBois, *Trojan Horses: Saving the Classics from Conservatives* (New York: New York University Press, 2001).

27. See, for example, the primer *Cultural Studies*, ed. L. Grossberg, C. Nelson, and P. A. Treichler (New York: Routledge, 1992), which like most work on cultural studies generally ignores historical and non-Anglophone examples; of forty essays, one discusses Shakespeare; another, gender and ethnicity in England in the 1830s and 1840s; another, *sati* in India during the nineteenth century.

28. See Alice Rains Trulock, *In the Hands of Providence: Joshua L. Chamberlain and the American Civil War* (Chapel Hill: University of North Carolina Press, 1992).

29. Cited in ibid., 83; from the manuscripts of Joshua Chamberlain collected at Bowdoin College.

30. *Basil Lanneau Gildersleeve, An American Classicist,* ed. Ward W. Briggs Jr. and Herbert W. Benario (Baltimore: Johns Hopkins University Press, 1986).

31. Thomas Habinek discusses Gildersleeve's ideological preference for Greece over Rome in *The Politics of Latin Literature: Writing, Identity, and Empire in Ancient Rome* (Princeton, N.J.: Princeton University Press, 1998), 18–25.

32. On classics in Germany, see Suzanne L. Marchand, *Down from Olympus: Archaeology and Philhellenism in Germany, 1750–1970* (Princeton, N.J.: Princeton University Press, 1996).

33. Letter 9 to Socrates Maupin, *The Letters of Basil Lanneau Gildersleeve,* ed. Ward W. Briggs Jr. (Baltimore: Johns Hopkins University Press, 1987), 39.

34. Letter 77 to Horace Elisha Scudder, The Cliff House, Kennebunkport, Maine, 10 August 1891, ibid.

35. *The Nation* called "Creed" "A poetical view of the Southern cause in the Civil War" (*Nation* 101 [8 July 1915]: 50).

36. B. L. Gildersleeve, *The Creed of the Old South, 1865–1915* (Baltimore: Johns Hopkins University Press, 1915), 184.

37. B. L. Gildersleeve, "The Creed of the Old South," *Atlantic Monthly* 69 (January 1892): 75–87, and "A Southerner in the Peloponnesian War," *Atlantic* 80 (September 1897), 330–42. Both were reprinted as *The Creed of the Old South, 1865–1915* (Baltimore: Johns Hopkins University Press, 1915). Thomas Jefferson had feared war over slavery and in 1821 asked John Adams: "Are we then to see again Athenian and Lacedaemonian confederacies? To wage another Peloponnesian War to settle the ascendancy between them?" Cited in Carl Richard, *The Founders and the Classics: Greece, Rome, and the American Enlightenment* (Cambridge, Mass.: Harvard University Press, 1994), 98.

38. Gildersleeve, *The Creed of the Old South,* 24.

39. Deborah Reeves Hopkins, "The Charleston Background," in *Basil Lanneau Gildersleeve, An American Classicist,* ed. Ward W. Briggs Jr. and Herbert W. Benario (Baltimore: Johns Hopkins University Press, 1986), 4.

40. Seth Schein, "Gildersleeve and the Study of Attic Tragedy," in *Basil Lanneau Gildersleeve: An American Classicist,* ed. Ward W. Briggs Jr. and Herbert W. Benario (Baltimore: Johns Hopkins University Press, 1986), 50–55; quotation taken from p. 54.

41. Hopkins, "The Charleston Background," 4.

42. On the antislavery arguments, see Thomas Bender, ed., *The Antislavery Debate: Capitalism and Abolitionism as a Problem in Historical Interpretation* (Berkeley and Los Angeles: University of California Press, 1992).

43. Louis Menand, *The Metaphysical Club* (New York: Farrar Straus and Giroux, 2001), 27.

44. Robin Blackburn, *The Making of New World Slavery: From the Baroque to the Modern 1492–1800* (London: Verso, 1997), 62.

45. David Brion Davis, *The Problem of Slavery in Western Culture* (Ithaca, N.Y.: Cornell University Press, 1966), 100–101.

46. George Fitzhugh, *Cannibals All! or Slaves without Masters,* ed. C. Vann

Woodward (Cambridge, Mass.: Harvard University Press, Belknap Press, 1960), 69.

47. "Lawmaker Says Bible Justifies Slavery," *Los Angeles Times*, 8 May 1996, Nation in Brief section.

48. Larry E. Tise, *Proslavery: A History of the Defense of Slavery in America, 1701–1840* (Athens: University of Georgia Press, 1987), 225.

49. For an excellent review of the intellectual history of views of ancient Athens, see Jennifer Tolbert Roberts, *Athens on Trial: The Antidemocratic Tradition in Western Thought* (Princeton, N.J.: Princeton University Press, 1994).

50. Cited in John White and Ralph Willett, eds., *Slavery in the American South* (London: Longmans, 1970), 113.

51. Eugene Genovese, *The Slave-Holders' Dilemma: Freedom and Progress in Southern Conservative Thought, 1820–1860* (Columbia: University Of South Carolina Press 1992), 5.

52. See, for example, Jean-Pierre Vernant and Pierre Vidal-Naquet's collection of articles, *Travail et esclavage en Grèce ancienne* (Paris: Ed. Complexe, 1988), in which the groundbreaking work of the French school, incorporating intellectual history, political theory, literary questions, and social history, takes the measure of ancient slavery; in Italian, L. Sichirollo, ed., *Schiavitù antica e moderna* (Naples: Guida, 1979), among others. See also J. Vogt: "Eastern European Marxist historians have applied themselves most energetically to the study of slavery in antiquity," in *Ancient Slavery and the Ideal of Man*, trans. T. Wiedemann (Cambridge, Mass.: 1975), 184. On the question of Marxism in the study of ancient history and slavery, see Yvon Garlan, *Slavery in Ancient Greece*, rev. ed., trans. Janet Lloyd (Ithaca, N.Y.: Cornell University Press, 1988), 219–24.

53. Ian Morris, introduction to Moses I. Finley, *The Ancient Economy*, updated ed. (Berkeley and Los Angeles: University of University of California Press, 1999), xviii.

54. Keith Bradley, "'The Regular, Daily Traffic in Slaves': Roman History and Contemporary History," *Classical Journal* (1992): 125–38.

55. Paul Cartledge, "Like a Worm I' the Bud?", *Greece and Rome* 40 (1993): 163–80.

56. The question of whether ancient Greece depended on a slave mode of production, in Marx's sense (although he used the term "ancient mode" [*Critique of Political Economy* (1859)]), and whether slaves can be considered a "class" engaged in class struggle in any technical sense, are addressed by G. E. M. de Sainte-Croix, *The Class Struggle in the Ancient Greek World from the Archaic Age to the Arab Conquests* (Ithaca, N.Y.: Cornell University Press, 1981); Moses I. Finley, *Ancient Slavery and Modern Ideology* (New York: Viking, 1980) and elsewhere (see bibliography); Yvon Garlan, *Slavery in Ancient Greece*, rev. ed., trans. Janet Lloyd (Ithaca, N.Y.: Cornell University Press, 1988); Jean-Pierre Vernant, "La lutte des classes" and Pierre Vidal-Naquet, "Les esclaves grecs étaient-ils une classe?," in Vernant and Vidal-Naquet, *Travail et esclavage* (Paris: Ed. Complexe, 1988); Perry Anderson, *Passages from Antiquity to Feudalism* (London: New Left Books, 1974); and Ellen M. Wood, *Peasant-Citizen and Slave: The*

Foundations of Athenian Democracy (London: Verso, 1988), among many others. The Messenian helots, collective slaves of the Spartans, did successfully revolt and found their own city, with the support of the Theban Epaminondas, in the fourth century BCE, but revolts of chattel slaves, who did not share a common language and culture as did the Messenians, are not recorded. Although slaves lacked consciousness of themselves as a "class," their labor and its value contributed to sustaining Athenian democracy and its citizenry.

57. As the philosopher Bernard Williams candidly and modestly remarks, in his discussion of slavery, justice, and identities in antiquity: "Much is known about ancient slavery, and much is not known; unfortunately, much of what is known is not known to me." *Shame and Necessity* (Berkeley and Los Angeles: University of California Press, 1993), 106.

58. A useful compendium of ancient texts on slaves and slavery is Thomas Wiedemann, *Greek and Roman Slavery* (Baltimore: Johns Hopkins University Press, 1981).

59. de Sainte-Croix, *The Class Struggle in the Ancient Greek World.* See also Perry Anderson, "Geoffrey de Ste. Croix and the Ancient World," in *A Zone of Engagement* (London: Verso, 1992), 1–24.

60. Ian Jenkins, *Greek and Roman Life* (London: British Museum Publications, 1986), 70.

61. Paul Cartledge, *The Greeks: A Portrait of Self and Others* (Oxford: Oxford University Press, 1993).

62. For a "cultural poetics" perspective on such questions, see the introduction to *Cultural Poetics in Archaic Greece: Cult, Performance, Politics,* ed. Carol Dougherty and Leslie Kurke (Cambridge: Cambridge University Press, 1993).

63. See Seth Schein, "Cultural Studies and Classics: Contrasts and Opportunities," in *Contextualizing Classics: Ideology, Performance, Dialogue,* ed. T. M. Falkner, N. Felson, and D. Konstan (Lanham, Md.: Rowman & Littlefield, 1999), 285–99. According to Schein, "Cultural Studies focuses on the nature and effects of the political in everyday social life, viewing individuals not merely as performing defined roles in a social system but as resisting this system and the order it entails" (285); "Cultural Studies aims not just to understand the world but, at least in limited ways, to change it by calling into question, critiquing, and intervening in the ways discourses are produced and circulated, so as to resist and transform existing structures and relations of power" (286); "[W]e simplify and dehistoricize Greek and Roman civilization, and we construct false genealogies of ourselves and our own cultural values, when . . . we isolate specific artifacts, texts and institutions, study them out of their historical and cultural contexts, or interpret them one-dimensionally, in positivist fashion, as if their meaning and validity were self-evident" (288).

64. Notable recent exceptions to this rule include Sandra R. Joshel and Sheila Murnaghan, eds., *Women and Slaves in Greco-Roman Culture: Differential Equations* (London: Routledge, 1998); William G. Thalmann, *The Swineherd and the Bow: Representations of Class in the "Odyssey"* (Ithaca, N.Y.: Cornell University Press, 1998); and Danielle Allen, *The World of Prometheus: The Politics*

of Punishing in Democratic Athens (Princeton, N.J.: Princeton University Press, 2000).

65. Fredric Jameson, "Marxism and Historicism," in *The Ideologies of Theory: Essays 1971–1986*, vol. 2, *The Syntax of History* (Minneapolis: University of Minnesota Press, 1988), 151–52.

66. Ira Berlin, in *Many Thousands Gone*, considers both diachronic and geographical differences in early American slavery.

67. Moses I. Finley, "Between Slavery and Freedom," *Comparative Studies in Society and History* 6 (1964),: 233–49.

68. Athenaeus, *The Deipnosophists*, vol. 3, trans. C. B. Gulick, Loeb Classical Library Series (Cambridge, Mass.: Harvard University Press, 1929), 6.265c.

69. See Pierre Vidal-Naquet, "Reflexions sur l'historiographie grecque de l'esclavage," in *Travail et esclavage*, 97–122.

70. Thucydides, *History of the Peloponnesian War*, trans. Rex Warner (Harmondsworth, England: Penguin Books, 1972), 5.116. Subsequent references are to this translation unless otherwise noted.

71. See duBois, *Torture and Truth;* and M. Gagarin, "The Torture of Slaves in Athenian Law," *Classical Philology* 91 (1996): 1–18. On slaves' roles in the legal networks of Athens, see Allen, *The World of Prometheus*, esp. 104–11.

72. Pseudo-Aristotle, *The Householder* 1.51.

73. Schol. to Aristophanes, *Acharnians* 54.

74. Aristotle, *Ath. Pol.* 50.2.

75. Demosthenes 27: *Against Aphobus* I, vol. 4, trans. A. T. Murray (Cambridge, Mass.: Harvard University Press, 1936). On the prices of slaves, see *IG* 1^3.421, col. 1, 33–49 (Meiggs and Lewis 79A): this text lists the prices of sixteen slaves sold at auction, ranging from 72 drachmas for "a little Carian child" to 301 drachmas for "a Syrian."

76. Xenophon, *Revenues* 1.14–17. Xenophon suggested that the state buy slaves and lease them to work in the mines, offering the practical suggestion: "how could anyone steal slaves who have been branded to show that they were state property?" (21)

77. *IG* 1^3.476, 199–218.

78. Pseudo-Xenophon, *Constitution of Athens* 1.10.

79. B.Williams, *Shame and Necessity*, x.

80. On this question in Rome, see Kathleen McCarthy, "Servitium amoris: Amor servitii," in *Women and Slaves in Greco-Roman Culture: Differential Equations*, ed. Sandra R. Joshel and Sheila Murnaghan (London: Routledge, 1998), 174–92. McCarthy calls "the task of mastery" "a very difficult project, one that could never be explicitly codified but existed only in practice" (181).

81. On citizenship, for example, see R. K. Sinclair, *Democracy and Participation in Athens* (Cambridge: Cambridge University Press, 1988), 28.

Chapter 1

1. Walter Benjamin, "No. 113," in *"One-Way Street" and Other Writings*, trans E. Jephcott and K. Shorter (London: New Left Books, 1979), 47.

2. See, for example, Boris Groys, "The Struggle against the Museum; or, The Display of Art in Totalitarian Space," in *Museum/Culture*, ed. D. J. Sherman and I. Rogoff (Minneapolis: University of Minnesota Press, 1994), 144–62; Philip Fisher, *Making and Effacing Art* (Oxford: Oxford University Press, 1991); Pierre Bourdieu and Alain Darbel with Dominique Schnapper, *The Love of Art: European Art Museums and Their Public*, trans. C. Beattie and N. Merriman (Cambridge: Polity, 1991).

3. Ian Jenkins, *Greek and Roman Life* (London: British Museum Publications, 1986), 70. Other books on everyday life treat the matter of slavery superficially. Robert Garland: "Abhorrent though the institution of slavery was in many respects, it nonetheless provided some measure of economic security." *Daily Life of the Ancient Greeks* (Westport, Conn.: Greenwood Press, 1998), 73. T. B. L. Webster: "No ancient society did without slaves, and therefore it is unhistorical to taunt the Athenians with having slaves. Secondly, the Athenians treated their slaves better than any other ancient society." *Everyday Life in Classical Athens* (London: Batsford, 1969), 43. Cyril E. Robinson: "there can be little doubt that the Athenians treated their slaves well." *Everyday Life in Ancient Greece* (Oxford: Clarendon Press, 1933), 88. C. B. Gulick: "As a rule, the treatment of slaves in Athens was not severe. . . . Kindly feelings of humanity also played their part, especially among the more enlightened Athenians." *The Life of the Ancient Greeks* (1902; reprint, New York: Cooper Square Publishers, 1973), 69.

4. Anne Pearson, *Everyday Life in Ancient Greece* (New York: Franklin Watts, 1994).

5. Marjorie Quennell and C. H. B. Quennell, *Everyday Things in Ancient Greece* (London: Batsford, 1930–33).

6. Henri Lefebvre, "The Everyday and Everydayness," trans. C. Levich, K. Ross, and A. Kaplan, *Yale French Studies* 73 (1987): 10. See also Lefebvre's *Critique de la vie quotidienne*, 3 vols. (Paris: L'Arche, 1958–81), in English as *Critique of Everyday Life*, trans. J. Moore, vol. 1 (New York: Verso, 1991); and *La vie quotidienne dans le monde moderne* (Paris: Gallimard, 1968).

7. Sigmund Freud, *The Psychopathology of Everyday Life*, trans. Alan Tyson (New York: Norton, 1966).

8. Fernand Braudel, *The Structures of Everyday Life: The Limits of the Possible*, rev. and trans. S. Reynolds (New York: Harper and Row, 1981).

9. Michel DeCerteau, *The Practice of Everyday Life*, trans. S. Rendall (Berkeley and Los Angeles: University of California Press, 1984).

10. See Carl Richard, *The Founders and the Classics: Greece, Rome, and the American Enlightenment* (Cambridge, Mass.: Harvard University Press, 1994), Jennifer Tolbert Roberts, *Athens on Trial: The Antidemocratic Tradition in Western Thought* (Princeton, N.J.: Princeton University Press, 1994).

11. See Ian Morris, *Archaeology as Cultural History: Words and Things in Iron Age Greece* (Oxford: Blackwell, 2000), who emphasizes conflict in ancient society, and ancient persons as actors in these conflicts.

12. Marcel Detienne, "Un ephèbe, un olivier," in *L'Ecriture d'Orphée* (Paris: Gallimard, 1989), 71–84.

13. Translation is from D. Grene and R. Lattimore, eds., *The Complete Greek Tragedies* (Chicago: University of Chicago Press, 1992).

14. See Lysias 7, "Before the Areopagus: Defence in the Matter of the Olive-Stump."

15. *Oxford Classical Dictionary*, ed. N. G. L. Hammond and H. H. Scullard, 2d ed. (Oxford: Oxford University Press, 1970), s.v. "cookery," 288.

16. See Page duBois, *Sowing the Body: Psychoanalysis and Ancient Representations of Women* (Chicago: University of Chicago Press, 1988).

17. Michael Jameson, "Domestic Space in the Greek City-State," in *Domestic Architecture and the Use of Space: An Interdisciplinary Study*, ed. Susan Kent, 92–113 (Cambridge: Cambridge University Press, 1990).

18. Jean-Pierre Vernant, "Hestia-Hermes: The Religious Expression of Space and Movement among the Greeks," trans. H. Piat, *Social Sciences Information* 8 (1969): 131–68.

19. Jameson, "Domestic Space in the Greek City-State," 106.

20. On the Greek house, see also Lisa C. Nevett, *House and Society in the Ancient Greek World* (Cambridge: Cambridge University Press, 1999): "The range of tasks carried out by household slaves also seems to have taken them into a variety of different parts of the house, and there is no evidence in either town or country for specific slave quarters." (40)

21. Ian Morris, "Remaining Invisible: The Archaeology of the Excluded in Classical Athens," in *Women and Slaves in Greco-Roman Culture*, ed. Sandra R. Joshel and Sheila Murnaghan (London: Routledge, 1998), 211. Morris makes a useful point in relation to the archaeological evidence of slavery in classical Athens: "As a tentative hypothesis, I suggest that the 'mainstream' material culture of Athens was so pervasive because Athenian male citizen culture as a whole was unusually hegemonic, filling every corner of the conceptual landscape, allowing no space for alternatives. . . . In Classical Athens, I suggest, the excluded remain invisible not just because of methodological problems, but because the dominant male citizens wanted them so. Slaves have no private spaces, no room in the house" (ibid.).

22. James Davidson, *Courtesans and Fishcakes: The Comsuming Passions of Classical Athens* (New York: HarperCollins, 1997), 86. See Ursula Knigge, *Der Kerameikos von Athen* (Athens: Krone Verlag, 1988).

23. Aristophanes, *Acharnians, Knights*, trans. Jeffrey Henderson, Loeb Classical Library Series (Cambridge, Mass.: Harvard University Press, 1998). All citations from Aristophanes except where otherwise noted come from the translations of Henderson.

24. Ian Morris, "Archaeologies of Greece," in *Classical Greece: Ancient Histories and Modern Archaeologies*, ed. Ian Morris (Cambridge: Cambridge University Press, 1994), 46.

25. Edward Miller, *That Noble Cabinet: A History of the British Museum* (London: André Deutsch, 1973), 309.

26. For the debate on the value, economic and aesthetic, of Greek vases, see Michael Vickers and David Gill, *Artful Crafts: Ancient Greek Silverware and Pot-*

tery (Oxford: Clarendon, 1994), and their critics. See, for example, *Looking at Greek Vases*, ed. T. Rasmussen and Nigel Spivey (Cambridge: Cambridge University Press, 1991), 134ff.

27. François Lissarrague, *The Aesthetics of the Greek Banquet: Images of Wine and Ritual*, trans. A. Szegedy-Maszak (Princeton, N.J.: Princeton University Press, 1990).

28. J. M. Roberts, *The Penguin History of the World* (London: Penguin Books, 1995), 22.

29. E. Marianne Stern and Birgit Schlick-Nolte, *Early Glass of the Ancient World, 1600 BC–AD 50* (Ostfildern: Verlag Gerd Hatje, 1994).

30. Lesley Stern, *The Smoking Book* (Chicago: University of Chicago Press, 1999), 222.

Chapter 2

1. Sigmund Freud, *The Interpretation of Dreams*, in *The Standard Edition of the Complete Psychological Works*, 24 vols. (London: Hogarth Press and the Institute of Psycho-Analysis, 1953–73).

2. See Karl Polanyi, *Primitive, Archaic, and Modern Economies: Essays of Karl Polanyi*, ed. G. Dalton (Garden City, N.Y.: Anchor Books, 1968). For a brilliant development of the cultural implications of this theoretical schema for analyzing ancient Greek society, see Leslie Kurke, *Coins, Bodies, Games, and Gold: The Politics of Meaning in Archaic Greece* (Princeton, N.J.: Princeton University Press, 1999).

3. See, in the bibliography, Duncan, Sherman and Rogoff, Pearce, Karp and Lavine, and P. Fisher, among others.

4. Carol Duncan, in her important book *Civilizing Rituals*, discusses only what she calls "art museums," and categorizes them as "princely galleries," public art museums, municipal art museums, and donor memorials. She moves, therefore, in one chapter from discussion of the Louvre, which includes in its vast collections broken pieces of the Parthenon frieze, to the National Gallery in London, a gallery of paintings. The Louvre became a museum in 1793 when "the French revolutionary government nationalized the king's art collection and declared the Louvre a public institution" (2). Duncan's discussion effaces the didactic, historical project of the Louvre, which contains a great deal of material from classical antiquity and from Egypt, and categorizes it as an "art museum": "In a relatively short time, the Louvre's directors (drawing partly on German and Italian precedents) worked out a whole set of practices that came to characterize art museums everywhere. In short, the museum organized its collections into art-historical schools and installed them so as to make visible the development and achievement of each school" (2). Interested as she is in art museums, she erases other ambitions of the Louvre, and so makes a transition not to the British Museum, a "universal survey museum" like the Louvre, but to London's National Gallery, the English analogue to the Louvre and an art historical museum established in the absence of a concern for ancient art and history.

Carol Duncan, *Civilizing Rituals: Inside Public Art Museums* (New York: Routledge, 1995).

5. Krzysztof Pomian, "The Collection: Between the Visible and the Invisible," in *Collectors and Curiosities: Paris and Venice, 1500–1800* (Cambridge: Polity Press, 1990), 7–44.

6. Salvatore Settis, lecture delivered at the Getty Museum, 1998.

7. See Marjorie Caygill, *The Story of the British Museum*, 2d ed. (London: British Museum Press for the Trustees of the British Museum, 1992); and Edward Miller, *That Noble Cabinet: A History of the British Museum* (London: André Deutsch, 1973).

8. The British Museum has recently, in its latest form, reincorporated the relics of so-called primitive societies, the objects of anthropological interest called ethnography in its didactic materials, into its displays. On such displays see James A. Boon, "Why Museums Make Me Sad," in *Exhibiting Cultures: The Poetics and Politics of Museum Display*, ed. Ivan Karp and Steven D. Lavine, 255–77 (Washington, D.C.: Smithsonian Institution Press, 1991); and Annie E. Coombes, "Blinded by 'Science': Ethnography at the British Museum," in *Art Apart: Art Institutions and Ideology across England and North America*, ed. Marcia Pointon (Manchester: Manchester University Press, 1994), 102–19.

9. This paradoxical position, characteristic of the "high" culture of ancient China as well, affects such comparative anthropological projects as that of Marcel Detienne. See, for example, his *Apollon le couteau à la main* (Paris: Gallimard, 1998); in the introduction Detienne discusses a collaborative project on polytheism involving an Africanist and other ethnographers, conducted in the CNRS and the Ecole pratique des Hautes Etudes. Detienne here distances himself from the comparativism early practiced with J.-P. Vernant, around "un solide noyau 'grec'" (17).

10. J. Paul Getty, *As I See It: The Autobiography of J. Paul Getty* (Englewood Cliffs, N.J.: Prentice-Hall, 1976), 279–80.

11. J. Paul Getty, *How to Be Rich* (Chicago: Playboy Press, 1966).

12. Duncan, *Civilizing Rituals*, 72–101. The villa is elsewhere referred to as "a robber-baron mansion" in Carol Duncan and Alan Wallach, "The Universal Survey Museum," *Art History* 3 (1980): 451.

13. Duncan and Wallach, "The Universal Survey Museum," 449.

14. Duncan and Wallach write of the Louvre: "No one can miss the point of the iconographic programme: France is the true heir of classical civilization" (ibid., 459). But Britain owns the lion's share.

15. On this frieze, see Page duBois, *Centaurs and Amazons* (Ann Arbor: University of Michigan Press, 1982), 64–66.

16. Mary Beard, "Souvenirs of Culture: Deciphering (in) the Museum," *Art History* 15 (1992), 523.

17. Mary Beard points out that the Horse of Selene, part of the east pediment of the Parthenon, was in 1988–89 the seventh most-often-purchased postcard image by museum visitors. Mary Beard, "Souvenirs of Culture," 509.

18. Caygill, *The Story of the British Museum*, 19.

19. On the removal of antiquities from Greece, see Caygill, *The Story of the British Museum;* Christopher Hitchens, *The Elgin Marbles: Should They Be Returned to Greece?* (London: Verso, 1997); C. P. Bracken, *Antiquities Acquired: The Spoliation of Greece* (Newton Abbot, England: David & Charles, 1975); Jeanette Greenfield, *The Return of Cultural Treasures*, 2d ed. (Cambridge: Cambridge University Press, 1995).

20. The label reads further: "Greek, made in Athens about 360–350 BC (attributed to the Apollonia Painter) from Cyrenaica. The woman descending the ladder drops incense and spices into bowl for dedication to Aphrodite and Adonis. The other women, accompanied by Pan and Eros, dance and play castanets." GR 1856. 10–1.16 BM Cat VasesE 241.

21. See Marcel Detienne, *The Gardens of Adonis: Spices in Greek Mythology*, trans. Janet Lloyd (Atlantic Highlands, N.J.: Humanities Press, 1977); John J. Winkler, *The Constraints of Desire: The Anthropology of Sex and Gender in Ancient Greece* (New York: Routledge, 1990), 188–209. On Pan, see Philippe Bourgeaud, *The Cult of Pan in Ancient Greece*, trans. K. Atlass and J. Redfield (Chicago: University of Chicago Press, 1988).

22. Duncan and Wallach, "The Universal Survey Museum," 457.

23. On modern Hellenism, see Artemis Leontis, *Topographies of Hellenism: Mapping the Homeland* (Ithaca, N.Y.: Cornell University Press, 1995); Gregory Jusdanis, *Belated Modernity and Aesthetic Culture: The Making of a National Literature* (Minneapolis: University of Minnesota Press, 1991); V. Lambropoulos, *Literature as National Institution: Studies in the Politics of Modern Greek Criticism* (Princeton, N.J.: Princeton University Press, 1988); M. Herzfeld, *Ours Once More: Folklore, Ideology, and the Making of Modern Greece* (New York: Pella Pubishing, 1986).

24. "Concise History of the National Museum," introduction to Semni Karouzou, *National Archaeological Museum: Collection of Sculpture* (Athens: General Direction of Antiquities and Restoration, 1968), vii.

25. Dr. Semni Karouzou, *National Museum: Illustrated Guide to the Museum* (Athens: Ekdotike Athenon, 1998), 56.

26. See especially Nicholas Himmelmann, *Archaologisches zum Problem der griechischen Sklaverei* (Wiesbaden: Verlag der Akademie der Wissenschaften und der Literatur, 1971).

27. See Ruth Leader, "In Death Not Divided: Gender, Family and State on Classical Athenian Grave Stelae," *American Journal of Archaeology* 101 (1997): 683–99; on the Hegeso stele, 689–90. See also Deborah Steiner, *Images in Mind: Statues in Archaic and Classical Greek Literature and Thought* (Princeton, N.J.: Princeton University Press, 2001), 155.

28. For bibliography, and an important discussion of this stele, see Andrew Stewart, *Art, Desire, and the Body in Ancient Greece* (Cambridge: Cambridge University Press, 1997), 124–29.

29. Himmelmann, *Archaologisches zum Problem der griechischen Sklaverei*, 38. The possession of a slave did not mark one as especially wealthy; later classical authors tend to assume that any Attic citizen, even of the lower classes, owns at

least one unfree servant. According to Himmelmann, "The purchase price for a not especially qualified person at the end of the fifth century amounted to 150–200 drachmas; in the same period the normal day's wages for a hand laborer amounted to 1 drachma per day" (6). Cited passage translated by Chris Hudson.

30. On the *hetaira*, see Kurke, *Coins, Bodies, Games, and Gold*, 175–219; James Davidson, *Courtesans and Fishcakes: The Consuming Passions of Classical Athens* (New York: HarperCollins, 1997), 109–36.

31. Stewart, *Art, Desire, and the Body in Ancient Greece*, 128.

32. See also object no. 4496—on the left side of a grave monument from the second half of the fourth century BCE, "a slave girl with a short mourning haircut."

33. There are other issues of interest brought up by the displays in this museum. One is the way in which the "national" museum appropriates the archaeological finds of various localities and displays them in the capital. Although ancient Greece was not a nation but a disparate, often warring set of city-states divided by land, sea, and dialectal differences, the national museum of the modern nation-state draws objects from every corner of its territory to display them as the nation's patrimony. The beautiful frescoes from the Minoan culture of Thira, from the island Santorini, named by the Italians who once possessed it, long promised to be returned to the island from which they were removed, grace the upper floor of the National Museum; one sees no sign of their imminent return to the Aegean Sea. Even when the objects themselves remain where they were discovered, often for other political and strategic reasons, they are made to serve the national project. When I was last in Greece, for example, one saw everywhere posters showing the golden diadem from the royal Macedonian tomb at Vergina, with the words "Macedonia/Greece" below—part of a national effort to claim and retain possession of Greek Macedonia and to counter the opposing claims of what is now called "Macedonia the Independent Nation of the Former State of Yugoslavia," which may have imperial designs on Greek Macedonia, not least because it was the home of Philip and Alexander the Great, ancestors of all Macedonians.

34. Fisher, *Making and Effacing Art*, 8.

35. M. Bernal, *Black Athena, The Afroasiatic Roots of Classical Civilization*, vol. 1, *The Fabrication of Ancient Greece 1785–1985* (New Brunswick, N.J.: Rutgers University Press, 1987), vol. 2, *The Archaeological and Documentary Evidence* (New Brunswick, N.J.: Rutgers University Press, 1991); see also Page duBois, *Trojan Horses: Saving the Classics from Conservatives* (New York: New York University Press, 2001).

36. Sigmund Freud, *The Standard Edition of the Complete Psychological Works* (London: Hogarth Press, 1953–73), 22:241.

37. Karouzou, *National Museum*, 6.

38. See Bracken, *Antiquities Acquired*; Hitchens, *The Elgin Marbles*.

39. An interesting art historical detail is the extensive exhibition in the nineteenth century of Hiram Powers's statue *Greek Slave*. Not a representation of an ancient slave, this marmoreal, very white figure depicts a Greek Christian

woman, with cross, imagined as enslaved by the Turks. See Joy S. Kasson, *Marble Queens and Captives: Women in Nineteenth-Century American Sculpture* (New Haven, Conn.: Yale University Press, 1990), 46–72. On the question of this statue and abolitionism, not a central issue for Kasson, see Vivien Green [Fryd], "Hiram Powers's *Greek Slave*, Emblem of Freedom," *American Art Journal* 14 (1982): 31–39.

40. Fred Wilson, *Mining the Museum, An Installation*, ed. Lisa G. Corrin (Baltimore: Contemporary, 1994).

Chapter 3

1. Michel Foucault, *The History of Sexuality*, vol. 2, *The Use of Pleasure*, trans. R. Hurley (New York: Vintage Books, 1990). Negative reactions included A. Richlin, "Zeus and Metis: Foucault, Feminism, Classics" *Helios* 18 (1991): 160–80; B. Thornton, "Constructionism and Ancient Greek Sex," *Helios* 18 (1991): 181–93; and more recently, James Davidson, *Courtesans and Fishcakes: The Consuming Passions of Classical Athens* (New York: HarperCollins, 1997), xxi–xxv, 313–14. The most prominent advocate of a Foucauldian perspective on Greek antiquity has been David Halperin; see *One Hundred Years of Homosexuality and Other Essays on Greek Love* (New York: Routledge, 1990) and *Saint Foucault* (New York: Oxford University Press, 1995).

2. Michel Foucault, *The History of Sexuality*, vol. 3, *The Care of the Self*, trans. Robert Hurley (New York: Pantheon Books, 1986).

3. See the works in the bibliography by Jean-Pierre Vernant, Pierre Vidal-Naquet, Nicole Loraux, Marcel Detienne, and Francois Lissarrague.

4. See, for example, *Before Sexuality: The Construction of Erotic Experience in the Ancient Greek World*, ed. D. Halperin, J. J. Winkler, and F. I. Zeitlin (Princeton, N.J.: Princeton University Press, 1990), in which slaves rarely figure.

5. Michel Foucault, *The Order of Things: An Archaeology of the Human Sciences* (New York: Pantheon Books, 1971), xv.

6. John Maxwell Edmonds, *The Fragments of Attic Comedy*, vol. 1 (Leiden: E. J. Brill, 1957).

7. Jeffrey Henderson, *The Maculate Muse: Obscene Language in Attic Comedy* (New Haven, Conn.: Yale University Press, 1975), 124.

8. Eva Keuls, *The Reign of the Phallus* (New York: Harper and Row, 1985).

9. See Alan Bray, *Homosexuality in Renaissance England* (London: Gay Men's Press, 1982); Jonathan Goldberg, ed, *Queering the Renaissance* (Durham, N.C.: Duke University Press, 1994), and *Sodometries: Renaissance Texts, Modern Sexualities* (Stanford, Calif.: Stanford University Press, 1992); Halperin, *One Hundred Years of Homosexuality*.

10. H. G. Liddell and Robert Scott, comps., *A Greek-English Lexicon*, 9th rev. ed., by H. S. Jones (Oxford: Oxford University Press, 1948) (1st ed, 1843).

11. Sigmund Freud, "Fetishism," in *The Standard Edition of the Complete Psychological Works* (London: Hogarth Press and the Institute of Psycho-Analysis,

1953–73). See also *Fetishism as Cultural Discourse?*, ed. B. Pietz and E. Apter (Ithaca, N.Y.: Cornell University Press, 1993).

12. Davidson, in *Courtesans and Fishcakes*, is critical of such an emphasis on penetration and domination (169ff.): "This theory has been overstated and presents a model of Athenian society which is not only simplistic and overschematic but quite misleading" (169). He focuses on the complexity of relations, "a nexus of exchanged values involving love, gifts, desirability and favours" (ibid.).

13. On plow and stilus, see Page duBois, *Sowing the Body: Psychoanalysis and Ancient Representations of Women* (Chicago: University of Chicago Press, 1988).

14. Henderson, *The Maculate Muse*.

15. Jürgen Habermas, "The Public Sphere," in *Jürgen Habermas on Society and Politics: A Reader*, ed. Steven Seidman (Boston: Beacon Press, 1989), 231.

16. David A. Campbell, ed. and trans., *Greek Lyric I, Sappho and Alcaeus*, Loeb Classical Library Series (Cambridge, Mass.: Harvard University Press, 1982).

17. Denys Page, *Sappho and Alcaeus* (Oxford: Oxford University Press, 1955), 144.

18. See Joan DeJean, *Fictions of Sappho, 1546–1937* (Chicago: University of Chicago Press, 1989); Page duBois, *Sappho Is Burning* (Chicago: University of Chicago Press, 1995).

19. *Plektidzomai*, "bandy blows," can mean "toy amorously," as at Aristophanes *Ekkleziadzousai* 964, Herodas *Mimiambi* 5.29 (LSJ).

20. M. L. West, "Burning Sappho," *Maia* 22 (1970): 307–33; Giuseppe Giangrande, "Sappho and the *Olisbos*," *Emerita* 48 (1980): 249–50.

21. See A. Guarino, "Professorenerotismus," *Labeo* 27 (1981): 439–40, and the response, Giuseppe Giangrande, "A che serviva l' 'olisbos' di Saffo?," *Labeo* 29 (1983): 154–55. K. J. Dover believes that if *olisbodokoisi* is the proper reading of the text, it is "tantalising but perhaps not important" to our understanding of Greek female homosexuality, because the olisbos "is associated essentially with solitary female masturbation." K. J. Dover, *Greek Homosexuality* (Oxford: Oxford University Press, 1978), 176, n. 9.

22. Giuseppe Giangrande, "Emendations to Callimachus," *Classical Quarterly*, n.s., 12 (1962): 212–22.

23. Campbell, *Greek Lyric I, Sappho and Alcaeus*, 125 n. 3.

24. *Aristophanes*, vol. 3, ed. and trans. Jeffrey Henderson, Loeb Classical Library Series (Cambridge, Mass.: Harvard University Press, 2000). Even in 1964, Douglass Parker, a refreshingly direct translator for his day, dodges the obscenity:

"Lovers can't be had for love or money,
not even synthetics. Why, since those beastly Milesians
revolted and cut off the leather trade, that handy
do-it-yourself kit's vanished from the open market."

Aristophanes, *Four Comedies*, trans. Douglass Parker (Ann Arbor: University of Michigan Press, 1969), 24 (Parker assigns this speech to "Kleonike.") See also Aristophanes, *Lysistrata*, ed. Jeffrey Henderson (Oxford: Oxford University Press, 1987).

25. Henderson, *The Maculate Muse*, 133.

26. Other mentions of dildos by ancient writers include the comic writer Sophron 24, *solenes*, for pipes and dildos; the *likhneuma* of widows, *gerra Naxia* (Epicharmus 174), for phallus, according to Henderson "a usage probably taken from the cult of Aphrodite at Naxos" (*The Maculate Muse*, 25), incidentally supporting Giangrande's argument ("Emendations to Callimachus") about the *gerra* in Callimachus. In an interesting passage from Eubulus (75.10), pastry is personified as the wife of Pluto, and the finger is compared to "the ramming beak of a trireme": "Demeter's girl, when kneaded, has a hollow cleft—like the swath of a trireme—made in her by the finger's poking: the excellent precursor to a meal!" Here the act of penetration is made equivalent both to the pastry cook's act of kneading, and the ramming action of a warship.

27. Henderson, *The Maculate Muse*, 111.

28. See duBois, *Sowing the Body*.

29. Edmonds, *The Fragments of Attic Comedy*, 1:132–33. The Herodotus passage reads as follows:

> After the battle (of Salamis) the Greeks towed over to Salamis all the disabled vessels which were adrift in the neighbourhood, and then prepared for a renewal of the fight, fully expecting that Xerxes would use his remaining ships to make another attack. Many of the disabled vessels and other wreckage were carried by the westerly wind to a part of the Attic coast called Colias, and in this way it came about that not only the prophecies of Bacis and Musaeus about this battle were fulfilled, but also another prophecy which had been uttered many years previously by an Athenian soothsayer named Lysistratus: the words of this one were, "The Colian women shall cook their food with oars."

Herodotus 8.96 (*The Histories*, rev. A. R. Burn and trans. A. de Selincourt [Harmondsworth, England: Penguin Books, 1972], 555).

30. Herodas, *Mimiambi*, ed. I. C. Cunningham (Oxford: Oxford University Press, 1971), 6.17–19; translation from Herodas, *The Mimes and Fragments*, with notes by W. Headlam, ed. A. D. Knox (Cambridge: Cambridge University Press, 1922).

31. Maurice Olender, "Aspects of Baubo: Ancient Texts and Contexts," in *Before Sexuality: The Construction of Erotic Experience in the Ancient Greek World*, ed. D. Halperin, J. J. Winkler, and F. I. Zeitlin (Princeton, N.J.: Princeton University Press, 1990), 83. On Gorgo-Baubo, see also J.-P. Vernant, *La mort dans les yeux. Figures de l'autre en Grèce ancienne* (Paris: Hachette, 1985).

32. For a mining of this and other texts on pleasure, see Davidson, *Courtesans and Fishcakes*.

33. Edmonds, *The Fragments of Attic Comedy*, 1:948–51.

34. On sex with slaves, especially helots, a more permissible form of intercourse in the Greek imaginary, see Pierre Vidal-Naquet, "Slavery and the Rule

of Women in Tradition, Myth and Utopia," in *Myth, Religion and Society: Structuralist Essays*, ed. R. L. Gordon (Cambridge: Cambridge University Press, 1981), 187–200.

35. Aristophanes, *Birds, Lysistrata, Women at the Thesmophoria*, trans. J. Henderson, Loeb Classical Library Series (Cambridge, Mass.: Harvard University Press, 2000).

Chapter 4

1. Nicholas Himmelmann, *Archaölogisches zum Problem der griechischen Sklaverei* (Wiesbaden: Verlag der Akademie der Wissenschaften und der Literatur, 1971), 42–43; on the iconography of slaves, see 8ff. Cited passage translated by Chris Hudson.

2. Dionysius Halicarnassensis, *Antiquitates Romanae* 7.2–12; Plutarch, *Moralia* 261e–262d. These slaves were probably like the Spartan helots, that is, enslaved collectively; see Pierre Vidal-Naquet, "Slavery and the Rule of Women in Tradition, Myth and Utopia," in *The Black Hunter*, trans. A. Szegedy-Maszak (Baltimore: Johns Hopkins University Press, 1986), 205–23; "servile power and female power are linked" (211).

3. Edith Hamilton and Huntington Cairns, eds., *The Collected Dialogues of Plato* (Princeton, N.J.: Bollingen, 1961), 1353.

4. Aristophanes, *Clouds, Wasps, Peace*, trans. J. Henderson, Loeb Classical Library Series (Cambridge, Mass.: Harvard University Press, 1998). Subsequent citations of these plays are to this translation unless otherwise noted.

5. Herodotus, *The Histories*, rev. A. R. Burn, trans. A. de Selincourt (Harmondsworth, England: Penguin Books, 1972). Subsequent citations are to this edition and translation.

6. W. R. M. Lamb, trans., *Plato*, vol. 3, Loeb Classical Library Series (Cambridge, Mass.: Harvard University Press, 1925).

7. James Davidson describes the bent-over position as the least expensive of prostitutes' offerings: "Bent-over . . . is the cheapest kind of sex, often priced at three obols." James Davidson, *Courtesans and Fishcakes: The Consuming Passions of Classical Athens* (New York: HarperCollins, 1997), 118.

8. See Page duBois, *Torture and Truth* (New York: Routledge, 1991).

9. See Davidson, *Courtesans and Fishcakes*, 93–95, 100–102, 105–6, 198–200; Jean-Pierre Vernant, "Marriage," in *Myth and Society in Ancient Greece*, trans. Janet Lloyd (New York: Zone Books, 1990), 57–58.

10. On torture, see Danielle Allen, *The World of Prometheus: The Politics of Punishing in Democratic Athens* (Princeton, N.J.: Princeton University Press, 2000), 104–5, 210–13; M. Gagarin, "The Torture of Slaves in Athenian Law," *Classical Philology* 91 (1996): 1–18; Virginia A. Hunter, *Policing Athens: Social Control in Attic Lawsuits* (Princeton, N.J.: Princeton University Press, 1994), 174–76, duBois, *Torture and Truth*.

11. C. P. Jones, "*Stigma:* Tattooing and Branding in Graeco-Roman Antiquity." *Journal of Roman Studies* 77 (1987): 141.

12. John Maxwell Edmonds, ed., *The Fragments of Attic Comedy* (Leiden: E. J. Brill, 1957), 1:591.

13. See C. P. Jones, "Stigma and Taboo," in *Written on the Body: The Tattoo in European and American History*, ed. Jane Caplan (Princeton, N.J.: Princeton University Press, 2000)

14. C. P. Jones ("Stigma and Taboo") translates this passage as "I have even heard that in addition he sent tattooers *(stigees)* to tattoo *(stixontes)* the Hellespont" (7), arguing that this verb refers to puncturing of the skin (4), not branding.

15. Ibid., 145. See K. Zimmermann, "Tatowierte Thrakerinnen auf griechischen Vasenbildern," *Jahrbuch. Deutsches Archaeologische Institut* 95 (1980): 163–96; *Dissoi logoi* (Diels 2.408) on tattoos as punishment; Asios of Samos mentions a *stigmatias*, a tattooed slave or criminal (Athenaeus 3.125). *Adikia*, "injustice," bears tattoos or circular marks on an Attic amphora of ca. 510 (Vienna 3722, Beazley ARV2 11 no.3).

16. J. F. Kindstrand, *Bion of Borysthenes* (Uppsala: S. Akademie Ubsaliensis, 1976), 179–80.

17. Aristotle, *Generation of Animals*, trans. A. L. Peck, Loeb Classical Library Series (Cambridge, Mass.: Harvard University Press, 1953).

18. See Aristotle, *Politics*.

19. *Aristophanes*, vol. 2, trans. B. B. Rogers, Loeb Classical Library Series (Cambridge, Mass.: Harvard University Press, 1924).

20. Jeffrey Henderson, *The Maculate Muse: Obscene Language in Attic Comedy* (New Haven, Conn.: Yale University Press, 1975), 175. K. J. Dover points out that "the passage is an interesting reminder that it is hard to keep secrets in a society where people constantly have slaves in attendance." Aristophanes, *Frogs*, ed. K. J. Dover (Oxford: Clarendon Press, 1993), 285.

21. Athenaeus, *The Deipnosophists*, trans. C. B. Gulick, Loeb Classical Library Series (Cambridge, Mass.: Harvard University Press, 1929).

22. On these texts, see Pierre Vidal-Naquet, "Esclavage et gynécocratie dans la tradition, le mythe, l'utopie," in *Travail et esclavage en Grèce ancienne*, by Jean-Pierre Vernant and Pierre Vidal-Naquet (Paris: Ed. Complexe, 1988), 123–46, and "Reflexions sur l'historiographie grecque de l'esclavage," in the same volume, 97–122.

23. In Rogers's translation of the *Thesmophoriazusae* (*Aristophanes*, vol. 2), lines 635–48 are simply omitted. The Loeb editor, unnamed, provides a Latin translation for the lines, which concern a *peos*, or "cock," in the footnotes; "643–648 are literally: *Cl. Sta erectus. Quo phallum trudis deorsum?*, etc." J. Henderson, in the new Loeb translation, gives us: "'Stand up straight. Where are you shoving your cock down there?,' etc." Aristophanes, *Birds, Lysistrata, Women at the Thesmophoria*, trans. J. Henderson, Loeb Classical Library (Cambridge, Mass.: Harvard University Press, 2000).

24. Patricia J. Williams, "My Best White Friend: Cinderella Revisited," *The New Yorker* 72, no. 2 (February 26 and March 4, 1996): 94.

25. See Page duBois, *Trojan Horses: Saving the Classics from Conservatives* (New York: New York University Press, 2001).

Chapter 5

1. Fredric Jameson, "Marxism and Historicism," in *The Ideologies of Theory: Essays 1971–1986*, vol. 2, *The Syntax of History* (Minneapolis: University of Minnesota Press, 1988), 151–52.

2. Ian Morris, foreword to Moses I. Finley, *The Ancient Economy*, updated ed. (Berkeley and Los Angeles: University of California Press, 1999), xxvi–vii.

3. Jameson, "Marxism and Historicism," 157. "Nor is there any reason that a contemporary Marxian model of social structure should not make a determinate place for the psychoanalytic 'instance'—the construction of a particular 'psychoanalytic' subject in this or that mode of production—and for the phenomenological—in particular the phenomenology of space and the organization of *Lebenswelt* or daily life in a given social formation. What needs to be stressed, however, is that all these various 'instances' are dialectically modified according to the structural place assigned to them in the various modes of production" (173).

4. J. Laplanche and J.-B. Pontalis, *The Language of Psychoanalysis*, trans. D. Nicholson-Smith (New York: Norton, 1973), 118. Freudian disavowal is a denial or disavowal of castration.

5. Glenn R. Morrow, *Plato's Law of Slavery in Its Relation to Greek Law* (New York: Arno, 1976), 45.

6. Paul Cartledge, *Aristophanes and His Theatre of the Absurd* (Bristol: Bristol Classical Press, 1990), 70.

7. Aristophanes, *Clouds, Wasps, Peace*, trans. Jeffrey Henderson, Loeb Classical Library Series (Cambridge, Mass.: Harvard University Press, 1998). This and subsequent translations are from this edition.

8. On this speech, see R. M. Harriot, *Aristophanes Poet and Dramatist* (London: Croom Helm, 1986), 37.

9. Ian Morris, "The Strong Principle of Equality and the Archaic Origins of Greek Democracy," in *Demokratia: A Conversation on Democracies, Ancient and Modern*, ed. Josiah Ober and Charles Hedrick (Princeton, N.J.: Princeton University Press, 1996), 19–48. See also Leslie Kurke, *Coins, Bodies, Games, and Gold: The Politics of Meaning in Archaic Greece* (Princeton, N.J.: Princeton University Press, 1999).

10. Page duBois, *Sowing the Body: Psychoanalysis and Ancient Representations of Women* (Chicago: University of Chicago Press, 1988), 121–23; see Jeffrey Henderson, *The Maculate Muse: Obscene Language in Attic Comedy* (New Haven, Conn.: Yale University Press, 1975), 39, 81–82, 201; on the tattooing of slaves, see chap. 4 of the present text, and C. P. Jones, "*Stigma*: Tattooing and Branding in Graeco-Roman Antiquity," *Journal of Roman Studies* 77 (1987): 139–55.

11. Kenneth Reckford, *Aristophanes' Old-and-New Comedy*, vol. 1 (Chapel Hill: University of North Carolina Press, 1987), 222–23). He does say, however, that Xanthias refers to the play as a whole as *logidion gnomen ekhon*, "a little story with a point." "The phrase suggests something like a fable of Aesop with its accompanying moral, or inherent lesson" (224).

12. A. M. Bowie, *Aristophanes: Myth, Ritual and Comedy* (Cambridge: Cambridge University Press, 1993), 78ff.

13. Cedric Whitman, *Aristophanes and the Comic Hero* (Cambridge, Mass.: Harvard University Press, 1964), 151.

14. K. J. Dover, *Aristophanic Comedy* (Berkeley and Los Angeles: University of California Press, 1972), 11.

15. See Michael Silk, "The People of Aristophanes," in *Characterization and Individuality in Greek Literature*, ed. Christopher B. R. Pelling (Oxford: Clarendon Press, 1990), 150–73; Victor Ehrenburg, *The People of Aristophanes* (Oxford: B. Blackwell, 1951).

16. Cf. David Konstan, *Greek Comedy and Ideology* (New York: Oxford University Press, 1995), 27–28.

17. Plutarch, *The Rise and Fall of Athens, Nine Greek Lives*, trans. Ian Scott-Kilvert (London: Penguin Books, 1960), 133.

18. "the barbarian came again with his great host against Hellas to enslave [*doulosomenos*] it" (1.18).

19. Josiah Ober, *Mass and Elite in Democratic Athens: Rhetoric, Ideology, and the Power of the People* (Princeton, N.J.: Princeton University Press, 1989). On the development of the concept of freedom, which he describes as a tripartite entity encompassing personal freedom, civic freedom, and sovereignal freedom, see Orlando Patterson, *Freedom*, vol. 1, *Freedom in the Making of Western* Culture (New York: Basic Books, 1991), 47–105.

20. Aristotle, *Nicomachean Ethics*, trans. H. Rackham, Loeb Classical Library Series (Cambridge, Mass.: Harvard University Press, 1934). On these passages, see Peter Garnsey, *Ideas of Slavery from Aristotle to Augustine* (Cambridge: Cambridge University Press, 1996), 118–21, with extensive bibliography on slavery. On friendship between women and slaves, see Lin Foxhall, "Emotional Attachments in Athenian Society," in *Kosmos*, ed. P. Cartledge, P. Millett, and S. von Reden (Cambridge: Cambridge University Press, 1998), 52–67; on women's intimate relationships with slaves, 64–65.

21. *Aristotle*, vol. 20, trans. H. Rackham, Loeb Classical Library Series (Cambridge, Mass.: Harvard University Press, 1952). The translator's diction here is suggestive; the slave is a "tool," a "member" of the master—language that in English slang points to a sexual usage of the slave.

22. See, for example, Peter Hunt's argument about the anxiety produced by the participation of slaves in Greek warfare in *Slaves, Warfare, and Ideology in the Greek Historians* (Cambridge: Cambridge University Press, 1998):

Slaves who fought trespassed upon the realm of the citizen. Such a blurring of categories could not be fully acknowledged because of the ideological function of the dichotomy between slave and citizen. All Athenian men, rich or poor, could think of themselves as united by the fact that they were not slaves and were indeed the very opposite of slaves. As wartime pressures led to acrimonious politics and even periods of civil war, the maintenance of the boundary between slaves and citizens became ever more critical. By glossing over slave participation Thucydides defended a threatened boundary and the increasingly shaky civic unity to which it was linked. (121)

Chapter 6

1. Euripides, *Hecuba*, trans. William Arrowsmith, in *The Complete Greek Tragedies, Centennial Edition*, vol. 3, ed. David Grene and Richmond Lattimore (Chicago: University of Chicago Press, 1992). Subsequent translations of tragedies come from this edition.

2. Françoise Frontisi-Ducroux and Jean-Pierre Vernant, *Dans l'oeil du miroir* (Paris: O. Jacob, 1997), esp. 183–84. Frontisi-Ducroux points out that this gaze in the mirror distinguishes the luxurious Trojans from the masculine, militarist Greeks.

3. On grief, lamentation, and tragedy as oratorio, see Nicole Loraux, *La voix endeuillée: Essai sur la tragédie grecque* (Paris: Gallimard, 1999).

4. See Nancy Sorkin Rabinowitz, *Anxiety Veiled: Euripides and the Traffic in Women* (Ithaca, N.Y.: Cornell University Press, 1993), and "Slaves with Slaves: Women and Class in Euripidean tragedy," in *Women and Slaves in Greco-Roman Culture: Differential Equations*, ed. Sandra R. Joshel and Sheila Murnaghan (London: Routledge, 1998), 56–68. On the *Hecuba*, see Froma Zeitlin, "The Body's Revenge: Dionysos and Tragic Action in Euripides' *Hekabe*," in *Playing the Other: Gender and Society in Classical Greek Literature* (Chicago: University of Chicago Press, 1996), 172–216.

5. "Blood and free birth obviously play a major role in Teucer's argument that enslavement is a sad fate but does not signify a lack of honour. We do not know, however, how much all this is based upon actual incidents." Christian Meier, *The Political Art of Greek Tragedy*, trans. A. Webber (Cambridge: Polity Press, 1993), 184.

6. On this question, see the volume of essays edited by Sheila Murnaghan and Sandra R. Joshel, *Women and Slaves in Greco-Roman Culture: Differential Equations* (London: Routledge, 1998), especially the introduction, 1–21. "Taken together, these essays show how thoroughly the ancient Greeks and Romans relied on the polarities of male/female and free/slave in order to understand themselves and to organize their societies, and they make it clear that these categories achieved their signifying power, not in tandem, but in combination with each other" (3).

7. On the historical course of slavery, see Moses I. Finley, "Between Slavery and Freedom," in *Economy and Society in Ancient Greece*, ed. B. Shaw and R. Saller (New York: Viking, 1982): [Ancient society] "moved from a society in which status ran along a continuum towards one in which statuses were bunched at the two ends, the slave and the free. . . . [U]nder the Roman Empire, the movement was reversed" (132).

8. On whether dependent characters in Homer are "slaves," precisely, see William G. Thalmann, "Female Slaves in the *Odyssey*," in *Women and Slaves*

in Greco-Roman Culture: Differential Equations, ed. Sandra R. Joshel and Sheila Murnaghan (London: Routledge, 1998), 24, and *The Swineherd and the Bow: Representations of Class in the "Odyssey"* (Ithaca, N.Y.: Cornell University Press, 1998).

9. *The Iliad of Homer,* trans. Richmond Lattimore (Chicago: University of Chicago Press, 1951). Subsequent translations come from this edition.

10. See Sheila Murnaghan and Sandra R. Joshel, introduction to *Women and Slaves in Greco-Roman Culture: Differential Equations* (London: Routledge, 1998), 4–5.

11. See Jean-Pierre Vernant, "Marriage," in *Myth and Society in Ancient Greece,* trans. Janet Lloyd (New York: Zone Books, 1990), 55–77; Louis Gernet, "Aspects mythiques de la valeur en Grèce," in *Anthropologie de la Grèce antique* (Paris: Maspero, 1968), 93–137.

12. The distinction between enslavement and ransoming is fuzzy here; often translators consider elite captives who are traded for money to be ransomed, that is, returned to their families, while nonelite others are "sold," more clearly slaves, purchased like other commodities.

13. Orlando Patterson, *Slavery and Social Death: A Comparative Study* (Cambridge, Mass.: Harvard University Press, 1982), defines "the slave, however recruited, as a socially dead person. Alienated from all 'rights' or claims of birth, he ceased to belong in his own right to any legitimate social order" (5).

14. On slavery in the *Odyssey,* see Thalmann, *The Swineherd and the Bow,* 49–107 and passim.

15. See Carol Dougherty, *The Raft of Odysseus: The Ethnographic Imagination of Homer's "Odyssey"* (New York: Oxford University Press, 2001), 45–46.

16. On this figure, see Helen P. Karydas, *Eurykleia and Her Successors: Female Figures of Authority in Greek Poetics* (Lanham, Md.: Roman & Littlefield, 1998).

17. See Thalmann, "Female Slaves in the *Odyssey,*" 22–34.

18. Herodotus, *The Histories,* rev., A. R. Burn, trans. A. de Selincourt (Harmondsworth, England: Penguin Books, 1972). Subsequent citations are from this edition and translation.

19. On pan-Hellenic aristocratic ties and strategies, see Mark Griffith, "Brilliant Dynasties: Power and Politics in the *Oresteia,*" *Classical Antiquity* 14 (1995): 62–129.

20. E. R. Dodds, *The Greeks and the Irrational* (Berkeley and Los Angeles: University of California Press, 1951).

21. Denise Eileen McCoskey's "'I, Whom She Detested So Bitterly': Slavery and the Violent Division of Women in Aeschylus' *Oresteia,*" in *Women and Slaves in Greco-Roman Culture: Differential Equations,* edited by Sandra R. Joshel and Sheila Murnaghan (London: Routledge, 1998), 35–55, considers the relationship between slave and free women, using evidence from American slavery. Her title comes from the American slave narrative of Harriet Jacobs.

22. Ibid.

23. Laura McClure, *Spoken like a Woman: Speech and Gender in Athenian Drama* (Princeton, N.J.: Princeton University Press, 1999).

24. See Rabinowitz, "Slaves with Slaves" and *Anxiety Veiled.*

25. On this play, see Page duBois, *Centaurs and Amazons: Women and the Prehistory of the Great Chain of Being* (Ann Arbor: University of Michigan Press, 1982).

26. See M. Davies, *Sophocles Trachiniae* (Oxford: Oxford University Press, 1991), 109.

27. "The Suppliant Women," trans. Frank Jones, in *Euripides IV*, ed. David Grene and Richmond Lattimore (Chicago: University of Chicago Press, 1958), 53–54.

28. On this play, see Zeitlin, "The Body's Revenge." Zeitlin interprets Hecuba's transformation in the course of the tragedy as a metamorphosis into "an avenging Erinys in the guise of a bacchant of Hades" (216).

29. See Helene P. Foley, *Ritual Irony: Poetry and Sacrifice in Euripides* (Ithaca, N.Y.: Cornell University Press, 1985).

30. On the bloody Apollo, see Marcel Detienne, *Apollon couteau à la main* (Paris: Gallimard, 1998).

31. Charles Segal, *The Theme of the Mutilation of the Corpse in the "Iliad"* (Leiden: Brill, 1971).

32. Thucydides, *The Peloponnesian War*, trans. Steven Lattimore (Indianapolis: Hackett, 1998), 7.87.

33. On such temple slaves, see Pierre Vidal-Naquet, "The Immortal Slave-Women of Athena Ilias," in *The Black Hunter: Forms of Thought and Forms of Society in the Greek World*, trans. A. Szegedy-Maszak (Baltimore: Johns Hopkins University Press, 1986), 189–204.

34. On ekphrasis, see P. duBois, *History, Rhetorical Description and the Epic* (Cambridge: Boydell and Brewer, 1982), and the essays on ekphrasis in Simon Goldhill and R. Osborne, eds., *Art and Text in Ancient Greek Culture* (Cambridge: Cambridge University Press, 1994).

35. See Sigmund Freud, "Family Romances," *The Standard Edition of the Complete Psychological Works of Sigmund Freud* (London: Hogarth Press and the Institute of Psycho-Analysis, 1953–73), 9:237ff.

Chapter 7

1. "Benjamin the Scrivener," trans. Richard Sieburth, in *Benjamin: Philosophy, Aesthetics, History*, ed. Gary Smith (Chicago: University of Chicago Press, 1989), 23. See also Joel Fineman, "The History of the Anecdote: Fiction and Fiction," in *The New Historicism*, ed. H. Aram Veeser (New York: Routledge, 1989), 49–76; and Richard Saller, "Anecdotes as Historical Evidence for the Principate," *Greece and Rome* 127 (1980): 69–84.

2. W. H. Porter, "The Sequel to Plato's First Visit to Sicily," *Hermathena* 61 (1943): 51–52; this episode raises the question, relevant elsewhere, concerning the difference between ransom and sale. In this case, the ancient texts refer to Plato often as a slave.

3. Alice Swift Riginos, *Platonica: The Anecdotes concerning the Life and Writings of Plato* (Leiden: E. J. Brill, 1976).

4. The life of Diogenes of Sinope is recounted by Diogenes Laertius, in *Lives of Eminent Philosophers*, trans. R. D. Hicks, vol. 2, Loeb Classical Library Series (Cambridge, Mass.: Harvard University Press, 1925).

5. On Lucian, see R. Bracht Branham, *Unruly Eloquence: Lucian and the Comedy of Traditions* (Cambridge, Mass.: Harvard University Press, 1989); and *The Cynics: The Cynic Movement in Antiquity and Its Legacy*, ed. R. B. Branham and M.-O. Goulet-Caze (Berkeley and Los Angeles: University of California Press, 1996).

6. *Lucian*, trans. A. M. Harmon, vol. 2, Loeb Classical Library Series (Cambridge, Mass.: Harvard University Press, 1915).

7. See Page duBois, "Violence, Apathy, and the Rhetoric of Philosophy," in *Rethinking the History of Rhetoric: Multidisciplinary Essays on the Rhetorical Tradition*, ed. Takis Poulakos (Boulder, Colo.: Westview Press, 1993), 119–34.

8. G. W. Most argues that the cock is for Plato himself, as heir to Sokrates. See "A Cock for Asclepius," *Classical Quarterly* 43 (1993): 96–111.

9. On the *Meno*, see, for background, see R. S. Bluck, ed., *Plato's "Meno"* (Cambridge: Cambridge University Press, 1961); R. W. Sharples, *Plato, "Meno"* (Chicago: Bolchazy-Carducci, 1985); J. E. Thomas, *Musings on the "Meno"* (The Hague: Martin Nijhoff, 1980), G. Vlastos, "Anamnesis in the *Meno*," *Dialogue* 4 (1981): 143–67; Norman Gulley, *Plato's Theory of Knowledge* (London: Methuen, 1962); Julius Moravcsik, "Learning as Recollection," in *Plato, A Collection of Critical Essays I*, ed. G. Vlastos (Garden City, N.J.: Anchor, 1971), 53–69; T. Irwin, "Recollection and Plato's Moral Theory," *Review of Metaphysics* 27 (1974): 752–72; Oded Balaban, "The Paradox of the *Meno* and Plato's Theory of Recollection," *Semiotica* 98 (1994): 265–75; Alexander Nehamas, "Meno's Paradox and Socrates as a Teacher," *Oxford Studies in Ancient Philosophy* (1985): 1–30.

10. H. H. Benson, "Meno, the Slave Boy, and the Elenchos," *Phronesis* 35 (1990): 128–58.

11. See L. Brandwood, *The Chronology of Plato's Dialogues* (Cambridge: Cambridge University Press, 1990), with bibliography.

12. See D. Ross, *Plato's Theory of Ideas* (Oxford: Clarendon Press, 1951); Norman Gulley, *Plato's Theory of Knowledge* (London: Methuen, 1962); Vlastos, "Anamnesis in the *Meno*"; J. T. Bedu-Addo, "Sense-Experience and Recollection in Plato's *Meno*," *American Journal of Philosophy* 104 (1983).

13. G. E. R. Lloyd, "The *Meno* and the Mysteries of Mathematics," *Phronesis* 37 (1992): 166–83: "What we are given, at this point in the *Meno*, is an ultra-obscure mathematical example . . . we find we have gone *through an initiation*" (178). See also M. Brown, "Plato Disapproves of the Slave-Boy's Answer," *Review of Metaphysics* 21 (1967–68): 57–93.

14. Marcus Giaquinto, "Diagrams: Socrates and Meno's Slave," *International Journal of Philosophical Studies* 1 (1993): 81–97, 96 n. 5. "The interchange between Socrates and Meno's slave in Plato's dialogue *Meno* has caught the attention of philosophers and psychologists past and present. That passage has been taken to illustrate something important about mathematical discovery by some of the best thinkers" (81).

15. The statues of Daedalus are mentioned elsewhere, in the *Euthyphro*, for example, where the character Euthyphro, engaged with Sokrates over his prosecution of his own father for killing a slave, is as paralyzed as Meno:

> Euthyphro: Somehow everything that we put forward keeps moving about us in a circle, and nothing will stay where we put it.
>
> Socrates: Your statements, Euthyphro, look like the work of Daedalus, founder of my line. If I had made them, and they were my positions, no doubt you would poke fun at me, and say that, being in his line, the figures I construct in words run off, as did his statues, and will not stay where they are put. . . .
>
> Euthyphro: . . . To my mind, it is you who are the Daedalus; so far as I am concerned, they would have held their place.
>
> Socrates: If so, my friend, I must be more expert in his art than he, in that he merely made his own works capable of moving, whereas I give this power not merely to my own, but, seemingly, to the works of other men as well. And the rarest thing about my talent is that I am an unwilling artist, since I would rather see our arguments stand fast and hold their ground than have the art of Daedalus plus all the wealth of Tantalus to boot. (11b–e)

The figures of Daedalus, automata, like slaves, existing at the bidding of their master and maker, will always flee if they can.

16. Bluck, *Plato's "Meno,"* 128; J. E. Thomas, *Musings on the "Meno,"* 24; Jane M. Day, *Plato's Meno in Focus* (London: Routledge, 1994), 16; Moravscik, "Learning as Recollection," 124. Francis Cornford's translation of the *Republic*, for example, in a philosophical version of expurgation, simply omits some of the question-and-answer form of the dialogue, turning the text into pure exposition (*The Republic of Plato*, trans. F. M. Cornford (London: Clarendon, 1945)). On the question of dialogical form in Plato's work, see G. A. Press, ed., *Who Speaks for Plato?: Studies in Platonic Anonymity* (Lanham, Md.: Rowman and Littlefield, 2000).

17. Peter Garnsey, *Ideas of Slavery from Aristotle to Augustine* (Cambridge: Cambridge University Press, 1996), 109ff.

18. Eugene Garver, "Aristotle's Natural Slaves: Incomplete *Praxeis* and Incomplete Human Beings," *Journal of the History of Philosophy* 32 (1994): 173–95.

19. Jacques Rancière, in *Le Philosophe et ses pauvres* (Paris: Fayard, 1983), argues that the slave here in the *Meno* is a pure proletarian, and that his ability to perform mathematically simply proves for Plato the uselessness of the popular teachings of the sophists, and the pointlessness of artisans' aspirations (64).

20. Martha Nussbaum, *The Fragility of Goodness: Luck and Ethics in Greek Tragedy and Philosophy* (Cambridge: Cambridge University Press, 1986), 421; Franco Volpi, "Dasein as *Praxis*: the Heideggerian Assimilation and the Radicalization of the Practical Philosophy of Aristotle," in *Critical Heidegger*, ed. C. Macann (London: Routledge, 1996), 27–66.

21. Bernard Williams, *Shame and Necessity* (Berkeley and Los Angeles: University of California Press, 1993), 110–11.

22. This judgment probably originates in (mis)readings of Jacques Derrida's "La pharmacie de Platon," in *La dissémination* (Paris: Éditions du Seuil, 1972). For analysis and bibliography see Catherine H. Zuckert, *Postmodern Platos: Nietzsche, Heidegger, Gadamer, Strauss, Derrida* (Chicago: University of Chicago Press, 1996).

23. See Peter Rose on Plato's resistance to the essentializing of women, in *Sons of the Gods, Children of Earth: Ideology and Literary Form in Ancient Greece* (Ithaca, N.Y.: Cornell University Press, 1992), 359–60.

24. Gregory Vlastos, "Slavery in Plato's Thought," in *Platonic Studies,* 147–63 (Princeton, N.J.: Princeton University Press, 1973), 152–53. Originally published as "Slavery in Plato's *Republic,*" *Philosophical Review* 50 (1941): 289–304.

25. Walter Benjamin, "Edward Fuchs, Collector and Historian," in *"One-Way Street" and Other Writings*, trans. E. Jephcott and K. Shorter (London: New Left Books, 1979), 351.

26. George Fitzhugh, *Sociology for the South or the Failure of Free Society* (Richmond, Va.: A. Morris, 1854), 244.

27. George Fitzhugh, *Cannibals All! or Slaves without Masters*, ed. C. Vann Woodward (Cambridge, Mass.: Harvard University Press, Belknap Press, 1960), 201.

28. Cited in Saidiya Hartman, *Scenes of Subjection: Terror, Slavery, and Self-Making in Nineteenth-Century America* (New York: Oxford University Press, 1997), 18.

29. On this issue, see Linda Williams, *Playing the Race Card: Melodramas of Black and White From Uncle Tom to O. J. Simpson* (Princeton, N.J.: Princeton University Press, 2001).

Chapter 8

1. J. D. Beazley, *Attic Red-Figure Vase-Painters*, 2d ed. (Oxford: Clarendon Press, 1963), 916.

2. Mary H. Swindler (*Ancient Painting* [New Haven, Conn.: Yale University Press, 1929], 178) discusses this vessel as an example of caricature, as does the *Enciclopedia dell'Arte Antica* (Rome: Istituto della Enciclopedia Italiana, 1958–66), 2:343, fig. 494. See also Karl Schefold et al., *Die Bildnisse der Antiken Dichter, Redner und Denker* (Basel: Schwabe, 1997): 86–87.

3. Leon Hermann argued that the caricature alludes to representations of Oedipus in colloquy with the sphinx, but that in this case a Cynic philosopher, dressed in his cloak, replaces the tyrant-to-be, and a fox stands in for the sphinx. He argues that the representation must not be Aesop, and also claims that the costume of the figure portrayed is not "servile," not a slave's costume, nor is he hunch-backed. He identifies the listener as Phaedrus, the Cynic fabulist, who compares himself to Sokrates, and in whose fables the fox figures prominently. Scholars writing subsequently, however, continue to identify the figure repre-

sented as Aesop. Leon Hermann, "Une caricature de Phèdre," in *Mélanges Charles Picard* (Paris: Presses universitaires de France, 1949), 1:435–37.

4. *Aesop without Morals: The Famous Fables, and a Life of Aesop*, trans. Lloyd W. Daly (New York: T. Yoseloff, 1961), 96–97. All translations of the *Life* and fables refer to this edition, unless otherwise noted.

5. Gregory Nagy, *Pindar's Homer* (Baltimore: Johns Hopkins University Press, 1990), 315.

6. Herodotus, *The Histories*, rev. A. R. Burn, trans. A. de Selincourt (Harmondsworth, England: Penguin Books, 1972). Subsequent references are to this edition and translation.

7. M. L. West, "The Ascription of Fables to Aesop in Archaic and Classical Greece," in *La Fable*, Entretiens sur l'antiquité clasique, vol. 30 (Geneva: Fondation Hardt, 1984), 116, 128. The important work of Gregory Nagy (see note 9 below) on the fable's connection with praise and blame, and with ritual, is an exception to this rule.

8. See B. E. Perry, ed., *Aesopica*, vol. 1, *Greek and Latin Texts* (Urbana: University of Illinois Press, 1952); Francisco R. Adrados, *Historia de la fabula greco-latina*, 2 vols. (Madrid: Editorial de la Universidad Complutense, 1979) [*History of the Graeco-Latin Fable*, vol. 1, rev. ed., trans. Leslie A. Ray (*Mnemosyne* suppl. 201) (Leiden: Brill, 1999)]; Gert-Jan van Dijk, *Ainoi, Logoi, Mythoi: Fables in Archaic, Classical and Hellenistic Greek Literature, with a Study of the Theory and Terminology of the Genre* (*Mnemosyne* suppl. 166) (Leiden: Brill, 1997).

9. Anton Wiechers, *Aesop in Delphi* (Meisenheim am Glan: A. Hain, 1961); Gregory Nagy, *The Best of the Achaeans: Concepts of the Hero in Archaic Greek Poetry* (Baltimore: Johns Hopkins University Press, 1979), *Pindar's Homer: The Lyric Possession of an Epic Past* (Baltimore: Johns Hopkins University Press, 1990), *Greek Mythology and Poetics* (Ithaca, N.Y.: Cornell University Press, 1990).

10. Antonio La Penna, "La morale della favola esopica come morale delle classi subalterne nell'antichità," *Società* 17 (1961): 459–537.

11. "La favola esopica, diremmo noi, è la mitologia razionale di Tersite, succeduta alla mitologia fantastica degli aedi" (ibid., 528).

12. Stefano Jedrkiewicz, *Sapere e paradosso nell'Antichità: Esopo e la favola* (Rome: Edizioni dell'Ateneo, 1989), 41; I am the translator of this and the other passages in this paragraph. For a further discussion of the argument for Aesop as a popular voice, see J. Cascajero, "Lucha de clases e ideologia: introduccion al estudio de la fabula esopica como fuente historica," *Gerion* 9 (1991): 11–58.

13. Adrados, *History of the Graeco-Latin Fable*, trans. Ray.

14. Annabel Patterson, *Fables of Power: Aesopian Writing and Political History* (Durham, N.C.: Duke University Press, 1991), 11.

15. See Doron Narkiss, "The Fox, the Cock, and the Priest: Chaucer's Escape from Fable," *Chaucer Review* 32 (1997): 46–63: "the classical model of fable may be defined as follows: a fable is an authoritarian allegorical form, which represents and enacts a hierarchical power system, relating deictically to implied or specified narratees" (46).

16. Keith Hopkins, "Novel Evidence for Roman Slavery," *Past and Present* 138 (1993): 3–27.

17. Nagy, *The Best of the Achaeans*, 316.

18. On the question of conflicting strains and their discursive manifestations in archaic and classical culture, see Ian Morris: "The middling ideology drew a line around a community of equal male citizens, and denied the importance of other communities. Elitists, by contrast, identified an international aristocracy, including (to varying degrees), men, women, Greeks, easterners, gods, and heroes. True excellence only existed in this community: the champions of local community were mere peasants." Ian Morris, *Archaeology as Cultural History: Words and Things in Iron Age Greece* (Oxford: Blackwell, 2000), 155.

19. S. A. Handford, trans., *Fables of Aesop* (Harmondsworth, England: Penguin Books, 1954), no. 25, p. 27 [Perry 450; Aristotle *Politics* 3.13].

20. See, for example, M. T. W. Arnheim, "The World of the Fable," *Studies in Antiquity* 1 (1980): 5.

21. Nagy, *The Best of the Achaeans*, 253.

22. See Kenneth S. Rothwell Jr., "Aristophanes' *Wasps* and the Sociopolitics of Aesop's Fables," *Classical Journal* 90 (1995): 233–54.

23. The character's use of the word *pepatekas* (*The Birds* 471), "peruse," is used as proof that there was a written text, a book, of Aesop's fables at the time of Aristophanes' writing (415 BCE): West, "The Ascription of Fables to Aesop," 121–26.

24. Here and elsewhere in the paragraph, references are to Aristophanes, *Clouds, Wasps, Peace*, trans. J. Henderson, Loeb Classical Library Series (Cambridge, Mass.: Harvard University Press, 1998).

25. See Rothwell Jr., "Aristophanes' *Wasps* and the Sociopolitics of Aesop's Fables."

26. van Dijk, *Ainoi, Logoi, Mythoi*: "Socrates' Aesopic versification in the face of death aptly illustrates his imperturbability" (318); he also connects this Aesopic moment with the "overall theme of music in the *Phaedo*" (319).

27. On the fable in *Alcibiades Major*, of which the Platonic authorship has been questioned, see Marie-Laurence Desclos, "'Le renard dit au lion . . . ' (Alcibiade Majeur 123A ou Socrate à la maniere d'Esope)," in *L'animal dans l'antiquité*, ed. Barbara Cassin, J.-L. Labarrière, G. Romeyer Dherbey (Paris: J. Vrin, 1997), 395–422.

28. See Veda Cobb-Stevens, "*Mythos* and *Logos* in Plato's *Phaedo*," *Analecta Husserliana* 12 (1982): 391–405.

29. See C. M. Bowra, "The Fox and the Hedgehog," *Classical Quarterly* 34 (1940): 26–29.

30. M. T. W. Arnheim, "The World of the Fable," *Studies in Antiquity* 1 (1980): 5.

31. Daly, trans., *Aesop without Morals*.

32. Alice Walker, "The Dummy in the Window: Joel Chandler Harris and the Invention of Uncle Remus," in *Living by the Word: Selected Writings 1973–1987* (San Diego: Harcourt Brace Jovanovich, 1988), 25–36. See Lawrence W.

Levine, *Black Culture and Black Consciousness: Afro-American Folk Thought from Slavery to Freedom* (New York: Oxford University Press, 1977); Florence E. Baer, *Sources and Analogues of the Uncle Remus Tales* (Helsinki: Suomalainen Tiedeakatemia, 1980). For a defense of Harris, see Wayne Mixon, "The Ultimate Irrelevance of Race: Joel Chandler Harris and Uncle Remus in Their Time," *Journal of Southern History* 56 (1990): 457–80.

33. Baer, *Sources and Analogues of the Uncle Remus Tales*.

34. Joel Chandler Harris, *Uncle Remus: His Songs and His Sayings*, ed. R. Hemenway (New York: Penguin Books, 1986), 57 [first published in 1881].

35. James C. Scott, *Domination and the Arts of Resistance: Hidden Transcripts* (New Haven, Conn.: Yale University Press, 1990), 4.

36. Mixon, "The Ultimate Irrelevance of Race," 470.

Chapter 9

1. Malcolm Bull, "Slavery and the Multiple Self," *New Left Review* 231 (1998): 94–131; see also M. Bull, *Seeing Things Hidden: Apocalypse, Vision and Totality* (London: Verso, 1999).

2. See Thomas C. Holt, "Marking: Race, Race-Making, and the Writing of History," *American Historical Review* 100 (1995): 1–20.

3. Peter Garnsey, *Ideas of Slavery from Aristotle to Augustine* (Cambridge: Cambridge University Press, 1996), 107.

4. Ibid., 127.

5. Orlando Patterson, *Slavery and Social Death: A Comparative Study* (Cambridge, Mass.: Harvard University Press, 1982), 88.

6. Christopher Gill, *Personality in Greek Epic, Tragedy, and Philosophy: The Self in Dialogue* (Oxford: Clarendon Press, 1996).

7. Gill also cites Martha Nussbaum, who draws a distinction between Plato and Aristotle on this point: Martha C. Nussbaum, *The Fragility of Goodness: Luck and Ethics in Greek Tragedy and Philosophy* (Cambridge: Cambridge University Press, 1986), 3–4.

8. See Helene P. Foley, "Medea's Divided Self," *Classical Antiquity* 8 (1989): 61–85.

9. See Page duBois, "Antigone and the Feminist Critic," *Genre* 19 (1986): 370–83.

10. On the *Politics*, see Josiah Ober, "Political Animals, Actual Citizens, and the Best Possible Polis: Aristotle's *Politics*," in *Political Dissent in Democratic Athens: Intellectual Critics of Popular Rule* (Princeton, N.J.: Princeton University Press, 1998), 290–351, with bibliography. "Women, slaves, and children, as 'incomplete humans,' simply disappear from the picture in book 3, when Aristotle is analyzing the polis as a composite made up of individual citizens" (298).

11. See M. Carrithers, Stephen Collins, and Steven Lukes, eds., *The Category of the Person: Anthropology, Philosophy, History* (Cambridge: Cambridge University Press, 1985). I use the word *person* here, with all its associative baggage, from possible Etruscan derivation to the Latin word for *mask*, and beyond. It remains

problematic, but preferable to *self*, with its suggestions of psychological interiority, and to *subject*, a word with a philosophical history and an inevitably trailing *object*.

12. Gill points to the important argument of Miles Burnyeat about a contrast between Cartesian and post-Cartesian notions of subject and object, and ancient thought: "Burnyeat suggests that the familiar modern (post-Cartesian) contrast between an inner world of subjective experience (to which we have privileged, authoritative access) and an external, objective world has no real equivalent in ancient thought. Even theories in which we might expect to find such a contrast . . . are in fact, 'realist' or 'objectivist' in assuming that what is at issue is our knowledge of the 'real' world, and not our access to a distinct zone of subjective experience" (Gill, *Personality in Greek Epic*, 409). Miles Burnyeat, "Idealism and Greek Philosophy: What Descartes Saw and Berkeley Missed," in *Idealism Past and Present*, ed. G. Vesey (Cambridge: Cambridge University Press, 1982), 19–50. See also S. Everson, "The Objective Appearance of Pyrrhonism," in *Psychology: Companions to Ancient Thought*, vol. 2, ed. S. Everson (Cambridge: Cambridge University Press, 1991), 121–47.

13. Gill, *Personality in Greek Epic*, 468.

14. Michel Foucault, *The Use of Pleasure*, trans. R. Hurley (New York: Vintage, 1985).

15. There is a vast bibliography on Aristotle, on the *Politics*, and on slavery in Aristotle's work. For an excellent beginning see Garnsey, *Ideas of Slavery*, 107–27 and bibliography.

16. Bernard Williams argues that the Greeks saw the female as a "necessary" identity, slave status as arbitrary, a calamity; yet his evidence for this latter point as a generally held view is not developed fully (*Shame and Necessity* [Berkeley and Los Angeles: University of California Press, 1993], 103–29).

17. Aristotle leaves the matter of slavery hanging, saying tantalizingly, in a promise that is left unfulfilled: "How slaves should be employed, and why it is advantageous that all slaves should have their freedom set before them as a reward we will say later"(1330a).

18. Leslie Kurke, *Coins, Bodies, Games, and Gold: The Politics of Meaning in Archaic Greece* (Princeton, N.J.: Princeton University Press, 1999), 22. On aristocratic hostility to money, and "disimbedded" wealth in the archaic period, relevant to later Greece as well, see her introduction, 3–23.

19. C. B. MacPherson, *The Political Theory of Possessive Individualism* (Oxford: Clarendon, 1962), 3.

20. Wendy Brown, *States of Injury: Power and Freedom in Late Modernity* (Princeton, N.J.: Princeton University Press, 1995).

Chapter 10

The original version of this chapter was the paper "Irate Greek Masters and Their Slaves," written for "Aspects of Anger in Antiquity," a conference at the Heidelberg University Seminar for Classical Philology, September 3–5, 1999.

1. Jacques Rancière, *Disagreement: Politics and Philosophy*, trans. Julie Rose (Minneapolis: University of Minnesota Press, 1999), 29.

2. Benjamin Quarles, ed., *Narrative of the Life of Frederick Douglass, an American Slave Written by Himself* (Cambridge, Mass.: Harvard University Press, Belknap Press, 1988), 97. The last version of the autobiography was published in 1880, the same year as Joel Chandler Harris's *Uncle Remus: His Songs and His Sayings.*

3. Paul Gilroy, *The Black Atlantic: Modernity and Double Consciousness* (Cambridge, Mass.: Harvard University Press, 1993), 60.

4. In a certain sense, this chapter is a response to Christopher Gill's remarks in an introduction to a volume on Roman "passions": "Another question that could be taken much further is that of the relationship between the social and political structures of Roman life and the presentation of emotion in literature and philosophy." Christopher Gill, "Introduction, II. The Emotions in Greco-Roman Philosophy," in *The Passions in Roman Thought and Literature*, ed. Christopher Gill and Susanna Morton Braund (Cambridge: Cambridge University Press, 1997), 5.

5. See William G. Thalmann, "Female Slaves in the *Odyssey*," in *Women and Slaves in Greco-Roman Culture: Differential Equations*, ed. Sandra R. Joshel and Sheila Murnaghan (London: Routledge, 1998), 22–34.

6. Aristophanes, *Clouds, Wasps, Peace*, trans. Jeffrey Henderson, Loeb Classical Library Series (Cambridge, Mass.: Harvard University Press, 1998). Subsequent citations of these plays are to this translation unless otherwise noted.

7. On this strange play, much has been written. See especially Christian Wolff, "Orestes," in *Oxford Readings in Greek Tragedy*, ed. C. Segal (Oxford: Oxford University Press, 1983), 340–56; Froma I. Zeitlin, "The Closet of Masks: Role-Playing and Myth-Making in the *Orestes* of Euripides," *Ramus* 9 (1980): 51–77; John R. Porter, *Studies in Euripides' "Orestes"* (Leiden: Brill, 1994).

8. See, for example, B. Gredley, "Is *Orestes* 1503–36 an Interpolation?," *Greek, Roman and Byzantine Studies* 9 (1968): 409–19, pointing to "substantial difficulties" with the scene.

9. The text is more accessible than any notion we can have of such a person. Retrospective projections of our ideas of authorial intentionality onto ancient drama seem to me only to obscure our encounters with the texts we have received. And the question of character in ancient drama is often misguided; it frequently takes for granted notions of consistency and coherent psychological subjectivity anachronistic and inappropriate to ancient culture.

10. See Porter, *Studies in Euripides' "Orestes,"* 199ff.; and Francis M. Dunn, *Tragedy's End: Closure and Innovation in Euripidean Drama* (Oxford: Oxford University Press, 1996), 178.

11. W. Arrowsmith, trans., *Orestes*, in *The Complete Greek Tragedies*, ed. David Grene and Richmond Lattimore, vol. 4, *Euripides* (Chicago: University of Chicago Press, 1992).

12. See Francis M. Dunn, "Comic and Tragic License in Euripides' Orestes," *Classical Antiquity* 8 (1989): 238–51; B. Seidensticker, *Palintonos Harmonia*

(Göttingen: Vandenhoeck & Ruprecht, 1982). M. L. West writes of lines 1503–36: "There is no funnier scene in Greek tragedy." Euripides, *Orestes*, ed. M. L. West (Warminster: Aris & Phillips, 1987). On the text, see also Euripides, *Orestes*, commentary by C. W. Willink (Oxford: Clarendon, 1986). On representations of barbarians in tragedy, see Edith Hall, *Inventing the Barbarian: Greek Self-Definition through Tragedy* (Oxford: Clarendon, 1989), esp. 110, 119, 131, 222: Helen Bacon, *Barbarians in Greek Tragedy* (New Haven, Conn.: Yale University Press, 1961); Page duBois, *Centaurs and Amazons: Women and the Prehistory of the Great Chain of Being* (Ann Arbor: University Of Michigan Press, 1982).

13. Hall, *Inventing the Barbarian*, 158, 209.

14. Karen Bassi, *Acting like Men: Gender, Drama, and Nostalgia in Ancient Greece* (Ann Arbor: University of Michigan Press, 1998), 247.

15. Diogenes Laertius, *Lives of Eminent Philosophers*, vol. 1, trans. R. D. Hicks, Loeb Classical Library Series (Cambridge, Mass.: Harvard University Press, 1938).

16. Peter Brown, "Late Antiquity," in *A History of Private Life*, vol. 1, *From Pagan Rome to Byzantium*, ed. Paul Veyne, trans. A. Goldhammer (Cambridge, Mass.: Harvard University Press, Belknap Press, 1987), 243.

17. On Aristotle, anger, and tragedy, see W. B. Stanford, *Greek Tragedy and the Emotions* (London: Routledge and Keegan Paul, 1983), 30–31.

18. On Roman philosophical arguments concerning anger, see D. P. Fowler, "Epicurean Anger," in *The Passions in Roman Thought and Literature*, ed. Susanna Morton Braund and Christopher Gill (Cambridge: Cambridge University Press, 1997), 16–35.

19. Rancière, *Disagreement*, 29.

Epilogue

1. On the obscene reference to blackened cooking pot and its props, see Sarah Morris, "*LASANA:* A Contribution to the Ancient Greek Kitchen," *Hesperia* 54 (1985): 398–99.

✛   BIBLIOGRAPHY

Adrados, Francisco R. *Historia de la fabula greco-latina*. 2 vols. Madrid: Editorial de la Universidad Complutense, 1979.

———. "The 'Life of Aesop' and the Origins of Novel in Antiquity." *Quaderni Urbinati di Cultura Classica*, n.s., 1 (1979): 93–112.

———. "Les collections de fables à l'époque hellenistique et romaine." In *La Fable*, 137–95. Entretiens sur l'antiquité classique, vol. 30. Geneva: Fondation Hardt, 1984.

———. *History of the Graeco-Latin Fable*. Rev. ed. Translated by Leslie A. Ray. Vol. 1, *Introduction* and *From the Origins to the Hellenistic Age. Mnemosyne; Bibliotheca classica batava*, suppl. 201. Leiden: Brill, 1999.

Aesop. *Fables*. Translated by S. A. Handford. Harmondsworth, England: Penguin Books, 1954.

Allen, Danielle. *The World of Prometheus: The Politics of Punishing in Democratic Athens*. Princeton, N.J.: Princeton University Press, 2000.

Anderson, Perry. *Passages from Antiquity to Feudalism*. London: New Left Books, 1974.

———. "Geoffrey de Ste. Croix and the Ancient World." In *A Zone of Engagement*, 1–24. London: Verso, 1992.

Appadurai, Arjun, ed. *The Social Life of Things*. Cambridge: Cambridge University Press, 1986.

Apter, E., and W. Pietz, eds. *Fetishism as Cultural Discourse*. Ithaca, N.Y.: Cornell University Press, 1993.

Archer, Léonie J., ed. *Slavery and Other Forms of Unfree Labour*. London: Routledge, 1988.

Aristophanes. *Four Comedies*. Translated by D. Parker. Ann Arbor: University of Michigan Press, 1969.

———. *Wasps*. Edited by D. M. MacDowell. Oxford: Clarendon Press, 1971.

———. *Wasps*. Edited by A. Sommerstein. Warminster, England: Aris & Phillips, 1983.

———. *Lysistrata*. Edited by J. Henderson. Oxford: Clarendon Press, 1987.

———. *Frogs*. Edited by K. J. Dover. Oxford: Clarendon Press, 1993.

———. *Acharnians, Knights*. Translated by Jeffrey Henderson. Loeb Classical Library Series. Cambridge, Mass.: Harvard University Press, 1998.

Arnheim, M. T. W. "The World of the Fable." *Studies in Antiquity* 1 (1980): 1–11.

Arnott, W. G. "Swan Songs." *Greece & Rome* 24 (1977): 149–53.

Athenaeus. *The Deipnosophists.* Translated by C. B. Gulick. Cambridge, Mass.: Harvard University Press, 1929.

Bacon, Helen. *Barbarians in Greek Tragedy.* New Haven, Conn.: Yale University Press, 1961.

Baer, Florence. *Sources and Analogues of the Uncle Remus Tales.* Helsinki: Suomalainen Tiedeakatemia, 1981.

Bailyn, Bernard, Oscar Handlin, Donald Fleming, and Stephen Thernstrom. *Glimpses of the Harvard Past.* Cambridge, Mass.: Harvard University Press, 1986.

Bain, David. *Masters, Servants and Orders in Greek Tragedy.* Manchester: Manchester University Press, 1981.

Bales, Kevin. *Disposable People: New Slavery in the Global Economy.* Berkeley and Los Angeles: University of California Press, 2000.

Ball, Edward. *Slaves in the Family.* New York: Farrar Straus and Giroux, 1998.

Bassi, Karen. *Acting Like Men: Gender, Drama and Nostalgia in Ancient Greece.* Ann Arbor: University of Michigan Press, 1998.

Beard, Mary. "Souvenirs of Culture: Deciphering (in) the Museum." *Art History* 15 (1992): 505–32.

Beard, Mary, and John Henderson. "That's Showbiz/Classics in the Museum." *Council of University Classical Departments Bulletin* 19 (1991): 23–28.

Beazley, J. D. *Attic Red-Figure Vase-Painters.* 2d ed. Oxford: Clarendon Press, 1963.

Bender, Thomas, ed. *The Antislavery Debate: Capitalism and Abolitionism as a Problem in Historical Interpretation.* Berkeley and Los Angeles: University of California Press, 1992.

Bengston, Hermann. *History of Greece.* Translated by E. F. Bloedow. Ottawa: University of Ottawa Press, 1988.

Benjamin, Andrew, ed. *Post-Structuralist Classics.* London: Routledge, 1988.

Benjamin, Walter. *"One-Way Street" and Other Writings.* Translated by E. Jephcott and K. Shorter. London: New Left Books, 1979.

Benveniste, Emile. "L'esclave, l'étranger." In *Economie, parenté, societé,* vol. 1 of *Le vocabulaire des institutions indo-européenes,* 355–61. Paris: Éditions de Minuit, 1969.

Beringer, Walter. "'Servile Status' in the Sources for Early Greek History." *Historia* 31, no. 1 (1982): 13–32.

Berlin, Ira. *Many Thousands Gone: The First Two Centuries of Slavery in North America.* Cambridge, Mass.: Harvard University Press, Belknap Press, 1998.

Bernal, Martin. *Black Athena, The Afroasiatic Roots of Classical Civilization.* Vol. 1, *The Fabrication of Ancient Greece 1785–1985.* New Brunswick, N.J.: Rutgers University Press, 1987.

———. *The Afroasiatic Roots of Classical Civilization.* Vol. 2, *The Archaeological and Documentary Evidence.* New Brunswick, N.J.: Rutgers University Press, 1991.

Bicknell, P. J. "Demosthenes 24.197 and the Domestic Slaves of Athens." *Mnemosyne* 21 (1968): 13–32.

Blackburn, Robin. *The Making of New World Slavery: From the Baroque to the Modern, 1492–1800.* London: Verso, 1997.

Bluck, R. S., ed. *Plato's "Meno."* Cambridge: Cambridge University Press, 1961.

Boardman, John. *The History of Greek Vases: Potters, Painters, and Pictures.* London: Thames & Hudson, 2001.

Bohrer, F. N. "The Times and Spaces of History: Representation, Assyria, and the British Museum." In *Museum/Culture: Histories Discourse Spectacles,* edited by D. J. Sherman and I. Rogoff, 197–222. Minneapolis: University of Minnesota Press, 1994.

Boon, James A. "Why Museums Make Me Sad." In *Exhibiting Cultures: The Poetics and Politics of Museum Display,* edited by Ivan Karp and Steven D. Lavine, 255–77. Washington, D.C.: Smithsonian Institution Press, 1991.

Borthwick, E. K. "Observations on the Opening Scene of Aristophanes' '*Wasps.*'" *The Classical Quarterly* 86 (1992): 274–78.

Bourdieu, Pierre, and Alain Darbel, with Dominique Schnapper. *The Love of Art: European Art Museums and their Public.* Translated by C. Beattie and N. Merriman. Cambridge: Polity Press, 1991.

Bowie, A. M. *Aristophanes: Myth, Ritual and Comedy.* Cambridge: Cambridge University Press, 1993.

Bowra, C. M. "The Fox and the Hedgehog." *The Classical Quarterly* 34 (1940): 26–29.

Bracken, C. P. *Antiquities Acquired: The Spoliation of Greece.* Newton Abbot, England: David & Charles, 1975.

Bradley, Keith. *Slaves and Masters in the Roman Empire.* Oxford: Oxford University Press, 1987.

———. "'The Regular, Daily Traffic in Slaves': Roman History and Contemporary History." *The Classical Journal* (1992): 125–38.

———. *Slavery and Society at Rome.* Cambridge: Cambridge University Press, 1994.

———. "The Problem of Slavery in Classical Culture." *Classical Philology* 92 (1997): 273–82.

———. *Slavery and Rebellion in the Roman World, 140 B.C.–70 B.C.* Bloomington: Indiana University Press, 1998.

Brandwood, L. *The Chronology of Plato's Dialogues.* Cambridge: Cambridge University Press, 1990.

Branham, Bracht. *Unruly Eloquence: Lucian and the Comedy of Traditions.* Cambridge, Mass.: Harvard University Press, 1989.

Braudel, F. *The Structures of Everyday Life: The Limits of the Possible.* Revised and translated by S. Reynolds. New York: Harper & Row, 1981.

Braund, S., and C. Gill, eds. *The Passions in Roman Thought and Literature.* Cambridge: Cambridge University Press, 1997.

Bray, Alan. *Homosexuality in Renaissance England.* London: Gay Men's Press, 1982.

Briggs, W. W. Jr., ed. *The Letters of Basil Lanneau Gildersleeve.* Baltimore: Johns Hopkins University Press, 1987.

Briggs, W. W. Jr., and H. W. Benario, eds. *Basil Lanneau Gildersleeve, An American Classicist*. Baltimore: Johns Hopkins University Press, 1986.

Briggs, W. W. Jr., and W. M. Calder III, eds. *Classical Scholarship: A Biographical Encyclopedia*. New York: Garland, 1990.

Brisson, Luc. *Platon, les mots et les mythes*. Paris: F. Maspero, 1982.

———. "La Lettre VII de Platon, une autobiographie?" In *L'Invention de l'Autobiographie d'Hésiode à Saint Augustin*, edited by Marie-Françoise Baslez, Philippe Hoffmann, and Laurent Pernot, 37–46. Paris: Presses de l'Ecole normale supérieure, 1993.

Brockmeyer, N. *Antike Sklaverei*. Darmstadt: Wisssenschaftliche Buchgesellschaft, 1979.

Brown, Wendy. *States of Injury: Power and Freedom in Late Modernity*. Princeton, N.J.: Princeton University Press, 1995.

Brunel, Pierre. "La fable est-elle une 'forme simple'?" *Revue de Littérature comparée*, n.s., 1 (1996): 9–19.

Brunschwig, B., and G. Lloyd, with P. Pellerin, eds. *Le savoir grec: dictionnaire critique*. Paris: Flammarion, 1996.

Brunt, P. A. "Aristotle and Slavery." In *Studies in Greek History and Thought*, 343–88. Oxford: Clarendon Press, 1993.

Bryson, Norman. *Looking at the Overlooked: Four Essays on Still Life Painting*. Cambridge, Mass.: Harvard University Press, 1990.

Bull, Malcolm. "Slavery and the Multiple Self." *New Left Review* 231 (1998): 94–131.

———. *Seeing Things Hidden: Apocalypse, Vision and Totality*. London: Verso, 1999.

Burckhardt, Jacob. *The Greeks and Greek Civilization*. Edited by O. Murray and translated by Sheila Stern. New York: St. Martin's Press, 1998.

Burford, A. *Land and Labor in the Greek World*. Baltimore: Johns Hopkins Press, 1993.

Burke, Kenneth. *Attitudes Toward History*. 3d ed. Berkeley and Los Angeles: University of California Press, 1984.

Burnyeat, Miles. "Idealism and Greek Philosophy: What Descartes Saw and Berkeley Missed." In *Idealism Past and Present*, edited by G. Vesey, 19–50. Cambridge: Cambridge University Press, 1982.

Burzachechi, M. "Oggetti parlanti nelle epigrafi greche." *Epigraphica* 24 (1962): 3–54.

Bush, M. L., ed. *Serfdom and Slavery: Studies in Legal Bondage*. London: Longman, 1996.

Cambiano, G. "Aristotle and the Anonymous Opponents of Slavery." In *Classical Slavery*, edited by Moses I. Finley, 21–41. London: F. Cass, 1987.

Canfora, L. "Posidonio nel VI libro di Ateneo: la schiavitù 'degenerata.'" *Index* 11 (1982): 43–56.

Carrière-Hervagault, Marie-Paule. "Esclaves et affranchis chez les orateurs attiques: Documents et étude." In *Actes du colloque 1971 sur l'esclavage*, 45–79. Paris: Les Belles Lettres, 1972.

Carrithers, M., Stephen Collins, and Steven Lukes, eds. *The Category of the*

Person: Anthropology, Philosophy, History. Cambridge: Cambridge University Press, 1985.

Cartledge, Paul. "Euphron and the *Douloi* Again." *Liverpool Classical Monthly* 5 (1980): 209–11.

———. "Rebels and *Sambos* in Classical Greece: A Comparative View." In *CRUX: Essays in Greek History Presented to G. E. M. de Sainte Croix on His 75th Birthday*, 17–46. Exeter: Imprint Academic, 1985.

———. *Aristophanes and His Theatre of the Absurd.* Bristol: Bristol Classical Press, 1990.

———. "Like a Worm I' the Bud?" *Greece and Rome* 40 (1993): 163–80.

———. *The Greeks: A Portrait of Self and Others.* Oxford: Oxford University Press, 1993.

Cascajero, J. "Lucha de clases e ideologia: introduccion al estudio de la fabula esopica como fuente historica." *Gerion* 9 (1991): 11–58.

Cassin, Barbara, J.-L. LaBarrière, and G. Romeyer Dherbey, eds. *L'animal dans l'antiquité.* Paris: J. Vrin, 1997.

Casson, L. "Galley Slaves." *Transactions and Proceedings of the American Philological Association* 97 (1966): 35–44.

Caygill, Marjorie. *The Story of the British Museum*, 2d ed. London: British Museum Press for the Trustees of the British Museum, 1992.

Chow, Rey. *Writing Diaspora: Tactics of Intervention in Contemporary Cultural Studies.* Bloomington: Indiana University Press, 1993.

Christensen, K. A. "The Theseion: A Slave Refuge at Athens." *American Journal of Ancient History* 9 (1984): 23–32.

Cobb-Stevens, Veda. "*Mythos* and *Logos* in Plato's *Phaedo*." *Analecta Husserliana* 12 (1982): 391–405.

Cole, Eve Browning. "Women, Slaves, and 'Love of Toil' in Aristotle's Moral Philosophy." In *Engendering Origins: Critical Feminist Readings in Plato and Aristotle*, edited by Bat-Ami Bar On. Albany, N.Y.: State University of New York Press, 1994.

Colvin, Stephen. *Dialect in Aristophanes and the Politics of Language in Ancient Greek Literature.* Oxford: Clarendon Press, 1999.

Compton, Todd. "The Trial of the Satirist: Poetic *Vitae* (Aesop, Archilochus, Homer) as Background for Plato's *Apology*." *American Journal of Philology* 111 (1990): 330–47.

Coombes, Annie E. "Blinded by 'Science': Ethnography at the British Museum." In *Art Apart: Art Institutions and Ideology across England and North America*, edited by Marcia Pointon, 102–19. Manchester: Manchester University Press, 1994.

Daitz, S. "Concepts of Freedom and Slavery in Euripides' *Hecuba*." *Hermes* 99 (1971): 217–26.

Daly, L. W., trans. *Aesop without Morals: The Famous Fables, and a Life of Aesop.* New York: T. Yoseloff, 1961.

Davidson, James. *Courtesans and Fishcakes: The Consuming Passions of Classical Athens.* New York: HarperCollins, 1997.

Davies, Malcolm, and Jeyaraney Kathirithamby. *Greek Insects.* New York: Oxford University Press, 1986.

Davis, D. B. *The Problem of Slavery in Western Culture.* Ithaca, N.Y.: Cornell University Press, 1966.

———. *The Problem of Slavery in the Age of Revolution, 1770–1823.* Ithaca, N.Y.: Cornell University Press, 1975.

———. *Slavery and Human Progress.* New York: Oxford University Press, 1984.

Day, Jane M. *Plato's Meno in Focus.* London: Routledge, 1994.

DeCerteau, Michel. *The Practice of Everyday Life.* Translated by S. Rendall. Berkeley and Los Angeles: University of California Press, 1984.

Demandt, A. "Politik in den Fabeln Aesops." *Gymnasium* 98 (1991): 397–419.

Demosthenes. *Orations.* Translated by N. DeWitt. Cambridge, Mass.: Harvard University Press, 1949.

Desclos, Marie-Laurence. "'Le renard dit au lion . . . ' (Alcibiade Majeur, 123A ou Socrate à la manière d'Esope." In *L'animal dans l'antiquité,* edited by Barbara Cassin, J.-L. Labarrière, and G. Romeyer Dherbey, 395–422. Paris: J. Vrin, 1997.

Detienne, Marcel. *The Gardens of Adonis: Spices in Greek Mythology.* Translated by J. Lloyd. Atlantic Highlands, N.J.: Humanities Press, 1977.

———. "Un ephèbe, un olivier." In *L'ecriture d'Orphée,* 71–84. Paris: Gallimard, 1989.

———. *Apollon le couteau à la main.* Paris: Gallimard, 1998.

Didi-Huberman, Georges. *Ce que nous voyons, ce qui nous regarde.* Paris: Editions de Minuit, 1992.

Dijk, Gert-Jan van. *Ainoi, Logoi, Mythoi: Fables in Archaic, Classical and Hellenistic Greek Literature, with a Study of the Theory and Terminology of the Genre. Mnemosyne; Bibliotheca classica batava,* supp. 166. Leiden: Brill, 1997.

Dillon, M., and L. Garland. *Ancient Greece: Social and Historical Documents from Archaic Times to the Death of Socrates (c. 800–399 BC).* London: Routledge, 1994.

Dilts, M. R., ed. *Scholia in Aeschinem.* Stuttgart: B. G. Teubner, 1992.

Diogenes Laertius. *Lives of Eminent Philosophers.* Translated by R. D. Hicks. Vol. 1. Cambridge, Mass.: Harvard University Press, 1938.

Dobbs, D. "Natural Right and the Problem of Aristotle's Defense of Slavery." *Journal of Politics* 56 (1994): 69–94.

Dougherty, Carol. *The Poetics of Colonization: From City to Text in Archaic Greece.* Oxford: Oxford University Press, 1993.

———. *The Raft of Odysseus: The Ethnographic Imagination of Homer's "Odyssey."* New York: Oxford University Press, 2001.

Dougherty, Carol, and L. Kurke, eds. *Cultural Poetics in Ancient Greece: Cult, Performance, Politics.* Cambridge: Cambridge University Press, 1993.

Dousougli, Angelika, and Sarah Morris. "Ancient Towers on Leukas, Greece." In *Structures Rurales et Societés Antiques: Actes du colloque de Corfou, 14–16 mai 1992,* edited by P. N. Doukelis and L. G. Mendoni, 215–25. Paris: Diffusé par Les Belles Lettres, 1994.

Dover, K. J. *Aristophanic Comedy*. Berkeley and Los Angeles: University of California Press, 1972.
———. *Greek Homosexuality*. London: Duckworth, 1978.
———. *Marginal Comment: A Memoir*. London: Duckworth, 1994.
duBois, P. *Centaurs and Amazons: Women and the Prehistory of the Great Chain of Being*. Ann Arbor: University of Michigan Press, 1982.
———. "Antigone and the Feminist Critic." *Genre* 19 (1986): 370–83.
———. *Sowing the Body: Psychoanalysis and Ancient Representations of Women*. Chicago: University of Chicago Press, 1988.
———. *Torture and Truth*. New York: Routledge, 1991.
———. "Violence, Apathy, and the Rhetoric of Philosophy." In *Rethinking the History of Rhetoric: Multidisciplinary Essays on the Rhetorical Tradition*, edited by Takis Poulakos, 119–34. Boulder, Colo.: Westview Press, 1993.
———. *Sappho Is Burning*. Chicago: University of Chicago Press, 1995.
———. *Trojan Horses: Saving the Classics from Conservatives*. New York: New York University Press, 2001.
Ducrey, P. *Le Traitement des prisonniers de guerre dans la Grèce ancienne*. Paris: E. de Boccard, 1968.
Duncan, Carol. *Civilizing Rituals: Inside Public Art Museums*. New York: Routledge, 1995.
Duncan, Carol, and Alan Wallach. "The Universal Survey Museum." *Art History* 3 (1980): 448–69.
Dunn, Francis M. "Comic and Tragic License in Euripides' *Orestes*." *Classical Antiquity* 8 (1989): 238–51.
———. *Tragedy's End: Closure and Innovation in Euripidean Drama*. Oxford: Oxford University Press, 1996.
Edmonds, J. M. *The Fragments of Attic Comedy*. Vol. 1, *Old Comedy*. Leiden: E. J. Brill, 1957.
Ehrenburg, V. *The People of Aristophanes*. Oxford: B. Blackwell, 1951.
Emerson, Ralph Waldo. *Emerson's Antislavery Writings*. Edited by L. Gougeon and J. Meyerson. New Haven, Conn.: Yale University Press, 1995.
Enciclopedia dell'Arte Antica. Rome: Istituto della Enciclopedia Italiana, 1958–66.
Euripides. *Orestes*. With commentary by C. W. Willink. Oxford: Clarendon, 1986.
———. *Orestes*. Edited by M. L. West. Warminster, England: Aris & Phillips, 1987.
Everson, S. "The Objective Appearance of Pyrrhonism." In *Psychology: Companions to Ancient Thought*, vol. 2, edited by S. Everson, 121–47. Cambridge: Cambridge University Press, 1991.
Fairweather, J. "Fiction in the Biographies of Ancient Writers." *Ancient Society* 5 (1974): 231–42.
Falkner, T. M., N. Felson, and D. Konstan, eds. *Contextualizing Classics*. Lanham, Md.: Roman and Littlefield, 1999.
Faust, Drew Gilpin, ed. *A Sacred Circle: The Dilemma of the Intellectual of the Old South*. Baltimore: Johns Hopkins University Press, 1977.

————. *The Ideology of Slavery: Proslavery Thought in the Antebellum South, 1830–1860*. Baton Rouge: Louisiana State University Press, 1981.

Fehr, Burkhard. "Wie der Korper zum Werkzeug der Seele wurde." In *Haltung-Gestik-Korpersprache: Der Menschliche Korper in der Kommunikation*, edited by Detlef Hoffmann, 55–89. Rehburg: Evangelische Akademie Loccum, 1997.

Fineman, Joel. "The History of the Anecdote: Fiction and Fiction." In *The New Historicism*, edited by H. Aram Veeser, 49–76. New York: Routledge, 1989.

Finley, Moses I. *Studies in Land and Credit, 500–200 B.C.: The Horos-Inscriptions*. New Brunswick, N.J.: Rutgers University Press, 1952.

————. *The Ancient Greeks*. New York: Viking Press, 1963.

————. "Between Slavery and Freedom." *Comparative Studies in Society and History* 6 (1964): 233–49.

————. *Slavery in Classical Antiquity: Views and Controversies*. New York: Barnes & Noble, 1968.

————. *The Ancient Economy*. Berkeley and Los Angeles University of California Press, 1973.

————. "Generalizations in Ancient History." In *The Use and Abuse of History*. London: Chatto and Windus, 1975.

————. *Aspects of Antiquity*. Harmondsworth, England: Penguin Books, 1977.

————. *Ancient Slavery and Modern Ideology*. New York: Viking Press, 1980.

————. "Was Greek Civilization Based on Slave Labor?" In *Economy and Society in Ancient Greece*, edited by B. Shaw and R. Saller, 24–40. New York: Viking Press, 1982.

————. *Politics in the Ancient World*. Cambridge: Cambridge University Press, 1983.

————. *The Ancient Economy*. 2d ed. Berkeley and Los Angeles: University of California Press, 1985.

————. *The Ancient Economy*. Rev. ed., with a foreword by Ian Morris. Berkeley and Los Angeles: University of California Press, 1999.

————, ed. *Classical Slavery*. London: F. Cass, 1987.

Fisher, N. R. E. *Slavery in Classical Greece*. Rev. ed. London: Bristol Classical Press, 1995.

Fisher, Philip. *Making and Effacing Art*. Oxford: Oxford University Press, 1991.

Fitzhugh, George. *Sociology for the South or the Failure of Free Society*. Richmond, Va.: A. Morris Publisher, 1854.

————. *Cannibals All! or Slaves without Masters*. Edited by C. Vann Woodward. Cambridge, Mass.: Harvard University Press, Belknap Press, 1960.

Foley, Helene. *Ritual Irony: Poetry and Sacrifice in Euripides*. Ithaca, N.Y.: Cornell University Press, 1985.

————. "Medea's Divided Self." *Classical Antiquity* 8 (1989): 61–85.

Fortenbaugh, W. "Aristotle on Slaves and Women." In *Articles on Aristotle*, vol. 2, *Ethics and Politics*, edited by J. Barnes, M. Schofield, and R. Sorabji. London: Duckworth, 1975.

Forty, Adrian. *Objects of Desire: Design and Society since 1750.* London: Thames and Hudson, 1986.

Foucault, M. *The Order of Things: An Archaeology of the Human Sciences.* New York: Pantheon Books, 1971.

———. *The History of Sexuality.* Vol. 3, *The Care of the Self,* translated by Robert Hurley. New York: Pantheon Books, 1986.

———. *The History of Sexuality.* Vol. 2, *The Use of Pleasure,* translated by Robert Hurley. New York: Vintage Books, 1990.

Fox, Robin Lane. "Aeschines and Athenian Democracy." In *Ritual, Finance, Politics,* edited by R. Osborne and S. Hornblower, 135–55. Oxford: Clarendon Press, 1994.

Foxhall, Lin. "Emotional Attachments in Athenian Society." In *Kosmos,* edited by P. Cartledge, P. Millett, and S. von Reden, 52–67. Cambridge: Cambridge University Press, 1998.

Fredrickson, George M. *The Inner Civil War: Northern Intellectuals and the Crisis of the Union.* New York: Harper & Row, 1965.

Freedberg, David. *The Power of Images: Studies in the History and Theory of Response.* Chicago: University of Chicago Press, 1989.

French, A. *The Growth of the Athenian Economy.* London: Routledge & Kegan Paul, 1964.

Freud, Sigmund. *The Standard Edition of the Complete Psychological Works.* 24 vols. London: Hogarth Press and the Institute of Psycho-Analysis, 1953–73.

Frontisi-Ducroux, Françoise, and Jean-Pierre Vernant. *Dans l'oeil du miroir.* Paris: O. Jacob, 1997.

[Fryd], Viven Green. "Hiram Powers's *Greek Slave,* Emblem of Freedom." *American Art Journal* 14 (1982): 31–39.

Fuks, M. "Slave War and Slave Troubles in Chios." In *Social Conflict in Ancient Greece,* 260–69. Leiden: E. J. Brill, 1984.

Gagarin, M. "The Torture of Slaves in Athenian Law," *Classical Philology* 91 (1996): 1–18.

Garlan, Yvon. *Slavery in Ancient Greece.* Rev. ed. Translated by Janet Lloyd. Ithaca, N.Y.: Cornell University Press, 1988.

Garland, Robert. *The Greek Way of Life: From Conception to Old Age.* Ithaca, N.Y.: Cornell University Press, 1990.

———. *Daily Life of the Ancient Greeks.* Westport, Conn.: Greenwood Press, 1998.

Garnsey, Peter. *Ideas of Slavery from Aristotle to Augustine.* Cambridge: Cambridge University Press, 1996.

———. "The Middle Stoics and Slavery." In *Hellenistic Constructs: Essays in Culture, History, and Historiography,* edited by P. Cartledge, P. Garnsey, and E. Gruen. Berkeley and Los Angeles: University of California Press, 1997.

———, ed. *Non-Slave Labour in the Greco-Roman World.* Cambridge: Cambridge University Press, 1980.

Garver, E. "Aristotle's Natural Slaves: Incomplete Praxeis and Incomplete Human Beings." *The Journal of the History of Philosophy* 32 (1994): 173–95.

Geary, Patrick. "Sacred Commodities: The Circulation of Medieval Relics." In *The Social Life of Things*, edited by Arjun Appadurai, 169–92. Cambridge: Cambridge University Press, 1986.

Genovese, Eugene. *Roll, Jordan, Roll: The World the Slaves Made*. New York: Vintage Books, 1976.

———. *Western Civilization through Slave-Holding Eyes: The Social and Historical Thought of Thomas Roderick Dew*. New Orleans: Graduate School of Tulane University, 1986.

———. *The Slaveholders' Dilemma: Freedom and Progress in Southern Conservative Thought, 1820–1860*. Columbia: University of South Carolina Press, 1992.

Gernet, Louis. *Anthropologie de la Grèce antique*. Paris: Maspero, 1968.

Getty, J. Paul. *How to Be Rich*. Chicago: Playboy Press, 1965.

———. *As I See It: The Autobiography of J. Paul Getty*. Englewood Cliffs, N.J.: Prentice-Hall, 1976.

Giangrande, Giuseppe. "Emendations to Callimachus." *Classical Quarterly*, n.s., 12 (1962): 212–22.

———. "Sappho and the *Olisbos*." *Emerita* 48 (1980): 249–50.

———. "A che serviva l' '*olisbos*' di Saffo?" *Labeo* 29 (1983): 154–55.

Gildersleeve, B. L. *The Creed of the Old South, 1865–1915*. Baltimore: Johns Hopkins University Press, 1915.

Gill, Christopher. "The Death of Socrates." *The Classical Quarterly* 23 (1973): 25–28.

———. *Personality in Greek Epic, Tragedy, and Philosophy: The Self in Dialogue*. Oxford: Clarendon Press, 1996.

———, ed. *The Person and the Human Mind: Issues in Ancient and Modern Philosophy*. Oxford: Clarendon Press, 1990.

Gill, Christopher, and Susanna Morton Braund, eds. *The Passions in Roman Thought and Literature*. Cambridge: Cambridge University Press, 1997.

Gilroy, Paul. *The Black Atlantic: Modernity and Double Consciousness*. Cambridge, Mass.: Harvard University Press, 1993.

Goff, Barbara, ed. *History, Tragedy, Theory: Dialogues on Athenian Drama*. Austin: University of Texas Press, 1995.

Goldberg, J., ed. *Sodometries: Renaissance Texts, Modern Sexualities*. Stanford: Stanford University Press, 1992.

———. *Queering the Renaissance*. Durham, N.C.: Duke University Press, 1994.

Golden, M. "Slavery and Homosexuality at Athens." *Phoenix* 38 (1984): 308–24.

———. "Pais, 'Child' and 'Slave.'" *L'Antiquité Classique* 54 (1985): 91–104.

———. "The Effects of Slavery on Citizen Households and Children: Aeschylus, Aristophanes and Athens." *Historical Reflections/Réflexions Historiques* 15 (1988): 455–75.

Golden, M., and P. Toohey. *Inventing Ancient Culture: Historicism, Periodization, and the Ancient World*. London: Routledge, 1997.

Goldhill, Simon, and R. Osborne, eds. *Art and Text in Ancient Greek Culture*. Cambridge: Cambridge University Press, 1994.

Gouldner, Alvin. *Enter Plato.* Pt. 1, *The Hellenic World.* New York: Basic Books, 1965.

———. *Enter Plato.* Pt. 2, *Classical Greece and the Origins of Social Theory.* New York: Basic Books, 1966.

Greenberg, Reesa, Bruce W. Ferguson, and Sandy Nairne, eds. *Thinking about Exhibitions.* London: Routledge, 1996.

Greenfield, Jeanette. *The Return of Cultural Treasures.* Cambridge: Cambridge University Press, 1965.

Gregory, Justina. *Euripides: Hecuba.* Atlanta: Scholars Press, 1999.

Grene, David, and Richmond Lattimore, eds. *The Complete Greek Tragedies.* Chicago: University of Chicago Press, 1992.

Griffith, Mark. "Brilliant Dynasties: Power and Politics in the *Oresteia.*" *Classical Antiquity* 14 (1995): 62–129.

———. "The King and Eye." *Proceedings of the Cambridge Philological Society* 44 (1998): 20–84.

Grossberg, L., C. Nelson, and P. Treichler, eds. *Cultural Studies.* New York: Routledge, 1992.

Groys, Boris. "The Struggle against the Museum; or, The Display of Art in Totalitarian Space." In *Museum/Culture: Histories Discourse Spectacles*, edited by D. J. Sherman and I. Rogoff, 144–62. Minneapolis: University of Minnesota Press, 1994.

Gschnitzer, Fritz. "Studien zur griechischen Terminologie der Sklaverei. Zweiter Teil: Untersuchen zur Alteren, insbesondere hoerischen sklaventerminologie." *Forschungen zur antiken Skaverei* 7. Wiesbaden: F. Steiner, 1976.

Guarino, A. "Professorenerotismus." *Labeo* 27 (1981): 439–40.

Gulick, C. B. *The Life of the Ancient Greeks.* 1902. Reprint, New York: Cooper Square Publishers, 1973.

Gulley, Norman. *Plato's Theory of Knowledge.* London: Methuen, 1962.

Gustafson, Mark. "*Inscripta in fronte;* Penal Tattooing in Late Antiquity." *Classical Antiquity* 16 (1997): 79–105.

———. "The Tattoo in the Later Roman Empire and Beyond." In *Written on the Body*, edited by J. Caplan, 17–31. Princeton, N.J.: Princeton University Press, 2000.

Guyot, Peter. *Eunuchen als Sklaven und Freigelassene in der griechisch-romischen Antike.* Stuttgart: Klett-Cotta, 1980.

Habermas, J. *Jürgen Habermas on Society and Politics: A Reader.* Edited by Steven Seidman. Boston: Beacon Press, 1989.

Habinek, Thomas N. *The Politics of Latin Literature: Writing, Identity, and Empire in Ancient Rome.* Princeton, N.J.: Princeton University Press, 1998.

Hall, Edith. *Inventing the Barbarian: Greek Self-Definition Through Tragedy.* Oxford: Clarendon Press, 1989.

Hall, Stuart, ed. *Representation: Cultural Representations and Signifying Practices.* London: Sage in association with the Open University, 1997.

Halperin, D. *One Hundred Years of Homosexuality and Other Essays on Greek Love*. New York: Routledge, 1990.

———. *Saint Foucault*. New York: Oxford University Press, 1995.

Hamilton, E., and H. Cairns, eds. *The Collected Dialogues of Plato*. Princeton, N.J.: Bollingen, 1961.

Hansen, M. H. *The Athenian Democracy in the Age of Demosthenes*. Oxford: B. Blackwell, 1991.

Hanson, V. D. "Thucydides and the Desertion of Attic Slaves during the Decelean War." *Classical Antiquity* 11 (1992): 209–28.

Harootunian, Harry. *History's Disquiet: Modernity, Cultural Practice, and the Question of Everyday Life*. New York: Columbia University Press, 2000.

Harriot, R. M. *Aristophanes Poet and Dramatist*. London: Croom Helm, 1986.

Harris, Joel Chandler. *Uncle Remus: His Songs and His Sayings*. Edited by R. Hemenway. New York: Penguin Books, 1982.

Harris, W. V. *Ancient Literacy*. Cambridge, Mass.: Harvard University Press, 1989.

Hartman, Saidiya. *Scenes of Subjection: Terror, Slavery, and Self-Making in Nineteenth-Century America*. New York: Oxford University Press, 1997.

Havelock, E. *The Liberal Temper in Greek Politics*. New Haven, Conn.: Yale University Press, 1957.

Henderson, Jeffrey. *The Maculate Muse: Obscene Language in Attic Comedy*. New Haven, Conn.: Yale University Press, 1975.

Hermann, Leon. "Une caricature de Phèdre." *Mélanges Charles Picard* (Paris: Presses universitaires de France, 1949), 1:435–37.

Herodas. *The Mimes and Fragments*. Edited by A. D. Knox. Cambridge: Cambridge University Press, 1922.

———. *Mimiambi*. Edited by I. C. Cunningham. Oxford: Clarendon Press, 1971.

Herodotus. *The Histories*. Translated by A. de Selincourt. Revised by A. R. Burn. Harmondsworth, England: Penguin Books, 1972.

Herzfeld, Michael. *Ours Once More: Folklore, Ideology, and the Making of Modern Greece*. New York: Pella Publishing, 1986.

Herzog, Reinhart. "On the Relation of Disciplinary Development and Historical Self-Presentation—The Case of Classical Philology since the End of the Eighteenth Century." In *Functions and Uses of Disciplinary Histories*, edited by L. Graham, W. Lepenies, and P. Weingart, 8:281–90. Dordrecht: D. Reidel, 1983.

Hetherington, Kevin. "Museum Topology and the Will to Connect." *Journal of Material Culture* 2 (1997): 199–218.

Hexter, Ralph, and Daniel Selden, eds. *Innovations of Antiquity*. New York: Routledge, 1992.

Himmelmann, N. *Archäologisches zum Problem der griechischen Sklaverei*. Wiesbaden: Verlag der Akademie der Wissenschaften und der Literatur, 1971.

———. *Reading Greek Art: Essays by Nikolaus Himmelmann*. Edited by W. Childs. Princeton, N.J.: Princeton University Press, 1998.

Hitchens, Christopher. *The Elgin Marbles: Should They Be Returned to Greece?* London: Verso, 1997.

Holzberg, N. *Die antike Fabel. Eine Einfuhrung.* Darmstadt: Wissenschaftliche Buchgesellschaft, 1993.

———. "Novel-like Works of Extended Prose Fiction II." In *The Novel in the Ancient World,* edited by G. Schmeling, 619–53. Leiden: E. J. Brill, 1996.

Hooper-Greenhill, Eilean. *Museums and the Shaping of Knowledge.* New York: Routledge, 1992.

Hopkins, Keith. "Slavery in Classical Antiquity." In *Caste and Race,* edited by A. de Rueck and J. Knight, 166–77. London: Churchill, 1967.

———. *Conquerors and Slaves.* Cambridge: Cambridge University Press, 1978.

———. *Death and Renewal.* Cambridge: Cambridge University Press, 1983.

———. "Everyday Life for the Roman Schoolboy." *History Today* 43 (1993): 25–30.

———. "Novel Evidence for Roman Slavery." *Past and Present* 138 (1993): 3–27.

Hunt, Peter. *Slaves, Warfare, and Ideology in the Greek Historians.* Cambridge: Cambridge University Press, 1998.

Hunter, Virginia A. *Policing Athens: Social Control in the Attic Lawsuits, 420–320 B.C.* Princeton, N.J.: Princeton University Press, 1994.

Jacob, O. *Les Esclaves publiques à Athenes.* Liège, Belgium: Imp. H. Vaillant-Carmanne, 1928.

Jameson, Fredric. *The Political Unconscious: Narrative as a Socially Symbolic Act.* Ithaca, N.Y.: Cornell University Press, 1981.

———. *The Ideologies of Theory: Essays 1971–1986.* Vol. 2, *The Syntax of History.* Minneapolis: University of Minnesota Press, 1988.

Jameson, Michael H. "Agriculture and Slavery in Classical Athens." *Classical Journal* 73 (1977): 122–41.

———. "Domestic Space in the Greek City-State." In *Domestic Architecture and the Use of Space: An Interdisciplinary Study,* edited by Susan Kent, 92–113. Cambridge: Cambridge University Press, 1990.

———. "Private Space and the Greek City." In *The Greek City from Homer to Alexander,* edited by O. Murray and S. Price Oxford: Clarendon Press, 1990.

Jedrkiewicz, Stefano. *Sapere e paradosso nell'Antichità: Esopo e la favola.* Rome: Edizioni dell'Ateneo, 1989.

———. "La funcion cultural originaria de la fabula de Esopo." *Revista de Occidente* 158 (1994): 122–34.

Jenkins, Ian. *Greek and Roman Life.* London: British Museum Publications for the Trustees of the British Museum, 1986.

Jenkins, W. S. *Pro-Slavery Thought in the Old South.* Gloucester, Mass.: P. Smith, 1960.

Johnston, S. "Virtuous Toil, Vicious Work: Xenophon on Aristocratic Style." *Classical Philology* 89 (1994): 219–40.

Jones, A. H. M. "Slavery in the Ancient World." *Economic History Review,* 2d ser., 9 (1956): 185–99.

———. *Athenian Democracy*. Oxford: B. Blackwell, 1957.

Jones, C. P. "*Stigma:* Tattooing and Branding in Graeco-Roman Antiquity." *Journal of Roman Studies* 77 (1987): 139–55.

———. "Stigma and Taboo." In *Written on the Body: The Tattoo in European and American History*, edited by J. Caplan, 1–16. Princeton, N.J.: Princeton University Press, 2000.

Joshel, Sandra R., and Sheila Murnaghan, eds. *Women and Slaves in Greco-Roman Culture: Differential Equations*. London: Routledge, 1998.

Jusdanis, Gregory. *Belated Modernity and Aesthetic Culture: The Making of a National Literature*. Minneapolis: University of Minnesota Press, 1991.

Just, Roger. "Freedom, Slavery and the Female Psyche." *History of Political Thought* 6 (1985): 169–88.

Kahrstedt, U. "Platons Verkauf in die Sklaverei." *Wurzburger Jbb.* 2 (1947): 295–300.

Karouzou, Semni. *National Archaeological Museum: Collection of Sculpture*. Athens: Ekdotike Athenon (General Direction of Antiquities and Restoration), 1968.

———. *National Museum: Illustrated Guide*. Athens: Ekdotike Athenon, 1980.

———. *National Museum: Illustrated Guide to the Museum*. Athens: Ekdotike Athenon, 1998.

Karp, Ivan, and Steven D. Lavine. *Exhibiting Cultures: The Poetics and Politics of Museum Display*. Washington, D.C.: Smithsonian Institution Press, 1991.

Karydas, Helen P. *Eurykleia and Her Successors: Female Figures of Authority in Greek Poetics*. Lanham, Md.: Rowman & Littlefield, 1998.

Kasson, Joy S. *Marble Queens and Captives: Women in Nineteenth-Century American Sculpture*. New Haven, Conn.: Yale University Press, 1990.

Kastely, James L. "Violence and Rhetoric in Euripides' *Hecuba*." *Publications of the Modern Language Association of America* 108 (1993): 1036–49.

Kelley, Brooks Mather. *Yale: A History*. New Haven, Conn.: Yale University Press, 1974.

Keuls, Eva. *The Reign of the Phallus*. New York: Harper and Row, 1985.

Kilmer, Martin F. *Greek Erotica on Attic Red-Figure Vases*. London: Duckworth, 1993.

Kindstrand, J. F. *Bion of Borysthenes*. Uppsala: S. Academie Ubsaliensis, 1976.

Klinger, D. M. *Erotische Kunst der Antike*. Nurnberg: DMK, 1983.

Knox, B. *Backing into the Future: The Classical Tradition and Its Renewal*. New York: Norton, 1994.

———. "Silent Reading in Antiquity." *Greek, Roman and Byzantine Studies* 9 (1968): 421–35.

Kofman, Sarah. *Socrate(s)*. Paris: Editions Galilée, 1989.

Konstan, David. "The Classics and Class Conflict." *Rethinking the Classical Canon, Arethusa* 27 (1994): 47–70.

———. *Greek Comedy and Ideology*. New York: Oxford University Press, 1995.

Kopff, E. Christian. *The Devil Knows Latin: Why America Needs the Classical Tradition*. Wilmington, Del.: ISI Books, 1999.

Kopytoff, Igor. "The Cultural Biography of Things: Commoditization as Process." In *The Social Life of Things*, edited by Arjun Appadurai, 64–91. Cambridge: Cambridge University Press, 1986.

Kurke, Leslie. *The Traffic in Praise: Pindar and the Poetics of Social Economy*. Ithaca, N.Y.: Cornell University Press, 1991.

———. *Coins, Bodies, Games and Gold: The Politics of Meaning in Archaic Greece*. Princeton, N.J.: Princeton University Press, 1999.

Lada, Ismene. "'Weeping for Hecuba': Is It a 'Brechtian' Act?" *Arethusa* 29 (1996): 87–124.

Lader, Lawrence. *The Bold Brahmins: New England's War against Slavery: 1831–1863*. New York: Dutton, 1961.

Lambropoulos, Vassilis. *Literature as National Institution: Studies in the Politics of Modern Greek Criticism*. Princeton, N.J.: Princeton University Press, 1988.

La Penna, Antonio. "La morale della favola esopica come morale delle classi subalterne nell'antichità." *Società* 17 (1961): 459–537.

Laplanche, J., and J.-B. Pontalis. *The Language of Psychoanalysis*. Translated by D. Nicholson-Smith. New York: Norton, 1974.

Lasserre, Francois. "La Fable en Grèce dans la Póesie archaïque." In *La Fable*, 51–103. Entretiens sur l'antiquité classique, vol. 30. Geneva: Fondation Hardt, 1984.

Lavelle, B. M. "Herodotos, Skythian Archers, and the *Doryphoroi* of the Peisistratids." *Klio* 74 (1992): 78–97.

Lazarus, Neil. "'Hating Tradition Properly.'" *New Formations* 38 (1999): 9–30.

Leader, Ruth E. "In Death Not Divided: Gender, Family , and State on Classical Athenian Grave Stelae." *American Journal of Archaeology* 101 (1997): 683–99.

Lefebvre, Henri. "The Everyday and Everydayness." Translated by C. Levich, K. Ross, and A. Kaplan. *Yale French Studies* 73 (1987): 7–12.

———. *Critique of Everyday Life*. Translated by J. Moore. Vol. 1. Paris: B. Grasset, 1947. New York: Verso, 1991.

Lekas, Padelis. *Marx on Classical Antiquity: Problems of Historical Methodology*. Brighton, England: Wheatsheaf Books, 1988.

Leontis, Artemis. *Topographies of Hellenism: Mapping the Homeland*. Ithaca, N.Y.: Cornell University Press, 1995.

Leveque, Pierre. "La dépendance dans la structure trifonctionelle indo-européenne." In *Antike Abhangigkeitsformen in den Griechischen Gebieten ohne Polisstruktur und den Romischen Provinzen, Actes du colloque sur l'esclavage, Iena, 1981*, 140–56. Berlin: Akademie-Verlag, 1985.

Levine, Lawrence. *Black Culture and Black Consciousness: Afro-American Folk Thought from Slavery to Freedom*. New York: Oxford University Press, 1977.

Levy, E. "Les Esclaves chez Aristophane." In *Actes de Colloque d'histoire sociale 1970 (Besançon)*, 29–46. Paris: Belles Lettres, 1970.

Lewis, D. "Public Property in the City." In *The Greek City from Homer to Alexander*, edited by O. Murray and S. Price, 245–63. Oxford: Clarendon Press, 1990.

Lewis, Sian. "Barbers' Shops and Perfume Shops: 'Symposia without Wine.'"

In *The Greek World*, edited by Anton Powell, 423–41. London: Routledge, 1995.

Lidchi, Henrietta. "The Poetics and the Politics of Exhibiting Other Cultures." In *Representation: Cultural Representations and Signifying Practices*, edited by Stuart Hall, 151–208. London: Sage in association with the Open University, 1997.

Lissarrague, François. *The Aesthetics of the Greek Banquet: Images of Wine and Ritual*. Translated by A. Szegedy-Maszak. Princeton, N.J.: Princeton University Press, 1990.

Lloyd, G. E. R. "The *Meno* and the Mysteries of Mathematics." *Phronesis* 37 (1992): 166–83.

Loraux, N. *The Invention of Athens: The Funeral Oration in the Classical City*. Translated by A. Sheridan. Cambridge, Mass.: Harvard University Press, 1986.

———. *La voix endeuillée: Essai sur la tragédie grecque*. Paris: Gallimard, 1999.

Lowenthal, David. *The Past Is a Foreign Country*. Cambridge: Cambridge University Press, 1985.

Lowry, S. Todd. *The Archaeology of Economic Ideas: The Classical Greek Tradition*. Durham, N.C.: Duke University Press, 1987.

Lubar, S., and W. D. Kingery, eds. *History from Things: Essays on Material Culture*. Washington, D.C.: Smithsonian Institution Press, 1993.

Macann, C., ed. *Critical Heidegger*. London: Routledge, 1996.

MacDowell, D. M. *The Law in Classical Athens*. London: Cornell University Press, 1978.

MacPherson, C. B. *The Political Theory of Possessive Individualism*. Oxford: Clarendon Press, 1962.

Mactoux, M.-M. *Douleia: Esclavage et Pratique discursive dans l'Athènes classique*. Paris: Belles Lettres, 1980.

Maleuvre, Didier. *Museum Memories: History, Technology, Art*. Stanford, Calif.: Stanford University Press, 1999.

Manville, P. B. *The Origins of Citizenship in Ancient Athens*. Princeton, N.J.: Princeton University Press, 1990.

Marchand, Suzanne. *Down from Olympus: Archaeology and Philhellenism in Germany, 1750–1970*. Princeton, N.J.: Princeton University Press, 1996.

Martin, Richard P. "The Seven Sages as Performers of Wisdom." In *Cultural Poetics in Ancient Greece: Cult, Performance, Politics*, edited by Carol Dougherty and Leslie Kurke, 108–28. Cambridge: Cambridge University Press, 1993.

Masson, O. "Les noms des esclaves dans la Grèce antique." In *Actes du colloque 1971 sur l'esclavage*. Paris: Belles Lettres, 1972.

Mastronarde, D. *Contact and Discontinuity: Some Conventions of Speech and Action on the Greek Tragic Stage*. Berkeley and Los Angeles: University of California Press, 1979.

McCarthy, Kathleen. "Servitium amoris: Amor servitii." In *Women and Slaves in*

Greco-Roman Culture: Differential Equations, edited by Sandra R. Joshel and Sheila Murnaghan, 174–92. London: Routledge, 1998.

McClure, Laura. *Spoken like a Woman: Speech and Gender in Athenian Drama.* Princeton, N.J.: Princeton University Press, 1999.

McCoskey, D. E. "'I, Whom She Detested So Bitterly': Slavery and the Violent Division of Women in Aeschylus' *Oresteia.*" In *Women and Slaves in Greco-Roman Culture*, edited by Sandra R. Joshel and Sheila Murnaghan, 33–55. London: Routledge, 1998.

McKitrick, Eric L., ed. *Slavery Defended: The Views of the Old South.* Englewood Cliffs, N.J.: Prentice-Hall, 1963.

Meier, Christian. *The Political Art of Greek Tragedy.* Translated by A. Webber. Cambridge: Polity, 1993.

———. "Gleichheit und Grenzen: Aristoteles, die Griechen, die Barbaren, die Sklaven." *Merkur* 49 (1995): 825–35.

Menand, Louis. *The Metaphysical Club.* New York: Farrar Straus and Giroux, 2001.

Menzel, Peter. *Material World: A Global Family Portrait.* San Francisco: Sierra Club Books, 1994.

Miller, Edward. *That Noble Cabinet: A History of the British Museum.* London: André Deutsch, 1973.

Millett, P. "Encounters in the Agora." In *Kosmos*, edited by P. Cartledge, P. Millett, and S. von Reden, 203–28. Cambridge: Cambridge University Press, 1998.

Mixon, W. "The Ultimate Irrelevance of Race: Joel Chandler Harris and Uncle Remus in Their Time." *Journal of Southern History* 56 (1990): 457–80.

Montiglio, Silvia. *Silence in the Land of Logos.* Princeton, N.J.: Princeton University Press, 2000.

Morgan, Edmund. *American Slavery, American Freedom: The Ordeal of Colonial Virginia.* New York: Norton, 1975.

Morison, Samuel Eliot. *Three Centuries of Harvard, 1636–1936.* Cambridge, Mass.: Harvard University Press, 1946.

Morris, Ian. *Death-Ritual and Social Structure in Classical Antiquity.* Cambridge: Cambridge University Press, 1992.

———. "The Strong Principle of Equality." In *Demokratia, A Conversation on Democracies, Ancient and Modern*, edited by Josiah Ober and Charles Hedrick, 19–48. Princeton, N.J.: Princeton University Press, 1996.

———. "Remaining Invisible: The Archaeology of the Excluded in Classical Athens." In *Women and Slaves in Greco-Roman Culture*, edited by Sandra R. Joshel and Sheila Murnaghan, 193–220. London: Routledge, 1998.

———. *Archaeology as Cultural History: Words and Things in Iron Age Greece.* Malden, Mass: Blackwell, 2000.

———, ed. *Classical Greece: Ancient Histories and Modern Archaeologies.* Cambridge: Cambridge University Press, 1994.

Morris, Sarah. "*LASANA:* A Contribution to the Ancient Greek Kitchen." *Hesperia* 54, no. 4 (October-December 1985): 393–409.

Morrow, Glenn R. *Plato's Law of Slavery in Its Relation to Greek Law*. New York: Arno Press, 1976.

Mossman, Judith. *Wild Justice: A Study of Euripides' "Hecuba."* Oxford: Clarendon Press, 1995.

Most, G. W. "A Cock for Asclepius." *Classical Quarterly* 43 (1993): 96–111.

Munn, Mark. *The School of History: Athens in the Age of Socrates*. Berkeley and Los Angeles: University of California Press, 2000.

Nagy, Gregory. *The Best of the Achaeans: Concepts of the Hero in Archaic Greek Poetry*. Baltimore: Johns Hopkins University Press, 1979.

———. *Greek Mythology and Poetics*. Ithaca, N.Y.: Cornell University Press, 1990.

———. *Pindar's Homer: The Lyric Possession of an Epic Past*. Baltimore: Johns Hopkins University Press, 1990.

———. *Poetry as Performance: Homer and Beyond*. Cambridge: Cambridge University Press, 1996.

Nails, Debra. *Agora, Academy and the Conduct of Philosophy*. Dordrecht: Kluwer Academic Publishers, 1995.

Narkiss, Doron. "The Fox, the Cock, and the Priest: Chaucer's Escape from Fable." *Chaucer Review* 32 (1997): 46–63.

Needler, Howard. "The Animal Fable among Other Medieval Literary Genres." *New Literary History* 22 (1991): 423–39.

Nevett, Lisa C. *House and Society in the Ancient Greek World*. Cambridge: Cambridge University Press, 1999.

Nichols, M. P. "The Good Life, Slavery, and Acquisition: Aristotle's Introduction to Politics." *Interpretation* 11 (1983): 171–83.

Nightingale, A. W. *Genres in Dialogue: Plato and the Construct of Philosophy*. Cambridge: Cambridge University Press, 1995.

Niranjana, Tejaswini. *Siting Translation: History, Post-Structuralism, and the Colonial Context*. Berkeley and Los Angeles: University of California Press, 1992.

Nöjgaard, M. *La Fable antique*. 2 vols. Copenhagen: A. Busck, 1964–67.

Nussbaum, Martha C. *The Fragility of Goodness: Luck and Ethics in Greek Tragedy and Philosophy*. Cambridge: Cambridge University Press, 1986.

Ober, Josiah. *Mass and Elite in Democratic Athens: Rhetoric, Ideology, and the Power of the People*. Princeton, N.J.: Princeton University Press, 1989.

———. *The Athenian Revolution: Essays on Ancient Greek Democracy and Political Theory*. Princeton, N.J.: Princeton University Press, 1996.

———. *Political Dissent in Democratic Athens: Intellectual Critics of Popular Rule*. Princeton, N.J.: Princeton University Press, 1998.

Ober, Josiah, and Charles Hedrick, eds. *Demokratia: A Conversation on Democracies, Ancient and Modern*. Princeton, N.J.: Princeton University Press, 1996.

Ogden, Daniel. *The Crooked Kings of Ancient Greece*. London: Duckworth, 1997.

Olender, M. "Aspects of Baubo: Ancient Texts and Contexts." In *Before Sexuality: The Construction of Erotic Experience in the Ancient Greek World*, edited by D. Halperin, J. J. Winkler, and F. I. Zeitlin. Princeton, N.J.: Princeton University Press, 1990.

Oliva, P. *Sparta and Her Social Problems*. Amsterdam: Academia, 1971.

Osborne, Robin. *Demos: The Discovery of Classical Attika*. Cambridge: Cambridge University Press, 1985.

———. *Classical Landscape with Figures: The Ancient Greek City and Its Countryside*. London: G. Philip, 1987.

———. "The Economics and Politics of Slavery at Athens." In *The Greek World*, edited by A. Powell, 27–43. London: Routledge, 1995.

Page, Denys. *Sappho and Alcaeus*. Oxford: Clarendon Press, 1955.

Patterson, Annabel. *Fables of Power. Aesopian Writing and Political History*. Durham, N.C.: Duke University Press, 1991.

Patterson, Orlando. *Slavery and Social Death*. Cambridge, Mass.: Harvard University Press, 1982.

———. *Freedom*. Vol. 1, *Freedom in the Making of Western Culture*. New York: Basic Books, 1991.

Pearce, Susan M., ed. *Interpreting Objects and Collections*. London: Routledge, 1994.

Pearson, Anne. *Everyday Life in Ancient Greece*. New York: Franklin Watts, 1994.

Pelling, Christopher B. R., ed. *Characterization and Individuality in Greek Literature*. Oxford: Clarendon Press, 1990.

Perry, B. E., ed. *Aesopica: A Series of Texts Relating to Aesop or Ascribed to Him or Closely Connected with the Literary Tradition that Bears His Name*. Vol. 1, *Greek and Latin Texts*. Urbana: University of Illinois Press, 1952.

Pesando, Fabrizio. *Oikos e Ktesis: La casa greca in età classica*. Rome: Quasar, 1987.

Pfeiffer, Rudolf. *History of Classical Scholarship from 1300–1850*. Oxford: Clarendon Press, 1976.

Plasa, C., and B. J. Ring. *The Discourse of Slavery: Aphra Behn to Toni Morrison*. London: Routledge, 1994.

Plato. *The Republic*. Translated by F. Cornford. London: Clarendon, 1945.

Pohlenz, Max. *Freedom in Greek Life and Thought: The History of an Ideal*. Translated by C. Rofmark. Dordrecht: D. Reidel, 1966.

Polanyi, Karl. *Primitive, Archaic, and Modern Economies*. Edited by G. Dalton. Garden City, N.J.: Anchor Books, 1968.

Pomeroy, S. *Goddesses, Whores, Wives and Slaves*. New York: Schocken Books, 1975.

Pomian, Krzysztof. "The Collection: Between the Visible and the Invisible." In *Collectors and Curiosities: Paris and Venice, 1500–1800*, 7–44. Cambridge: Polity Press, 1990.

Porter, James I. *The Invention of Dionysus: An Essay on the Birth of Tragedy*. Stanford, Calif.: Stanford University Press, 2000.

———. *Nietzsche and the Philology of the Future*. Stanford, Calif.: Stanford University Press, 2000.

Porter, John R. *Studies in Euripides' "Orestes."* Leiden: E. J. Brill, 1994.

Porter, W. H. "The Sequel to Plato's First Visit to Sicily." *Hermathena* 61 (1943): 51–52.

Powell, Anton, ed. *Euripides, Women, and Sexuality*. New York: Routledge, 1990.

Press, G. A., ed. *Who Speaks for Plato? Studies in Platonic Anonymity.* Lanham, Md.: Rowman and Littlefield, 2000.

Quarles, B., ed. *Narrative of the Life of Frederick Douglass, an American Slave Written by Himself.* Cambridge, Mass.: Harvard University Press, Belknap Press, 1988.

Quennell, Marjorie, and C. H. B. Quennell. *Everyday Things in Ancient Greece.* 3 vols. London: Batsford, 1930–33.

Raaflaub, K. A. "Democracy, Oligarchy, and the Concept of the 'Free Citizen' in Late Fifth-Century Athens." *Political Theory* 11 (1983): 517–44.

———. *Die Entdeckung der Freiheit.* Munich: Beck, 1985.

Rabinowitz, Nancy Sorkin. *Anxiety Veiled: Euripides and the Traffic in Women.* Ithaca, N.Y.: Cornell University Press, 1993.

———. "Slaves with Slaves: Women and Class in Euripidean Tragedy." In *Women and Slaves in Greco-Roman Culture: Differential Equations,* edited by Sandra R. Joshel and Sheila Murnaghan, 56–68. London: Routledge, 1998.

Rancière, J. *Le philosophe et ses pauvres.* Paris: Fayard, 1983.

———. *Disagreement: Politics and Philosophy.* Translated by J. Rose. Minneapolis: University of Minnesota Press, 1999.

Randall, R. H. "The Erechtheum Workmen." *American Journal of Archaeology* 57 (1953): 199–210.

Rasmussen, T., and Nigel Spivey, eds. *Looking at Greek Vases.* Cambridge: Cambridge University Press, 1991.

Reckford, K. *Aristophanes' Old-and-New Comedy.* Vol. 1, *Six Essays in Perspective.* Chapel Hill: University of North Carolina Press, 1987.

———. "Pity and Terror in Euripides' *Hecuba.*" *Arion* 1 (1991): 24–43.

Reden, Sitta von. *Exchange in Ancient Greece.* London: Duckworth, 1995.

Reilly, Linda Collins. *Slaves in Ancient Greece: Slaves from Greek Manumission Inscriptions.* Chicago: Ares, 1978.

Reinhold, Meyer. *Classica Americana: The Greek and Roman Heritage in the United States.* Detroit: Wayne State University Press, 1984.

Richard, Carl. *The Founders and the Classics: Greece, Rome, and the American Enlightenment.* Cambridge, Mass.: Harvard University Press, 1994.

Riginos, Alice Swift. *Platonica: The Anecdotes concerning the Life and Writings of Plato.* Leiden: E. J. Brill, 1976.

Rihll, Tracey. "War, Slavery and Settlement in Early Greece." In *War and Society in the Greek World,* edited by J. Rich and G. Shipley, 77–107. London: Routledge, 1993.

———. "The Origin and Establishment of Ancient Greek Slavery." In *Serfdom and Slavery: Studies in Legal Bondage,* edited by M. L. Bush, 89–111. London: Longman, 1996.

Roberts, J. M. *The Penguin History of the World.* London: Penguin, 1995.

Roberts, J. T. *Athens on Trial: The Antidemocratic Tradition in Western Thought.* Princeton, N.J.: Princeton University Press, 1994.

Robinson, Cyril E. *Everyday Life in Ancient Greece.* Oxford: Clarendon Press, 1933.

Robinson, D., ed. *Excavations at Olynthus*. 14 vols. Baltimore: Johns Hopkins University Press, 1929–52.

Rose, Peter W. *Sons of the Gods, Children of Earth: Ideology and Literary Form in Ancient Greece*. Ithaca, N.Y.: Cornell University Press, 1992.

Rosenbloom, David. "Myth, History, and Hegemony in Aeschylus." In *History, Tragedy, Theory*, edited by B. Goff, 91–130. Austin: University of Texas Press, 1995.

Rosivach, Vincent J. "Agricultural Slavery in the Northern Colonies and in Classical Athens: Some Comparisons." *Comparative Studies in Society and History* 35 (1993): 551–67.

Rothwell, Kenneth S. Jr. "Aristophanes' *Wasps* and the Sociopolitics of Aesop's Fables." *The Classical Journal* 90 (1995): 233–54.

Sainte-Croix, G. E. M. de. *The Origins of the Peloponnesian War*. London: Duckworth, 1972.

———. *The Class Struggle in the Ancient Greek World from the Archaic Age to the Arab Conquests*. Ithaca, N.Y.: Cornell University Press, 1981.

———. "Slavery and Other Forms of Unfree Labor." In *Slavery and Other Forms of Unfree Labour*, edited by Léonie J. Archer, 19–32. London: Routledge, 1988.

Sallares, R. *The Ecology of the Ancient Greek World*. London: Duckworth, 1991.

Saller, Richard. "Anecdotes as Historical Evidence for the Principate." *Greece and Rome* 127 (1980): 69–84.

Salmon, J. *Wealthy Corinth: A History of the City to 339 BC*. Oxford: Clarendon Press, 1984.

Sandys, John Edwin. *A History of Classical Scholarship*. 3 vols. Cambridge: Cambridge University Press, 1903–8.

Saxonhouse, Arlene. *Fear of Diversity: The Birth of Political Science in Ancient Greek Thought*. Chicago: University of Chicago Press, 1992.

Sayer, Derek. *The Violence of Abstraction: The Analytic Foundations of Historical Materialism*. Oxford: B. Blackwell, 1987.

Schefold, K., et al. *Die Bildnisse der Antiken Dichter, Redner und Denker*. Basel: Schwabe, 1997.

Schein, Seth. "Gildersleeve and the Study of Attic Tragedy." In *Basil Lanneau Gildersleeve: An American Classicist*, edited by W. W. Briggs Jr. and H. W. Benario, 50–55. Baltimore: Johns Hopkins University Press, 1986.

———. "Cultural Studies and Classics: Contrasts and Opportunities." In *Contextualizing Classics: Ideology, Performance, Dialogue. Essays in Honor of John J. Peradotto*, edited by T. M. Falkner, N. Felson, and D. Konstan, 285–99. Lanham, Md.: Rowman & Littlefield, 1999.

Schlaifer, R. "Greek Theories of Slavery from Homer to Aristotle." *Classical Philology* 47 (1936): 165–204.

Schnapp, Alain. *The Discovery of the Past*. Translated by I. Kinnes and G. Varndell. New York: Harry N. Abrams, 1997.

Schofield, M. "Ideology and Philosophy in Aristotle's Theory of Slavery." In

Aristoteles' "Politik," XI Symposium Aristotelicum, edited by G. Patzig. Göttingen: Vandenhoeck & Ruprecht, 1990.

Schrempp, Gregory. "Aristotle's Other Self: The Boundless Subject of Anthropological Discourse." In *Romantic Motives: Essays on Anthropological Sensibility*, edited by George W. Stocking Jr., 10–43. Madison: University of Wisconsin Press, 1989.

Scott, James C. *Domination and the Arts of Resistance: Hidden Transcripts*. New Haven, Conn.: Yale University Press, 1990.

Segal, Charles. *The Theme of the Mutilation of the Corpse in the "Iliad."* Leiden: Brill, 1971.

———. *Euripides and the Poetics of Sorrow: Art, Gender and Commemoration in "Alcestis," "Hippolytus," and "Hecuba."* Durham, N.C.: Duke University Press, 1993.

Seidensticker, B. *Palintonos Harmonia*. Göttingen: Vandenhoeck & Ruprecht, 1982.

Severyns, A. "Deux graffiti de Délos." *Bulletin de Correspondance Hellénique* 51 (1927): 234–43.

Shanks, Michael. *Classical Archaeology of Greece: Experiences of the Discipline*. London: Routledge, 1996.

Shaw, B., and R. Saller, eds. *Economy and Society in Ancient Greece*. New York: Viking Press, 1982.

Sherman, D. J., and I. Rogoff, eds. *MuseumCulture: Histories Discourses Spectacles*. Minneapolis: University of Minnesota Press, 1994.

Sichirollo, L., ed. *Schiavitù antica e moderna*. Naples: Guida, 1979.

Sicking, C. M. J. "The Classicists' Nostalgia." In *Distant Companions*, 209–44. Leiden: E. J. Brill, 1998.

Silk, Michael. "The People of Aristophanes." In *Characterization and Individuality in Greek Literature*, edited by Christopher B. R. Pelling, 150–73. Oxford: Clarendon Press, 1990.

Sinclair, R. K. *Democracy and Participation in Athens*. Cambridge: Cambridge University Press, 1988.

Sinn, U. "Greek Sanctuaries as Places of Refuge." In *Greek Sanctuaries: New Approaches*, edited by N. Marinatos and R. Hagg, 88–109. London: Routledge, 1993.

Skillen, Anthony. "Aesop's Lessons in Literary Realism." *Philosophy* 67 (1992): 169–181.

Smith, N. D. "Aristotle's Theory of Natural Slavery." *Phoenix* 37 (1983): 109–22.

Snodgrass, Anthony M. *An Archaeology of Greece: The Present State and Future Scope of a Discipline*. Berkeley and Los Angeles: University of California Press, 1987.

Sollors, Werner, et al., eds. *Blacks at Harvard*. New York: New York University Press, 1993.

Sophocles. *Trachiniae*. Edited by Malcolm Davies. Oxford: Clarendon Press, 1991.

Spencer, Nigel, ed. *Time, Tradition and Society in Greek Archaeology: Bridging the "Great Divide."* London: Routledge, 1995.

Spivey, Nigel. "Bionic Statues." In *The Greek World*, edited by Anton Powell, 442–59. London: Routledge, 1995.

Stallybrass, Peter, and Allon White. *The Politics and Poetics of Transgression.* Ithaca, N.Y.: Cornell University Press, 1986.

Stanford, W. B. *Greek Tragedy and the Emotions.* London: Routledge & Kegan Paul, 1983.

Starr, Chester G. "An Overdose of Slavery." *Journal of Economic History* (1958): 17–32.

———. *Past and Future in Ancient History.* Lanham, Md.: University Press of America, 1987.

Steiner, Deborah. *The Tyrant's Writ: Myths and Images of Writing in Ancient Greece.* Princeton, N.J.: Princeton University Press, 1994.

———. *Images in Mind: Statues in Archaic and Classical Greek Literature and Thought.* Princeton: Princeton University Press, 2001.

Stern, E. Marianne, and Birgit Schlick-Nolte. *Early Glass of the Ancient World, 1600 B.C.–A.D. 50.* Ostfildern: Verlag Gerd Hatje, 1994.

Stewart, Andrew. "Reflections." In *Sexuality in Ancient Art: Near East, Egypt, Greece, and Italy*, edited by Nathalie Boymel Kampen. Cambridge: Cambridge University Press, 1996.

———. *Art, Desire, and the Body in Ancient Greece.* Cambridge: Cambridge University Press, 1997.

Stewart, Douglas. "Socrates' Last Bath." *Journal of the History of Philosophy* 10 (1972): 253–59.

Stocking, George W. Jr., ed. *Objects and Others: Essays on Museums and Material Culture.* Madison: University of Wisconsin Press, 1985.

Stray, Christopher. *Classics Transformed: Schools, Universities and Society in England, 1830–1960.* Oxford: Clarendon Press, 1998.

Sultan, Nancy. *Exile and the Poetics of Loss in Greek Tradition.* Lanham, Md.: Rowman & Littlefield, 1999.

Svenbro, Jesper. *Phrasikleia: l'anthropologie de la lecture en Grèce ancienne.* Paris: La Découverte, 1988.

Swindler, Mary H. *Ancient Painting.* New Haven, Conn.: Yale University Press, 1929.

Synodinou, K. *On the Concept of Slavery in Euripides.* Ioannina: University of Ioannina, 1977.

Taillardat, J. *Les Images d'Aristophane.* Paris: Société d'édition Les Belles Lettres, 1965.

Talbert, R. J. A. "The Role of the Helots in the Class Struggle at Sparta." *Historia* 38 (1989): 22–40.

Thalmann, William G. "Euripides and Aeschylus: The Case of the *Hekabe.*" *Classical Antiquity* 12 (1993): 126–59.

———. "Female Slaves in the *Odyssey.*" In *Women and Slaves in Greco-Roman*

Culture: Differential Equations, edited by Sandra R. Joshel and Sheila Murnaghan, 22–34. London: Routledge, 1998.

———. *The Swineherd and the Bow: Representations of Class in the "Odyssey."* Ithaca, N.Y.: Cornell University Press, 1998.

Theodorou, Z. "Subject to Emotion: Exploring Madness in *Orestes*." *Classical Quarterly* 43 (1993): 32–46.

Thomas, J. E. *Musings on the "Meno."* The Hague: Martin Nijhoff, 1980.

Thomas, Rosalind. *Literacy and Orality in Ancient Greece*. Cambridge: Cambridge University Press, 1992.

Thomson, George. *Aeschylus and Athens*. 2d ed. London: Lawrence & Wishart, 1946.

Thucydides. *History of the Peloponnesian War*. Translated by Rex Warner. Harmondsworth, England: Penguin Books, 1972.

———. *The Peloponnesian War*. Translated by S. Lattimore. Indianapolis: Hackett, 1998.

Tilley, Christopher, ed. *Reading Material Culture*. Oxford: B. Blackwell, 1990.

Tise, Larry. *Proslavery: A History of the Defense of Slavery in America, 1701–1840*. Athens: University of Georgia Press, 1987.

Trulock, Alice Rains. *In the Hands of Providence: Joshua L. Chamberlain and the American Civil War*. Chapel Hill: University of North Carolina Press, 1992.

Tsigakou, Fania-Maria. *The Rediscovery of Greece: Travellers and Painters of the Romantic Era*. New Rochelle, N.Y.: Caratzas Brothers, 1981.

Turner, Jeffrey. "The Images of Enslavement and Incommensurability in Plato's *Meno*." *Interpretation* 20 (1992–93): 117–34.

Vergo, Peter, ed. *The New Museology*. London: Reaktion Books, 1989.

Vernant, Jean-Pierre. *La mort dans les yeux*. Paris: Hachette, 1985.

———. *Myth and Society in Ancient Greece*. Translated by Janet Lloyd. New York: Zone Books, 1990.

———. *Entre mythe et politique*. Paris: Seuil, 1996.

Vernant, Jean-Pierre, Marc Augé, Cornélius Castoriadis, Maria Daraki, Philippe Descola, Claude Mossé, André Motte, Marie-Henriette Quet, and Gilbert Romeyer-Dherbey. *La Grèce pour penser l'avenir*. Paris: L'Harmattan, 2000.

Vernant, Jean-Pierre, and Pierre Vidal-Naquet. *Myth and Tragedy in Ancient Greece*. Translated by Janet Lloyd. New York: Zone Books, 1990.

———. *Travail et esclavage en Grèce ancienne*. Paris: Ed. Complexe, 1988.

———. ed. *The Greeks*. Translated by C. Lambert and T. L. Fagan. Chicago: University of Chicago Press, 1995.

Veyne, Paul, ed. *A History of Private Life*. Vol. 1, *From Pagan Rome to Byzantium*, translated by A. Goldhammer. Cambridge, Mass.: Harvard University Press, Belknap Press, 1987.

Vickers, Michael, and David Gill. *Artful Crafts: Ancient Greek Silverware and Pottery*. Oxford: Clarendon Press, 1994.

Vidal-Naquet, Pierre. "Slavery and the Rule of Women in Tradition, Myth and

Utopia." In *Myth, Religion and Society: Structuralist Essays*, edited by R. L. Gordon, 187–200. Cambridge: Cambridge University Press, 1981.

——. "The Immortal Slave Women of Athena Ilias." In *The Black Hunter: Forms of Thought and Forms of Society in the Greek World*, translated by A. Szegedy-Maszak, 189–204. Baltimore: Johns Hopkins University Press, 1986.

——. "Reflections on Greek Historical Writing about Slavery." In *The Black Hunter*, 168–80.

——. "Were Greek Slaves a Class?" In *The Black Hunter*, 159–67.

Vlastos, Gregory. "Slavery in Plato's *Republic*." *Philosophical Review* 50 (1941): 289–304.

——. "Did Slavery Exist in Plato's *Republic*?" *Classical Philology* 63 (1968): 291–95.

——. "Slavery in Plato's Thought." In *Platonic Studies*, 146–63. Princeton, N.J.: Princeton University Press, 1973.

——. "The Individual as an Object of Love in Plato." In *Platonic Studies*, 2d ed., 3–34. Princeton, N.J.: Princeton University Press, 1981.

——, ed. *Plato, A Collection of Critical Essays*. Vol. 1. Garden City, N.J.: Anchor, 1971.

Vogt, Joseph. *Ancient Slavery and the Ideal of Man*. Translated by T. Wiedemann. Cambridge, Mass.: Harvard University Press, 1975.

Vogt, J., and H. Bellen, eds. *Bibliographie zur antiken Sklaverei*. Revised by E. Hermann and N. Brockmeyer. Bochum: N. Brockmeyer, 1983.

Volpi, Franco. "Dasein as Praxis: the Heideggerian Assimilation and the Radicalization of the Practical Philosophy of Aristotle." In *Critical Heidegger*, edited by C. Macann, 27–66. London: Routledge, 1996.

Walker, Alice. "The Dummy in the Window: Joel Chandler Harris and the Invention of Uncle Remus." In *Living by the Word: Selected Writings 1973–1987*, 25–32. San Diego: Harcourt Brace Jovanovich, 1988.

Walker, Peter. *Moral Choices: Memory, Desire, and Imagination in Nineteenth-Century American Abolition*. Baton Rouge: Louisiana State University Press, 1978.

Walters, Ronald G. *The Antislavery Appeal: American Abolitionism after 1830*. Baltimore: Johns Hopkins University Press, 1976.

Warch, Richard. *School of the Prophets: Yale College, 1701–1740*. New Haven, Conn.: Yale University Press, 1973.

Webster, T. B. L. *Everyday Life in Classical Athens*. London: Batsford, 1969.

Welskopf, E. Ch. "Loisir et esclavage dans la Grèce antique." In *Actes du colloque 1973 sur l'Esclavage*, 161–78. Paris: Belles Lettres, 1976.

Welwei, K. W. *Unfreie im Antiken Kriegsdienst*. 3 vols. Wiesbaden: Steiner, 1974–88.

West, M. L. "The Ascription of Fables to Aesop in Archaic and Classical Greece." In *La Fable*, 105–36. Entretiens sur l'antiquité classique, vol. 30. Geneva: Fondation Hardt, 1984.

Westermann, W. L. *Slave Systems of Greek and Roman Antiquity*. Philadelphia: American Philosophical Society, 1955.

Whitby, M. "Images of Spartans and Helots." In *The Shadow of Sparta*, edited by A. Powell and S. Hodkinson, 87–126. London: Routledge for The Classical Press of Wales, 1994.

White, John, and Ralph Willett. *Slavery in the American South*. Harlow: Longmans, 1970.

Whitman, Cedric. *Aristophanes and the Comic Hero*. Cambridge, Mass.: Harvard University Press, 1964.

Wickersham, John. *Hegemony and Greek Historians*. Lanham, Md.: Rowman & Littlefield, 1994.

Wiechers, A. *Aesop in Delphi*. Meisenheim am Glan: A. Hain, 1961.

Wiedemann, Thomas. *Greek and Roman Slavery*. Baltimore: Johns Hopkins University Press, 1981.

———. *Slavery. Greece and Rome: New Surveys in the Classics*, no. 19. Oxford: Clarendon Press for the Classical Association, 1987.

Wilamowitz-Moellendorff, Ulrich von. *History of Classical Scholarship*. Translated by A. Harris. London: Duckworth, 1982.

Wiles, David. *Tragedy in Athens: Performance Space and Theatrical Meaning*. Cambridge: Cambridge University Press, 1997.

Wilkins, John. *The Boastful Chef: The Discourse of Food in Ancient Greek Comedy*. Oxford: Oxford University Press, 2000.

Williams, Bernard. *Shame and Necessity*. Berkeley and Los Angeles: University of California Press, 1993.

Williams, Linda. *Playing the Race Card: Melodramas of Black and White from Uncle Tom to O. J. Simpson*. Princeton, N.J.: Princeton University Press, 2001.

Williams, Patricia J. "My Best White Friend: Cinderella Revisited." *The New Yorker* 72, no. 2 (1996): 94.

Wilson, Fred. *Mining the Museum, An Installation*. Edited by Lisa G. Corrin. Baltimore: Contemporary, 1994.

Winkler, John J. *The Constraints of Desire: The Anthropology of Sex and Gender in Ancient Greece*. New York: Routledge, 1990.

Winkler, John J., and Froma I. Zeitlin, eds. *Nothing to Do with Dionysos?: Athenian Drama in Its Social Context*. Princeton, N.J.: Princeton University Press, 1990.

Wise, Jennifer. *Dionysus Writes: The Invention of Theatre in Ancient Greece*. Ithaca, N.Y.: Cornell University Press, 1998.

Wolff, C. "Orestes." In *Oxford Readings in Greek Tragedy*, edited by Charles Segal, 340–56. Oxford: Oxford University Press, 1983.

Wood, Ellen M. *Peasant-Citizen and Slave: The Foundations of Athenian Democracy*. London: Verso, 1988.

Wright, M. R. "Presocratic Minds." In *The Person and the Human Mind: Issues in Ancient and Modern Philosophy*, edited by Christopher Gill, 207–25. Oxford: Clarendon Press, 1990.

Wyatt-Brown, Bertram. *Yankee Saints and Southern Sinners*. Baton Rouge: Louisiana State University Press, 1985.

Xenophon. *Recollections of Socrates*. Translated by A. Benjamin. New York: Macmillan, 1965.

———. *Oeconomicus, A Social and History Commentary.* Translated by Sarah B. Pomeroy. Oxford: Clarendon Press, 1994.

———. *Xenophon.* Vol. 8. Cambridge, Mass.: Harvard University Press, 1968.

Young, R. "An Industrial District of Ancient Athens." *Hesperia* 20 (1951): 135–288.

Zeitlin, Froma. "The Closet of Masks: Role-Playing and Myth-Making in the *Orestes* of Euripides." *Ramus* 9 (1980): 51–77.

———. "The Body's Revenge: Dionysos and Tragic Action in Euripides' *Hekabe*." In *Playing the Other: Gender and Society in Classical Greek Literature*, 172–216. Chicago: University of Chicago Press, 1996.

———. "Mysteries of Identity and Designs of the Self in Euripides' *Ion*." In *Playing the Other*, 285–338.

Zinato, A. "Possibile e impossibile nella favola esopica." In *Il meraviglioso e il verosimile tra antichità e medioevo*, edited by D. Lanza and O. Longo. Florence: L. S. Olschki, 1989.

INDEX